D1121676

PARALLEL COMPUTING ON HETEROGENEOUS NETWORKS

**WILEY SERIES ON PARALLEL
AND DISTRIBUTED COMPUTING**

Editor: Albert Y. Zomaya

A complete list of titles in this series appears at the end of this volume.

PARALLEL COMPUTING ON HETEROGENEOUS NETWORKS

Alexey Lastovetsky
University College, Dublin, Ireland

WILEY-
INTERSCIENCE

A JOHN WILEY & SONS, INC., PUBLICATION

Published by John Wiley & Sons, Inc., Hoboken, New Jersey.
Published simultaneously in Canada.

For general information on our other products and services please contact our Customer Care Department within the U.S. at 877-762-2974, outside the U.S. at 317-572-3993 or fax 317-572-4002.

Wiley also publishes its books in a variety of electronic formats. Some content that appears in print, however, may not be available in electronic format.

Library of Congress Cataloging-in-Publication Data:

ISBN: 0-471-22982-2

Printed in the United States of America.

10 9 8 7 6 5 4 3 2 1

To my wife Gulnara, my daughters Olga and Oksana, and my parents Leonid and Lyudmila.

■■■■■ CONTENTS

ACKNOWLEDGMENTS

I would like to express my deep appreciation to my colleagues and friends Alexey Kalinov, Ilya Ledovskih, Dmitry Arapov, and Mikhail Posypkin for the happy days when we were working together on the mpC programming language. Their skills, devotion, and creativity created the basis for its successful implementation. I am very grateful to Victor Ivannikov for his persistent support of both the mpC project and myself in good and bad times. I am also very grateful to Ted Lewis without whose support and contribution the mpC project would not be possible at all. My special thanks are to Hesham El-Rewini and Albert Zomaya for their positive and encouraging attitude to the idea of this book. I also wish to thank Ravi Reddi for his comments and valuable contribution in the material presented in Sections 8.2, 9.1.1.3, and 9.1.1.4.

Introduction

The current situation with parallel programming resembles computer programming before the appearance of personal computers. Computing was concentrated in special computer centers, and computer programs were written by nerds. Soon after PCs appeared, computer programming became available to millions of ordinary people. The result of the change can be clearly seen now.

Similarly parallel computing is now concentrating mainly in supercomputer centers established around specialized high-performance parallel computers or clusters of workstations, and only highly trained people write parallel programs for the computer systems. At the same time, local networks of computers have become personal supercomputers available to millions of ordinary people. They only need appropriate programming languages and tools to write fast and portable parallel applications for the networks. The release of the huge performance potential currently hidden in networks of computers might have even a more significant impact on science and technology than the invention of more powerful processors and supercomputers.

The intent of this book is to introduce into the area of parallel computing on common local networks of computers NoCs.

Nowadays NoCs are a common and widespread parallel architecture. In general, a NoC comprises PCs, workstations, servers, and sometimes supercomputers interconnected via mixed communication equipment. Traditional parallel software was developed for homogeneous multiprocessors. It tries to distribute computations evenly over available processors and therefore cannot utilize the performance potential of this heterogeneous architecture. A good parallel program for a NoC should distribute computations and communications over the NoC unevenly, taking into account actual performances of both processors and communication links. This book mainly introduces in parallel programming for heterogeneous, in other words, NoCs in heterogeneous parallel programming.

To present both basic and advanced concepts of heterogeneous parallel programming, the book extensively uses the mpC language. This is a high-level

Parallel Computing on Heterogeneous Networks, by Alexey Lastovetsky
ISBN 0-471-22982-2   Copyright © 2003 by John Wiley & Sons, Inc.

language aimed at programming portable parallel computations on NoCs. The design of this language allows easy expression in portable form of a wide range of heterogeneous parallel algorithms. The introduction to the mpC language and the accompanying programming model and language constructs serves also to introduce the area of heterogeneous parallel programming. A representative series of mpC programs was carefully selected to illustrate all of the presented concepts. All of the programs can be compiled and executed on a local network of workstations or even on a single workstation with the freely available mpC programming system installed. While the basic concepts are illustrated by very simple programs, a representative set of real-life problems and their portable parallel solutions on NoCs are also included. The problems studied here involve linear algebra, modeling of oil extraction, integration, *N*-body applications, data mining, business applications, and distributed software testing.

It is important for any book to clearly define from the beginning basic terms, especially if the terms are in common use but are understood differently. This is particularly true in parallel computing on distributed memory architectures, where a specific case is parallel computing on heterogeneous networks. Indeed, it is easy to confuse parallel computing on distributed memory architectures with distributed computing, especially high-performance distributed computing. In a distributed memory computer system both parallel and distributed applications are nothing more than a number of processes running in parallel on different computing nodes and interacting via message passing. They both can use the same communication protocols (e.g., TCP/IP) and the same basic software (e.g., sockets).

The key difference between parallel computing technologies and distributed computing technologies lies in the main goal of each of the technologies. The main goal of distributed computing technologies is to make software components, inherently located on different computers, work together. The main goal of parallel computing technologies is to speed up the solution of a single problem on the available computer hardware. Correspondingly, in the case of parallel computing, the partition of an application into a number of distributed components located on different computers is just a way to speed up its execution on the distributed memory computer system; it is not an intrinsic feature of the application nor of the problem that the application solves. The book presents the technology of heterogeneous parallel computing proceeding from this basic understanding of the main goal of parallel computing technologies.

Thus the target computer hardware is the material basis of any parallel computing technology. Correspondingly the evolution of computer hardware is followed by the evolution of parallel computing technologies. In general, the resulting trajectory of computer hardware is aimed at higher performance, that is, at the ability to compute faster and store more data. There exist two ways to make computer systems execute the same volume of computations faster: reduce the time of execution of a single instruction (i.e., to increase the processor clock rate), and increase the number of instructions executed in parallel. The first way is determined by the level of microelectronic technology, and it has some natural limits conditioned by universal physical constants such as the velocity of light. Nowadays the clock rates have reached the magnitude of gigacycles per second. But it is not the higher clock rate that distinguishes high-performance computer systems. Rather, at any stage of the development of microprocessor technology, this index is approximately the same for most manufactured microprocessors. The high-performance computer systems can handle a higher parallelism of computations. Therefore high-performance computer systems are always of parallel architecture.

Part I provides an overview of the evolution of parallel computer architectures in relation to the evolution of parallel programming models and tools. The starting-point of all parallel architectures is the serial scalar processor. Main architectural milestones include vector and superscalar processors, a shared memory multiprocessor, a distributed memory multiprocessor, and a common heterogeneous network of computers. The parallel architectures represent the logic of a parallel architecture development rather than its chronology. They represent the main stream of architectural ideas that have proved their viability and effectiveness and made a major impact on the real-life hardware. Compared to a historical approach, the logical approach gives a concise and conceptually clear picture of the evolution of parallel architectures, throwing off a good deal of secondary, nonviable, or simply erroneous architectural decisions, and separating more strictly different architectural concepts often mixed in real hardware. In the series of parallel architectures, each next architecture contains the preceding one as a particular case, and provides more parallelism and, hence, more performance potential.

For each of the listed parallel architectures, its intrinsic model of parallel program is presented and followed by outline of programming tools implementing the model. The models represent all main paradigms of parallel programming. Apart from optimizing compilers for traditional serial programming languages, the programming tools outlined include parallel libraries and parallel programming languages. The book does not pretend to cover all aspects of parallel programming. Many important topics such as debugging of parallel applications and maintenance of fault tolerance of parallel computations are beyond the scope of this book. The book focuses on basic parallel programming models and their implementation by the most popular parallel programming tools.

In Chapter 2 vector and superscalar processors are presented. The architectures provide instruction-level parallelism, which is best exploited by applications with intensive operations on arrays. Such applications can be written in a serial programming language, such as C or Fortran 77, and complied by dedicated optimizing compilers performing some specific loop optimizations. Array libraries allow the programmers to avoid the use of dedicated compilers performing sophisticated optimizations. Instead, the programmers express operations on arrays directly, using calls to carefully implemented subroutines implementing the array operations. Parallel languages, such as Fortran 90 or C[ ], combine advantages of the first and second approaches. They allow the programmer explicitly express operations on arrays, and they therefore do not need to use sophisticated algorithms to recognize parallelized loops. They are able to perform global optimization of combined array operations. Last, unlike existing array libraries, they support general-purpose programming.

In Chapter 3 the shared memory multiprocessor architecture is shown to provide a higher level of parallelism than the vector and superscalar architectures via multiple parallel streams of instructions. Nevertheless, the SMP architecture is not scalable. The speedup provided by this architecture is limited by the bandwidth of the memory bus. Multithreading is the primary programming model for the SMP architecture. Serial languages, such as C and Fortran 77, may be used in concert with optimizing compilers to write efficient programs for SMP computers. Unfortunately, only a limited and simple class of multithreaded algorithms can be implemented in an efficient and portable way by this approach. Thread libraries directly implement the multithreading paradigm and allow the programmers to explicitly write efficient multithreaded programs independent of optimizing compilers. Pthreads are standard for Unix platforms supporting thus efficiently portable parallel programming Unix SMP computers. Thread libraries are powerful tools supporting both parallel and distributed computing. The general programming model underlying the thread libraries is universal and seen too powerful, complicated, and error-prone for parallel programming. OpenMP is a high-level parallel extension of Fortran, C, and C++, providing a simplified multithreaded programming model based on the master/slave design strategy, and aimed specifically at parallel computing on SMP architectures. OpenMP significantly facilitates writing parallel mutlithreaded applications.

In Chapter 4 the distributed memory mutltiprocessor architecture, also known as the MPP architecture, is introduced. It provides much more parallelism than the SMP architecture. Moreover, unlike all other parallel architectures, the MPP architecture is scalable. It means that the speed increase provided by this architecture is potentially infinite. This is due to the absence of principal bottlenecks, such as might limit the number of efficiently interacting processors. Message passing is the dominant programming model for the MPP architecture. As the MPP architecture is farther away from the serial scalar architecture than the vector, superscalar, and even SMP architectures, it is very difficult to automatically generate an efficient message-passing code for the serial source code written in C or Fortran 77. In fact, optimizing C or Fortran 77 compilers for MPPs would involve solving the problem of automatic synthesis of an efficient message-passing program using the source serial code as a specification of its functional semantics. This problem is still a challenge for researchers. Therefore no industrial optimizing C or Fortran 77 compiler for the MPP architecture is now available. Basic programming tools for MPPs are message-passing libraries and high-level parallel languages. Message-passing libraries directly implement the message-passing paradigm and allow the programmers to explicitly write efficient parallel programs for MPPs. MPI is a standard message-passing interface supporting efficiently portable parallel programming MPPs. Unlike the other popular message-passing library, PVM, MPI supports modular parallel programming and hence can be used for development of parallel libraries. MPI is a powerful programming tool for implementing a wide range of parallel algorithms on MPPs in highly efficient and portable message-passing applications. Scientific programmers, who find the explicit message passing provided by MPI tedious and error-prone, can use data parallel programming languages, mainly HPF, to write programs for MPPs. When programming in HPF, the programmer specifies the strategy for parallelization and data partitioning at a higher level of abstraction, based on the single-threaded data parallel model with a global name space. The tedious low-level details of translating from an abstract global name space to the local memories of individual processors and the management of explicit interprocessor communication are left to the compiler. Data parallel programs are easy to write and debug. However, the data parallel programming model allows the programmer to express only a limited class of parallel algorithms. HPF 2.0 addresses the problem by extending purely data-parallel HPF 1.1 with some task parallel features. The resulting multi-paradigm language is more complicated and not as easy to use as pure data parallel languages. Data parallel languages (i.e., HPF) are difficult to compile. Therefore it is hard to get top performance via data parallel programming. The efficiency of data parallel programs strongly depends on the quality of the compiler.

In Chapter 5 we analyze challenges associated with parallel programming for common networks of computers (NoCs) that are, unlike dedicated parallel computer systems, inherently heterogeneous and unreliable. This analysis results in description of main features of an ideal parallel program running on a NoC. Such a program distributes computations and communications unevenly across processors and communications links during the execution of the code of the program. The distribution may be different for different NoCs and for different executions of the program on the same NoC, depending on the work load of its elements. The program keeps running even if some resources in the executing network fail. In the case of resource failure, it is able to reconfigure itself and resume computations from some point in the past. The program takes into account differences in machine arithmetic on different computers and avoids erroneous behaviour of the program that might be caused by the differences.

Part II is the core of the book and presents the mpC parallel programming language.

In Chapter 6 a basic subset of the mpC language is described. It addresses some primary challenges of heterogeneous parallel computing, focusing on uneven distribution of computations in heterogeneous parallel algorithms, and the heterogeneity of physical processors of NoCs. The programmers can explicitly specify the uneven distribution of computations across parallel processes dictated by the implemented heterogeneous parallel algorithm. The mpC compiler will use the provided information to map the parallel processes to the executing network of computers. A simple model of the executing network is used when parallel processes of the mpC program are mapped to physical processors of the network. The relative speed of the physical processors is a key parameter in the model. In heterogeneous environments the speed parameter is sensitive to both the code executed by the processors and the current work load due to external computations. The programmers can control the accuracy of this model at runtime and adjust its parameters to their particular applications. The implementation of the basic version of the mpC language is freely available at *http://www.ispras.ru/~mpc*.

In Chapter 7 some advanced features of the mpC language are presented. In general, the mC language allows the user not only to program computations and communications of the heterogeneous parallel algorithm but also to specify the performance model of the algorithm. This performance model takes into account all the main features of the algotihm that affect its execution time, including the number of parallel processes executing the algorithm, the absolute volume of computations performed by each of the processes, the absolute volume of data transferred between each pair of processes, and the interactions between the parallel processes during the execution of the algorithm. This information is used at runtime to map the algorithm to physical processors of the network of computers. The mpC programming system performs the mapping to minimize the execution time of the algorithm. The implementation of the full mpC language is freely available for research and educational purposes from the author of this book.

In Chapter 8 we very briefly consider how the mpC language approach to optimal heterogeneous distribution of computations and communications can be implemented in the form of a message-passing library. In so doing, we provide a small extension of the standard MPI for heterogeneous NoCs.

Part III presents a number of advanced mpC applications solving different problems on heterogeneous clusters.

In Chapter 9 we demonstrate that a wide range of scientific problems can be efficiently solved on heterogeneous networks of computers. We consider in details the design of the parallel block cyclic algorithm of matrix multiplication on heterogeneous NoCs and its portable implementation in the mpC language. We also consider parallel algorithms solving on heterogeneous NoCs a more demanding linear algebra problem: Cholesky factorization of a symmetric, positive-definite matrix. We present a relatively simple approach to assessment of a heterogeneous parallel algorithm via comparing its efficiency with the efficiency of its homogeneous prototype. We present two approaches to design of parallel algorithms solving regular problems on heterogeneous NoCs. The first approach supposes a one process per processor configuration of the parallel program with the work load unevenly distributed over the processes. The second approach assumes a mutliple processes per processor configuration of the parallel program, when the work load is evenly distributed over the processes while the number of processes on each processor is proportional to its speed. We experimentally compare the approaches and describe their portable mpC implementation. We present an N-body mpC application, which is an example of inherently irregular problem. A heterogeneous parallel algorithm solving such a problem is naturally deduced from the problem itself rather than from the parallel environment executing the algorithm. We also consider in detail the design of the parallel adaptive quadrature routine for numerical approximation to definite integrals on heterogeneous NoCs and its portable mpC implementation. We end with an experience of solving a real-life regular problem—simulation of oil extraction—in a heterogeneous parallel environment.

In Chapter 10 we demonstrate that heterogeneous parallel computing can be used not only to solve scientific problems but also to improve the performance of business distributed applications. Heterogeneous parallel computing also has application in software engineering practice to optimize the maintenance process. An experience of integration of the mpC-based technology of heterogeneous parallel computing and the CORBA-based technology of distributed computing is demonstrated.

The book does not pretend to be an encyclopedia of parallel computing. It presents a subjective view on parallel programming technologies, but Part I of the book can nevertheless be a good basis for an introductory university course on parallel programming systems. All the source code given in this book was carefully tested.

EVOLUTION OF
PARALLEL COMPUTING

## CHAPTER 1

Serial Scalar Processor

1.1. SERIAL SCALAR PROCESSOR AND PROGRAMMING MODEL

The starting-point of evolution of parallel architectures is the traditional serial scalar von Neumann architecture. This traditional architecture provides single control flow with serially executed instructions operating on scalar operands. Figure 1.1 depicts schematically the architecture. The processor has one instruction execution unit (IEU). Execution of an instruction can be only started after execution of the previous instruction in the flow is terminated. Except for a relatively small number of special instructions for data transfer between main memory and registers, the instructions take operands from and put results to scalar registers (a scalar register is a register that holds a single integer or float number). The total time of program execution is equal to the sum of execution times of the instructions. Performance of that architecture is determined by the clock rate.

1.2. BASIC PROGRAM PROPERTIES

Many languages and tools have been designed for programming traditional serial scalar processors, but C and Fortran have undoubtedly proved to be the most popular among professionals. What is so special in these two languages that makes them so successful and generally recognized? The answer is that both C and Fortran support and facilitate development of software whose properties are considered basic and necessary by most professionals.

While Fortran is mostly used for scientific programming, the C language is more general purpose widely used for system programming. The C language can be adapted for programming in the Fortran-like style. Moreover any Fortran 77 program can be easily converted into an equivalent C program (in particular, the GNU Fortran 77 compiler is implemented as such a convertor). So it is reasonable to assume that apart from the traditional affection of scientific programmers for Fortran, the same properties make Fortran attractive

Parallel Computing on Heterogeneous Networks, by Alexey Lastovetsky
ISBN 0-471-22982-2   Copyright © 2003 by John Wiley & Sons, Inc.

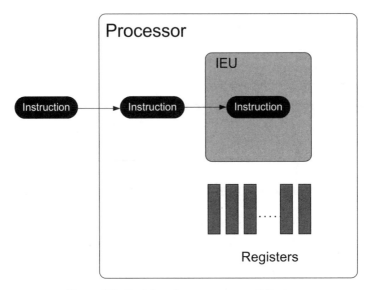

Figure 1.1. Serial scalar processor architecture.

for scientific programming and C for general purpose and especially for system programming. Therefore we will refer mostly to C while analyzing basic software properties that are to be supported by successful programming tools.

First of all, the C language allows one to develop highly efficient software for any particular serial scalar processor. This is because the language reflects all of the main features of the architecture having an effect on the program efficiency such as machine-oriented data types (short, char, unsigned, etc.), indirect addressing and address arithmetics (arrays, pointers and their correlation), and other machine-level notions (increment/decrement operators, the sizeof operator, cast operators, bit-fields, bitwise operators, compound assignments, etc.). The traditional serial scalar architecture is reflected in the C language with a completeness that allows programmers to write, for each serial scalar processor, programs having practically the efficiency of assembly code. In other words, the C language supports efficient programming.

Second, the C language is standardized as ANSI C, and all good C compilers support the standard. This allows programmers to write in C applications that, once developed and tested on one particular platform, will run properly on all platforms. In other words, the C language supports portable programming. Portability of C applications is determined not only by the portability of their source code but by the portability of used libraries as well. The C language provides especially high level of portability for computers running either the same operating system or operating systems of the same family (e.g., different clones of Unix). The point is that in addition to standard ANSI C libraries, a lot of other libraries are de facto standard in the framework of the corresponding family of operating systems. As for Unix systems, the high-quality portable GNU C compiler is often used on many platforms instead of native C compilers, which provides still more portability for source C code.

Third, the C language allows programmer to develop program units that can be separately compiled and correctly used by other programmers, while developing their applications, without knowledge of their source code. In other words, the C language supports modular programming. Obviously packages and libraries can only be developed with tools supporting modular programming.

Fourth, the C language provides a clear and easy-in-use programming model that ensures reliable programming. In addition to modularity it facilitates the development of really complex and useful applications. It is very difficult to find a balance between efficiency and lucidity as well as to combine lucidity and expressiveness. The C language is an exceptionally rare example of such harmony.

Finally, the C language supports not only efficient and portable but efficiently portable programming the serial scalar processors. It has been stressed that the C language reflects all the main features of this architecture that affect program efficiency. On the other hand, the C language hides such peculiarities of each particular processor that have no analogs in other processors of the architecture (the peculiarities of register storage, details of stack implementation, details of instruction sets, etc.). It allows writing portable applications that run efficiently on any particular serial scalar platform having both a high-quality C compiler and efficiently implemented libraries.

Note that any tool supporting efficiently portable programming also supports both efficient and portable programming. However, not every tool enabling both efficient and portable programming of its target architecture, has to enable efficiently portable programming of this architecture as well. Indeed, if some tool allows one to write a portable application as well as manually to optimize the application for every particular representative of the architecture, it does not mean that the application will run efficiently on every system of the architecture without changes in its source code.

Of course, the five properties above do not exhaust all possible properties that can appear important for one or another kind of software (fault tolerance for controlling software, scalability for parallel software, etc.). But these five are primary, and can be summarized in plain language as follows. Not too many programmers will want to use programming tools that subject them to these disadvantages.

- Do not allow them to utilize efficiently the performance potential of their computers.
- Do not allow them to write programs that can run on different computers.

- Do not allow them to write program modules that can be used by other programmers.
- Are based on a sophisticated set of ideas that make applications complex and tedious and also error-prone.
- Do not allow them to write portable applications running efficiently over a target group of computers.

In this book parallel programming tools are mainly assessed from the point of view of how well they support these basic program properties.

## CHAPTER 2

Vector and Superscalar Processors

2.1. VECTOR PROCESSOR

The vector processor provides a single control flow with serially executed instructions operating on both vector and scalar operands. The parallelism of this architecture is at the instruction level. Figure 2.1 depicts the architecture. Like the serial scalar processor the vector processor has only one IEU, and this IEU does not begin executing the next instruction until the execution of the current one is completed. Unlike the serial scalar processor, its instructions can operate both on scalar operands and on vector operands. The vector operand is an ordered set of scalars that is generally located on a vector register.

While a number of different implementations of this architecture exist, such as ILLIAC-IV, STAR-100, Cyber-205, Fujitsu VP 200, and ATC, probably the most elegant is the vector computer Cray-1 designed by Seymour Cray in 1976. Its processor employs a data pipeline to execute the vector instructions.

The idea of this approach is that the instruction to be executed performs some binary vector operation, say, multiplication, taking operands from vector registers **a** and **b** and putting the result on vector register **c**. Most vector operations, such as multiplication of two vector operands, are just elementwise extensions of the corresponding scalar operations. For example, in our case, ith element of the resulting vector **c** is equal to the product of ith elements of vectors **a** and **b**

$$c_i = a_i \times b_i.$$

This instruction is executed by a pipelined unit able to multiply scalars. The multiplication of two scalars is partitioned into m stages, and the unit can simultaneously perform different stages for different pairs of scalar elements of the vector operands. The execution of vector instruction $\mathbf{c} = \mathbf{a} \times \mathbf{b}$, where **a**, **b**, and **c** are n-element vector registers, by the pipelined unit can be summarized as follows:

Parallel Computing on Heterogeneous Networks, by Alexey Lastovetsky
ISBN 0-471-22982-2   Copyright © 2003 by John Wiley & Sons, Inc.

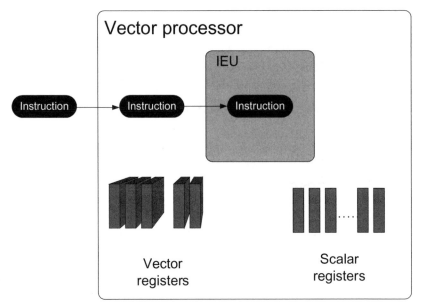

Figure 2.1. Vector processor architecture.

- At the first step, the unit performs stage 1 of the multiplication of elements a_1 and b_1:

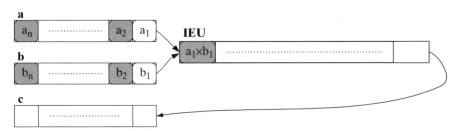

- At the ith step ($i = 2, \ldots, m - 1$), the unit performs in parallel stage 1 of the multiplication of elements a_i and b_i, stage 2 of the multiplication of elements a_{i-1} and b_{i-1}, etc., and stage i of the multiplication of elements a_1 and b_1,

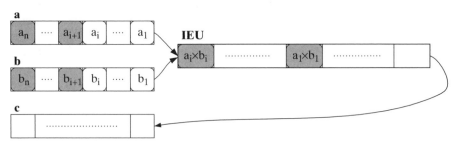

- At the mth step, the unit performs in parallel stage 1 of the multiplication of elements a_m and b_m, stage 2 of the multiplication of elements a_{m-1} and b_{m-1}, etc., as well as the final stage m of the multiplication of elements a_1 and b_1, resulting in $a_1 \times b_1$ put into element c_1 of vector register **c**:

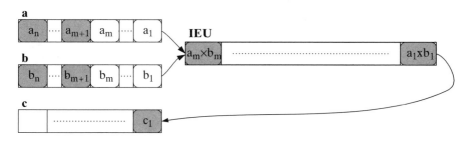

- At the $(m + j)$-th step $(j = 1, \ldots, n - m)$, the unit performs in parallel stage 1 of the multiplication of elements a_{m+j} and b_{m+j}, stage 2 of the multiplication of elements a_{m+j-1} and b_{m+j-1}, etc., as well as the final stage m of the multiplication of elements a_{j+1} and b_{j+1}, resulting in $a_{j+1} \times b_{j+1}$ put into element c_{j+1} of vector register **c**:

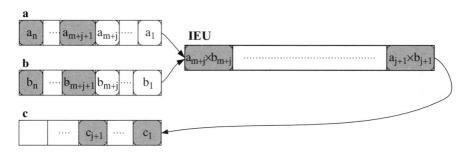

- At the $(n + k - 1)$-th step $(k = 2, \ldots, m - 1)$, the unit performs in parallel stage k of the multiplication of elements a_n and b_n, stage $k + 1$ of the multiplication of elements a_{n-1} and b_{n-1}, etc., as well as the final stage m of the multiplication of elements a_{n-m+k} and b_{n-m+k}, resulting in $a_{n-m+k} \times b_{n-m+k}$ put into element c_{n-m+k} of vector register **c**:

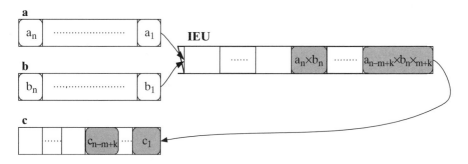

- At the $(n + m - 1)$-th step, the unit only performs the final stage m of the multiplication of elements a_n and b_n, resulting in $a_n \times b_n$ put into element c_n of vector register **c**:

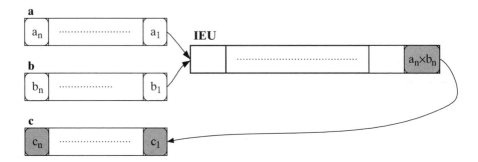

In total, it takes $n + m - 1$ steps to execute this instruction. The pipeline of the unit is fully loaded only from the mth to the nth step of the execution. Serial execution of n scalar multiplications with the same unit would take $n \times m$ steps. Thus the speedup provided by this vector instruction is

$$S = \frac{n \times m}{n + m - 1} = \frac{m}{1 + [(m-1)/n]}.$$

If n is large enough, the speedup is approximately equal to the length of the unit's pipeline, $S \approx m$.

Vector architectures are able to speed up such applications, a significant part of whose computations falls into the basic elementwise operations on arrays. Vector architecture includes the serial scalar architecture as a particular case ($n = 1, m = 1$).

2.2. SUPERSCALAR PROCESSOR

The superscalar processor provides a single control flow with instructions operating on scalar operands and being executed in parallel. Figure 2.2 depicts this architecture. In general, the superscalar processor has several instruction execution units executing instructions in parallel. Except for a small number of special instructions for data transfer between main memory and registers, the instructions operate on scalar operands located on the scalar registers.

Two successive instructions can be executed in parallel by two different IEUs if they do not have conflicting operands, that is, if they do not write in the same register and neither instruction uses a register in which the other writes. In any case, the parallel execution should not change the functional semantics of a serial execution of successive instructions.

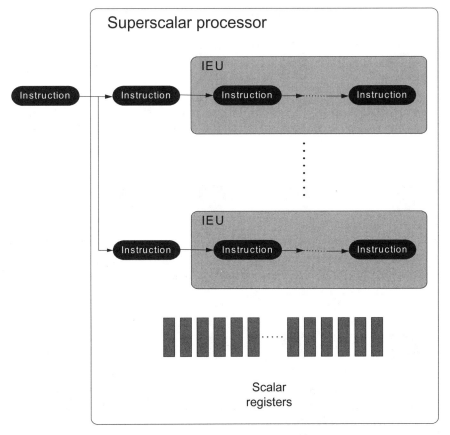

Figure 2.2. Superscalar processor architecture.

One can imagine a dispatcher unit directing instructions to relevant IEUs based on their type. Each IEU is characterized by the set of instructions that it executes. So the entire set of instructions is divided into a number of non-intersecting subsets each associated with some IEU.

Additionally each IEU can be a pipelined unit; that is, it can simultaneously execute several successive instructions, each being on its stage of execution. That parallel execution also should not change functional semantics of serial execution of the successive instructions. Consider the work of the pipelined unit executing a number of successive independent instructions. Let the pipeline of the unit consist of m stages. Let n successive instructions of the program, $I_1, \ldots, I_n$, be performed by the unit. Instruction I_k takes operands from registers a_k, b_k and puts the result on register c_k $(k = 1, \ldots, n)$. Let no two instructions have conflicting operands. Then the work of the unit can be summarized as follows:

- At the first step, the unit performs stage 1 of instruction I_1:

- At the ith step ($i = 2, \ldots, m - 1$), the unit performs in parallel stage 1 of instruction I_i, stage 2 of instruction I_{i-1}, etc., and stage i of instruction I_1,

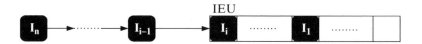

- At the mth step, the unit performs in parallel stage 1 of instruction I_m, stage 2 of instruction I_{m-1}, etc., as well as the final stage m of instruction I_1; after completion of this, register c_1 contains the result of instruction I_1:

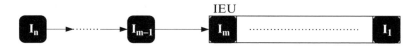

- At the $(m + j)$-th step ($j = 1, \ldots, n - m$), the unit performs in parallel stage 1 of instruction I_{m+j}, stage 2 of instruction I_{m+j-1}, etc., as well as the final stage m of instruction I_{j+1}; after completion of this, register c_{j+1} contains the result of instruction I_{j+1}:

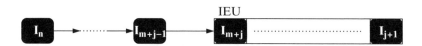

- At the $(n + k - 1)$-th step ($k = 2, \ldots, m - 1$), the unit performs in parallel stage k of instruction I_n, stage $k + 1$ of instruction I_{n-1}, etc., as well as the final stage m of instruction I_{n-m+k}; after completion of this, register c_{n-m+k} contains the result of instruction I_{n-m+k}:

- At the $(n + m - 1)$-th step, the unit only performs the final stage m of instruction I_n; after completion of this, register c_n contains the result of instruction I_n:

IEU

In total, it takes $(n + m-1)$ steps to execute n instruction. The pipeline of the unit is fully loaded only from the mth to the nth step of the execution. Strictly serial execution by the unit of n successive instructions takes $n \times m$ steps. Thus the maximal speedup provided by this pipelined unit is

$$S_{\text{IEU}} = \frac{n \times m}{n+m-1} = \frac{m}{1+[(m-1)/n]}.$$

If n is large enough, the speedup is approximately equal to the length of the unit's pipeline, $S_{\text{IEU}} \approx m$.

The maximal speedup provided by the entire superscalar processor having K parallel IEUs is approximately equal to the sum of lengths of pipelines of the IEUs:

$$S_{\text{proc}} \approx \sum_{i=1}^{K} m_i.$$

The obvious type of computation that can be speeded up by the superscalar processor is the basic elementwise operation on arrays when successive instructions execute the same operation on successive elements of the arrays. To efficiently support that type of computation, the processor should have at least $R \times \Sigma_{i=1}^{K} m_i$ registers, as this guarantees that no two of $\Sigma_{i=1}^{K} m_i$ simultaneously executed instructions share the same register. Hence the operations can be safely executed in parallel (provided that each instruction uses R registers).

CDC 6600 (1964) was the first processor with several IEUs functioning in parallel. CDC 7600 (1969) was the first processor with several pipelined IEUs functioning in parallel. Nowadays practically all manufactured microprocessors have many IEUs, each of which is normally a pipelined unit, and we can hardly imagine other microprocessor architectures.

Superscalar architecture includes the serial scalar architecture as a particular case ($K = 1, m = 1$).

2.3. PROGRAMMING MODEL

Vector and superscalar architectures are united in a single group for a number of reasons. One is that the most successful vector architectures are very close to superscalar architectures both ideologically and in implementation. Indeed, the vector pipelined unit presented above can be seen as a specialized clone of the general-purpose superscalar pipelined unit, which is optimized for pipelined execution of n successive instructions performed as the same operation but on different operands. The optimization is that due to its specialization the vector pipelined unit does not need a decoding stage and therefore uses a more effective data pipeline instead of the instruction pipeline. On the other hand, the design of some advanced superscalar processors, such as Intel i860, is obviously influenced by the vector-pipelined architecture.

But the most important reason is that these architectures share the same programming model. Namely a good portable program that can take full advantage of the performance potential of superscalar processors is defined in the same way as for vector processors. Indeed, what makes this a good program for vector processors? It is the program's use of a wide range of vector instructions that implement basic operations on arrays. Like wise a program intensively using basic operations on arrays is perfectly suitable for superscalar processors in that it allows a very high level of utilization of their pipelined units.

Of course, unlike vector processors, superscalar processors allow more sophisticated mixtures of operations to efficiently load their pipelined units than just basic array operations. But normally such mixtures are rather specific for each superscalar processor and therefore are not portable. Second, most of the mixtures are quite esoteric and rarely relevant in real-life applications. Last, even in the odd case where a real-life application is potentially able to load the pipelined units of the superscalar processor with some complex mixture of operations, the problem of writing/generating the corresponding efficient code may seem too difficult to justify undertaking its solution. Therefore, even if the superscalar architecture looks richer than the vector architecture, the real programming model used for superscalar processors should be the same as the programming model for vector processors.

2.4. OPTIMIZING COMPILERS

Vector and superscalar architectures provide more performance potential than the serial scalar architecture. Vector and superscalar architectures are an evolution of this traditional architecture and include the latter as a particular case. For this reason programming tools for the architectures are mainly based on C and Fortran.

These tools include optimizing C and Fortran 77 compilers. The main specific optimization is loop vectorization. The compilers try to recognize the loops, which are in fact a sequential form of vector operations, and compile the loops in the most efficient way. For example, consider the following loop:

```
for(i=0;  i<64;  i++)
   c[i]  =  a[i]  +  b[i]  ;
```

This implements addition of two real vectors. Straightforward compilation of the loop leads to the target code of the form

```
        r0 <- 0
begin:  if(r0>=64) goto end
        r1 <- a[r0]
        r2 <- b[r0]
        r3 <- r1 + r2
        c[r0] <- r3
        r0 <- r0 + SIZE_OF_TYPE
        goto begin
end:    continue
```

where r0, r1, r2, r3 are scalar registers, a, b, c are address constants (addresses of the first element of the corresponding arrays), and SIZE_OF_TYPE is a integer constant (the size of elements of real arrays a, b, and c). The target code takes no advantage of the vector processor because it does not use vector instructions. It is also not able to load pipelined units of the superscalar processor because the instructions of the program, which could be executed in parallel by the same IEU, have conflicting operands: namely the addition instruction

```
r3 <- r1 + r2
```

writes in the same register r3 at successive iterations of the loop. In addition, in the control flow, the instructions are separated by several other instructions and hence cannot fully load the corresponding pipeline even in the absence of conflicting operands.

Thus the straightforward compilation scheme is not able to accelerate the execution of the array operation. At the same time, for the vector processor, the loop could be efficiently implemented with vector instructions of the processor by the target code of the form

```
v1 <- a
v2 <- b
v3 <- v1 + v2
c <- v3
```

where v1, v2, v3 are vector registers (for simplicity, we assume that the size of the vector registers is 64).

For the superscalar processor, the loop could be efficiently implemented by unrolling the loop in order to load the best possible pipelined units of the processor. For example, an optimizing compiler for the superscalar processor could generate the following target code

```
         r0 <- 0
begin:   if(r0>=64) goto end
         r1 <- a[r0]
         r2 <- a[r0+SIZE_OF_TYPE]
         r3 <- a[r0+2*SIZE_OF_TYPE]
         r4 <- a[r0+3*SIZE_OF_TYPE]
         r5 <- a[r0+4*SIZE_OF_TYPE]
         r6 <- a[r0+5*SIZE_OF_TYPE]
         r7 <- a[r0+6*SIZE_OF_TYPE]
         r8 <- a[r0+7*SIZE_OF_TYPE]
         r9 <- b[r0]
         r10 <- b[r0+SIZE_OF_TYPE]
         r11 <- b[r0+2*SIZE_OF_TYPE]
         r12 <- b[r0+3*SIZE_OF_TYPE]
         r13 <- b[r0+4*SIZE_OF_TYPE]
         r14 <- b[r0+5*SIZE_OF_TYPE]
         r15 <- b[r0+6*SIZE_OF_TYPE]
         r16 <- b[r0+7*SIZE_OF_TYPE]
         r17 <- r1 + r9
         r18 <- r2 + r10
         r19 <- r3 + r11
         r20 <- r4 + r12
         r21 <- r5 + r13
         r22 <- r6 + r14
         r23 <- r7 + r15
         r24 <- r8 + r16
         c[r0] <- r17
         c[r0+SIZE_OF_TYPE] <- r18
         c[r0+2*SIZE_OF_TYPE] <- r19
         c[r0+3*SIZE_OF_TYPE] <- r20
         c[r0+4*SIZE_OF_TYPE] <- r21
         c[r0+5*SIZE_OF_TYPE] <- r22
         c[r0+6*SIZE_OF_TYPE] <- r24
         c[r0+7*SIZE_OF_TYPE] <- r24
         r0 <- r0 + 8*SIZE_OF_TYPE
         goto begin
end:     continue
```

This code is able to load the pipeline unit executing reading from memory into registers, the pipeline unit executing addition of two registers, and the pipeline unit executing writing into memory from registers. Some compilers for superscalar processors perform a more general loop parallelization—the loop pipelining, including loop vectorization as a particular case.

The most difficult problem to be solved by the optimizing compilers is recognition of the loops, whether parallelized or vectorized. The solution is based on the analysis of data dependencies in loops. In general, there are three classes of data dependence between statements in sequential programs that must be determined for the statements to be executed in parallel: flow dependence (or true dependence), anti-dependence, and output dependence. True dependence exists between a statement of the form

```
x = a + b ;
```

and a statement of the form

```
c = x + d ;
```

In other words, true dependence exists between statement *s1*, which writes in some variable, and statement *s2*, which follows (in control flow) statement *s1* and uses this variable. In graphical form this dependence is depicted as follows:

Anti-dependence exists between a statement of the form

```
a = x + b ;
```

and a statement of the form

```
x = c + d ;
```

In other words, anti-dependence exists between statement *s1*, which uses some variable, and statement *s2*, which follows (in control flow) statement *s1* and writes in this variable. In graphical form this dependence is depicted as follows:

Output dependence exists between a statement of the form

```
x = a + b ;
```

and a statement of the form

```
x = c + d ;
```

In other words, output dependence exists between statement *s1*, which writes in some variable, and statement *s2*, which follows (in control flow) statement *s1* and also writes in this variable. In graphical form this dependence is depicted as follows:

To decide if a loop can be parallelized or vectorized, its dependence graph should be built. The dependence graph for the loop is built as a summary of the dependence graph for the result of the unrolling of the loop. For example, the full "unrolled" dependence graph for the loop

```
for (i=0; i<n; i++) {
    c = a[i] + b[i] ; /* statement s1 */
    d[i] = c + e[i] ; /* statement s2 */
}
```

looks as follows:

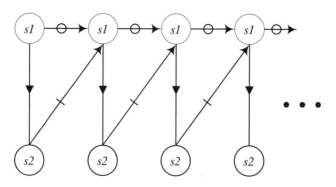

This potentially infinite graph is summarized in the form of the finite graph

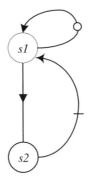

Usually during the summarizing some information is lost. For example, the loop

```
for(i=0; i<n; i++) {
  c[i] = a[i] + b ;      /* statement s1 */
  d[i] = c[i] + e[i] ; /* statement s2 */
}
```

has the same dependence graph of the form

as the loop

```
for(i=0; i<n; i++) {
  c[i+1] = a[i] + b ;    /* statement s1 */
  d[i] = c[i] + e[i] ; /* statement s2 */
}
```

However, their unrolled dependence graphs are different. The unrolled dependence graph for the first loop is

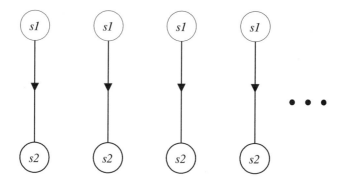

The unrolled dependence graph for the second loop is

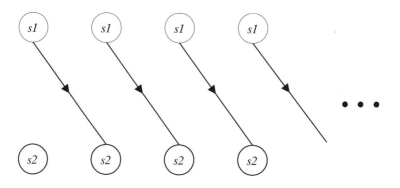

The importance of the dependence analysis of loops is explained by a simple fact: A loop whose dependence graph is cycle-free can be parallelized or vectorized. The reason is that if there are no cycles in the dependence graph, then there will be no races in parallel execution of the same statement from different iterations of the loop.

Note that the presence of cycles in the dependence graph does not mean that the loop cannot be vectorized or parallelized. The point is that some cycles in the dependence graph can be eliminated by using elementary transformations. For example, the loop

```
for(i=0; i<n; i++) {
    c = a[i] + b[i] ; /* statement s1 */
    d[i] = c + e[i] ; /* statement s2 */
}
```

whose dependence graph is

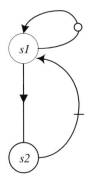

can be transformed into the loop

```
for(i=0; i<n; i++) {
   cc[i] = a[i] + b[i] ; /* statement s1 */
   d[i] = cc[i] + e[i] ; /* statement s2 */
}
c = cc[n-1] ;
```

whose dependence graph has no cycle:

The transformation is known as *scalar expansion*.

Another transformation that eliminates cycles in dependence graphs is *induction variable recognition*. This transformation is used to transform the loop

```
for(i=0; i<n; i++) {
   a = a + b ;          /* statement s1 */
   c[i] = c[i] + a ; /* statement s2 */
}
```

whose dependence graph is

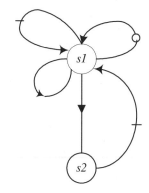

into the loop

```
for(i=0;  i<n;  i++)  {
  d[i]  =  a  +  b*i  ;        /*  statement  s1  */
  c[i]  =  c[i]  +  d[i]  ;  /*  statement  s2  */
}
```

whose dependence graph has no cycle:

So far building the dependence graph for a loop has proved not so difficult. This is explained by simplicity of subscript expressions in the loops we have analyzed. But the problem of testing dependences in loops can be very complex and expensive. To see this, let us define some dependences in loops in a more general and formal way. For a loop of the form

```
for(i=0;  i<n;  i++)  {
  c[f(i)]  =  a[i]  +  b[i]  ;  /*  statement  s1  */
  d[i]  =  c[g(i)]  +  e[i]  ;  /*  statement  s2  */
}
```

a true dependence between statement *s1* and statement *s2* exists if and only if $\exists i, j \in [0, n-1]: i \leq j$ & $f(i) = g(j)$, and an anti-dependence between statement *s2* and statement *s1* exists if and only if $\exists i, j \in [0, n-1]: i > j$ & $f(i) = g(j)$. For a loop of the form

```
for(i=0; i<n; i++) {
  c[i] = a[g(i)] + b[i] ; /* statement s1 */
  a[f(i)] = d[i] + e[i] ; /* statement s2 */
}
```

a true dependence between statement *s2* and statement *s1* exists if and only if $\exists i, j \in [0, n-1]: i < j \ \& \ f(i) = g(j)$.

The problem of testing these conditions can be NP-complete and hence very expensive. Therefore the practical tests used in optimizing compilers usually assume that subscript expressions are simple: namely that $f(i) = a_1 \times i + a_0$ and $g(i) = b_1 \times i + b_0$. Then $f(i) = g(j)$ if and only if $a_1 \times i - b_1 \times j = b_0 - a_0$. The approach that has traditionally been used is to try to *break* a dependence, that is, to try to prove that the dependence does not exist.

One simple practical test is the GCD test. The test breaks the dependence if there is no integer solution to the equation $a_1 \times i - b_1 \times j = b_0 - a_0$, ignoring the loop limits. A solution to the equation $a_1 \times i - b_1 \times j = b_0 - a_0$ exists if and only if the greatest common divisor (GCD) of a_1 and b_1 divides $b_0 - a_0$. The test is *conservative*. That is, it may not break a dependence that does not exist. Indeed, the equation could have solutions outside the iteration space only. A conservative test can guarantee the absence of the dependence but may not guarantee its presence. In other words, if the test fails to prove the absence of the dependence, it does not necessarily mean that the dependence is present. Practical tests are usually conservative.

A more accurate test taking into account the loop limits is Banerjee's test. It proceeds by finding an upper bound U, and a lower bound L of $a_1 \times i - b_1 \times j$ under the constraints that $0 \leq i < n$ and $0 \leq j < n$. If either $L > b_0 - a_0$ or $U < b_0 - a_0$, then the functions do not intersect, and therefore there is no dependence. For example, consider the loop

```
for(i=0; i<10; i++) {
  c[i+10] = a[i] + b[i] ; /* statement s1 */
  d[i] = c[i] + e[i] ;    /* statement s2 */
}
```

The GCD test will not break the dependence between statements *s1* and *s2* because there is a solution to the equation $a_1 \times i - b_1 \times j = b_0 - a_0$ or $i - j = -10$. However, the lower bound of $a_1 \times i - b_1 \times j = i - j$ is -9, which is greater than $b_0 - a_0$, and therefore the dependence would be broken by the Banerjee test.

The same procedure for the loop

```
for(i=0; i<10; i++) {
  c[i+9] = a[i] + b[i] ; /* statement s1 */
  d[i] = c[i] + e[i] ;   /* statement s2 */
}
```

will not break the dependence because the lower bound of $a_1 \times i - b_1 \times j = i - j$ is -9, which is not greater than $b_0 - a_0 = -9$. In this case the accuracy of dependence analysis can be increased by testing possible dependences between statements $s1$ and $s2$ separately. Namely, to test the anti-dependence between statements $s2$ and $s1$, the restriction $i > j$ should be added to the loop limits when computing the upper and lower bounds. Then the lower bound of $a_1 \times i - b_1 \times j = i - j$ is 1, which is greater than $b_0 - a_0 = -9$ and therefore the anti-dependence is broken by the test. To test the true dependence between statements $s1$ and $s2$, the restriction $i \leq j$ should be added to the loop limits when computing the upper and lower bounds of $a_1 \times i - b_1 \times j$. Then the lower bound of $a_1 \times i - b_1 \times j = i - j$ is -9, which is not greater than $b_0 - a_0$, and therefore the true dependence is not broken. This more accurate analysis allows us to conclude that even though there may exist a true dependence between statements $s1$ and $s2$, other dependences between the statements do not exist, and therefore the dependence graph for the loop is cycle-free, which means that the loop can be parallelized or vectorized.

This more accurate test can be formulated in terms of *directions*. Note that testing all types of dependence between statements $s1$ and $s2$ reduces to computing an upper bound U, and a lower bound L of $a_1 \times i - b_1 \times j$ under the constraints that $0 \leq i < n$ and $0 \leq j < n$. Testing different types of dependence only differs in the direction of the dependence in the iteration space: at the same iteration ($i = j$), between different iterations in forward direction ($i < j$), and between different iterations in backward direction ($i > j$).

In general, given a loop nest

```
for(i1=...)
  for(i2=...)
    . . .
      for(ik=...){
      a[f(i1,i2,...,ik)]  = ...     /* statement s1 */
      ... = a[g(i1,i2,...,ik)] ;  /* statement s2 */
}
```

the complete Banerjee test would check dependencies for each possible *direction*. Namely, for all valid direction vectors $(\Psi_1, \Psi_2, \ldots, \Psi_k)$ with each Ψ_i is either $<, >,$ or $=$, the test tries to show that there is no solution to the equation

$$f(i_1, i_2, \ldots, i_k) = g(j_1, j_2, \ldots, j_k)$$

within the loop limits, with the restrictions

$$i_1 \Psi_1 j, i_2 \Psi_2 j_2, \ldots, i_k \Psi_k j_k$$

These restrictions are taken into account when computing the upper and lower bounds (in the complete test, there is a pair of lower and upper bounds for each loop index).

There are at least three reasons why Banerjee's test is conservative. First, it only checks that there is a real-valued solution to the equation. The solution does not have to be integer. Therefore failure to break the dependence does not imply that the dependence exists.

Second, for multiple subscript arrays, each subscript equation is tested separately. A dependence will be assumed if there is a solution for each separate equation. This is conservative because the system of equations may not have a solution even though each equation has a solution.

Third, it is assumed that the loop limits and the coefficients are known constants. This assumption can be relaxed as the test will still work if loop limit are set to infinity. However, dependence is assumed if one of the coefficients is not known.

Apart from the GCD test and the Banerjee inequalities test, there are some other practical dependence tests such as the Rice partition-based test, the Stanford cascade test, and the Maryland Omega test.

Different optimizing compilers use different algorithms to recognize parallelizable loops. Each compiler has its own class of parallelizable loops, and the classes for different compilers can differ significantly. Therefore, although optimizing C and Fortran 77 compilers are able to generate efficient codes for vector and superscalar architectures, the writing of the corresponding source codes is often not trivial. The programmer must know the particular compiler very well to use exactly those forms of parallelizable loops that are recognized by the compiler. As a result some applications that run efficiently on one vector or superscalar processor, due to their careful tuning to the corresponding compiler, may run much slower on other vector and superscalar processors of the same potential performance. Although there are some simple classes of parallelizable loops that are recognized by any normal optimizing compiler for vector or superscalar processor, these classes are quite restricted and do not include many real-life loop patterns.

Our analysis of optimizing C and Fortran 77 compilers for vector and superscalar processors can be summarized as follows:

- Like those for the serial architecture, the compilers support modular, portable, and reliable programming.
- The compilers support efficient programming but for rather restricted class of applications; the efficient programming is quite demanding for the programmer and often leads to such source code that is difficult to read and understand.
- The support for portable efficiency provided by the compilers is limited to some very simple classes of application.

2.5. ARRAY LIBRARIES

As we have seen, the most difficult problem to be solved by optimizing C and Fortran 77 compilers is the recognition of the loops, which can be parallelized or vectorized. Function extensions of C and Fortran 77 with array or vector libraries allow the programmer to use regular C and Fortran 77 compilers, which perform no optimizations specific for vector and superscalar architectures, for efficient programming those architectures. Instead, the programmer can use library functions or subroutines efficiently implementing operations on arrays for each particular vector or superscalar processor.

One well-known and well-designed array library is the Basic Linear Algebra Subprogram (BLAS). This library provides basic array operations for numerical linear algebra, and it is aimed, first of all, at vector and superscalar architectures. The functionality of the library covers all main operations on vectors and matrices used for the numerical solution of linear algebra problems.

Highly efficient machine-specific implementations of the BLAS are available for most modern computers, and this is what makes parallel programming with the library efficiently portable.

BLAS routines are divided into three main categories, commonly referred to as Levels 1, 2, and 3 BLAS, depending on the type of implemented operation. Level 1 addresses scalar-vector operations, Level 2 addresses matrix-vector operations, and Level 3 addresses matrix-matrix operations.

2.5.1. Level 1 BLAS

Routines of Level 1 do vector reduction operations, vector rotation operations, elementwise and combined vector operations, and data movement with vectors. An example of vector reduction operation is the addition of the scaled dot product of two real vectors x and y into a scaled scalar r. The mathematical formulation of the operation is

$$ r \leftarrow \beta r + \alpha x^T y = \beta r + \alpha \sum_{i=0}^{n-1} x_i y_i, $$

where $\alpha, \beta, r \in \Re$, $x, y \in \Re^n$, x^T denotes the transposition of vector x, and $\leftarrow$ stands for the assignment statement. The BLAS provides both Fortran 77 and C interfaces to its routines. The C interface of the routine implementing the above operation is

```
void BLAS_ddot( enum blas_conj_type conj, int n,
                double alpha, const double *x,
                int incx, double beta, const double *y,
                int incy, double *r );
```

The n-length vector operand x is specified by two arguments—x and incx, where x is an array that contains the entries of the n-length vector x, and incx is the stride within x between two successive elements of the vector x. The argument conj has no effect and is only added to keep interfaces of different routines but implementing similar operations generic. This optional argument specifies for the function BLAS_cdot, which implements the same operation but on complex vectors x and y, if the vector components x_i are used unconjugated or conjugated. Other routines of the group compute different vector norms of vector x, compute the sum of the entries of vector x, find the smallest or biggest component of vector x, computes the sum of squares of the entries of vector x. Level 1 routines doing rotation operations generate Givens plane rotation, Jacobi rotation, and Householder transformation.

An example of elementwise vector operation is the scaled addition of two real vectors x and y. The mathematical formulation of the operation is

$$w \leftarrow \alpha x + \beta y,$$

where $\alpha, \beta \in \Re$, and $x, y, w \in \Re^n$. The C interface of the routine implementing this operation is

```
void BLAS_dwaxpby( int n, double alpha, const double *x,
                   int incx, double beta, const double *y,
                   int incy, double *w, int incw );
```

The routine scales vector x by α and vector y by β, adds these two vectors, and stores the result in vector w. Function BLAS_cwaxpby does the same operation but on complex vectors. Other routines of the group scale the entries of a vector x by the real scalar $1/\alpha$; scale a vector x by α and a vector y by β, add these two vectors to one another, and store the result in vector y; combine a scaled vector accumulation and a dot product; and apply a plane rotation to vectors x and y.

An example of data movement with vectors is the interchange of real vectors x and y. The C interface of the routine implementing this operation is

```
void BLAS_dswap( int n, double *x, int incx, double *y,
                 int incy );
```

Function BLAS_cswap does the same operation but on complex vectors. Other routines of the group copy vector x into vector y; sort the entries of real vector x in increasing or decreasing order, and overwrite this vector x with the sorted vector as well as compute the corresponding permutation vector p; permute the entries of vector x according to permutation vector p.

2.5.2. Level 2 BLAS

Routines of Level 2 compute different matrix vector products, do addition of scaled matrix vector products, compute multiple matrix vector products, solve triangular equations, and perform rank 1 and rank 2 updates. Matrix operands of the operations are dense or banded. In addition some operations use symmetric, Hermitian, or triangular matrices. To store matrices, the following schemes are used:

- Column-based and row-based storage in a contiguous way (conventional storage).
- Packed storage for symmetric, Hermitian or triangular matrices.
- Band storage for band matrices.

So, for the C language interfaces, matrices may be stored in columns or rows: an $m \times n$ matrix A is stored in a one-dimensional array a, with matrix element a_{ij} stored columnwize in an array element a[i+j*s] or row-wize in an array element a[j+i*s]. That is, it is assumed that for row-wize storage, elements within a row are contiguous in memory, while elements within a column are separated by s memory elements. If s is equal to n, the rows will be contiguous in memory. If s is greater that n, there will be a gap of $(s - n)$ memory elements between two successive rows. Similarly, for column-wize storage, elements within a column are contiguous in memory, while elements within the rows are separated by s memory elements. If s is equal to m, rows will be contiguous in memory. If s is greater that m, there will be a gap of $(s - n)$ memory elements between two successive rows.

If a matrix is triangular, only the elements of the upper or lower triangle are accessed. The remaining elements of the array need not be set. Routines that handle symmetric or Hermitian matrices allow for either the upper or lower triangle of the matrix to be stored in the corresponding elements of the array; the remaining elements of the array need not be set.

Symmetric, Hermitian, or triangular matrices are allowed to be stored more compactly, with the relevant triangle being packed by columns or rows in a one-dimensional array. For example, in the case of the C language and row storage scheme, the upper triangle of an $n \times n$ matrix A may be stored in a one-dimensional array a in such a way, that matrix element a_{ij} $(i \leq j)$ is stored in array element a[j+i*(2*n-i-1)/2]. Thus matrix

$$\begin{pmatrix} a_{00} & a_{01} & a_{02} \\ 0 & a_{11} & a_{12} \\ 0 & 0 & a_{22} \end{pmatrix}$$

may be stored compactly in a one-dimensional array as follows:

$$a_{00} \quad a_{01} \quad a_{02} \quad a_{11} \quad a_{12} \quad a_{22}$$

Compared to general matrices, band matrices are allowed to be stored more compactly. For example, in Fortran and the column-wize storage scheme, an $m \times n$ band matrix A with l subdiagonals and u superdiagonals may be stored in a two-dimensional array A with $l + u + 1$ rows and n columns. Columns of matrix A are stored in corresponding columns of array A, and diagonals of matrix A are stored in rows of array A in such a way that matrix element a_{ij} is stored in array element A$(u+i-j,j)$ for $\max(0, j - u) \leq i \leq \min(m - 1, j + l)$. Thus band matrix

$$\begin{pmatrix} a_{00} & a_{01} & 0 & 0 & 0 \\ a_{10} & a_{11} & a_{12} & 0 & 0 \\ a_{20} & a_{21} & a_{22} & a_{23} & 0 \\ 0 & a_{31} & a_{32} & a_{33} & a_{34} \\ 0 & 0 & a_{42} & a_{43} & a_{44} \end{pmatrix}$$

may be stored compactly in a two-dimensional array as follows:

$$\begin{array}{cccccc} * & a_{01} & a_{12} & a_{23} & a_{34} \\ a_{00} & a_{11} & a_{22} & a_{33} & a_{44} \\ a_{10} & a_{21} & a_{32} & a_{43} & * \\ a_{20} & a_{31} & a_{42} & * & * \end{array}$$

The elements marked by an * in the upper left and lower right corners of this array need not be set because they are not referenced by BLAS routines.

There are also special storage schemes for compact storing triangular, symmetric, and Hermitian band matrices. An example of matrix vector multiplication operation is the scaled addition of a real n-length vector y, and the product of a general real $m \times n$ matrix A and a real n-length vector x. The mathematical formulation of the operation is

$$y \leftarrow \alpha A x + \beta y,$$

where $\alpha, \beta \in \mathfrak{R}$. The C interface of the routine implementing this operation is

```
void BLAS_dgemv( enum blas_order_type order,
                 enum blas_trans_type trans, int m, int n,
                 double alpha, const double *a, int stride,
                 const double *x, int incx, double beta,
                 const double *y, int incy );
```

If order is set to blas_rowmajor, it is assumed that the matrix A is stored row-wise in the array a with elements within array columns separated by stride memory elements. If this parameter is set to blas_colmajor, it is assumed that A is stored columnwise with elements within array rows separated by stride memory elements. The argument trans should be set to `blas_no_trans`. If the parameter is set to `blas_trans`, the routine will perform the operation

$$y \leftarrow \alpha A^T x + \beta y$$

instead of the operation above. Function `BLAS_cgemv` performs the same operation but on complex operands. If matrix A is a general band matrix with l subdiagonals and u superdiagonals, the use of the function

```
void BLAS_dgbmv ( enum blas_order_type order,
                  enum blas_trans_type trans,
                  int m, int n, int l, int u,
                  double alpha, const double *a, int stride,
                  const double *x, int incx, double beta,
                  const double *y, int incy );
```

instead of `BLAS_dgemv` leads to better use of memory. Function `BLAS_dgbmv` assumes that a band storage scheme is used to store matrix A. Other routines of Level 2 do the following:

- Multiply vector x by a real symmetric, complex symmetric, or Hermitian matrix A; scale the resulting vector and add it to the scaled vector operand y, that is, perform the operation

$$y \leftarrow \alpha A x + \beta y,$$

  where $A = A^T$ or $A = A^H$.
- Multiply vector x by a general triangular matrix A, or its transpose, or its conjugate transpose, and copy the resulting vector in the vector operand x, that is, perform one of the operations

$$x \leftarrow \alpha A x, \quad x \leftarrow \alpha A^T x, \quad \text{or} \quad x \leftarrow \alpha A^H x.$$

- Add the product of two scaled matrix vector products, that is, perform the operation

$$y \leftarrow \alpha A x + \beta B x.$$

- Multiply vector y by a general matrix A^T, scale the resulting vector, and add the result to z, storing the result in the vector operand x; then multiply the matrix A by x, scale the resulting vector, and store it in the vector operand w; that is, perform the pair of operations

$$x \leftarrow \beta A^T y, \quad w \leftarrow \alpha A x.$$

- Multiply vector y by a triangular matrix A^T, storing the result as x, as well as multiply matrix A by vector z, storing the result as w; that is, perform the pair of operations

$$x \leftarrow A^T y, \quad w \leftarrow Az.$$

- Precede a combined matrix vector and a transposed matrix vector multiply by a rank 2 update—namely update a matrix A by $u_1 v_1^T$ and $u_2 v_2^T$, then multiply the updated matrix by a vector y, then add the scaled resulting vector to the vector operand z, storing the result as x, then multiply the operand x by the updated matrix A, and then scale the resulting vector and store it as w; that is, perform the sequence of operations

$$\hat{A} \leftarrow A + u_1 v_1^T + u_2 v_2^T, \quad x \leftarrow \beta \hat{A}^T y + z, \quad \text{and} \quad w \leftarrow \alpha \hat{A} x.$$

- Solve one of the systems of equations

$$x \leftarrow \alpha A^{-1} x \quad \text{or} \quad x \leftarrow \alpha A^{-T} x,$$

where x is a vector and matrix A is a unit, non-unit, upper or lower triangular (or triangular banded) matrix.

- Perform the rank 1 operation

$$A \leftarrow \alpha x y^T + \beta A,$$

where x is a vector and A is a unit, non-unit, upper or lower triangular (or triangular banded) matrix.

- Perform the symmetric rank 1 update

$$A \leftarrow \alpha x x^T + \beta A,$$

where α and β are scalars, x is a vector, and A is a symmetric matrix.

- Perform the Hermitian rank 1 update

$$A \leftarrow \alpha x x^H + \beta A,$$

where α and β are real scalars, x is a complex vector, and A is a Hermitian matrix.

- Perform the symmetric rank 2 update

$$A \leftarrow \alpha x y^T + \alpha y x^T + \beta A,$$

where α and β are scalars, x and y are vectors, and A is a symmetric matrix.

- Perform the Hermitian rank 2 update

$$A \leftarrow \alpha x y^H + \overline{\alpha} y x^H + \beta A,$$

where α is a complex scalar and β is a real scalar, x and y are complex vectors, and A is a Hermitian matrix.

For any matrix-vector operation that has a specific matrix operand (triangular, symmetric, banded, etc.), there is a routine implementing the operation for each storage scheme that can be used to store the operand.

2.5.3. Level 3 BLAS

Routines of Level 3 do $O(n^2)$ matrix operations (norms, diagonal scaling, scaled accumulation, and addition), $O(n^3)$ matrix-matrix operations (multiplication, solving matrix equations, symmetric rank k and $2k$ updates), and data movement with matrices.

Routines implementing $O(n^2)$ matrix operations allow the programmers to use different storage schemes to store matrix operands. Depending on the form of the matrix operands, different conventional, packed, or band storage schemes can be used. For example, to add two symmetric band matrices, we can pick a routine using the general conventional storage scheme, a routine using the band storage scheme, a routing using the conventional symmetric storage scheme, a routine using the symmetric band storage scheme, or a routine using the symmetric packed storage scheme.

An example of the $O(n^2)$ matrix operation is

$$C \leftarrow \alpha A + \beta B,$$

which scales two real $m \times n$ matrices A and B and stores their sum in a matrix C. The C interface of the routine implementing this operation under assumption that the matrices A, B, and C are of the general form is

```
void BLAS_dge_add( enum blas_order_type order, int m,
                   int n, double alpha, const double *a,
                   int stride_a, double beta,
                   const double *b, int stride_b,
                   double *c, int stride_c );
```

There are other 15 routines performing this operation for different types and forms of the matrices A, B, and C. For example, function BLAS_cge_add performs this operation on complex matrices of the general form, and function BLAS_dtp_add performs this operation on real triangular matrices, which are stored using the packed storage scheme.

An example of $O(n^3)$ matrix-matrix operation is

$$C \leftarrow \alpha A B + \beta C,$$

where α, β are scalars, A is an $m \times n$ matrix, B is an $n \times k$ matrix, and C is an $m \times k$ matrix. The C interface of the routine implementing this operation under assumption that A, B and C are real matrices of the general form is

```
void BLAS_dgemm( enum blas_order_type order,
                 enum blas_trans_type trans_a,
                 enum blas_trans_type trans_b,
                 int m, int n, int k, double alpha,
                 const double *a, int stride_a,
                 const double *b, int stride_b,
                 double beta, const double *c,
                 int stride_c ) ;
```

Arguments `trans_a` and `trans_b` should be set to `blas_no_trans`. If, say, the parameter `trans_a` is set to `blas_trans`, the routine will perform the operation

$$C \leftarrow \alpha A^T B + \beta C$$

instead of the operation above. Function `BLAS_cgemm` performs the same operation but on complex operands. Other routines of the group do the following:

- Perform one of the symmetric (or Hermitian) matrix-matrix operations

$$C \leftarrow \alpha AB + \beta C \quad \text{or} \quad C \leftarrow \alpha BA + \beta C,$$

  where α and β are scalars, A is a symmetric (or Hermitian) matrix, and B and C are general matrices.
- Perform one of the matrix-matrix operations

$$C \leftarrow \alpha AB, \quad \text{or} \quad C \leftarrow \alpha BA,$$
$$\text{or} \quad C \leftarrow \alpha A^T B, \quad \text{or} \quad C \leftarrow \alpha BA^T,$$
$$\text{or} \quad C \leftarrow \alpha A^H B, \quad \text{or} \quad C \leftarrow \alpha BA^H,$$

  where α is a scalar, B is a general matrix, and A is a triangular (or triangular band) matrix.
- Solve one of the matrix equations

$$B \leftarrow \alpha A^{-1} B, \quad \text{or} \quad B \leftarrow \alpha BA^{-1},$$
$$\text{or} \quad B \leftarrow \alpha A^{-T} B, \quad \text{or} \quad B \leftarrow \alpha BA^{-T},$$
$$\text{or} \quad B \leftarrow \alpha A^{-H} B, \quad \text{or} \quad B \leftarrow \alpha BA^{-H},$$

  where α is a scalar, B is a general matrix, and A is a triangular matrix.

- Perform one of the symmetric rank k and $2k$ updates

$$C \leftarrow \alpha A A^T + \beta C, \quad \text{or} \quad C \leftarrow \alpha A^T A + \beta C,$$

$$\text{or} \quad C \leftarrow \alpha A J A^T + \beta C, \quad \text{or} \quad C \leftarrow \alpha A^T J A + \beta C,$$

$$\text{or} \quad C \leftarrow (\alpha A) B^T + B(\alpha A)^T + \beta C,$$

$$\text{or} \quad C \leftarrow (\alpha A) B^T + B^T (\alpha A) + \beta C,$$

$$\text{or} \quad C \leftarrow (\alpha A J) B^T + B(\alpha A J)^T + \beta C,$$

$$\text{or} \quad C \leftarrow (\alpha A J)^T B + B^T (\alpha A J) + \beta C,$$

where α is a scalar, C is a symmetric matrix, A and B are general matrices, and J is a symmetric tridiagonal matrix.

- Perform one of the Hermitian rank k and $2k$ updates

$$C \leftarrow \alpha A A^H + \beta C, \quad \text{or} \quad C \leftarrow \alpha A^H A + \beta C,$$

$$\text{or} \quad C \leftarrow \alpha A J A^H + \beta C, \quad \text{or} \quad C \leftarrow \alpha A^H J A + \beta C,$$

$$\text{or} \quad C \leftarrow (\alpha A) B^H + B(\alpha A)^H + \beta C,$$

$$\text{or} \quad C \leftarrow (\alpha A)^H B + B^H (\alpha A) + \beta C,$$

$$\text{or} \quad C \leftarrow (\alpha A J) B^H + B(\alpha A J)^H + \beta C,$$

$$\text{or} \quad C \leftarrow (\alpha A J)^H B + B^H (\alpha A J) + \beta C,$$

where α is a scalar, C is a Hermitian matrix, A and B are general matrices, and J is a symmetric tridiagonal matrix.

Data movement with matrices include

- copying matrix A (or its transpose or conjugate transpose), with storing the result in matrix B,

$$B \leftarrow A, \quad B \leftarrow A^T, \quad \text{or} \quad B \leftarrow A^H;$$

- transposition or conjugate-transposition of a square matrix A with the result overwriting matrix A,

$$A \leftarrow A^T \quad \text{or} \quad A \leftarrow A^H;$$

- permutation of the rows or columns of matrix A by a permutation matrix P,

$$A \leftarrow PA \quad \text{or} \quad A \leftarrow AP.$$

Routines implementing the operations support different types and forms of matrix operands as well as different storage schemes.

2.5.4. Sparse BLAS

Apart from the Dense and Banded BLAS outlined above, there is a library called the Sparse BLAS providing computational routines for *unstructured* sparse matrices, that is, such matrices that contain many zero entries not making up a regular sparsity pattern (e.g., banded or triangular).

The Sparse BLAS functionality is much poorer than that of the Dense and Banded BLAS and only includes matrix multiply and triangular solve, along with sparse vector update, dot product, and gather/scatter (the basic array operations used in solving large sparse linear equations by iterative techniques).

The Sparse BLAS does not specify a method to store the sparse matrix. The storage format is dependent on the algorithm being used, the original sparsity pattern of the matrix, the underlying computer architecture, among other considerations about the format in which the data exists, and so on. Therefore sparse matrix arguments to the Sparse BLAS routines are not really data components but placeholders, or *handles*, that refer to an abstract representation of the matrix. Several routines are provided to create Sparse BLAS matrices, but the internal representation is implementation dependent, which provides Sparse BLAS library developers with the best opportunity for optimizing and fine-tuning their kernels for specific situations. As a result programmers can write numerical algorithms using the Sparse BLAS independently of the matrix storage scheme, relying on the scheme provided by each particular implementation of the library.

The typical use of the Spase BLAS consists of three phases:

- Create an internal sparse matrix representation and return its handle.
- Use the handle as a parameter in computational Sparse BLAS routines.
- Call a cleanup routine to free resourses associated with the handle, when the matrix is no longer needed.

The C program below illustrates the use of the Sparse BLAS library to multiply a sparse 4×4 matrix

$$A = \begin{pmatrix} 1.1 & 0 & 0 & 0 \\ 0 & 2.2 & 0 & 2.4 \\ 0 & 0 & 3.3 & 0 \\ 4.1 & 0 & 0 & 4.4 \end{pmatrix}$$

with the vector

$$x = \begin{pmatrix} 1.0 \\ 1.0 \\ 1.0 \\ 1.0 \end{pmatrix}$$

performing the operation $y \leftarrow Ax$:

```c
#include <blas_sparse.h>
int main() {
  const int n = 4;
  const int nonzeros = 6;
  double values[] = {1.1, 2.2, 2.4, 3.3, 4.1, 4.4};
  int index_i[] = {0, 1, 1, 2, 3, 3};
  int index_j[] = {0, 1, 3, 2, 0, 3};
  double x[] = {1.0, 1.0, 1.0, 1.0};
  double y[] = {0.0, 0.0, 0.0, 0.0};

  blas_sparse_matrix A;
  int k;
  double alpha = 1.0;

  /* Create Sparse BLAS handle */
  A = BLAS_duscr_begin(n, n);

  /* Insert entries one by one */
  for(k=0; k < nonzeros; k++)
    BLAS_duscr_insert_entry(A, values[k], index_i[k],
    index_j[k]);

  /* Complete construction of sparse matrix */
  BLAS_uscr_end(A);

  /* Compute matrix-vector product y = A*x */
  BLAS_dusmv(blas_no_trans, alpha, A, x, 1, y, 1);

  /* Release matrix handle */
  BLAS_usds(A);
}
```

2.6. PARALLEL LANGUAGES

C and Fortran 77 cannot be used the same way for vector and superscalar processors as they are for serial scalar ones. These languages do not reflect certain essential features of these architectures, and thus make the writing of efficiently portable programs for vector and superscalar processors difficult or even impossible.

Optimizing compilers can only solve this problem for a simple and limited class of applications. Array libraries are able to provide efficient implementation for a relatively small number of array operations, not covering all possible operations on arrays that may be needed for an algorithm. More complex array operations can only be expressed as a combination of the locally optimized library array operations. This approach excludes global optimization of combined array operations and therefore can only provide a relatively slow implementation for many algorithms, potentially suitable for a much more efficient execution on vector and superscalar processors.

Parallel extensions of C and Fortran 77, which allow the programmer to explicitly express in a portable way array-based computations that can be efficiently implemented for any vector and superscalar processor, provide a comprehensive solution to the problem of efficiently portable programming of these architectures. The compiler for a parallel language does not recognize what portions of source code are suitable for efficient execution on vector and superscalar processors. The compiler just focuses on the generation of efficient target code for the array operations specified by the programmer. In generating the target code, the compiler is potentially able to optimize the array-based computations as global as it is allowed by the modular structure of source code.

A number of parallel supersets of C and Fortran 77 have been designed for efficiently portable programming vector and superscalar processors. In the book, we outline two of them: Fortran 90 and C[ ].

2.6.1. Fortran 90

Fortran 90 is a new standard of the Fortran language released in 1991. It has been widely implemented in recent years. Fortran 90 adds many powerful extensions to the Fortran language. The new features of Fortran 90 can be divided into two categories based on their motivation. The first category unites the features aimed at modernization of the language according to the state-of-the-art in serial programming languages in order to make Fortran competitive with computer languages created later (e.g., C and C++). The features of the category include

- free-format source code and some other simple improvements;
- dynamic memory allocation (automatic arrays, allocatable arrays, and pointers and associated heap storage management);
- user-defined data types (structures);
- generic user-defined procedures (functions and subroutines) and operators;
- recursive procedures;

- new control structures to support structured programming;
- a new program unit, `MODULE`, for encapsulation of data and a related set of procedures.

These extensions upgrade the archaic syntax of Fortran 77 and introduce modern storage management, a control structure, a procedural structure, and a basic support for object-oriented programming. The new features are very important for Fortran programmers, but they are not directly related to parallel programming vector and superscalar architectures.

The second category of added features includes the extensions made to support explicit expression of operations on arrays. Unlike Fortran 77, Fortran 90 considers arrays first-class objects and allows whole-array operations, assignments, and functions. In the case of arrays, operations and assignments are extended in an obvious way—element by element. So, for the arrays

REAL, DIMENSION(3,4,5) :: a, b, c

the statement

```
c = a + b
```

performs elementwise addition of the arrays a and b, storing the result in the array c.

Similarly all appropriate intrinsic functions are array-valued for array arguments. They operate elementwise if given an array as their argument. Therefore the statement

```
c = SQRT(a)
```

is legal in Fortran 90 and has the obvious semantics. Fortran 90 also allows the programmers to write array-valued functions themselves.

Array expressions may also include scalar constants and variables, which are replicated (or expanded) to the required number of elements. For example, the statement

```
c = a + 2.0
```

increases all elements of the array a by 2.0, storing the result in the array c.

Occasionally some elements of arrays in an array-valued expression must be treated specially. This is done by using the `WHERE` structure. For example, to avoid division by zero in the statement

```
a = 1./a
```

where a is an array, the `WHERE` statement

WHERE (a / = 0.) a = 1./a

or the WHERE construct

WHERE (a / = 0.)
    a = 1./a
ELSEWHERE
    a = HUGE(a)
END WHERE

can be used.

All the array elements in an array-valued expression or array assignment must be *conformable*. That means that they must have the same *shape*, that is, the same number of axes as well as the same number of elements along each axis. For example, all the arrays a, b, and c

REAL :: a(3,4,5), b(0:2,4,5), c(3,4,-1:3)

have the same *rank* of 3, *extents* of 3, 4, and 5, *shape* of {3, 4, 5}, and *size* of 60. They only differ in the lower and upper dimension bounds. The first dimension of the array b ranges from 0 to 2, while that of the arrays a and c ranges from 1 to 3. The third dimension of the array c ranges from -1 to 3, while that of the arrays a and b ranges from 1 to 5. Thus the statement

c = b/SQRT(ABS(a)+1.)

is correct because all of its array elements are conformable.

Whole arrays are not the only array-valued objects allowed in Fortran 90. An *array section* can be used everywhere in array assignments and array-valued expressions where a whole array is allowed. In general, an array section is specified with triplets of the form

lower : upper : stride

used as subscripts. The triplet designates an ordered set of integer values $i_1, \ldots, i_k$ such that $i_1 = lower$ and $i_{j+1} = i_j + stride$ $(j = 1, \ldots, k - 1)$, and $| i_k - upper | < stride$. Thus for the array

REAL :: a(50,50)

the expression

a(i,1:50:1) or a(i,1:50) or a(i,:)

designates the *i*th row of array a. This rank 1 section has a shape of {50}. Note that the third component of the triplet expression along with the preceding semicolon may be omitted. In that case the stride is set to 1. The first and/or the second components may also be omitted. In that case the lower and/or upper bounds will be taken from the array's declaration. The expression

```
a(i,1:50:3)
```

selects every third element of this row. The shape of this section is {16}. The expression

```
a(i,50:1:-1)
```

designates this row in reverse order. The section is also of rank 1 and has a shape of {50}. The expression

```
a(11:40,j)
```

designates a part of the *j*th column (a section of the shape {30}). The expression

```
a(1:10,1:10)
```

designates the left upper 10×10 block of a, which is a rank 2 section of the shape {10, 10}.

Along with triplets, *vector subscripts* may also be used to specify array sections. Any expression whose value is a rank 1 integer array may be used as a vector subsript. For example, the code

```
REAL :: a(5,5), b(5)
INTEGER :: index(5)
index = (/5,4,3,2,1/)
b = a(index,1)
```

assigns the reversed first column of array a to array b. The array-valued variable index is used as a vector subscript in expression a(index,1) designating an array section.

Whole arrays and array sections of the same shape can be mixed in expressions and assignments. Note that unlike a whole array, an array section may not occupy contiguous storage locations.

Along with array variables and array-valued expressions, Fortran 90 introduces array constants, which is quite natural as soon as arrays are considered first-class objects. Array constants may appear in any array expression. The simplest form of array constant is just a list of elements enclosed in (/ and /). Such an array constant was used in the example above to initialize the array index. In general, array constants, also known as *array constructors*, may contain lists of scalars, lists of arrays, and implied-DO loops familiar from I/O lists. Some examples of correct array constants are

```
(/ 0, i=1,50 /)
(/ (3.14*i, i=4,100,3) /)
(/ ( (/ 5,4,3,2,1 /), i=1,5 ) /)
```

The array constructors are only able to produce one-dimensional arrays. In order to construct arrays of higher rank, the function RESHAPE can be used. The second argument of the function is the shape of the output array, while its first argument specifies the array whose elements should be used for constructing the output array of the specified shape. For example, in order to assign zeros to all elements of the array a,

REAL :: a(500,500)

the statement

```
a = RESHAPE( (/ (0., i=1,250000) /), (/ 500,500 /) )
```

can be used.

User-defined procedures implementing operations on arrays normally use *assumed-shape* arrays as formal array arguments. For example, the subprogram

```
SUBROUTINE swap(a,b)
REAL, DIMENSION(:,:) :: a, b
REAL, DIMENSION(SIZE(a,1), SIZE(a,2)) :: temp
temp = a
a = b
b = temp
END SUBROUTINE swap
```

has two formal array arguments a and b, whose specification only defines their type and rank, but bounds are just marked with colons. This means that the actual shape is taken from that of the array arguments each time the subroutine is called. The local array temp is an example of the *automatic* array. Its size is set at runtime with the intrinsic function SIZE, which returns the number of elements in the dimension, specified by the second argument, of the array specified by the first argument. The automatic array are released as soon as control leaves the procedure in which it is defined.

In addition to extension of such intrinsic functions as SQRT and SIN to array arguments, Fortran 90 introduces a number of specific array intrinsic functions. The functions do the following:

- Compute the scalar product of two vectors (the function DOT_PRODUCT) and the matrix product of two matrices (the function MATMUL).
- Perform diverse reduction operations on an array, such as logical multiplication (the function ALL) and addition (the function ANY) of the elements of the array, counting the number of true elements in the array, arithmetical multiplication (the function PRODUCT) and addition (the function SUM) of its elements, and finding the smallest (the function MINVAL) or the largest (the function MAXVAL) element of the array.
- Return diverse attributes of an array such as its shape (the function SHAPE), the lower-dimension bounds of the array (the function LBOUND), the upper-dimension bounds (the function UBOUND), the number of elements (the function SIZE), and the allocation status of the array (the function ALLOCATED).
- Construct arrays by means of merging two arrays under mask (the function MERGE), or packing an array into a vector (the function PACK), or replication of an array by adding a dimension (the function SPREAD), or unpacking a vector (a rank 1 array) into an array under mask (the function UNPACK).
- Reshape arrays (the function RESHAPE).
- Move array elements performing the circular shift (the function CSHIFT), or the end-off shift (the function EOSHIFT), or the transpose of a rank 2 array (the function TRANSPOSE).
- Locate the first maximum (the function MAXLOC) or minimum (the function MINLOC) element in an array.

2.6.2. The C[ ] Language

The C[ ] (C "brackets") language is a strict ANSI C superset allowing programmers to explicitly describe operations on arrays.

2.6.2.1. Vector Value and Vector Object.
A basic new notion of the C[ ] language is *vector value*, or simply *vector*. Vector value is an ordered sequence of values (or vector values) of any one type. Any vector type is characterized by two attributes: the number of elements and the type of elements.

ANSI C defines object as the region of data storage whose contents can represent values. The C[ ] language introduces the notion of *vector object* as the region of data storage whose contents can represent vector values. Namely C[ ] defines vector object as an ordered sequence of objects (or vector objects) of any one type.

ANSI C does not define the notion of value of array object. The C[ ] language does, and this value is a vector. For example, the value of the array defined with the declaration

```
int a[3][2] = {0,1,2,3,4,5};
```

is the vector

```
{ {0,1}, {2,3}, {4,5} }
```

consisting of three vectors, each composed of two integers. This vector type is named by the type name int[3][2]. We also say that the vector has the *shape* {3, 2}. By definition, the shape of the array is the same as that of its vector value. Thus, in C[], array object is a particular case of vector object.

2.6.2.2. Arrays and Pointers. In C, an array comprises a contiguously allocated set of elements of any one type of object. In C[ ], an array comprises a set of elements of any one type of object sequentially allocated with a positive *stride*. The stride is a distance between successive elements of the array measured in units equal to the size of array element. If stride is not specified, it is assumed to be 1.

Thus a C[ ] array has at least three attributes: the type of elements, the number of elements, and the allocation stride. For example, both the declaration

int a[3];

and the declaration

int a[3:1];

define an array of the form

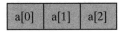

The declaration

int a[3:3];

defines an array of the form

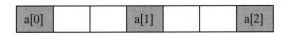

The size of the slot between array elements is 2 × *sizeof* (int) bytes.

In C, a pointer has only one attribute—the type of object it points to. This attribute is necessary for the correct interpretation of the value of the object it points to as well as the address operators + and −. These operators are correct only if the pointer's operands and the pointer's results point to elements of the same array object. The same rule is valid for the C[ ] language. Therefore, to support the correct interpretation of the address operators, C[ ] introduces one more attribute of the pointer; this attribute is *stride*. If stride is not specified, it is equal to 1.

In C, when an expression that has integer type is added to or subtracted from a pointer, the integer value is first multiplied by the size of the object pointed to. In C[ ], the multiplier is equal to the product of the pointer's stride and the size of the object pointed to. In C, when two pointers to elements of the same array object are subtracted, the difference is divided by the size of an element. In C[ ], the divisor is equal to the product of the pointer's stride and the size of an element.

For example, the declarations

```
int      a[]  = {0,1,2,3,4};
int *    p1   = (void*)a;
int *:2  p2   = (void*)&a[4];
```

form the following structure of storage

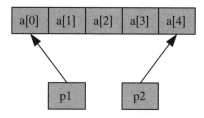

The address expressions p1+2 and p2-1 point to the same element of the array a, namely a[2]. Indeed, the offset from p1 specified by the expression p1+2 is equal to $(1 \times sizeof \text{(int)}) \times 2 = 2 \times sizeof \text{(int)}$ bytes, and the offset from p2 specified by the expression p2-1 is equal to $(2 \times sizeof \text{(int)}) \times (-1) = -2 \times sizeof \text{(int)}$ bytes.

In C[ ], access to the *e2*-th element of an array object *e1* is obtained with using one of the expressions *e1*[*e2*] or (*e2*)[*e1*]. Both are identical to (*(((*e1*)+(*e2*)))). Here, *e2* is an integer expression, *e1* is an lvalue that has the type "array of *type*." This lvalue is converted to an expression that has the type "pointer to *type*" and that points to the intial element of the array object (the attribute *stride* of the pointer is identical to that of the array object).

In C[ ], an integer nonconstant expression may be used to specify the size of an automatic array, or the stride of an atomatic array or pointer. The following fragment of C[ ] code, which initializes with units the diagonal elements of an $n \times n$ matrix, illustrates the use of such *dynamic* arrays and pointers:

```
typedef int (*pDiag)[n:n+1];
int a[n][n];
int j;
pDiag p = (void*)a;
...
for(j=0; j<n; j++)
  (*p)[j]=1;
```

2.6.2.3. Lvector. In C[ ], the value of an array object is a vector. The *i*th element of the vector is the value of the *i*th element of the array object.

To support access to an array as the whole, C[ ] introduces the postfix [ ] operator (the blocking operator). The operand of the operator has the type "array of *type*." The [ ] operator blocks the conversion of the operand to a pointer. For example, if the arrays a, b, and c are declared as

```
int a[5], b[5:2], c[5:3];
```

then expressions a[], b[], and c[] designate arrays a, b, and c as a whole; and expression c[]=a[]+b[] assigns the sum of the vectors that are the values of arrays a and b to the array c. Note that expression a[]+b[] has type "vector of 5 ints."

In C, an *lvalue* is an expression designating an object. For example, if the array d is declared as

```
int d[5][5];
```

then expressions d[i][j], d, and d[0] are lvalues, while expressions d[i][j]+1 and &d[0] are not. A *modifiable* lvalue is an lvalue that is allowed as the left operand of an assignment operator. So, while d[i][j] is a modifiable lvalue, d and d[0] are not.

In addition to lvalue, C[ ] introduces the notion of *lvector* as an expression designating a vector object. *Modifiable lvector* is an lvector that can be used as the left operand of an assignment operator. Array object is a particular case of vector object. Therefore expressions d, d[0], d[], and d[0][] are lvectors. At the same time, d[] and d[0][] are modifiable lvectors, meanwhile d and d[0] are not.

In principal, the extended notions of array and pointer in concert with the [ ] operator support the access to whole arrays and subarrays. For example, if array a is declared as

```
int a[4][4];
```

then the modifiable lvector

```
(*(int(*)[4:5])a)[]
```

designates an array of four `ints` allocated with stride 5 that contains the main diagonal of matrix *a*:

a[0][0]	a[0][1]	a[0][2]	a[0][3]
a[1][0]	a[1][1]	a[1][2]	a[1][3]
a[2][0]	a[2][1]	a[2][2]	a[2][3]
a[3][0]	a[3][1]	a[3][2]	a[3][3]

We say that an object *belongs* to an array if it is an element of the array or belongs to an element of the array. By definition, a set of objects belonging to an array is a *subarray* of the array if and only if the set is an array itself. The main diagonal above is a subarray of array a because it is an array object of the type `int[4:5]`.

The modifiable lvector

```
(*(int(*)[3:5])(&a[0][1]))[]
```

designates a subarray of the array a that contains the first superdiagonal of the matrix *a*:

a[0][0]	a[0][1]	a[0][2]	a[0][3]
a[1][0]	a[1][1]	a[1][2]	a[1][3]
a[2][0]	a[2][1]	a[2][2]	a[2][3]
a[3][0]	a[3][1]	a[3][2]	a[3][3]

Not every, even regular, set of objects belonging to an array is its subarray. For example, if array a is declared as

```
int a[5][5];
```

then the inner elements of matrix *a*,

a[0][0]	a[0][1]	a[0][2]	a[0][3]	a[0][4]
a[1][0]	a[1][1]	a[1][2]	a[1][3]	a[1][4]
a[2][0]	a[2][1]	a[2][2]	a[2][3]	a[2][4]
a[3][0]	a[3][1]	a[3][2]	a[3][3]	a[3][4]
a[4][0]	a[4][1]	a[4][2]	a[4][3]	a[4][4]

do not make up a subarray. Therefore there is no constant modifiable lvector similar to those used for designation of the "diagonal" subarrays that designates this "inner square."

In order to support access to such array sections of general form, C[ ] introduces the [:] operator (the grid operator). In the general case, this quaternary operator has the following syntax:

```
e[l:r:s]
```

where expression e may have type "array of *type*" or "pointer to *type*" and expressions l, r, and s have integer types and denote the left bound, right bound, and stride respectively. In that case the expression designates a vector object consisting of $(r - s)/l + 1$ elements of type *type*. The ith element of the resulting vector object is $e[l + s \cdot i]$. Expression $e[l:r:s]$ is an lvector. It will be a modifiable lvector, if all the expressions $\{e[l + s \cdot i]\}_{i=0,1,\ldots}$ are either modifiable lvalues or modifiable lvectors. If stride s is equal to 1, the corresponding operand along with the preceding semicolon may be omitted (i.e., $e[l:r]$ may be used as a short form of $e[l:r:1]$).

The first operand e of the grid operator may have a vector type. In that case the operator is applied elementwise to each element of the vector value of e. For example, let the vector value be $\{u_1, \ldots, u_k\}$. Then the expression $e[l:r:s]$ will designate a vector of k vectors with the ith element of the jth vector being $u_j[l + s \cdot i]$ ($j = 1, \ldots, k$). This successive application of several grid operations allows the programmer to construct modifiable lvectors designating diverse sections of multidimensional arrays (or more precisely, arrays of arrays).

Thus the array section above can be designated with the modifiable lvector a[1:3][1:3]. Indeed, expression a[1:3] is an unmodifiable lvector designating a vector object consisting of three arrays a[1], a[2], and a[3] of type int[5] that correspondingly contain the second, third, and fourth rows of the 5×5 matrix a:

a[0][0]	a[0][1]	a[0][2]	a[0][3]	a[0][4]
a[1][0]	a[1][1]	a[1][2]	a[1][3]	a[1][4]
a[2][0]	a[2][1]	a[2][2]	a[2][3]	a[2][4]
a[3][0]	a[3][1]	a[3][2]	a[3][3]	a[3][4]
a[4][0]	a[4][1]	a[4][2]	a[4][3]	a[4][4]

This lvector is unmodifiable because a[1], a[2], and a[3] are unmodifiable lvalues.

In expression a[1:3][1:3], the second grid operator [1:3] is applied to each of these three arrays selecting their second, third, and forth elements. Therefore expression a[1:3][1:3] designates a vector object consisting of three arrays of the type int[3] that contain the inner 3×3 square of the 5×5 matrix a:

a[0][0]	a[0][1]	a[0][2]	a[0][3]	a[0][4]
a[1][0]	a[1][1]	a[1][2]	a[1][3]	a[1][4]
a[2][0]	a[2][1]	a[2][2]	a[2][3]	a[2][4]
a[3][0]	a[3][1]	a[3][2]	a[3][3]	a[3][4]
a[4][0]	a[4][1]	a[4][2]	a[4][3]	a[4][4]

The second operand l and/or the third operand r of the grid operator may be omitted. If l is omitted, the left bound is set to 0. If r is omitted, the right bound is set to $n - 1$ if the first operand e is an n-element array, or determined from the context if e is a pointer. So expression a[:][:] is a modifiable lvector designating as a whole the 5×5 array a above. Note that the more compact modifiable lvector a[] also designates this array.

2.6.2.4. Elementwise Vector Operators. The operand of the scalar cast operator and the unary operators &, *, +, −, ~, !, ++, and −− may have a vector type. In that case the operators are applied elementwise to each element of the vector operand to produce the vector result.

For example, if array p is defined with declarations

```
int  j,  k,  l,  m,  n;
int  *p[5]  =  {  &j,  &k,  &l,  &m,  &n  };
```

then expression p[1:3] is a modifiable lvector designating a vector object consisting of three variables p[1], p[2], and p[3] of the type int*, and expression *(p[1:3]) is a modifiable lvector designating a vector object consisting of three integer variables k, l, and m.

Any of the binary operators *, /, %, +, -, <<, >>, <, >, <=, ,>=, ==, !=, &, ^, |, &&, and || may have vector operands. If the operands have the same shape, then the operator is executed elementwise to produce the result of this shape.

In general, the operands have different shapes. However, the operands must be *conformable* in that the beginning of the shape of one operand must be identical to the shape of the other operand. For example, two vectors of shapes {9, 8, 7, 6} and {9, 8} are conformable. A nonvector operand is always conformable with any vector operand because all nonvectors have the empty shape { }. If the rank of one operand *a* is less than that of the other operand *b*, then the execution of the operator starts from *conformable extension* of the vector value of operand *a* to the shape of operand *b*. The conformable extension just replicates the vector value by adding dimensions. For example, conformable extension of the vector

```
{  {1,2,3},  {4,5,6}  }
```

of the shape {2, 3} to the shape {2, 3, 2} is vector

```
{  {  {1,1},  {2,2},  {3,3}  },  {  {4,4},  {5,5},  {6,6}  }  }
```

Then the operator is applied elementwise to the result of the conformable extension of the value of operand *a* and the value of operand *b*, producing the result of the same shape as that of operand *b*.

C[ ] introduces two new binary operators, ?> and ?<. The result of the ?> operator is the maximum of its operands. The result of the ?< operator is the minimum of the operands. The operators may also have vector operands. In that case they are executed in the same manner as other binary arithmetic operators.

The assignment operators =, *=, +=, etc., may have vector operands. In that case the left operand of an assignment operator must be a modifiable lvector. Its rank must be not less than the rank of the right operand, and the operands must be conformable. If the rank of the right operand is less than that of the left operand before the elementwise execution of the assignment operator, the value of the right operand is conformably extended to the shape of the left one. For example, the C[ ] code

```
int a[m][n], b[m];
...
a[:][:] = b[:];
```

assigns the value of the *i*th element of the array b to all elements of the *i*th row of the array a ($i = 0, \ldots, m - 1$). The following is a fragment of the C[ ] application performing the LU factorization of the square $n \times n$ matrix *a* by using the Gaussian elimination:

```
double a[n][n], t;
int i, j;
...
for(i=0; i<n; i++) {
  for(j=i+1; j<n; j++) {
    t = a[j][i]/a[i][i];
    if(a[j][i]!=0.)
      a[j][i:n-1]-=4*a[i][i:n-1];
  }
}
```

The definition of the subscript operator [ ] is that *e1*[*e2*] is identical to (*((*e1*) + (*e2*))), and the expressions *e1* and *e2* may be of vector type. This allows the programmer to construct lvectors designating irregular array sections. For example, the C[ ] code

```
int a[m][n], ind[] = {0, 1, 6, 18};
...
a[ind[:]][:] = 0;
```

zeros the elements of the 0th, 1st, 6th, and 18th rows of array a. The expression a[ind[:]][:] is a modifiable lvector that designates a vector object of shape {4, *n*} consisting of rows a[0], a[1], a[6], and a[18] of array a.

The first operand of the . operator may have a vector type. The second operand must name a member of a structure or union type. In that case the operator is executed elementwise, and the result will have the same shape as the first operand. Expression $e \rightarrow id$ is identical to expression (*e).*id*.

2.6.2.5. Reduction operators. For the binary operators *, +, &, ^, |, &&, ||, ?<, and ?>, the C[ ] language introduces *reduction* operators [*], [+], [&],[^], [|],[&&],[||],[?<], and [?>]. The reduction operators are unary prefix operators only applicable to vector operands. The definition of the reduction operator [∘] is that if $v_1, \ldots, v_n$ are the elements of the vector value of expression e, then the value of expression $[\circ]e$ is that of expression $v_1 \circ v_2 \circ \ldots \circ v_n$. For example, the C[ ] code

```
double a[n];
double b[n];
double c;
...
c = [+](a[]*b[]);
```

computes the dot product of vectors a and b. The code

```
int a[m][n];
int max;
...
max = [?>][?>]a[];
```

computes the maximum element of matrix a. The value of expression a[] is an m-element vector, whose elements are n-element vectors of integers. The value of expression [?>] a[] is an n-element vector whose ith element is the maximum element of the ith column of matrix a. Finally, the application of operator [?>] to this vector yields the maximum of the column maximums, that is, the maximum element of the entire matrix a.

The code

```
double a[m][l];
double b[l][n];
double c[m][n];
int i;
...
for(i=0; i<m; i++)
  c[i][] = [+](a[i][]*b[]);
```

multiplies matrices a and b storing the result into matrix c.

2.7. MEMORY HIERARCHY AND PARALLEL PROGRAMMING TOOLS

Our consideration of vector and superscalar architectures would not be complete without a brief outline of the basic approaches to efficient management of such an important resource as memory. Although the optimal use of memory is not directly related to parallel computing technologies, there are at least two reasons to take a closer look at this issue in the context of parallel programming vector and superscalar architectures. First, all parallel programming systems for the architectures take into account their modern memory structure, and the speedup due to more optimal use of the memory often appears more significant than that due to better use of parallel instruction execution units. Second, the approaches, models, and techniques aimed at efficient use of the memory appear surprisingly similar to those aimed at efficient use of parallel facilities of the architectures.

Vector and superscalar processors, as they were presented in Sections 2.1 and 2.2, have a simple two-level memory hierarchy:

- Small and fast register memory.
- Large and relatively slow main memory.

This memory hierarchy is reflected in instruction sets and directly visible to the programmers. At the same time, physically modern uniprocessor architectures provide more complex memory hierarchy, although not directly reflected in their instruction sets. That actual memory hierarchy is organized into several levels with higher levels being substantially faster and smaller than lower ones.

A simple actual memory hierarchy includes the following levels:

- Register memory
- Cache memory
- Main memory
- Disk memory

Cache is a buffer memory between the main memory and the registers. A cache holds copies of some data from the main memory. To read a data item from the main memory into a register, the instruction is first to check if a copy of the item is already in the cache. If so, the data item will be actually transferred into the register not from the main memory but from the cache. If not, the data item will be transferred into the register from the main memory, and a copy of the item will appear in the cache. Therefore, if the next data transfer instruction reads the same data item, it will be taken from the cache rather than from the main memory resulting in a faster execution of the instruction.

Cache is partitioned into blocks called *cache lines*. A cache line is a minimum unit of data transfer between the cache and the main memory. So scalar data items may be transferred between the cache and the main memory only as a part of a cache line. The cache memory is much smaller than the main memory and hence it may not be able to hold copies of all the data items from the main memory, which are processed by the program. Therefore, at different moments of the program execution, the same cache line may reflect different data blocks from the main memory, because a copy of the data block, which is not reflected in the cache and contains a required data item, will replace a copy of some other data block.

A cache is said to be *direct mapped* if each block of the main memory has only one place it can appear in the cache. If a block can be placed anywhere in the cache, the cache is said to be *fully associative*. If a block can be placed in a restricted set of places in the cache, the cache is said to be *set associative*. A set is a group of two or more cache lines. A block is first mapped onto a set, and then the block can be placed anywhere within the set. If there are n blocks in a set, the cache is called n-way associative.

The situation when a data item being referenced is not in the cache is called *cache miss*. If the contribution of data transfer instructions into the total execution time of a program is substantial, a low number of cache misses will significantly accelerate the execution of the program. An obvious class of programs suitable for such optimization includes programs intensively using basic operations on arrays. Note that exactly the same class of programs is perfectly suitable for vector and superscalar processors allowing a very high level of utilization of their parallel units.

The main specific optimization performed by optimizing C and Fortran 77 compilers in order to minimize the number of cache misses is *loop tiling*. Consider the following loop nest:

```
for(i=0;  i<m;  i++)      /* loop 1 */
   for(j=0;  j<n;  j++)    /* loop 2 */
      if(i==0)
         b[j]=a[i][j];
      else
         b[j]+=a[i][j];
```

which computes the sum of rows of the $m \times n$ matrix a, storing the resulting n-element vector b in array b. Data items accessed by reference b[j] are repeatedly used by successive interations of loop 1. If the number n of iterations of loop 2 is large enough, the data items may be flushed from the cache by the moment of their repeated use. In order to minimize the flushing of repeatedly used data items, the number of iterations of loop 2 may be decreased. In order to keep the total number of iterations of this loop nest unchanged, an additional controlling loop is introduced. As a result the transformed loop nest looks as follows:

```
for(k=0;  k<n;  k+=T)                  /* additional
                                          controlling loop 0 */
   for(i=0;  i<m;  i++)                 /* loop 1 */
      for(j=k;  j<min(k+T,n);  j++)     /* loop 2 */
         if(i==0)
            b[j]=a[i][j];
         else
            b[j]+=a[i][j];
```

This transformation is called tiling, and T is the tile size.

In general, the loop tiling is applied to loop nests of the form

```
for(i1=...)            /* loop 1 */
   for(i2=...)         /* loop 2 */
   ...
      for(in=...) {    /* loop n */
      ...
      e[i2] ... [in]
      ...
      }
```

in order to minimize the number of cache misses for reference e[i2] ... [in], which is repeatedly used by succesive iterations of loop 1. Thus loop tiling improves temporal locality of nested loops by decreasing the number of iterations between repeatedly used array elements.

The recognition of tilable loop nests is a difficult problem that should be solved by optimizing C and Fortran 77 compilers. Its solution is based on an analysis of data dependencies in the loop nests. For example, loop tiling is legitimately applicable to the loop nest given above if and only if the loops from loop 2 to loop *n* are fully interchangeable, that is, provided that any two loops from this set may be safely interchanged without any change of the functional semantics of this code. To prove the interchangability of the loops, an analysis of dependence between different iterations of the above loop nest is needed.

Maximization of data reuse in the upper levels of the memory hierarchy can be achieved by partitioning the matrix or matrices into blocks, and performing the computation with matrix-matrix operations on the blocks. The Level 3 BLAS were specified in such a way to support the implementation of such algorithms, and they have been successfully used as the building blocks of a number of applications, including LAPACK. (LAPACK is a linear algebra package written in Fortran 77 that provides routines for solving systems of simultaneous linear equations, least-squares solutions of linear systems of equations, eigenvalue problems, and singular value problems.)

Compilers for parallel languages such as Fortran 90 and C[ ] do not need to recognize loops suitable for tiling in order to improve the reuse of data held in the cache. Instead, they may translate explicit operations on arrays into loop nests with the best possible temporal locality.

As a rule the address space provided by the instruction set of a modern uniprocessor computer is larger than its physical main memory. In fact, the instructions address *virtual memory* rather than real physical memory. The virtual memory is partitioned into *pages* of a fixed size. Each page is stored on a disk until it is needed. When the page is needed, the operating system copies it from disk to main memory, translating the virtual addresses into real addresses. The process of translating virtual addresses into real addresses is called *mapping*. The copying of virtual pages from disk to main memory is known as paging or *swapping*.

Programs processing large enough arrays do not fit into main memory. Therefore during execution of such programs the swapping takes place every time the required data are not in the main memory. As copying of a virtual page from disk to main memory is an expensive operation, minimization of the number of swappings can significantly accelerate the programs. The problem is similar to the problem of minimizing the cache misses, and it can be therefore approached similarly.

2.8. SUMMARY

Vector and superscalar processors provide intstruction-level parallelism, which is best exploited by applications with intensive operations on arrays. Such applications can be written in a serial programming language, such as C or Fortran 77, and complied by dedicated optimizing compilers performing some specific loop optimizations. This approach supports modular, portable, and reliable programming. The efficiency and portable efficiency are also supported but only for a limited class of programs.

Array libraries, such as the BLAS, allow the programmers to avoid the use of dedicated compilers performing sophisticated optimizations. Instead, the programmers express operations on arrays directly, using calls to carefully implemented subroutines for the array operations. This approach also supports modular, portable, and reliable programming as well as limited efficiency and portable efficiency because it excludes global optimization of combined array operations.

Parallel languages, such as Fortran 90 or C[ ], combine advantages of the first and second approaches. They allow the programmer to explicitly express operations on arrays, and they therefore do not require sophisticated algorithms that recognize parallelizable loops. They can perform global optimization of combined array operations. And, finally, unlike existing array libraries, they support general-purpose programming. Thus general-purpose parallel extensions of C and Fortran 77 support modular, reliable, and efficienly portable programming for vector and superscalar architectures.

CHAPTER 3

Shared Memory Multiprocessors

3.1. SHARED MEMORY MULTIPROCESSOR ARCHITECTURE AND PROGRAMMING MODELS

The shared memory multiprocessor (SMP) architecture, shown in Figure 3.1, consists of a number of identical processors sharing a global main memory. In general, the processors of an SMP computer framework are of the vector or superscalar architecture.

The primary model of a program efficiently utilizing the performance potential of the architecture is parallel *threads* of control, each running on a separate processor of the SMP and sharing memory with other threads in the framework of the same process. Such a program is called a *multithreaded* (MT) program. All threads within the process share the same process-level structures and data, such as file descriptors and user ID. Therefore the threads have access to all the same functions, data, open files, and so on.

An MT program starts up with one initial *main* thread. That main thread may create new threads by calling the create routine, passing a routine for that new thread to run. The new thread now runs the routine and provides another stream of instructions operating on data in the same address space. When several threads all make use of the same data, they coordinate their usage via synchronization variables, such as a mutual exclusion lock (a *mutex*). Another way for threads to synchronize their work is to direct signals internally to individual threads.

The secondary model of a program for the SMP architecture is parallel processes, each running on a separate processor, not sharing main memory with other processes and using message passing to communicate with the others in order to coordinate their work. This message-passing parallel programming model is a primary one for the distributed memory multiprocessor architecture, and is considered in the next chapter.

The SMP architecture provides more parallel potentialities to speed up computations. This is done by adding parallel streams of instructions to the

Parallel Computing on Heterogeneous Networks, by Alexey Lastovetsky
ISBN 0-471-22982-2   Copyright © 2003 by John Wiley & Sons, Inc.

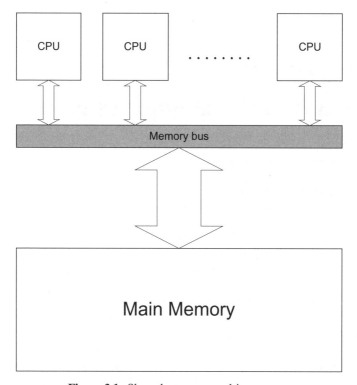

Figure 3.1. Shared memory multiprocessor.

instruction-level parallelism provided by the vector and superscalar architectures. How significant is the performance potential of the SMP architecture? It might be expected that an n-processor SMP computer would be able to perform the same volume of computations approximately n times as fast compared to the one-processor configuration of the computer. But the real picture is quite different. If you start from a one-processor configuration and add processors one by one, you will find that each next processor is adding only a fraction of the performance that you got from the first; and the fraction is becoming smaller and smaller. Eventually there is a point where adding one more processor will just decrease performance.

This limitation on speedup provided by the SMP architecture cannot be explained by the so-called Amdahl law, which is a formulation of a rather obvious observation, that if a program has one section that is parallelizable and another section that must run serially, then the program can never run faster than the serial section:

$$t_{\text{total}} = t_{\text{serial}} + \frac{t_{\text{parallel}}}{n},$$

where n is the number of processors. This fact is of no interest for any but the most simplistic of programs. "Normal" programs encounter other limitations far before they ever reach this one.

The real bottleneck of the SMP architecture putting limits on speedup is the memory bus. For example, heavy matrix multiplication programs come up against the limited memory bandwidth very quickly. If, say, 30 possible processors on a SMP computer average one main memory reference every 90 bus cycles, which is quite possible for such programs, then there will be a reference every third cycle. If a request/reply occupies the bus, say, for about 6 cycles, then that will be already twice what the bus can handle (and we are ignoring bus contention and possible I/O activity).

3.2. OPTIMIZING COMPILERS

Optimizing C and Fortran 77 compilers are widely used for parallel programming SMP architectures. The main optimization they perform is loop parallelization where different iterations of a loop are simultaneously executed by different parallel threads.

The most difficult problem that must be solved by optimizing compilers is recognition of the loops that can be parallelized. Solution of the problem is based on an analysis of the data dependencies in the loops. Optimizing compilers for the SMP architecture and for the vector and superscalar architectures share the same methods and algorithms for recognition of parallelizable loops as outlined in Section 2.4. The two groups of compilers actually share the same advantages and disadvantages of the "optimizing C or Fortran 77 compilers" approach to the problem of efficiently portable programming of the target parallel architectures as we saw in the analysis of Chapter 2.

To that analysis we want to add a few more words about the problem of porting serial legacy code to parallel architectures. Most serial C and Fortran 77 programs cannot be efficiently implemented on SMP computers by just optimizing the C and Fortran 77 compilers. A good serial algorithm maximizes the re-use of information, computed at each loop iteration, by all subsequent iterations, thus minimizing redundant computations. This results in strong, profound, and sophisticated interiteration data dependences without the optimizing compilers having to parallelize the most principal and time-consuming loops. Industrial C and Fortran 77 optimizing compilers parallelize a very small fraction of loops in such programs (e.g., about 3% for an actual Fortan 77 modeling of physical phenomena), and the parallelizable loops very often only initialize arrays and do not contribute much to the total execution time. Therefore most serial programs must be re-designed so that optimizing compilers can generate a code that runs efficiently on SMP computers.

3.3. THREAD LIBRARIES

Thread libraries are used to directly implement a thread parallel programming model and allow the programmers to explicitly write MT programs not relying on the optimizing compilers. The basic paradigm of multithreading implemented in different thread libraries (POSIX, NT, Solaris, OS/2, etc.) is the same as that briefly summarized in Section 3.1. The libraries just differ in the implementation details of the same basic model.

The POSIX thread library we use is also known as Pthreads. The main reason we focus on this library is that in 1995 the specification of Pthreads became a part of the IEEE POSIX standard, and hence it is considered the standard for all Unix systems. Most hardware vendors now offer Pthreads in addition to their proprietary thread libraries.

Pthreads are originally defined as a C language library. The standard Fortran interface to this library is not yet complete. Pthreads introduce three classes of objects and operations on the objects:

- Threads
- Mutexes
- Condition variables

Any thread of an MT program is represented by its ID, which is a reference to an opaque data object holding full information about the thread. This information is used and modified by operations on threads. The operations can create threads, terminate threads, join threads, and so on. There are also operations to set and query thread attributes.

Mutex is an abbreviation for *mut*ual *ex*clusion. Mutex variables (or simply mutexes) are one of the primary means of thread synchronization, normally used when several threads update the same global data. A mutex acts as a lock protecting access to the shared data resource. Only one thread can lock a mutex at any given time. Thus, even if several threads simultaneously try to lock a mutex, only one of them will succeed and claim ownership of that mutex. No other thread can lock that mutex until the owning thread unlocks it. Thus mutexes serialize access to the shared resource by concurrent threads. Operations on mutexes include creating, destroying, locking, and unlocking mutexes. There are also operations that set and modify the attributes associated with mutexes.

Condition variables are yet another way for threads to synchronize their work. A condition variable is a global variable shared by several threads and used by those threads to signal each other that some condition is satisfied. Namely a thread that waits for some condition to be satisfied may block itself on a condition variable, and then do nothing until some other thread unblocks it by performing a corresponding operation on the same condition variable as soon as the condition is satisfied. Without condition variables the thread would be constantly polling to check if the condition is met, which is very resource-consuming since the thread would be continuously busy in this activity. Thus condition variables allow the programmer to use "cold" waiting, which does not keep processors busy, instead of "hot" waiting. Operations on condition variables include creating condition variables, waiting on and signaling condition variables, and destroying condition variables. There are also operations to set and query condition variable attributes.

3.3.1. Operations on Threads

An MT program starts up with one initial thread running the function `main`. All other threads must be explicitly created. Creation of a new thread is performed by the following Pthreads function:

```
int pthread_create(pthread_t *thread,
                   const pthread_attr_t *attr,
                   void *(*start_routine)(void*),
                   void *arg)
```

This function creates a new thread that runs concurrently with the calling thread. The new thread executes the function `start_routine`. Only one argument can be passed to this function via `arg`. For cases where multiple arguments must be passed, this limitation is easily overcome by creating a structure that contains all of the arguments and then passing a pointer to that structure in the `pthread_create` function.

The `attr` argument specifies thread attributes to be applied to the new thread. The `attr` argument can also be NULL, in which case default attributes are used. On success, the ID of the newly created thread is stored in the location pointed by the `thread` argument, and 0 is returned. On error, a nonzero error code is returned. Once created, threads become peers and so can create other threads.

Upon successful completion, `pthread_create` stores the ID of the created thread in the location referenced by `thread`. The caller can use this thread ID to perform various operations on the thread. Any thread may learn its own ID with the function

```
pthread_t pthread_self(void)
```

returning the unique, system assigned thread ID of the calling thread. Function

```
int pthread_equal(pthread_t t1, pthread_t t2)
```

compares two thread IDs `t1` and `t2`. The `pthread_equal` function returns a nonzero value if `t1` and `t2` are equal. Otherwise, 0 is returned.

The new thread terminates either explicitly, by calling the function

```
void pthread_exit(void *status)
```

or implicitly, by returning from the start_routine function. The latter is equivalent to calling pthread_exit with the result returned by start_routine as exit code. If function main finishes before the threads it has created, and exits with pthread_exit, the other threads will continue to execute. Otherwise, they will be automatically terminated when main finishes. A termination *status* may be optionally specified. If the thread is not detached (see below), the exit status specified by status is made available to any successful join with the terminating thread. The pthread_exit function does not close files. Any file opened inside the thread will remain open after the thread is terminated.

Joining is a synchronization operation on threads. The operation is implemented by function

int pthread_join(pthread_t t, **void** **status)

which blocks the calling thread until the specified thread t terminates. There are two types of threads: joinable and detached. It is impossible to join a detached thread (see below). Several threads cannot wait for the same thread to complete; one thread will complete successfully and the others will terminate with an error. The pthread_join function will not block processing of the calling thread if the specified thread t has already terminated. This function returns successfully when thread t terminates. If a pthread_join call returns successfully with a non-null status argument, the value passed to the pthread_exit function by the terminating thread will be placed in the location referenced by status.

When a thread is created, one of its possible attributes defines whether or not the thread may be joined. If the thread is created *detached*, then it cannot be joined; that is, use of the ID of the newly created thread by the pthread_join function is an error. If the thread is created *joinable*, then it can be joined. A detached or joinable state of the thread is set by using the attr argument in the pthread_create function. The argument points to a thread attribute variable, that is, a variable of the pthread_attr_t type.

The attribute variable is an opaque data object holding all attributes of the thread. Typically this variable is first initialized by the function

int pthread_attr_init(pthread_attr_t *attr)

to set the default value for all of the individual attributes used by a given implementation. Then the *detached status* attribute is set in the attribute object with the function

int pthread_attr_setdetachstate(pthread_attr_t *attr,
                               int detstat)

where detstat can be set to either PTHREAD_CREATE_DETACHED or PTHREAD_CREATE_JOINABLE. A value of PTHREAD_CREATE_DETACHED causes all threads created with attr to be in the detached state, whereas using a value of PTHREAD_CREATE_JOINABLE causes all threads created with attr to be in the joinable state. The default value of the *detached status* attribute is PTHREAD_CREATE_JOINABLE. The *detached status* attribute can be retrieved using the function

```
int pthread_attr_getdetachstate(const pthread_attr_t *attr,
                                int *pdetstat)
```

which stores the value of the *detached status* attribute in the location pointed by pdetstat, if successful.

A single attribute object can be used in multiple simultaneous calls to the pthread_create function. Other attributes held in the attribute object, for example, may specify the address and size for a thread's stack (allocated by system by default), priority of the thread (0 by default).

The function

```
int pthread_attr_destroy(pthread_attr_t *attr)
```

releases resources used by the attribute object attr, which cannot be reused until it is reinitialized. The function

```
int pthread_detach(pthread_t *t)
```

can be used to explicitly detach thread t even though it was created as joinable. The only reason for using detached threads is some reduction in the Pthreads overhead.

3.3.2. Operations on Mutexes

A typical sequence of operations on a mutex is as follows:

1. Create a mutex.
2. Initialize the mutex.
3. Lock the mutex by one of several competing threads. The winner starts owning the mutex, and the losers act depending on the type of lock operation used. The blocking lock operation blocks the calling thread until the mutex becomes available and this thread locks the mutex. The non-blocking lock operation terminates even if the mutex has been already locked by another thread. On completion, the operation informs the calling thread whether or not it has managed to lock the mutex.
4. Unlock the mutex by its current owner. The mutex becomes available for locking by other competing threads.
5. Destroy the mutex. The mutex cannot be re-used without re-initialization.

To create a mutex, a variable of the `pthread_mutex_t` type must be declared. The variable is an opaque data object that contains all information about the mutex in an implementation-dependent form.

The mutex can be initialized dynamically by the function

```
int pthread_mutex_init(pthread_mutex_t *mutex,
                const pthread_mutexattr_t *mutexattr)
```

which initializes the mutex referenced by `mutex` with attributes specified by `mutexattr`. Typically `mutexattr` is specified as NULL to accept the default mutex attributes. Upon successful initialization, the state of the mutex becomes initialized and unlocked.

The mutex may also be initialized statically, when the mutex variable is declared, by the macro PTHREAD_MUTEX_INITIALIZER. For example,

```
pthread_mutex_t a_mutex = PTHREAD_MUTEX_INITIALIZER;
```

The effect is equivalent to dynamic initialization by a call to the `pthread_mutex_init` function with argument `mutexattr` specified as NULL, except that no error checks are performed.

The function

```
int pthread_mutex_destroy(pthread_mutex_t *mutex)
```

destroys the mutex object, freeing the resources it might hold.

The function

```
int pthread_mutex_lock(pthread_mutex_t *mutex);
```

locks the mutex object referenced by `mutex`. If the mutex is already locked, the calling thread blocks until the mutex becomes available. This operation returns with the mutex object referenced by `mutex` in the locked state with the calling thread as its owner.

The function

```
int pthread_mutex_trylock(pthread_mutex_t *mutex);
```

behaves identically to the `pthread_mutex_lock` function except that if the mutex object referenced by `mutex` is currently locked, the call returns immediately. The `pthread_mutex_trylock` function returns 0 if it succeeds to lock the mutex. Otherwise, a nonzero error is returned.

The function

```
int pthread_mutex_unlock(pthread_mutex_t *mutex);
```

releases the mutex object referenced by `mutex`, resulting in the mutex becoming available. If a signal is delivered to a thread waiting for a mutex, upon return from the signal handler the thread resumes waiting for the mutex as if it was not interrupted.

3.3.3. Operations on Condition Variables

A condition variable (or simply a condition) is a synchronization device that allows threads to suspend execution and relinquish the processors until some predicate on shared data is satisfied. A condition variable must always be associated with a mutex, to avoid a race whereby a thread prepares to wait on a condition variable, and another thread signals the condition variable just before the first thread actually waits on it.

A typical sequence of operations on a condition variable can be depicted as follows:

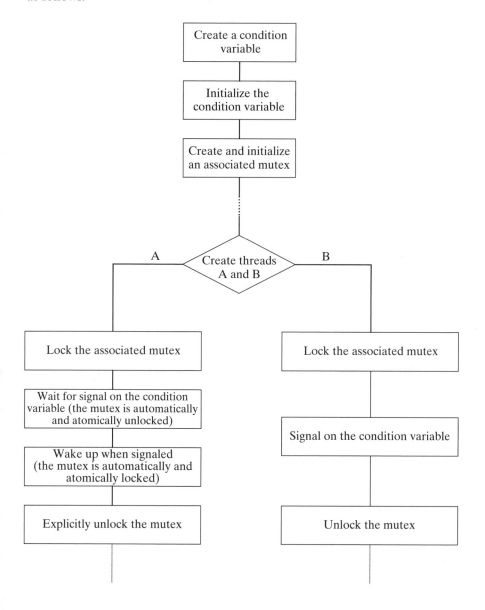

To create the condition, a variable of the pthread_cond_t type must be declared. The variable is an opaque data object that contains all information about the condition in an implementation-dependent form.

The condition variable can be initialized dynamically, with function

```
int pthread_cond_init(pthread_cond_t *cond,
                      const pthread_condattr_t *condattr)
```

which initializes the condition variable pointed by cond, using the condition attributes specified in condxattr. Typically condattr is specified as NULL to accept the default condition attributes.

The condition variable may also be initialized statically, when it is declared, with the macro PTHREAD_COND_INITIALIZER. For example,

```
pthread_cond_t a_cond = PTHREAD_COND_INITIALIZER ;
```

The effect is equivalent to dynamic initialization by a call to the pthread_cond_init function with argument condattr specified as NULL, except that no error checks are performed.

The function

```
int pthread_cond_signal(pthread_cond_t *cond)
```

restarts one of the threads that are waiting on the condition variable pointed by cond. If no threads are waiting on this condition variable, nothing happens. If several threads are waiting on the condition, only one is restarted, but it is not specified which thread should proceed.

The function

```
int pthread_cond_broadcast(pthread_cond_t *cond)
```

restarts all the threads that are waiting on the condition variable pointed by cond. Nothing happens if no threads are waiting on this condition.

The function

```
int pthread_cond_wait(pthread_cond_t *cond,
                      pthread_mutex_t *mutex)
```

atomically unlocks the mutex pointed by mutex (as per pthread_unlock_mutex) and waits for the condition variable pointed by cond to be signaled. The thread execution is suspended and does not consume any processor time until the condition variable is signaled. The mutex must be locked by the calling thread on entrance to the pthread_cond_wait function. Before returning to the calling thread, `pthread_cond_wait` re-acquires the mutex (as per `pthread_lock_mutex`). Unlocking the mutex and suspending on the condition variable is done atomically. Thus, if all threads always acquire the mutex before signaling the condition, this guarantees that the condition cannot be signaled (and thus ignored) between the time a thread locks the mutex, and the time it waits on the condition variable.

The function

```
int pthread_cond_timedwait(pthread_cond_t *cond,
                           pthread_mutex_t *mutex,
                           const struct timespec *abstime)
```

atomically unlocks the mutex pointed by mutex and waits on the condition variable pointed by `cond`, as `pthread_cond_wait` does, but it also bounds the duration of the wait. If the condition variable has not been signaled within the amount of time specified by `abstime`, the mutex is re-acquired and `pthread_cond_timedwait` returns error `ETIMEDOUT`. The `abstime` argument specifies an absolute time.

The function

```
int pthread_cond_destroy(pthread_cond_t *cond)
```

destroys the condition variable pointed by `cond`, freeing the resources it might hold. No threads must be waiting on the condition variable on entrance to `pthread_cond_destroy`.

3.3.4. Example of MT Application: Multithreaded Dot Product

We consider a Pthreads application computing the dot product of two real m-length vectors x and y to illustrate parallel programming an n-processor SMP computer with thread libraries. This MT application divides vectors x and y into n subvectors. While the first $n - 1$ subvectors are of the same length m/n, the last nth subvector may be shorter if m is not a multiple of n. This application uses n parallel threads with ith thread computing its fraction of the total dot product by multiplying subvectors x_i and y_i. The n parallel threads share a data object that accumulates as the dot product, and synchronize their access to the data object by a mutex. The main thread creates the n threads, waits for them to complete their computations by joining with each of the threads, and then puts out the result.

The source code of the application is as follows:

```
#include <stdio.h>
#include <stdlib.h>
#include <pthread.h>
```

```
#define MAXTHRDS 124


typedef struct {
            double *my_x;
            double *my_y;
            double my_dot_prod;
            double *global_dot_prod;
            pthread_mutex_t *mutex;
            int my_vec_len;
} dot_product_t;


void *serial_dot_product(void *arg) {
    dot_product_t *dot_data;
    int i;

    dot_data = arg;
    for(i=0; i<dot_data->my_vec_len; i++)
      dot_data->my_dot_prod += dot_data->my_x[i] *dot_data->my_y[i];
    pthread_mutex_lock(dot_data->mutex);
    *(dot_data->global_dot_prod) += dot_data->my_dot_prod;
    pthread_mutex_unlock(dot_data->mutex);

    pthread_exit(NULL);
}


int main()
{
    double *x, *y, dot_prod;
    pthread_t *working_thread;
    dot_product_t *thrd_dot_prod_data;
    void *status;
    pthread_mutex_t *mutex_dot_prod;

    int num_of_thrds;
    int vec_len;
    int subvec_len;
    int i;

    printf("Number of processors = ");
    if(scanf("%d", &num_of_thrds) < 1 || num_of_thrds > MAXTHRDS) {
    printf("Check input for number of processors. Bye.\n");
      return -1;
```

```
}
printf("Vector length = ");
if(scanf("%d", &vec_len)<1) {
 printf("Check input for vector length. Bye.\n");
 return -1;
}
subvec_len = vec_len/num_of_thrds;
x = malloc(vec_len*sizeof(double));
y = malloc(vec_len*sizeof(double));
for(i=0; i<vec_len; i++) {
 x[i] = 1.;
 y[i] = 1.;
}


working_thread = malloc(num_of_thrds*sizeof(pthread_t));
thrd_dot_prod_data = malloc(num_of_thrds*sizeof (dot_product_t));


mutex_dot_prod = malloc(sizeof(pthread_mutex_t));
pthread_mutex_init(mutex_dot_prod, NULL);


for(i=0; i<num_of_thrds; i++) {
   thrd_dot_prod_data[i].my_x = x + i*subvec_len;
   thrd_dot_prod_data[i].my_y = y + i*subvec_len;
   thrd_dot_prod_data[i].global_dot_prod = &dot_prod;
   thrd_dot_prod_data[i].mutex = mutex_dot_prod;
   thrd_dot_prod_data[i].my_vec_len =
     (i==num_of_thrds-1)? vec_len-(num_of_thrds-1)*subvec_len
                    : subvec_len;
pthread_create(&working_thread[i], NULL, serial_dot_product,
            (void*)&thrd_dot_prod_data[i]);
}
for(i=0; i<num_of_threds; i++
   pthread_join(working_thread[i], &status);


printf("Dot product = %f\n", dot_prod);
free(x);
free(y);
free(working_thread);
free(thrd_dot_prod_data);
pthread_mutex_destroy (mutex_dot_prod);
free(mutex_dot_prod);
}
```

3.4. PARALLEL LANGUAGES

Optimizing C and Fortran 77 compilers do not solve the efficiently portable parallel programming of the SMP architecture. In using those compilers, the programmers can only implement simple multithreaded applications.

Thread libraries do solve this efficiency problem. In particular, Pthreads are a powerful tool by which programmers can implement a wide range of parallel algorithms on SMP computers in highly efficient, portable multithreaded applications.

However, some programmers find the power of thread libraries redundant for parallel programming purposes. The reason is that the multithreaded programming model underlying the libraries is universal and supports both parallel and diverse distributed computing technologies. There are a number of high-level design approaches to writing MT programs with thread libraries, most of which are used in distributed programming, in particular, when implementing servers in server/client applications.

The master/slave design is common to many tasks, and it is widely used in multithreaded parallel programming. Its idea is that one thread does most work of the program, occasionally creating other threads to help in some portion of the work.

Apart from this basic design strategy there exist other design strategies used in distributed programming and not in parallel programming. One such strategy is the producer/consumer design where some threads create work and put it in a queue, and other threads take the work items off the queue and execute them. Other examples are the pipeline design whereby each thread performs some part of an entire tack and passes it partially completed to the next thread, and the personal servant design whereby a thread is assigned to each client and serves only that client.

Thus the programming model underlying the thread libraries is considered to be too powerful and complicated (and hence, error-prone) for use in parallel programming. For this reason a number of high-level parallel extensions of Fortran 77 and C have been designed to provide a simplified multithreaded programming model based on the master/slave strategy, and specifically directed at parallel computing on SMP architectures. Next, we look at two such parallel language forms: Fortran 95 and OpenMP.

3.4.1. Fortran 95

Fortran 95 is the latest version of the standard Fortran language released by ISO in December 1997. Fortran 95 is seen as a relatively minor enhancement of Fortran 90, and it includes a small number of new features. The major new feature added to support parallel programming SMP computers is the FORALL statement and construct.

The FORALL statement is introduced as an alternative to the DO-loop. The idea is that the FORALL statement can be executed in any order, independent of the index. It therefore gives the possibility of parallel implementation of the statement, in particular, with parallel threads for the SMP architecture.

For example, the FORALL statement

FORALL (I = 1:N, J = 1:N) H(I,J) = 1./**REAL**(I+J-1)

defines a Hilbert matrix of order N. The FORALL statement

FORALL (I = 1:N, J = 1:N, Y(I,J).**NE**.0.) X(I,J) = 1./Y(I,J)

inverts the elements of a matrix, avoiding division with zero.

In the statements above, FORALL can be considered as a double loop, which can be executed in arbitrary order. The general form of the FORALL statement is

FORALL ($v_1=l_1:u_1:s_1, \ldots, v_n=l_n:u_n:s_n,$ mask) a($e_1, \ldots, e_m$) = expr,

and it is evaluated according to certain well specified rules. Namely, first the left bound, right bound and stride expressions for each triplet are evaluated in any order. All possible pairings of indexes form the set of combinations. For example, given the statement

FORALL (I=1:3, J=4:5) A(I,J) = A(J,I)

the set of combinations of I and J is

{ (1,4), (1,5), (2,4), (2,5), (3,4), (3,5) }

Second, the *mask* expression for the set of combinations is evaluated, in any order, producing a set of active combinations (those for which *mask is* evaluated to .TRUE.). For example, if mask (I+J.NE.6) is applied to the set above, the set of active combinations is

{ (1,4), (2,5), (3,4), (3,5) }

Then expressions $e_1, \ldots, e_m$, and *expr* are evaluated in any order for all active combinations of indexes. Finally, the computed values of *expr* are assigned to the corresponding elements of *a* in any order for all active combinations of indexes.

In addition there is a FORALL construct that has to be distinguished from the single-line FORALL statement. The construct is interpreted in the same way as if its internal statements were written as FORALL statements in the same order. This restriction is important in order to achieve a unique computational result. For example, when the statements in the below FORALL construct

```
REAL, DIMENSION(N, N) :: A, B
...
FORALL (I = 2:N-1, J = 2:N-1)
   A(I,J) = 0.25*(A(I,J-1)+A(I,J+1)+A(I-1,J)+A(I+1,J))
   B(I,J) = A(I,J)
END FORALL
```

have been executed, arrays A and B have identical values in the internal points, while B has kept its previous values on the boundaries.

In general, Fortran 95 procedures may have side effects. Side effects that may occur include a change in value of an argument or global variable. However, FORALL statements and constructs by design require that all referenced functions be free of side effects. Therefore, to avoid problems associated with side effects, Fortran 95 enables the programmers to specify a procedure as side effect free. These procedures are referred to as PURE functions. Within FORALL statements and constructs calls of PURE functions are only permitted.

A restricted form of a PURE procedure is called ELEMENTAL. In Fortran 90, to provide a procedure that operated elementally, the programmer had to produce eight versions of the procedure: one to operate on scalars, and one for each rank of the array from one to seven. If two array arguments were used, as many as 16 versions could be required. Using ELEMENTAL, the programmer can write a single procedure with the same functionality.

3.4.2. OpenMP

OpenMP is a recent application program interface (API) for writing multi-threaded applications based on the master/slave design strategy. OpenMP supports parallel programming in C, C++, and Fortran on all SMP architectures, including Unix platforms and Windows NT platforms. OpenMP is jointly defined by a group of major computer hardware and software vendors such as Intel, HP, SGI, IBM, SUN, Compaq, KAI, PGI, and NAG, among many others. First specifications of OpenMP appeared in late 1998.

Technically OpenMP specifies a set of language extensions in the form of compiler directives, library procedures, and environmental variables. OpenMP is semantically the same between Fortran and C/C++ differing mainly in syntax. In this book we use the C/C++ API to present OpenMP.

An OpenMP compiler directive is just a C/C++ preprocessing pragma directive of the form

```
#pragma omp directive-name list-of-clauses
```

Such syntax allows C/C++ compilers that do not support OpenMP to compile an OpenMP program. OpenMP also specifies stubs for the runtime library functions in order to enable portability to platforms that do not support the OpenMP C/C++ API. On these platforms, OpenMP programs must be linked with a library containing the stub functions. The stub functions assume that the directives in the OpenMP program are ignored. As such, they emulate serial semantics.

As a rule an OpenMP directive applies to a *structured block*, that is, a statement (single or compound) that has a single entry and a single exit. No statement is a structured block if there is a jump into or out of that statement. A compound statement is a structured block if its execution always begins at the opening *{*, and always ends at the closing *}* or at a call to the `exit` function.

The directive and the subsequent structured block to which it applies make up an OpenMP *construct*. Note that some directives are not part of a construct.

A typical sequence of OpenMP's constructs and single directives do the following:

- Define a structured block, which is to be executed by multiple threads in parallel, and create the parallel threads; in OpenMP that structured block is called a *parallel region*.
- Distribute the execution of the parallel region among the parallel threads.
- Synchronize the work of the parallel threads during the execution of the parallel region.
- Control the data environment during the execution of the parallel region via specification of shared data, private data, accumulating variables, and so on.

3.4.2.1. Parallel Regions. A `parallel` construct is the fundamental construct that starts parallel execution of a parallel region. It has the following form:

```
#pragma omp parallel list-of-clauses
structured-block
```

When a thread encounters a `parallel` construct, a team of threads is created. This thread becomes the master thread of the team, with a thread number of 0, and all threads, including the master thread, execute the region in parallel.

By default, the number of threads that are requested is implementation-defined. To explicitly determine the number of threads requested, the `num_threads` clause may be used in the `parallel` directive. Alternatively, the `omp_set_num_threads` library function may be called before activization of the parallel region.

For example, the following OpenMP code

```
int a[5][5];
omp_set_num_threads(5);
#pragma omp parallel
{
    int thrd_num = omp_get_thread_num();
    zero_init(a[thrd_num], 5);
}
```

defines a parallel region executed by five parallel threads. The omp_get_thread_num library function returns the thread number, within its team, of the thread executing the function. The thread number lies between 0 and 4. The master thread of the team is thread 0. Array a is shared among all the threads. Variable thrd_num is private to each thread in the team. Each thread calls a user-defined zero_init function to initialize with zeros the corresponding row of the array in parallel.

There is an implicit barrier at the end of a parallel region, that is, a synchronization point that must be reached by all threads in the team. Each thread waits until all threads in the team arrive at this point. Only the master thread of the team continues execution at the end of the parallel region.

If a thread in a team executing a parallel region encounters another parallel construct, it creates a new team, and it becomes the master of that new team. Nested parallel regions are serialized by default. As a result, by default, a nested parallel region is executed by a team composed of one thread. The default behavior may be changed by using either the omp_set_nested library function or the OMP_NESTED environment variable. However, the number of threads in a team that execute a nested parallel region is implementation-defined.

3.4.2.2. Work-Sharing Constructs. A work-sharing construct distributes the execution of the associated statement among the members of the team that encounter it. The work-sharing directives do not launch new threads, and there is no implicit barrier on entry to a work-sharing construct.

The sequence of work-sharing constructs and barrier directives encountered must be the same for every thread in a team.

A for construct of the form

```
#pragma omp for list-of-clauses
for-loop
```

specifies that the iterations of the associated loop will be executed in parallel. The iterations of the for loop are distributed across threads that already exist in the team executing the parallel region to which the team binds.

The associated for loop must be of the following *canonical* form

```
for(var = lb; var logical-op rb; incr-expr)
```

where *var* is a signed integer variable that must not be modified within the body of the `for` statement; *incr-expr* is one of ++*var*, —*var*, *var*++, *var*—, *var*+=*incr*, *var*-=*incr*, *var*=*var*+*incr*, *var*=*var*–*incr*, or *var*=*incr*+*var*; *lb*, *lb*, and *incr* are loop invariant integer expressions; and *logical-op* is one of $<, >, <=$, or $>=$. The canonical form allows the number of loop iterations to be computed upon entry to the loop.

The `schedule` clause of the form

```
schedule(kind [, chunk-size])
```

specifies how iterations of the `for` loop are divided among threads of the team. If *kind* is `static`, iterations are divided into chunks of a size specified by *chunk-size*. The chunks are statically assigned to threads in a round-robin fashion in the order of the thread number. When no *chunk-size* is specified, the iteration space is divided into chunks that are approximately equal in size, with one chunk assigned to each thread. For example, code

```
int a[10][10], k;
omp_set_num_threads(5);
#pragma omp parallel
#pragma omp for schedule(static)
for(k=0; k<10; k++)
    zero_init(a[k], 10);
```

specifies that each of five threads, executing the `for` statement, will execute two successive iterations of the loop. Namely thread *i* will execute 2*i*th and (2*i* + 1)-th iterations of the loop calling the `zero_init` function to initialise with zeros the 2*i*th and (2*i*+1)-th rows of array a. Note that variable *k* will be private to each of the threads.

If *kind* is `dynamic`, the iterations are divided into a series of chunks, each containing *chunk-size* iterations. Each chunk is assigned to a thread that is waiting for an assignment. The thread executes the chunk of iterations and then waits for its next assignment, until no chunks remain to be assigned. When no *chunk-size* is specified, it defaults to 1. For example, code

```
int a[10][10], k;
omp_set_num_threads(5);
#pragma omp parallel
#pragma omp for schedule(dynamic, 2)
for(k=0; k<10; k++)
    zero_init(a[k], 10);
```

also specifies that each of five threads, executing the `for` statement, will execute two successive iterations of the loop. But which thread will execute which pair of iterations is decided at run time.

If *kind* is guided, the iterations are assigned to threads in chunks with decreasing sizes. When a thread finishes its assigned chunk of iterations, it is dynamically assigned another chunk, until none remains. For a *chunk-size* of 1, the size of each chunk is approximately the number of unassigned iterations divided by the number of threads. These sizes decrease approximately exponentially to 1. For a *chunk-size* greater than 1, the sizes decrease approximately exponentially to *chunk-size*, except that the last chunk may be fewer than *chunk-size* iterations. When no *chunk-size* is specified, it defaults to 1.

Finally, if *kind* is runtime, the decision regarding scheduling is deferred until runtime. The schedule kind and size of the chunks can be chosen at run time by setting the environment variable OMP_SCHEDULE. If this environment variable is not set, the resulting schedule is implementation-defined. No *chunk-size* must be specified.

In the absence of an explicitly defined schedule clause, the default schedule is implementation-defined. An OpenMP compliant program should not rely on a particular schedule for correct execution. There is an implicit barrier at the end of a for construct unless a nowait clause is specified.

A sections construct of the form

```
#pragma omp sections list-of-clauses
{
  [#pragma omp section]
   structured-block
  [#pragma omp section
   structured-block]
...
}
```

specifies a set of constructs that are to be divided among threads in a team. Each section is executed once by a thread in the team. Except for the first section, each section must be preceded by a section directive. For example, code

```
int a[10][10];
omp_set_num_threads(5);
#pragma omp parallel
#pragma omp sections
{
{
  zero_init(a[0], 10);
  zero_init(a[1], 10);
}
#pragma omp section
{
```

```
      zero_init(a[2], 10);
      zero_init(a[3], 10);
    }
  #pragma omp section
    {
      zero_init(a[4], 10);
      zero_init(a[5], 10);
    }
  #pragma omp section
    {
      zero_init(a[6], 10);
      zero_init(a[7], 10);
    }
  #pragma omp section
    {
      zero_init(a[8], 10);
      zero_init(a[9], 10);
     }
    }
```

specifies that each of five threads, executing the parallel region, will execute a section containing two calls to the `zero_init` function initializing with zeros two corresponding rows of array a. There is an implicit barrier at the end of a `sections` construct unless a `nowait` clause is specified.

A `single` construct of the form

```
#pragma omp single list-of-clauses
structured-block
```

specifies that the associated structured block is executed by only one thread in the team (not necessarily the master thread). There is an implicit barrier after a `single` construct unless a `nowait` clause is specified.

A `master` construct of the form

```
#pragma omp master
structured-block
```

specifies that the associated structured block is executed by the master thread of the team. Other threads of the team do not execute this statement. There is no implicit barrier on entry to or exit from the master section.

OpenMP provides shortcuts to specifying a parallel region that contains only one work-sharing construct. The combined parallel work-sharing constructs are

```
#pragma omp parallel for list-of-clauses
for-loop
```

for a parallel region that contains a single `for` construct, and

```
#pragma omp parallel sections list-of-clauses
{
  [#pragma omp section]
   structured-block
  [#pragma omp section
   structured-block]
  . . .
}
```

for a parallel region containing a single `sections` construct.

3.4.2.3. Synchronization Directives and Constructs. In addition to implicit barriers implied on some OpenMP constructs, the `barrier` directive

```
#pragma omp barrier
```

is provided to explicitly synchronize all the threads in a team. When encountered, each thread of the team waits until all of the others have reached this point.

An `ordered` construct of the form

```
#pragma omp ordered list-of-clauses
structured-block
```

specifies that the associated structured block is executed in the order in which iterations would be executed in a sequential loop.

In order to synchronize access to shared data, a `critical` construct

```
#pragma omp critical [(name)]
structured-block
```

is provided that restricts execution of the associated structured block to a single thread at a time. A thread waits at the beginning of a critical region until no other thread is executing a critical region (anywhere in the program) with the same name *name*. All unnamed critical regions have the same unspecified name. For example, code

```
int a[100], ind[100], b[100], k;
. . .
omp_set_num_threads(5);
#pragma omp parallel for
for(k=0; k<100; k++) {
    #pragma omp critical
```

```
  {
     a[ind[k]]  +=  f(k);
  }
  b[k]  +=  g(k);
}
```

specifies that five threads execute in parallel the iterations of the above `for` loop. During the execution they are updating elements of the shared array a. An element of a to be updated by an iteration is specified by an element of array `ind`. Therefore different iterations of the loop may update the same element of a. The `critical` directive is used to serialize execution of the corresponding statement by the parallel threads, and thus the threads avoid race conditions (simultaneous updates of an element of a by multiple threads).

An `atomic` construct of the form

```
#pragma omp atomic
expression-statement
```

may be seen as a special case of a critical section. Unlike the `critical` directive, the `atomic` directive does not prevent simultaneous execution by multiple threads of the associated statement. Instead, it ensures that a specific memory location is updated atomically, that is, prevents simultaneous access to the memory location by multiple threads.

In the `atomic` construct, *expression-statement* must have one of the following forms: x op= $expr$, x++, ++x, x—, or —x, where x is an lvalue of scalar type, $expr$ is an expression of scalar type not referencing the object designated by x, and op is one of the binary operators +, *, -, /, &, ^, |, <<, or >>. Only the load and store of the object designated by x are atomic. The evaluation of $expr$ is not atomic. To avoid race conditions, all updates of the location in parallel should be protected with the `atomic` directive, except those that are known to be free of race conditions.

When supported by hardware instructions, `atomic` directives allow more efficient implementation than via straightforward replacement of all `atomic` directives with `critical` directives that have the same unique name. For example, code

```
int a[100], ind[100], b[100], k;
...
omp_set_num_threads(5);
#pragma omp parallel for
for(k=0; k<100; k++) {
    #pragma omp atomic
       a[ind[k]]  +=  f(k);
    b[k]  +=  g(k);
}
```

only differs from the previous example code in the way it avoids race conditions—the `atomic` directive is used instead of the `critical` directive. The advantage of using the `atomic` directive in this example is that it allows updates of two different elements of *a* to occur in parallel. The use of the `critical` directive leads to all updates to elements of *a* are executed serially.

A flush directive of the form

```
#pragma omp flush [(variable-list)]
```

specifies a sequence point at which all threads in a team must have a consistent view of memory. This means that all memory operations (both reads and writes) specified before the sequence point must complete. For example, variables in registers or write buffers must be updated in memory. All memory operations specified after the point would not have yet begun. The directive provides an explicit mechanism to ensure consistency of shared data not depending on particular algorithms of cache management implemented in one or another underlying SMP computer.

A flush directive without a *variable-list* synchronizes all shared objects except in accessible automatic variables. It is implied for the `barrier` directive, at entry to and exit from `critical` and `ordered` constructs, and at exit from `parallel`, `for`, `sections`, and `single` constructs. The directive is not implied if a `nowait` clause is present.

A flush directive with a *variable-list* synchronizes only the objects designated by variables in the *variable-list*.

3.4.2.4. Data Environment. There are two kinds of variable in an OpenMP program. A *shared* variable designates a single region of storage. All threads in a team that access this variable will access this single region of storage. By default, if a variable is defined outside a `parallel` construct and is visible when the `parallel` construct is encountered, then the variable is shared within the `parallel` construct. Static variables declared within a parallel region are shared. Heap-allocated memory is shared.

A *private* variable designates a region of storage that is unique to the thread making the reference. Automatic variables declared within a `parallel` construct are private. Other ways to specify that a variable is private are

- a `threadprivate` directive;
- a `private`, `firstprivate`, `lastprivate`, or `reduction` clause;
- use of the variable as a `for` loop control variable immediately following a `for` or `parallel for` directive.

The `threadprivate` directive

```
#pragma omp threadprivate [(variable-list)]
```

makes the variables specified in the *variable-list* private to a thread. Each copy of a `threadprivate` variable is initialized once, at an unspecified point of the program before the first reference to that copy, and in the usual manner (i.e., as the master copy would be initialized in a serial execution of the program). Only global variables or static block-scope variables may appear in the *variable-list*. For example, the following code

```
int count()
{
   static int counter = 0;
   #pragma omp threadprivate(counter)
   counter++;
   return counter;
}
```

uses the `threadprivate` directive to give each thread calling the `count` function a separate counter.

The `parallel` directive and most work-sharing directives accept clauses that allow the programmer to explicitly specify whether a variable is private or shared, how the variable is initialized, and so on.

A `copyin` clause of the form

```
copyin(variable-list)
```

provides a mechanism to assign the same value to `threadprivate` variables for each thread in the team executing the parallel region. For each variable specified in a `copyin` clause, the value of the variable in the master thread of the team is copied, as if by assignment, to the thread-private copies at the beginning of the parallel region.

A `private` clause of the form

```
private(variable-list)
```

declares the variables in *variable-list* to be private to each thread in a team. The behavior of a variable specified in a `private` clause is as follows: A new object with automatic storage duration is allocated for the construct. The size and alignment of the new object are determined by the type of the variable. This allocation occurs once for each thread in the team; the initial value of the object is indeterminate. The original object designated by the variable has an indeterminate value upon entry to the construct, must not be modified within the construct, and has an indeterminate value upon exit from the construct. Within the construct the variable designates the new private object allocated by the thread. Note that unlike the `threadprivate` directive, which replicates a global or local static variable preserving its static nature within each thread, the `private` clause creates private automatic variables overriding the original (possibly, global or local static) variable.

A `firstprivate` clause of the form

firstprivate(*variable-list*)

is a special case of the `private` clause, which additionally initializes each new private object. The initialization happens as if it were done once per thread, before the thread's execution of the construct. For a `firstprivate` clause on a `parallel` construct, the initial value of the new private object is the value of the original object that exists immediately before the `parallel` construct for the thread that encounters it. For a `firstprivate` clause on a work-sharing construct, the initial value of the new private object for each thread that executes the work-sharing construct is the value of the original object that exists before the point in time that the same thread encounters the work-sharing construct.

A `lastprivate` clause of the form

lastprivate(*variable-list*)

is a special case of the `private` clause, which additionally determines the original object upon exit from the work-sharing construct. Namely the value of each `lastprivate` variable from the sequentially last iteration of the associated loop, or the lexically last section, is assigned to the variable's original object. Variables that are not assigned a value by the last iteration of the `for` or `parallel for`, or by the lexically last section of the `sections` or `parallel sections` construct, have indeterminate values after the construct.

A `shared` clause of the form

shared(*variable-list*)

shares variables that appear in the *variable-list* among all the threads in a team. All threads within a team access the same region of storage for `shared` variables.

A `copyprivate` clause of the form

copyprivate(*variable-list*)

provides a mechanism to use a private variable to broadcast a value from one member of a team to the other members. This clause may only appear on the `single` directive. After the execution of the structured block associated with the `single` directive and before any of the threads in the team have left the barrier at the end of this `single` construct, a `copyprivate` variable becomes defined (as if by assignment) in all other threads of the team with the value of the corresponding variable in the thread that executed the construct's structured block. The mechanism is an alternative to using a shared variable for the value, when providing such a shared variable would be difficult.

A reduction clause of the form

```
reduction(op:variable-list)
```

specifies the way a reduction operation with the operator *op* on a scalar variable in the *variable-list* is performed in the corresponding parallel or work-sharing construct. Namely inside the construct a private copy of each variable in the *variable-list* is created, one for each thread, as if the private clause had been used, and initialized depending on the *op* (0 for +, -, |, ^, and ||; 1 for * and &&; and ~0 for &). Then each thread updates its private copy of the variable. At the end of the region for which the reduction clause was specified, the original object is updated to reflect the result of combining its original value with the final value of each of the private copies using the operator *op*. For example, the code

```
int k;
double sum, a[1000];
...
sum = 0.;
#pragma omp parallel for reduction(+: sum)
for(k=0; k<1000; k++)
  sum += a[k];
```

uses the reduction clause to compute efficiently the sum of elements of the array a by parallel threads.

A default clause of the form

```
default(none)
```

may be used in the parallel directive. When specified, the clause repeals all defaults for implicit specification of shared variables in the corresponding parallel region, and requires explicit specification of their shared status.

3.4.2.5. Runtime Library Functions. The OpenMP runtime library functions are divided into the following two non-intersecting classes:

- Functions controlling and querying the parallel execution environment like the omp_set_num_threads function.
- Functions (and data types) implementing a mutexlike explicit synchronization mechanism.

Examples of functions that affect and monitor threads, processors, and the parallel environment are omp_set_num_threads, omp_get_num_threads, omp_get_max_threads, omp_get_thread_num, and omp_get_num_procs.

The function

void omp_set_num_threads(**int** num_threads)

sets the default number of threads to use for subsequent parallel regions that do not specify a num_threads clause.
The function

int omp_get_num_threads(**void**)

returns the number of threads currently in the team executing the parallel region from which it is called.
The function

int omp_get_max_threads(**void**)

returns the maximum value that can be returned by calls to omp_get_num_threads.
The function

int omp_get_thread_num(**void**)

returns the thread number, within its team, of the thread executing the function.
The function

int omp_get_num_procs(**void**)

returns the maximum number of processors that could be assigned to the program.

The part of the OpenMP runtime library providing a mutexlike synchronization mechanism declares two types of *lock* variables (an analogue of mutex variables of Pthreads) as well as functions for

- initializing a lock variable;
- destroying the lock variable;
- setting the lock variable (an analogue of locking a mutex in Pthreads);

- unsetting the lock variable (an analogue of unlocking a Pthreads mutex);
- testing the lock variable (an analogue of the Pthreads's `trylock`).

3.4.2.6. Example of OpenMP Application: Multithreaded Dot Product.
To illustrate parallel programming SMP computers with OpenMP, we consider an application for computing the dot product of two real vectors x and y. The OpenMP application implements the same parallel algorithm as that of Pthreads presented in Section 3.3.4.

The source code of the application is as follows:

```c
#include <stdio.h>
#include <stdlib.h>
#include <omp.h>

#define MAXTHRDS 124

int main()
{
    double *x, *y, dot_prod;
    int num_of_thrds, vec_len, i;

    num_of_thrds = omp_get_num_procs();
    omp_set_num_threads(num_of_thrds);
    printf("Vector length = ");
    if(scanf("%d", &vec_len)<1) {
        printf("Check input for vector length. Bye.\n");
        return -1;
    }

    x = malloc(vec_len*sizeof(double));
    y = malloc(vec_len*sizeof(double));
    for(i=0; i<vec_len; i++) {
        x[i] = 1.;
        y[i] = 1.;
    }

    dot_prod = 0.;
    #pragma omp parallel for reduction(+: dot_prod)
    for(i=0; i<vec_len; i++) {
        dot_prod += x[i]*y[i];
    }

    printf("Dot product = %f\n", dot_prod);
```

```
    free(x);
    free(y);
}
```

Obviously this OpenMP code is much simpler and more compact than the Pthreads code.

3.5. SUMMARY

The shared memory multiprocessor architecture provides a higher-level parallelism than the vector and superscalar architecture via multiple parallel streams of instructions. However, the SMP architecture is not scalable. The speedup provided by this architecture is limited by the bandwidth of the memory bus.

Multithreading is the primary programming model for the SMP architecture. Serial languages, such as C and Fortran 77, may be used in concert with optimizing compilers to write efficient programs for SMP computers. Unfortunately, only a limited and simple class of multithreaded algorithms can be implemented in an efficient and portable way by that approach.

Thread libraries directly implement the multithreading paradigm and allow the programmers to write efficient MT programs that do not rely on optimizing compilers. For Unix platforms Pthreads are standard and efficiently support portable parallel programming Unix SMP computers.

Thread libraries are powerful tools that support both parallel and distributed computing. The general programming model underlying the thread libraries is universal and considered too powerful, complicated, and error-prone for just the goals of parallel programming. OpenMP is a high-level parallel extension of Fortran, C, and C++ providing a simplified multithreaded programming model based on the master/slave design strategy and aimed specifically at parallel computing on SMP architectures. OpenMP significantly facilitates writing parallel MT applications and efficiently supports portable programming for all the range of SMP computers including NT computers and Unix computers, among others.

## CHAPTER 4

Distributed Memory Multiprocessors

4.1. DISTRIBUTED MEMORY MULTIPROCESSOR ARCHITECTURE: PROGRAMMING MODEL AND PERFORMANCE MODELS

A computer system of the distributed memory multiprocessor architecture, shown in Figure 4.1, consists of a number of identical processors not sharing global main memory and interconnected via a communication network. The architecture is also called the *massively parallel processors* (MPP) architecture.

The primary model of a program for the MPP architecture is parallel processes, each running on a separate processor and using message passing to communicate with each other. There are two main reasons for parallel processes of a message-passing program to send messages among themselves. The first one is that some processes may use data computed by other processes. As this occurs, the data must be delivered from processes producing the data to processes using the data. The second reason is that the processes may need to synchronize their work. Messages are exchanged to inform the processes that some event has happened or some condition has been satisfied.

Since MPPs provide much more parallelism, they have more performance potential than SMPs. Indeed, although the number of processors in SMPs rarely exceeds 32, MPPs often have hundreds and even thousands of processors. Modern communication technologies allow a manufacturer to build such an MPP whose $(p+1)$-processor configuration executes "normal" message-passing programs faster than a p-processor configuration for a practically arbitrary p. This means that unlike the SMP architecture, the MPP architecture is *scalable*.

Many different protocols, devices, physical communications bearers, and the like, may be used to implement communication networks in MPPs. Nonetheless, whatever technical solutions are employed in the particular communication network of an MPP, its main goal is to provide a communication layer that is fast, well balanced with the number and performance of processors, and homogeneous. The structure of the network should cause no degradation in communication speed even when all processors of the MPP simultaneously

Parallel Computing on Heterogeneous Networks, by Alexey Lastovetsky
ISBN 0-471-22982-2   Copyright © 2003 by John Wiley & Sons, Inc.

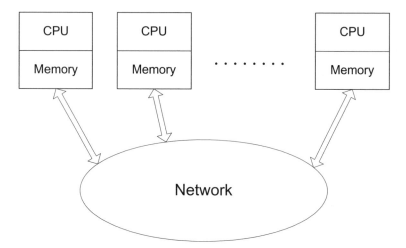

Figure 4.1. Distributed memory multiprocessor.

perform intensive data transfer operations. The network should also ensure the same speed of data transfer between any two processors of the MPP.

The MPP architecture is implemented in the form of parallel computer or in the form of dedicated cluster of workstations. A real MPP implementing the ideal MPP architecture is normally a result of compromise between the cost and quality of its communication network.

To see how the MPP architecture is scalable, consider parallel matrix-matrix multiplication on the ideal MPP. Recall that we have used matrix-matrix multiplication in Chapter 3 to demonstrate that the SMP architecture is not scalable.

The simplest parallel algorithm implementing matrix operation $C = A \times B$ on a p-processor MPP, where A, B are dense square $n \times n$ matrices, can be summarized as follows:

- Each element c_{ij} in C is computed as $c_{ij} = \sum_{k=0}^{n-1} a_{ik} \times b_{kj}$.
- The A, B, and C matrices are evenly (and identically) partitioned into p horizontal slices (for simplicity we assume that n is a multiple of p). There is one-to-one mapping between these slices and the processors. Each processor is responsible for computing its C slice (see Figure 4.2).
- In order to compute elements of its C slice, each processor requires all elements of the B matrix. Therefore, during the execution of the algorithm, each processor receives from each of $p - 1$ other processors n^2/p matrix elements (shown in gray in Figure 4.2).

In total, the matrix-matrix multiplication involves $O(n^3)$ operations. Therefore the contribution of computation to the total execution time of the parallel algorithm above is

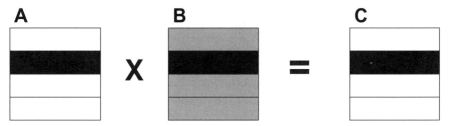

Figure 4.2. Matrix-matrix multiplication with matrices A, B, and C evenly partitioned in one dimension. The slices mapped onto a single processor are shaded in black. During execution, this processor requires all of matrix B (shown shaded in gray).

$$t_{\text{comp}} = \frac{t_{\text{proc}} \times n^3}{p},$$

where t_{proc} characterizes the speed of a single processor.

To estimate the contribution of communication to the total execution time, assume that the time of transfer of a data block is a linear function of the size of the data block. Thus the cost of transfer of a single horizontal slice between two processors is

$$t_{\text{slice}} = t_s + t_e \times \frac{n^2}{p},$$

where t_s is the start-up time and t_e is the time per element.

During the execution of the algorithm, each processor sends its slice to $p - 1$ other processors as well as receives their slices. Assume that at any given time the processor can be simultaneously sending a single message and receiving another single message (a double-port model). Then, under the pessimistic assumption that the processor sends its slice to other processors in $p - 1$ sequential steps, the estimation of the per-processor communication cost is

$$t_{\text{comm}} = (p-1) \times t_{\text{slice}} \approx t_s \times p + t_e \times n^2.$$

For simplicity, assume that communications and computations do not overlap. Namely first all of the communications are performed in parallel, and then all of the computations are performed in parallel. So the total execution time of the parallel algorithm on the ideal p-processor MPP is

$$t_{\text{total}} \approx t_{\text{proc}} \times \frac{n^3}{p} + t_s \times p + t_e \times n^2.$$

What restrictions must be satisfied to ensure faster execution of the algorithm on a $(p + 1)$-processor configuration of the MPP compared with the

p-processor configuration ($p = 1, 2, \ldots$)? First of all, the algorithm must ensure speedup at least while upgrading the MPP from a one-processor to a two-processor configuration. It means that

$$t_{\text{proc}} \times n^3 - \left(t_{\text{proc}} \times \frac{n^3}{2} + t_s + t_e \times n \frac{n^2}{2} \right) = t_{\text{proc}} \times \frac{n^3}{2} - t_s - t_e \times \frac{n^2}{2} > 0.$$

Typically $t_s/t_{\text{proc}} \sim 10^3$ and $t_e/t_{\text{proc}} \sim 10^1$. Therefore, the inequality

$$n^3 > 2 \times \frac{t_s}{t_{\text{proc}}} + \frac{t_e}{t_{\text{proc}}} \times n^2$$

will be comfortably satisfied if $n > 100$. Second, the algorithm will be scalable, if t_{total} is a monotonically decreasing function of p, that is, if

$$\frac{\partial t_{\text{total}}}{\partial p} = t_s - t_{\text{proc}} \times \frac{n^3}{p^2} < 0,$$

or

$$\frac{t_s}{t_{\text{proc}}} \times \left(\frac{p}{n} \right)^2 \times \frac{1}{n} < 1.$$

The inequality above will be true if n is reasonably larger than p.

The efficiency of the parallel algorithm above can be significantly improved by using a two-dimensional decomposition of matrices A, B, and C instead of the one-dimensional decomposition. The resulting algorithm of parallel matrix-matrix multiplication can be summarized as follows:

- Each element c_{ij} in C is computed as $c_{ij} = \sum_{k=0}^{n-1} a_{ik} \times b_{kj}$.
- The A, B, and C matrices are identically partitioned into p equal $n/\sqrt{p} \times n/\sqrt{p}$ squares so that each row and each column contain $\sqrt{p}$ squares (for simplicity we assume that p is a square number and n is a multiple of $\sqrt{p}$). There is one-to-one mapping between these squares and the processors. Each processor is responsible for computing its C square (see Figure 4.3).
- To compute elements of its C square, each processor requires the corresponding row of squares of the A matrix and column of squares of the B matrix (shown in gray in Figure 4.3). Therefore, during the execution of the algorithm, each processor receives from each of its $\sqrt{p} - 1$ horizontal and $\sqrt{p} - 1$ vertical neighbors n^2/p matrix elements.

The total per-processor communication cost,

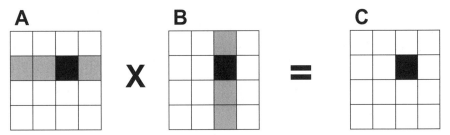

Figure 4.3. Matrix-matrix multiplication with matrices A, B, and C evenly partitioned in two dimensions. The blocks mapped onto a single processor are shaded black. During execution, this processor requires corresponding rows of matrix A and columns of matrix B (shown shaded in gray).

$$t_{\text{comm}} = 2 \times (\sqrt{p} - 1) \times \left(t_s + t_e \times \frac{n^2}{p} \right) \approx 2 \times t_s \times \sqrt{p} + 2 \times t_e \times \frac{n^2}{\sqrt{p}},$$

and the total execution time of that parallel algorithm,

$$t_{\text{total}} \approx t_{\text{proc}} \times \frac{n^3}{p} + 2 \times t_s \times \sqrt{p} + 2 \times t_e \times \frac{n^2}{\sqrt{p}},$$

are considerably less than in the one-dimensional algorithm. Some further improvements can be made to achieve overlapping communications and computations as well as better locality of computation during execution of the algorithm. As a result the carefully designed two-dimensional algorithm appears efficient and scalable, practically, for any reasonable task size and number of processors.

Summarizing the analysis, we can conclude that the ideal MPP proved to be scalable when executing carefully designed and highly efficient parallel algorithms. In addition, under quite weak, reasonable, and easily satisfied restrictions even very straightforward parallel algorithms make the MPP architecture scalable.

The model of the MPP architecture used in the preceding performance analysis is indeed simplistic. We used three parameters t_{proc}, t_s, and t_e, and a straightforward linear communication model to describe an MPP. The model was quite satisfactory for the goal of that analysis—to demonstrate the scalability of the MPP architecture. It may also be quite satisfactory for performance analysis of coarse-grained parallel algorithms with simple structure of communications and mainly long messages sent during the communications. However, the accuracy of the model becomes unsatisfactory if one needs to predict performance of a message-passing algorithm with nontrivial communication structure and frequent communication operations transferring mainly short messages, especially if communications prevail over computations.

A more realistic model of the MPP architecture that addresses this issue is the LogP model. It is simple but sufficiently detailed for accurate prediction of the performance of message-passing algorithms with a fine-grained communication structure. In this model the processors communicate by point-to-point short messages. The model specifies the performance characteristics of the interconnection network, but does not describe the structure of the network. The model has four basic parameters:

- L: an upper bound on the *latency*, or delay, incurred in sending a message from its source processor to its target processor.
- o: the *overhead*, defined as the length of time that a processor is engaged in the transmission or reception of each message; during this time the processor cannot perform other operations.
- g: the *gap* between messages, defined as the minimum time interval between consecutive message transmissions or consecutive message receptions at a processor. The reciprocal of g corresponds to the available per-processor communication bandwidth for short messages.
- P: the number of processors.

The model assumes a unit time for local operations and calls it a processor cycle. The parameters L, o, and g are measured as multiples of the processor cycle.

It is assumed that the network has a finite capacity, such that at most L/g messages can be in transit from any processor or to any processor at any time. If a processor attempts to transmit a message that would exceed this limit, it stalls until the message can be sent without exceeding the capacity limit.

The model is asynchronous, that is, processors work asynchronously, and the latency experienced by any message is unpredictable but is bounded above by L in the absence of stalls. Because of variations in latency, the messages directed to a given target processor may not arrive in the same order as they are sent.

The parameters of the LogP model are not equally important in all situations; often it is possible to ignore one or more parameters and work with a simpler model. For example, in algorithms that communicate data infrequently, it is reasonable to ignore the bandwidth and capacity limits. In some algorithms messages are sent in long streams, which are pipelined through the network, so that message transmission time is dominated by the intermessage gaps, and the latency may be disregarded. In some MPPs the overhead dominates the gap, so g can be eliminated.

As an illustration of the role of various parameters of the LogP model, consider the problem of optimal broadcasting a single data unit from one processor to $P - 1$ others. The main idea is that all processors that have received the data unit transmit it as quickly as possible, while ensuring that no processor receives more than one message.

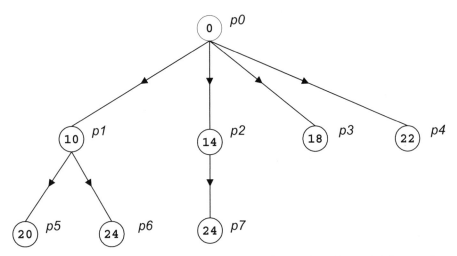

Figure 4.4. Optimal broadcast tree $P = 8$, $L = 6$, $g = 4$, and $o = 2$. The number shown for each node is the time at which it has received the data unit and can begin sending it.

The source of the broadcast begins transmitting the data unit at time 0. The first data unit enters the network at time o, takes L cycles to arrive at the destination, and is received by the processor at time $L + 2 \times o$. Meanwhile the source will have initiated transmission to other processors at time g, $2 \times g$, ..., assuming $g \geq o$, each of which acts as the root of a smaller broadcast tree.

The optimal broadcast tree for p processors is unbalanced with the fan-out at each node determined by the relative values of $L, o,$ and g. Figure 4.4 depicts the optimal broadcast tree for $P = 8, L = 6, g = 4,$ and $o = 2$. The number shown for each node is the time at which it has received the data unit and can begin sending it on. Notice that the processor overhead of successive transmissions overlaps the delivery of previous messages. Processors may experience idle cycles at the end of the algorithm while the last few messages are in transit.

The algorithm above does no computation. As an example of the usage of the LogP model to analyze a parallel algorithm doing both computation and communication, consider the problem of summation of as many values as possible within a fixed amount of time T. The pattern of communication among the processors again forms a tree. In fact the tree has the same shape as an optimal broadcast tree. Each processor has the task of summing a set of the elements and then (except for the root processor) transmitting the result to its parent. The elements to be summed by a processor consist of original inputs stored in its memory, together with partial results received from its children in the communication tree. To specify the algorithm, first determine the optimal schedule of communication events and then determine the distribution of the initial inputs.

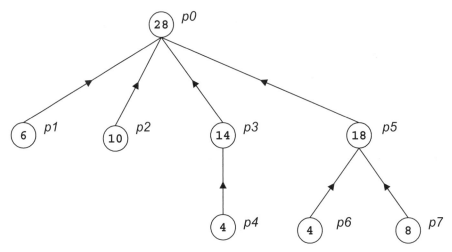

Figure 4.5. Communication tree for optimal summing for $T = 28$, $P = 8$, $L = 5$, $g = 4$, and $o = 2$.

If $T \leq L + 2 \times o$, the optimal solution is to sum $T + 1$ values on a single processor, since there is not sufficient time to receive data from another processor. Otherwise, the last step performed by the root processor (at time $T - 1$) is to add a value it has computed locally to a value it just received from another processor. The remote processor must have sent the value at time $T - 1 - L - 2 \times o$, and we assume recursively that it forms the root of an optimal summation tree with this time bound. The local value must have been produced at time $T - 1 - o$. Since the root can receive a message every g cycles, its children in the communication tree should complete their summations at times $T - (2 \times o + L + 1)$, $T - (2 \times o + L + 1 + g)$, $T - (2 \times o + L + 1 + 2 \times g)$, and so on. The root performs $g - o - 1$ additions of local input values between messages, as well as the local additions before it receives its first message. This communication schedule must be modified by the following consideration: since a processor invests o cycles in receiving a partial sum from a child, all transmitted partial sums must represent at least o additions. Based on this schedule, it is straightforward to determine the set of input values initially assigned to each processor and the computation schedule. Figure 4.5 shows the communication tree for optimal summing for $T = 28$, $P = 8$, $L = 5$, $g = 4$, and $o = 2$.

The LogP model assumes that all messages are of a small size. A simple extension of the model dealing with longer messages is called the LogGP model. It introduces one more parameter, G, which is the *gap per byte* for long messages, defined as the time per byte for a long message. The reciprocal of G characterizes the available per-processor communication bandwidth for long messages.

The presented performance models make up a good mathematical basis for designing portable parallel algorithms that run efficiently on a wide range of MPPs via a parametrizing of the algorithms with the parameters of the models. The MPP architecture is much far away from the serial scalar architecture than the vector, superscalar, and SMP architectures. Therefore it is very difficult to automatically generate an efficient message-passing target code for the serial source code written in C or Fortran 77. In fact, optimizing C or Fortran 77 compilers for MPPs would have to solve the problem of automatic synthesis of an efficient message-passing program using the source serial code as a specification of its functional semantics. Although some interesting research results have been obtained in this direction (e.g., during the work on the experimental PARADIGM compiler), they are still far away from practical use. No industrial optimizing C or Fortran 77 compiler for the MPP architecture is available.

Basic programming tools for MPPs are message-passing libraries and high-level parallel languages.

4.2. MESSAGE-PASSING LIBRARIES

Message-passing libraries directly implement the message-passing parallel programming model and allow programmers to explicitly write message-passing programs. The basic paradigm of message passing implemented in different libraries (PARMACS, Chameleon, CHIMP, PICL, Zipcode, p4, PVM, MPI, etc.) is the same and was briefly summarized in Section 4.1. The libraries differ in details of implementation of the same basic model. The most popular libraries are MPI (Message-Passing Interface) and PVM (Parallel Virtual Machine). Absolute majority of existing message-passing code is written using one of the libraries.

In this book we outline MPI. The main reason we focus on this library is that it has been standardized (in 1995) as MPI 1.1 and widely implemented in compliance with the standard. Practically all hardware vendors offer MPI. In addition there exist free high-quality MPI implementations such as LAM MPI from Ohio Supercomputing Center (currently supported by Open System Laboratory at Indiana University) and MPICH from Argonne National Laboratory and Mississippi State University. MPI supports parallel programming in C and Fortran on all MPP architectures, including Unix and Windows NT platforms.

Some extensions to MPI 1.1, known as MPI 2.0, were released in 1997. The extensions include Fortran 90 and C++ bindings, parallel I/O, one-sided communications, etc. A typical MPI library fully implements MPI 1.1 and optionally supports some features of MPI 2.0. Our introduction into MPI will be based on the C interface to MPI 1.1.

4.2.1. Basic MPI Programming Model

An MPI program consists of a fixed number of processes, executing their own code in their own address space. The codes executed by each process do not need to be identical. The processes communicate via calls to MPI communication primitives.

MPI does not provide mechanisms to specify the number of processes of an MPI program, the code to be executed by each of the processes, and the allocation of the processes to physical processors. Such mechanisms are external to the MPI program and must be provided by particular MPI implementations. Instead MPI provides inquiring operations allowing the processes of the MPI program to determine their total number and identify themselves in the program.

MPI provides two types of communication operation: point-to-point and collective operations. A point-to-point operation involves two processes, one of which sends a message and other receives the message. A collective operation, such as barrier synchronization and broadcast, involves a group of processes.

In MPI a *process group* is defined as an ordered collection of processes, each with a *rank*. Groups define the scope of collective communication operations. That allows collective operations to avoid unnecessarily synchronizing uninvolved processes (potentially running unrelated code). In point-to-point communication operations, groups define a scope for process names; that is, participating processes are specified by their rank in the same process group.

MPI does not provide a mechanism to build a group from scratch, but only from other, previously defined groups. There are operations to construct new groups by subsetting and supersetting existing groups. Immediately after MPI is initialized, only one group consisting of all processes that make up the MPI program is available. This group is the base group upon which all other groups are defined.

MPI provides a mechanism that allows the programmer to safely separate messages that do not have to be logically mixed, even when the messages are transferred between processes of the same group. The mechanism is called *communicators*. Logically a communicator may be seen as a separate communication layer associated with a group of processes. There may be several communicators associated with the same group, providing nonintersecting communication layers. Communication operations explicitly specify the communicator, which will be used to transmit messages. Messages transmitted over different communicators cannot be mixed; that is, a message sent through a communicator is never received by a process not communicating over the communicator.

Technically the creation of a communicator consists in generation of a unique tag that becomes attached to all messages sent through the communicator and used by processes to filter incoming messages. The tag is generated at runtime and shared by all processes of the group, with which the communicator is associated.

This feature of MPI is important. It is the very feature that allows the programmer to use MPI for writing parallel libraries. In other words, the programmer can write an MPI subprogram that can be safely used by other programmers in their MPI programs without any knowledge of the details of its implementation. In contrast, the other popular message-passing library, PVM, does not have the capacity to separate safely communication layers for message passing, and therefore it cannot be used for implementation of parallel libraries. The point is that the only unique attribute characterizing a PVM process is its ID assigned at runtime to each process of the PVM program. All other communication attributes, which could be used to separate messages, such as groups and tags, are user-defined. Therefore they do not have to be unique at runtime, especially if different modules of the program are written by different programmers.

To see more precisely why the PVM approach does not allow the programmer to safely localize communications inside a parallel module, consider the following message-passing pseudocode:

```
extern Proc();
if(my process ID is A)
  Send message M with tag T to process B
Proc();
if(my process ID is B)
  Receive a message with tag T from process A
```

The code is supposed to ensure the following scenario. First, the process A sends a message M to the process B. Then all processes of the message-passing program, including processes A and B, execute the externally defined parallel procedure Proc. Then, after the process B has left the procedure Proc, it receives the message M. This desirable semantics of the program may be broken if the procedure Proc performs a point-to-point communication operation also sending a message from the process A to the process B. In that case the message M sent by the process A from the outside of the procedure Proc may be intercepted inside this procedure by the process B. Correspondingly the message sent by the process A from the inside of the procedure Proc will be received by the process B outside. The user-defined tag T cannot solve the problem of matching the sending and receiving operations, since there is no guarantee that the programmer who coded the procedure Proc has not used the same tag.

The mechanism of communicators provided by MPI easily solves the problem, allowing for the following safe implementation of the program above:

```
extern Proc ();
Create communicator C for a group including processes A and B
```

```
if(my process ID is A)
   Send message M to process B through communicator C
Proc();
if(my process ID is B)
   Receive a message from process A through communicator C
```

A unique tag attached to any message sent over the communicator C prevents the interception of the message inside the procedure Proc, since a communication operation sending or receiving messages with the same tag cannot occur in this procedure.

The following sections present in more detail the operations on groups and communicators, point-to-point and collective communication operations, and operations for MPI environmental management.

4.2.2. Groups and Communicators

A *group* is an ordered set of processes. Each process in a group is associated with an integer *rank*. Ranks are contiguous and start from zero. Groups are represented by opaque *group objects* of the type MPI_Group, and hence cannot be directly transferred from one process to another.

A *context* is a unique, system-generated tag that differentiates messages. The MPI system manages this differentiation process.

A *communicator* brings together the concepts of group and context. MPI communication operations reference communicators to determine the scope and the "communication universe" in which a point-to-point or collective operation is to operate. A communicator contains an instance of a group, a context for point-to-point communication, and a context for collective communication.

The group associated with the communicator always includes the local process. The source and destination of a message is identified by process rank within that group. For collective communication, the communicator specifies the set of processes that participate in the collective operation. Thus the communicator restricts the "spatial" scope of communication, and provides machine-independent process addressing through ranks. Communicators are represented by opaque *communicator objects* of the type MPI_Comm, and hence they cannot be directly transferred from one process to another.

Communicators described above are also called *intracommunicators*. They are used for point-to-point communication between processes of the same group and for collective communication. In addition to intracommunicators, MPI introduces *intercommunicators* used specifically for point-to-point communication between processes of different groups. We do not consider those communication operations in the book, and hence only deal with intracommunicators.

An initial pre-defined communicator `MPI_COMM_WORLD` is a communicator of all processes making up the MPI program. This communicator has the same value in all processes. The base group, upon which all other groups are defined, is the group associated with the initial communicator `MPI_COMM_WORLD`. This group does not appear as a pre-defined constant, but it may be accessed using the function

```
int MPI_Comm_group(MPI_Comm comm, MPI_Group *group),
```

which returns in `group` a handle to the group of `comm`.

Other group constructors provided by MPI either explicitly list the processes of an existing group, which make up a new group, or do set-like binary operations (union, intersection, and difference) on existing groups to construct a new group.

The function

```
int MPI_Group_incl(MPI_Group group, int n, int *ranks,
                   MPI_Group *newgroup)
```

creates a group `newgroup` that consists of the n processes in `group` with ranks `rank[0]`,..., `rank[n-1]`. The process with rank k in `newgroup` is the process with rank `rank[k]` in `group`.

The function

```
int MPI_Group_excl(MPI_Group group, int n, int *ranks,
                   MPI_Group *newgroup)
```

creates a group `newgroup` that is obtained by deleting from `group` those processes with ranks `rank[0]`,..., `rank[n-1]`. The ordering of processes in `newgroup` is identical to the ordering in `group`.

The function

```
int MPI_Group_range_incl(MPI_Group group, int n,
                         int ranges[][3], MPI_Group *newgroup)
```

assumes that `ranges` consist of triplets

$$(f_0, l_0, s_0), \ldots, (f_{n-1}, l_{n-1}, s_{n-1})$$

and constructs a group `newgroup` consisting of processes in `group` with ranks

$$f_0, f_0 + s_0, \ldots, f_0 + \left[\frac{l_0 - f_0}{s_0}\right] \times s_0, \ldots, f_{n-1}, f_{n-1} + s_{n-1}, \ldots, f_{n-1} + \left[\frac{l_{n-1} - f_{n-1}}{s_{n-1}}\right] \times s_{n-1}.$$

We may have $f_i > l_i$, and s_i may be negative but cannot be zero. The process with rank k in newgroup is the process with kth rank in the list of ranks above. The function

```
int MPI_Group_range_excl(MPI_Group group, int n,
                         int ranges[][3], MPI_Group *newgroup)
```

constructs newgroup by deleting from group those processes with ranks

$$f_0, f_0 + s_0, \ldots, f_0 + \left[\frac{l_0 - f_0}{s_0} \right] \times s_0, \ldots, f_{n-1}, f_{n-1} + s_{n-1}, \ldots, f_{n-1} + \left[\frac{l_{n-1} - f_{n-1}}{s_{n-1}} \right] \times s_{n-1}.$$

The ordering of processes in newgroup is identical to the ordering in group. The function

```
int MPI_Group_union(MPI_Group group1, MPI_Group group2,
                    MPI_Group newgroup)
```

creates a group newgroup that consists of all processes of group1, followed by all processes of group2. The function

```
int MPI_Group_intersection(MPI_Group group1,
                           MPI_Group group2, MPI_Group newgroup)
```

creates a group newgroup that consists of all processes of group1 that are also in group2, ordered as in group1. The function

```
int MPI_Group_difference(MPI_Group group1, MPI_Group group2,
                         MPI_Group newgroup)
```

creates a group newgroup that consists of all processes of group1 that are not in group2, ordered as in group1.

Note that for these three set-like operations the order of processes in the output group is determined primarily by the order in the first group and then, if necessary, by the order in the second group. Therefore neither union nor intersection is commutative, but both are associative.

Like groups, new communicators are created from previously defined communicators. Unlike group constructors, which are local operations, communicator constructors are collective operations that must be performed by all processes in the group associated with the existing communicator, which is used for creation of a new communicator.

The function

```
int MPI_Comm_dup(MPI_Comm comm, MPI_Comm *newcomm)
```

creates a communicator `newcomm` with the same group but with a new context.
The function

```
int MPI_Comm_create(MPI_Comm comm, MPI_Group group,
                    MPI_Comm *newcomm)
```

creates a communicator `newcomm` with associated group defined by `group`
and a new context. The function returns `MPI_COMM_NULL` to processes that
are not in `group`. The call is to be executed by all processes in `comm`, even if
they do not belong to the new group. All `group` arguments must have the
same value (in particular, this is guaranteed if all processes build `group`
exactly in the same way), and `group` must be a subset of the group associated
with `comm`.
The function

```
int MPI_Comm_split(MPI_Comm comm, int color, int key,
                   MPI_Comm *newcomm)
```

partitions the group associated with `comm` into disjoint subgroups, one for
each nonnegative value of `color`. Each subgroup contains all processes of
the same color. Within each subgroup the processes are ranked in the order
defined by the value of the argument `key`. If, for a fixed color, the keys are
not unique, the operation will order processes that supply the same key
according to their rank in the parent group. A new communicator is created
for each subgroup and returned in `newcomm`. A process may supply the color
value `MPI_UNDEFINED`, in which case `newcomm` returns `MPI_COMM_NULL`.

There are two local operations allowing any member of the group associated with a communicator to determine its rank in the group and the total
number of processes in the group. The function

```
int MPI_Comm_size(MPI_Comm comm, int *size)
```

returns in `size` the number of processes in the group of `comm`. The function

```
int MPI_Comm_rank(MPI_Comm comm, int *rank)
```

returns in `rank` the rank of the calling processes in the group of `comm`.
In the MPI program below, each process first determines the total number
of processes executing the program and its rank in the global group associated with `MPI_COMM_WORLD`. Then two new communicators are created:
one containing processes with even global ranks, and the other containing

processes with odd global ranks. Next each process determines its local rank in the group associated with one of the newly created communicators. The source code of the program is

```
#include <mpi.h>
int main(int argc, char **argv) {
  int my_global_rank, my_rank_in_a, my_rank_in_b;
  int global_size, size_a, size_b;
  MPI_Comm comm_a, comm_b;

  MPI_Init(&argc, &argv);

  MPI_Comm_size(MPI_COMM_WORLD, &global_size);
  MPI_Comm_rank(MPI_COMM_WORLD, &my_global_rank);

  MPI_Comm_split(MPI_COMM_WORLD,
                 my_global_rank%2 ? 0 : MPI_UNDEFINED,
                 my_global_rank, &comm_a);
  MPI_Comm_split(MPI_COMM_WORLD,
                 my_global_rank%2 ? MPI_UNDEFINED : 0,
                 my_global_rank, &comm_b);

  if(comm_a != MPI_COMM_NULL) {
    MPI_Comm_size(comm_a, &size_a);
    MPI_Comm_rank(comm_a, &my_rank_in_a);
  }
  if(comm_b != MPI_COMM_NULL) {
    MPI_Comm_size(comm_b, &size_b);
    MPI_Comm_rank(comm_b, &my_rank_in_b);
  }
  . . .
  if(comm_a != MPI_COMM_NULL)
    MPI_Comm_free(&comm_a);
  if(comm_b != MPI_COMM_NULL)
    MPI_Comm_free(&comm_b);
  MPI_Finalize();
}
```

Note that in this program all MPI library functions are called after MPI_Init and before MPI_Finalize. This is a general rule. The function

```
int MPI_Init(int *argc, char ***argv)
```

initializes the MPI environment and must be called by all processes of the program before any other MPI function is called. The function must be called at most once; subsequent calls are erroneous. The function

```
int MPI_Finalize(void)
```

cleans up all MPI state. Once the function is called, no MPI function (even `MPI_Init`) may be called.

The program above also uses group and communicator destructors. The operations are collective. They mark the corresponding group or communicator object for deallocation. Any ongoing operations that use this object will complete normally; the object is actually deallocated only if there are no other active references to it. The function

```
int MPI_Comm_free(MPI_Comm *comm)
```

marks the communication object for dealocation. The handle is set to `MPI_COMM_NULL`. The function

```
int MPI_Group_free(MPI_Group *group)
```

marks the group object for deallocation. The handle is set to `MPI_GROUP_NULL`.

4.2.3. Point-to-Point Communication

Point-to-point communication operations are the basic MPI communication mechanism. MPI provides a wide range of send and receive operations allowing the programmer to implement different modes of point-to-point communication such as blocking and nonblocking and synchronous and asynchronous.

Among all this diversity, there are two basic operations that are predominantly used in MPI applications. The two operations implement a clear and reliable model of point-to-point communication and allow the programmers to write portable MPI code. These two operations are a *blocking send* and a *blocking receive*.

The function

```
int MPI_Send(void *buf, int n, MPI_Datatype datatype,
             int dest, int tag, MPI_Comm comm)
```

implements a standard blocking send operation. The operation forms a message and sends it to the addressee.

The *message* consists of a data to be transferred and an envelope into which the data are put. The data part of the message may be empty (n=0). In that case the message consists only of the message envelope. The message envelope is a fixed part of message that carries information used to distinguish messages and selectively receive them. This information includes the message *source*, the message *destination*, the message *tag*, and the *communicator*.

The message source is implicitly determined by the identity of the message sender. The other fields are specified by arguments in the send operation.

The comm argument specifies the communicator that is used for the send operation. The message destination is specified by the dest argument as a rank of the destination process within the group associated with the communicator specified by comm.

The integer-valued message tag is specified by the tag argument. This integer can be used by the program to distinguish different types of messages. A valid tag value is nonnegative.

The data part of the message consists of a sequence of n values of the type specified by datatype. These values are taken from a send buffer, which consists of n entries of the type specified by datatype, starting at the entry at address buf. The argument datatype can specify a basic datatype, which corresponds to one of the basic datatypes of the C language, or a derived datatype, which is constructed from basic ones using datatype constructors provided by MPI.

In general, a *datatype* is an opaque object of the type MPI_Datatype. MPI provides pre-defined constants of that type for the basic datatypes such as MPI_CHAR (corresponds to **signed char**), MPI_SHORT (**signed short int**), MPI_INT (**signed int**), and MPI_FLOAT (**float**). Using basic datatypes can specify only contiguous buffers containing a sequence of elements of the same basic type. More general communication buffers are specified by using derived datatypes.

A *derived datatype* is constructed from basic datatypes and specifies two things:

- A sequence of basic datatypes.
- A sequence of integer displacements.

The displacements are not required to be positive, distinct, or in increasing order. Therefore the order of items need not coincide with their order in store, and an item may appear more than once. All methods of constructing derived datatypes can be applied recursively. Thus the derived datatypes can specify buffers that contain different datatypes (e.g., an integer count, followed by a sequence of real numbers) and noncontiguous buffers (e.g., a buffer containing a diagonal of a matrix).

A derived datatype is characterized by a sequence of pairs of the form

$$\{(type_0, disp_0), \ldots, (type_{n-1}, disp_{n-1})\},$$

where $type_i$ are basic types, and $disp_i$ are displacements. This sequence is called a *type map*. The sequence of basic datatypes (displacements are ignored)

$$\{type_0, \ldots, type_{n-1}\}$$

is called the *type signature* of the datatype. This type map, together with a base address *buf*, specifies a communication buffer that consists of n entries, where the ith entry is at address $buf+disp_i$ and has type $type_i$. A data message assembled from such a communication buffer will consist of n values of the types defined by the type signature above. The *extent* of the datatype is defined to be the span from the first byte to the last byte occupied by entries in the datatype, and rounded up to satisfy alignment requirements.

A basic datatype can be characterized by a type map with one entry of the corresponding basic type and displacement zero. For example, the type map for MPI_INT is { (**int**, 0) }.

The simplest datatype constructor allows replication of a datatype into contiguous locations. It is implemented by the function

```
int MPI_Type_contiguous(int count, MPI_Datatype oldtype,
                        MPI_Datatype *newtype),
```

which concatenates count copies of oldtype to obtain newtype. Concatenation is defined using extent as the size of the concatenated copies. For example, if oldtype has type map

{ (**double**, 0), (**char**, 8) }

with extent 16, and count=3, then the type map of the datatype returned by newtype will be

{ (**double**, 0), (**char**, 8), (**double**, 16), (**char**, 24), (**double**, 32), (**char**, 40) }.

The function

```
int MPI_Type_vector(int count, int blocklen, int stride,
                    MPI_Datatype oldtype,
                    MPI_Datatype *newtype)
```

implements a more general constructor, which creates newtype by replication of oldtype into a sequence of count equally spaced blocks. Each block is obtained by concatenating blocklen copies of oldtype. The spacing between blocks is equal to stride extents of oldtype. For example, assume again that oldtype has type map

{ (**double**, 0), (**char**, 8) }

with extent 16. Then a call to MPI_Type_vector(2,3,4,oldtype, &newtype) will create the datatype with type map {(**double**, 0), (**char**, 8), (**double**, 16), (**char**, 24), (**double**, 32), (**char**, 40), (**double**, 64), (**char**, 72), (**double**, 80), (**char**, 88), (**double**, 96), (**char**, 104)}.

The function

```
int MPI_Type_hvector(int count, int blocklen,
                     MPI_Aint stride, MPI_Datatype oldtype,
                     MPI_Datatype *newtype)
```

is identical to `MPI_Type_vector`, except that `stride` is given in bytes rather than in elements. `MPI_Aint` is an opaque MPI type used specifically for integers specifying the size in bytes.

The function

```
int MPI_Type_indexed(int count, int *array_of_blocklens,
                     int array_of_disps, MPI_Datatype oldtype,
                     MPI_Datatype *newtype)
```

creates `newtype` by replication of `oldtype` into a sequence of `count` blocks (each block is a concatenation of `oldtype`), where each block can contain a different number of copies and have a different displacement. The ith block contains `array_of_blocklens[i]` elements, which start at displacement `array_of_disps[i]` measured in multiples of the `oldtype` extent. The function

```
int MPI_Type_hindexed(int count, int *array_of_blocklens,
                      MPI_Aint *array_of_disps,
                      MPI_Datatype oldtype,
                      MPI_Datatype *newtype)
```

is identical to `MPI_Type_indexed`, except that block displacements in `array_of_disps` are given in bytes rather than in multiples of the `oldtype` extent.

The function

```
int MPI_Type_struct(int count, int *array_of_blocklens,
                    MPI_Aint *array_of_disps,
                    MPI_Datatype *array_of_types,
                    MPI_Datatype *newtype)
```

implements the most general constructor. It further generalizes the previous constructor in that it allows each block to consist of replications of different datatypes. Namely `array_of_types[i]` specifies the type of elements in ith block.

A derived datatype has to be *committed* before it can be used in a communication operation. A committed datatype can still be used as an argument in datatype constructors. The function

```
int MPI_Type_commit(MPI_Datatype *datatype)
```

implements the commit operation. The function

```
int MPI_Type_free(MPI_ Datatype *datatype)
```

marks the datatype object for deallocation and sets `datatype` to `MPI_DATATYPE_NULL`. Derived datatypes that were defined from the freed datatype are not affected.

The function

```
int MPI_Recv(void *buf, int n, MPI_Datatype datatype,
             int source, int tag, MPI_Comm comm,
             MPI_Status *status)
```

implements a standard blocking receive operation. The receive buffer consists of the storage containing n consecutive elements of the type specified by `datatype`, starting at address `buf`. The length of the data part of the received message must not be greater than the length of the receive buffer.

The selection of a message by a receive operation is governed by the value of the message envelope. A message can be received by a receive operation if its envelope matches the `source`, `tag`, and `comm` values specified by the receive operation. The receiver may specify a wildcard `MPI_ANY_SOURCE` value for `source`, and/or a wildcard `MPI_ANY_TAG` value for `tag`, indicating that any source and/or tag are acceptable. It cannot specify a wildcard value for `comm`. Thus a message can be received by a receive operation only if it is addressed to the receiving process, has a matching communicator, has matching source (unless any source is explicitly specified as acceptable), and has a matching tag (unless any tag is explicitly specified as acceptable). The argument `source`, if different from `MPI_ANY_SOURCE`, is specified as a rank within the process group associated with the communicator specified by `comm`.

Note the asymmetry between send and receive operations: a send operation always sends a message to a unique receiver, whereas a receive operation may accept messages from an arbitrary sender. That communication driven by the sender is known as a *push* communication (unlike a *pull* communication driven by the receiver).

The source or tag of a received message may not be known if wildcard values were used in the receive operation. In that case the information is returned by the `status` argument of the type `MPI_Status`, which is a structure that contains at least three fields named `MPI_SOURCE`, `MPI_TAG`, and

MPI_ERROR. The fields contain the source, tag, and error code, respectively, of the received message. An error, for example, occurs if all incoming data do not fit, without truncation, into the receive buffer. Status variables need to be allocated by the user; that is, they are not system objects.

We have specified the presented send and receive operations as *blocking* communication operations. In general, return from a blocking operation means that resources used by the operation are allowed to be re-used.

In case of the receive operation, the blocking simply means that MPI_Recv returns only after the data part of the incoming message has been stored in the receive buffer. In case of the send operation, it means that MPI_Send does not return until the message data and envelope have been safely stored away so that the sender is free to access and overwrite the send buffer. The message might be copied directly into the matching receive buffer, or it might be copied into a temporary system buffer.

Message buffering decouples the send and receive operations. A blocking send can complete as soon as the message was buffered, even if no matching receive has been executed by the receiver.

MPI_Send uses the *standard* communication mode. In this mode it is up to MPI to decide whether outgoing messages will be buffered. MPI may buffer outgoing messages. In such a case the send call may complete before a matching receive is invoked. On the other hand, buffer space may be unavailable, and MPI may choose not to buffer outgoing messages, for performance reasons. In this case the send call will not complete until a matching receive has been posted, and the data have been moved to the receiver.

Thus a send in standard mode can be started whether or not a matching receive has been posted. It may complete before a matching receive is posted. The standard mode send is *nonlocal*. In general, an operation is nonlocal if its completion requires the execution of some MPI procedure on another process. In the send operation its completion may depend on the occurrence of a matching receive.

While the standard communication mode is predominantly used, it is not the only mode of send operation supported by MPI. There are three additional communication modes.

In *buffered* mode, if a send is executed and no matching receive is posted, then MPI must buffer the outgoing message, allowing the send to complete. Thus a buffered mode send operation is *local* because its completion does not depend on the occurrence of a matching receive. However, this mode is not as safe as standard mode because an error will occur if there is insufficient buffer space.

In *synchronous* mode, a send will complete successfully only if a matching receive was posted, and the receive operation has started to receive the message sent by the synchronous send. Thus the completion of a synchronous send not only indicates that the send buffer can be re-used but also that the receiver has reached a certain point in its execution, namely that it has started executing the matching receive. The blocking synchronous send and the blocking receive provide synchronous communication semantics: a communication does not complete at either end before both processes *rendezvous* at the communication. The synchronous send is obviously nonlocal.

In *ready* mode, a send may be started only if the matching receive is already posted. Otherwise, the operation is erroneous and its outcome is undefined.

The functions of the form

```
int MPI_xsend(void *buf, int n, MPI_Datatype datatype,
              int dest, int tag, MPI_Comm comm)
```

are provided for the three additional communication modes, where x is B for buffered, S for synchronous, and R for ready mode.

Any valid MPI implementation guarantees certain properties of point-to-point communication. First of all, it guarantees a certain *order* in receiving messages sent from the same source. If a sender sends two messages in succession to the same destination, and both match the same receive, then this operation cannot receive the second message while the first one is still pending. If a receiver posts two receives in succession, and both match the same message, then the second receive operation cannot be satisfied by this message while the first is still pending. Briefly, we can say that messages do not overtakes each other. This requirement facilitates matching of sends to receives and hence helps writing deterministic message-passing code. Notice that the LogP model is more liberal allowing messages directed to a given process not to arrive in the same order as they are sent.

Second, a certain *progress* in the execution of point-to-point communication is guaranteed. If a pair of matching send and receive has been initiated on two processes, then at least one of these two operations will complete, independently of other actions in the system: the send operation will complete, unless the receive is satisfied by another message, and completes; the receive operation will complete, unless the message sent is consumed by another matching receive that was posted at the same destination process.

Unfortunately, MPI makes no guarantee of *fairness* in the handling of communication. Suppose that a send is posted. Then it is possible that the destination process repeatedly posts a receive that matches this send, yet the message is never received because it is each time overtaken by another message sent from another source. It is the programmer's responsibility to prevent such unfairness (e.g., by creatively using tags or communicators).

In many MPPs, communication can be executed autonomously by an intelligent communication controller. This allows communication to overlap computation, which results in more efficient parallel programs. However, the blocking communication operations do not support this type of optimization. Suppose that a blocking receive is posted. It can complete only after the matching send has started and the received message is stored in the receive buffer. So, during this time slot, which can be quite significant, the calling process is actually doing nothing except waiting for a message to arrive.

Similarly suppose that a standard mode send is posted. In the case of limited buffer space, the send may not complete until a matching receive has been posted, and the data have been moved to the receiver. Again, the calling process will be doing nothing during a significant time slot.

A possible mechanism for achieving such overlap is multithreading. One way would be to use parallel threads, some responsible for communication and some responsible for computation. This mechanism is external to MPI.

MPI provides its own alternative mechanism to approach the problem. The mechanism is *nonblocking* communication. The idea underlying nonblocking communication is to split a one-piece communication operation into two suboperations. The first suboperation just initiates the entire communication operation but does not complete it. So, immediately after the suboperation returns, the calling process will be able to do computations concurrently with the communication operation as it is being executed. The second suboperation completes this communication operation.

More specifically, a nonblocking *send start* call initiates the send operation but does not complete it. The send start call will return before the message was copied out of the send buffer. A separate *send complete* call is needed to complete the communicatin, namely to verify that the data has been copied out of the send buffer. Similarly a nonblocking *receive start* call initiates the receive operation but does not complete it. The call will return before a message is stored into the receive buffer. A separate *receive complete* call is needed to complete the receive operation and verify that the data have been received into the receive buffer.

Nonblocking send start calls can use the same four communication modes as blocking sends: standard, buffered, synchronous, and ready. These carry the same meaning. A nonblocking ready send can be started only if a matching receive is posted. Nonblocking sends of other modes can be started whether or not a matching receive has been posted. In all cases the send start call is local: it returns immediately, independent of the status of other processes.

If the send mode is *synchronous*, then the send complete call can return only if a matching receive has started. If the send mode is *buffered*, then the message must be buffered if there is no pending receive, and the send complete call must return independent of the status of a matching receive. If the send mode is *standard*, then the send complete call may return before a matching receive occurred if the message is buffered. On the other hand, the send complete may not return until a matching receive occurred, and the message was copied into the receive buffer.

Note that nonblocking sends can be matched with blocking receives, and vice-versa. Nonblocking communications use opaque *request* objects of the type `MPI_Request` to identify communication operations and match the operation that initiates the communication with the operation that completes it. These are system objects that are accessed via a handle. A request object identifies various properties of a communication operation, such as the send mode, the communication buffer that is associated with it, its context, the tag and destination arguments, to be used for a send, or the tag and source arguments to be used for a receive. In addition this object stores information about the status of the pending communication operation.

The functions of the form

```
int MPI_Ixsend(void *buf, int n, MPI_Datatype datatype,
               int dest, int tag,
               MPI_Comm comm, MPI_Request *request)
```

are used to start a nonblocking send, where x is empty for standard, B for buffered, S for synchronous, and R for ready mode. A nonblocking send call indicates that the system may start copying data out of the send buffer. The sender should not access any part of the send buffer after a nonblocking send operation is called, until the send completes.

The function

```
int MPI_Irecv(void *buf, int n, MPI_Datatype datatype,
              int source, int tag, MPI Comm comm,
              MPI_Request *request)
```

starts a nonblocking receive. A nonblocking receive call indicates that the system may start writing data into the receive buffer. The receiver should not access any part of the receive buffer after a nonblocking receive operation is called, until the receive completes.

All these calls allocate a communication request object and associate it with the request handle request. The request can be used later to query the status of the communication or wait for its completion.

The function

```
int MPI_Wait(MPI_Request *request, MPI_Status *status)
```

is used to complete a nonblocking communication. It returns when the operation identified by request is complete. The request object associated with request is de-allocated and the request handle is set to MPI_REQUEST_NULL. The call returns, in status, information on the completed operation. MPI_Wait is a blocking nonlocal operation.

MPI provides another function

```
int MPI_Test(MPI_Request *request, int *flag,
             MPI_Status *status),
```

that also can be used to complete a nonblocking communication. Unlike MPI_Wait, MPI_Test is a nonblocking operation. It returns in flag either *true* ($\neq 0$) or *false* ($= 0$). It returns *true* if the operation identified by request is complete. In such a case MPI_Test acts exactly as MPI_Wait. If *false* is returned, it means that the operation identified by `request` is not complete. In this case the value of the status object is undefined. The use of the nonblocking `MPI_Test` call allows the user to schedule alternative activities within a single thread of execution. An event-driven thread scheduler can be emulated with periodic calls to `MPI_Test`.

In addition to the two basic complete operations, MPI provides various complete operations that can be used to wait for the completion of any, some, or all the operations in a list, rather than having to wait for a specific message. The remaining point-to-point communications operations are aimed mainly at better optimisation of computer resources such as memory and processor cycles. `MPI_Probe` and `MPI_Iprobe` operations allow for incoming messages to be checked without actually receiving them. The user can then decide how to receive them, based on the information returned by the probe. In particular, the user may allocate memory for the receive buffer according to the length of the probed message.

Often a communication with the same argument list is repeatedly executed within the inner loop of a parallel computation. The loop may be optimized by binding the list of communication arguments to a so-called *persistent communication request* once, out of the loop, and then repeatedly using the request to initiate and complete messages in the loop.

4.2.4. Collective Communication

Collective communication is communication that involves a group of processes. The basic collective communication operations are as follows:

- Barrier synchronization across all group members
- Broadcast from one member to all members of a group
- Data from all group members gathered to one member
- Data from one member scattered to all members of a group
- Global reduction operations such as sum, max, min, and user-defined functions.

MPI also provides a few advanced variations and combinations of the basic collective operations.

In order to execute a collective operation, all processes in the group must call the corresponding communication function with matching arguments. Several collective operations such as broadcast and gather have a single originating or receiving process. Such a process is called the *root*.

A barrier call returns only after all group members have entered the call. Other collective communication calls can return as soon as their participation in the collective communication is complete. The completion of a call indicates that the caller is now free to access locations in the communication buffer. It does not indicate that other processes in the group have completed or even started the operation. Therefore a portable MPI program should not count on the effect of synchronizing all calling processes for all collective communication calls, except barrier calls.

Collective communication calls may use the same communicators as point-to-point communication. MPI guarantees that messages generated on behalf of collective communication calls will not be confused with messages generated by point-to-point communication. This separation is achieved by using separate contexts for point-to-point and collective communications (see Section 4.2.2 for the communicator structure).

The function

```
int MPI_Barrier(MPI_Comm comm)
```

blocks the caller until all members of the group associated with comm have called it. The call returns at any process only after all group members have entered the call.

The function

```
int MPI_Bcast(void *buf, int count, MPI_Datatype datatype,
              int root, MPI_Comm comm)
```

broadcasts a message from the process with rank root to all processes of the group, itself included. It is called by all members of the group using the same arguments for comm, root. On return, the contents of root's communication buffer have been copied to all processes. General, derived datatypes are allowed for datatype. The type signature obtained by count-fold replication of the type signature of datatype on any process must be equal to that at the root. This implies that the amount of data sent must be equal to the amount received, pairwise, between each process and the root. Distinct type maps between sender and receiver are allowed.

The function

```
int MPI_Gather(void *sendbuf, int sendcount,
               MPI_Datatype sendtype, void *recvbuf,
               int recvcount, MPI_Datatype recvtype,
               int root, MPI_Comm comm)
```

implements the basic gather operation. Each process (the root process included) sends the contents of its send buffer to the root process. The root process receives the messages and stores them in rank order. The outcome is as if each of n processes in the group (including the root process) had sent a message to the root by executing a call to

```
MPI_Send(sendbuf, sendcount, sendtype, root,...),
```

and the root had executed n receives,

```
MPI_Recv(recvbuf+i*recvcount*recvtype_extent,
         recvcount, recvtype, i,...),
```

where `recvtype_extent` is the extent of `recvtype`, i=0,1,...,n-1.

The receive buffer is ignored for all nonroot processes. General, derived datatypes are allowed for both `sendtype` and `recvtype`. The type signature obtained by `sendcount`-fold replication of the type signature of `sendtype` on process i must be equal to the type signature obtained by `recvcount`-fold replication of the type signature of `recvtype` at the root.

All arguments to the function are significant on the root process, while on other processes, only arguments `sendbuf`, `sendcount`, `sendtype`, `root`, and `comm` are significant. The arguments `root` and `comm` must have identical values on all processes. The specification of counts and types should not cause any location on the root to be written more than once. Note that `recvcount` is the number of items the root receives from each process, not the total number of items it receives.

The function

```
int MPI_Gatherv(void *sendbuf, int sendcount,
                MPI_Datatype sendtype, void *recvbuf,
                int *recvcounts, int *displs,
                MPI_Datatype recvtype, int root, MPI_Comm comm)
```

extends the functionality of `MPI_Gather` by allowing a varying count of data from each process, since `recvcounts` is now an array. It also allows more flexibility as to where the data are placed on the root, by providing the new argument `displs`. The outcome is as if each of n processes in the group (including the root process) had sent a message to the root,

```
MPI_Send(sendbuf, sendcount, sendtype, root,...),
```

and the root had executed n receives,

```
MPI_Recv(recvbuf+disp[i]*recvtype_extent,
         recvcounts[i], recvtype, i,...).
```

Messages are placed in the receive buffer of the root process in rank order, that is, the data sent from process i is placed in the i-th portion of `recvbuf`. This i-th portion begins at offset `displs[i]` elements (in terms of `recvtype`) into `recvbuf`.

The function

```
int MPI_Scatter(void *sendbuf, int sendcount,
                MPI_Datatype sendtype, void *recvbuf,
                int recvcount, MPI_Datatype recvtype,
                int root, MPI_Comm comm)
```

is the inverse operation to `MPI_Gather`. The outcome is as if the root executes n sends,

```
MPI_Send(sendbuf+i*sendcount*sendtype_extent,
         sendcount, sendtype, i,...),
```

where `sendtype_extent` is the extent of `sendtype`, and each process executes a receive,

```
MPI_Recv(recvbuf, recvcount, recvtype, root,...).
```

The function

```
int MPI_Scatterv(void *sendbuf, int *sendcounts,
                 int *displs, MPI_Datatype sendtype,
                 void *recvbuf, int recvcount,
                 MPI_Datatype recvtype, int root, MPI_Comm comm)
```

is the inverse operation to `MPI_Gatherv`. It extends the functionality of `MPI_Scatter` by allowing a varying count of data to be sent to each process, since `sendcounts` is now an array. It also allows more flexibility as to where the data are taken from the root by providing the new argument `displs`. The outcome is as if the root executes n sends,

```
MPI_Send(sendbuf+displs[i]*sendtype_extent,
         sendcounts[i], sendtype, i,...),
```

and each process executes a receive,

```
MPI_Recv(recvbuf, recvcount, recvtype, root,...).
```

The function

```
int MPI_Reduce(void *inbuf, void *outbuf, int count,
               MPI_Datatype datatype, MPI_Op op,
               int root, MPI_Comm comm)
```

combines the elements provided in the input buffer of each process in the group, using the operation op, and returns the combined value in the output buffer of root. The input buffer is defined by the arguments inbuf, count, and datatype. The output buffer is defined by the arguments outbuf, count, and datatype. Both buffers have the same number of elements, with the same type. The arguments count, datatype, op, root, and comm must have identical values on all processes. Thus all processes provide input buffers and output buffers of the same length, with elements of the same type. Each process can provide one element, or a sequence of elements, in which case the combine operation is executed elementwise on each entry of the sequence.

The operation op can be either one of a pre-defined list of operations, or a user-defined operation. In general, an operation is an opaque object of the type MPI_Op. MPI provides the following pre-defined constants of that type for pre-defined operations: MPI_MAX (maximum), MPI_MIN (minimum), MPI_SUM (sum), MPI_PROD (product), MPI_LAND (logical and), MPI_BAND (bitwise and), MPI_LOR (logical or), MPI_BOR (bitwise or), MPI_LXOR (logical exclusive or), MPI_BXOR (bitwise exclusive or), MPI_MAXLOC (maximum value and its location), MPI_MINLOC (minimum value and its location).

For all the pre-defined operations, except MPI_MAXLOC and MPI_MINLOC, the datatype argument is an appropriate basic datatype. For example, the following function uses MPI_Reduce to compute the dot product of two real vectors that are distributed across a group of processes (for simplicity we assume that the length of the vectors is a multiple of the number processes in the group):

```
double dot_product(double *x, double *y, int m,
MPI_Comm comm) {
    double local_dot_prod;
    double global_dot_prod; /* result (at process zero) */
    int i;

    local_dot_prod = 0.;
    for(i=0; i<m; i++)
     local_dot_prod += x[i]*y[i];

    MPI_Reduce(&local_dot_prod, &global_dot_prod, 1,
              MPI_DOUBLE, MPI_SUM, 0, comm);
    return global_dot_prod;
}
```

The argument m is the length of local subvectors x and y of the entire distributed vectors. The function returns the result at the process with rank zero.

The operation `MPI_MAXLOC` (`MPI_MINLOC`) computes a global maximum (minimum) and the rank of the process containing this value. The operation is applied to reduce a sequence of pairs. Each process supplies a value and its rank within the group, and the reduce operation will return the maximum (minimum) value and the rank of the first process (in rank order) with that value. Each pair is supplied in the form of a structure that contains two fields: one for value and other for rank. The rank field is always of the **int** type. The value field has distinct types depending on the type of value. In order to use `MPI_MAXLOC` and `MPI_MINLOC` in a reduce operation, one must provide a `datatype` argument that represents a pair (value and rank). MPI provides seven such pre-defined datatypes: `MPI_FLOAT_INT` (for **float** values), `MPI_DOUBLE_INT` (for **double** values), `MPI_LONG_INT` (for **long** values), `MPI_2INT` (for **int** values), `MPI_SHORT_INT` (for **short** values), `MPI_LONG_DOUBLE_INT` (for **long double** values).

The following function `normloc` uses `MPI_Reduce` to compute the maximum element of a real vector that is distributed across a group of processes and the rank of the process containing the largest element (for simplicity we assume that the length of the vector is a multiple of the number of processes in the group):

```
typedef struct {double val; int rank;} double_int;

double_int normloc(double *vec, int m, MPI_Comm comm)
{
 double_int *in, *out, res;
 int i, myrank;
 in = calloc(m, sizeof(double_int));
 out = calloc(m, sizeof(double_int));
 MPI_Comm_rank(comm, &myrank);
 for(i=0; i<m; i++) {
  in[i].val = vec[i];
  in[i].rank = myrank;
 }
 MPI_Reduce(in, out, m, MPI_DOUBLE_INT, MPI_MAXLOC, 0, comm);
 if(myrank == 0) {
  res = out[0];
  for(i=1; i<m; i++)
   if(res.val < out[i].val) {
    res.val = out[i].val;
    res.rank = out[i].rank;
   }
   else if(res.val == out[i].val && res.rank > out [i].rank)
    res.rank = out[i].rank;
 }
```

```
free(in);
free(out);
return res;
}
```

The argument m is the length of the local subvector vec of the entire distributed vector. The function returns the result at process with rank zero.

All pre-defined operations are assumed to be associative and commutative. User-defined operations are assumed to be associative but may not be commutative. MPI provides the function

```
int MPI_Op_create(MPI_User_function *fun, int commute, MPI_Op *op)
```

which binds a user-defined operation to an op handle that can subsequently be used in MPI_Reduce. If commute is zero (false), then the user-defined operation is assumed to be not commutative. In this case the order of operands is fixed and is defined to be in ascending process rank order, beginning with process zero. The order of evaluation can be changed, which takes advantage of the associativity of the operation. If commute is nonzero (true), the operation should be both commutative and associative. In that case, the order of evaluation can be changed, which takes advantage of commutativity and associativity.

The argument fun is the user-defined function, which type can be specified as follows:

```
typedef void MPI_User_function(void *invec,
                               void *inoutvec, int len,
                               MPI_Datatype datatype);.
```

The datatype argument is a handle to the data type that was passed into the call to MPI_Reduce. The arguments invec and inoutvec are arrays of len elements of the type specified by datatype that the function fun is combining. The result of the reduction overwrites values in inoutvec. Each invocation of the function results in the pointwise evaluation of the reduce operator on len elements; that is, the function fun returns in inoutvec[i] the value invec[i]o inoutvec[i], for i=0,...,len-1, where o is the combining operation computed by the function.

General datatypes may be passed to the user-defined function. No MPI communication function may be called inside the user-defined function.

The function

```
int MPI_Op_free(MPI_Op *op)
```

marks a user-defined reduction operation for deallocation and sets `op` to `MPI_OP_NULL`.

4.2.5. Environmental Management

MPI provides a few functions for various parameters that relate to the MPI implementation and the execution environment. For example, the function

```
int MPI_Get_processor_name(char *name, int *resultlen)
```

returns the name of the processor, on which it was called, in the form of a character string. The argument `name` must represent storage that is at least `MPI_MAX_PROCESSOR_NAME` characters long. The number of characters actually written is returned in `resultlen`.

The function

```
double MPI_Wtime(void)
```

returns a floating-point number of seconds, representing elapsed wall-clock time since some time in the past. This *time in the past* is guaranteed not to change during the life of the process. The times returned are local to the node that called them. There is no requirement that different nodes return *the same time*.

The function

```
double MPI_Wtick(void)
```

returns the resolution if `MPI_Wtime` in seconds. That is, it returns, as a double precision value, the number of seconds between sucessive clock ticks.

4.2.6. Example of an MPI Application:
Parallel Matrix-Matrix Multiplication

In order to illustrate parallel programming MPPs with MPI, we consider an application implementing the simplest parallel algorithm of matrix-matrix multiplication presented in Section 4.1. The source code of the application is as follows:

```
#include <stdio.h>
#include <stdlib.h>
#include <float.h>
#include <mpi.h>

int n, p;

int main(int argc, char **argv) {
```

```
int myn, myrank;
double *a, *b, *c, *allB, start, sum, *allC, sumdiag;
int i, j, k;



n = atoi(argv[1]);
MPI_Init(&argc, &argv);
MPI_Comm_size(MPI_COMM_WORLD,&p);
MPI_Comm_rank(MPI_COMM_WORLD,&myrank);
myn = n/p;
a = malloc(myn*n*sizeof(double));
b = malloc(myn*n*sizeof(double));
c = malloc(myn*n*sizeof(double));
allB = malloc(n*n*sizeof(double));
for(i=0; i<myn*n; i++) {
    a[i] = 1.;
    b[i] = 2.;
}
MPI_Barrier(MPI_COMM_WORLD);
if(myrank==0)
 start = MPI_Wtime();
for(i=0; i<p; i++)
 MPI_Gather(b, myn*n, MPI_DOUBLE, allB, myn*n,
            MPI_DOUBLE, i, MPI_COMM_WORLD);
for(i=0; i<myn; i++)
 for(j=0; j<n; j++) {
  sum = 0.;
  for(k=0; k<n; k++)
   sum += a[i*n+k]*allB[k*n+j];
  c[i*n+j] = sum;
 }
free(allB);
MPI_Barrier(MPI_COMM_WORLD);
if(myrank==0)
 printf("It took %f seconds to multiply 2 %dx%d matrices.\n",
        MPI_Wtime()-start, n, n);
if(myrank==0)
 allC = malloc(n*n*sizeof(double));
MPI_Gather(c, myn*n, MPI_DOUBLE, allC, myn*n,
           MPI_DOUBLE, 0, MPI_COMM_WORLD);
if(myrank==0) {
 for(i=0, sumdiag=0.; i<n; i++)
  sumdiag += allC[i*n+i];
```

```
    printf("The trace of the resulting matrix is %f\n", sumdiag);
    }
if(myrank==0)
    free(allC);
    MPI_Finalize();
    free(a);
    free(b);
    free(c);
}
```

It is assumed that via an external parameter, the user supplies the value for n and that this value is a multiple of the total number of processes executing the program, p. It is also assumed that process zero (myrank=0) runs on the node with I/O available. Each process has the following arrays on heap:

- a, b, and c to store its horizontal *myn* × *n* slice of matrices *A*, *B*, and *C* respectively.
- allB to store the full matrix *B*. This array is deallocated as soon as the process has computed all elements of its *C* slice.

The array allC is allocated on process zero after the parallel multiplication itself has been complete. This array is used as a receive buffer by the collective operation that gathers all slices of the resulting matrix *C* on process zero. After the matrix *C* is gathered on process zero in the array allC, this process computes the trace of the matrix and outputs it (for the user to check the correctness of the computations).

By the way, the loop

```
for(i=0; i<p; i++)
    MPI_Gather(b, myn*n, MPI_DOUBLE, allB, myn*n,
               MPI_DOUBLE, i, MPI_COMM_WORLD);
```

which results in all processes receiving the matrix *B*, can be replaced by a single call of the form

```
MPI_Allgather(b, myn*n, MPI_DOUBLE, allB, myn*n,
              MPI_DOUBLE, MPI_COMM_WORLD);.
```

MPI_Allgather is an example of an advanced variation of the basic gather operation. It is assumed that MPI can implement MPI_Allgather more efficiently than via successive calls to MPI_Gather.

4.3. PARALLEL LANGUAGES

Message-passing libraries solve the problem of efficiently portable programming MPPs. In particular, MPI is a well designed, powerful, and widespread library that allows the programmers to implement a wide range of parallel algorithms on MPPs in the form of highly efficient and portable message-passing applications.

However, many end-users that do scientific computing on MPPs find the explicit message passing provided by MPI and other libraries tedious and error-prone. They are accustomed to writing their applications mainly in Fortran, and they consider parallel primitives provided by the message-passing libraries too low level, creating unnecessary detailed description of parallel algorithms they would like to implement on MPPs. Indeed, many of the algorithms are straightforward and based on the *data parallel* paradigm.

In the data parallel programming model, processors perform the same work on different parts of data. It is the distribution of the data across the processors that determines distribution of computational work and interprocessor communication. This programming style is characterized by single threaded control, global name space, loosely synchronous processes, and parallelism implied by operations on data. It is mainly supported by high-level parallel languages, and the responsibility of a compiler is to generate the explicit message-passing code, which will be executed in parallel by all participating processors (the single-program multiple-data model, or SPMD for short).

The main advantage of the data parallel programming style is that it is easy to use. First, it is relatively simple to write data parallel applications. Second, due to the single thread of control, a data parallel program is easy to debug. Third, as conceptually data parallel programming is not too far removed from serial programming, it is easy to port legacy serial code to MPPs using the data parallel programming approach.

A number of data parallel languages have been designed for portable programming MPPs, among which HPF (High Performance Fortran) is the most popular and well known. In the book we only outline HPF.

High Performance Fortran consists in a set of extensions to Fortran aimed at writing data parallel programs for architectures where the distribution of data impacts performance, that is, mainly for MPPs. The extensions were defined by the High Performance Fortran Forum (HPFF) in which over 40 organizations participated. There are two main versions of HPF produced by HPFF: a version known as HPF 1.1, which is dated November 10, 1994, and a version known as HPF 2.0, which was released on January 31, 1997. While HPF is widely implemented and available, it is not accepted in an official standard form as yet.

HPF 1.1 is based on Fortran 90 and specifies a number of language constructs, which are now included in Fortran 95 (i.e., the FORALL construct and statement, PURE procedures). HPF 2.0 is defined as an extension of Fortran 95 and hence inherits all of its data parallel constructs.

Thus the language features provided by HPF to express data parallelism are the following: whole-array operations, assignments, and functions; the FORALL construct and statement; PURE and ELEMENTAL procedures. In addition to these inherited data parallel features, HPF introduces one more way to specify computation, which can be executed in parallel. It provides a directive of the form

```
!HPF$  INDEPENDENT
```

that can precede an indexed DO loop or FORALL statement. The directive asserts to the compiler that the iterations in the following DO loop or the operations in the following FORALL statement may be executed independently— that is, in any order, or interleaved, or concurrently—without changing the semantics of the program. Such information is valuable as it enables compiler optimization without complex data dependence analysis. The INDEPENDENT directive allows the programmer to directly pass on his or her knowledge of the application to the compiler. The compiler relies on the assertion in its translation process. If the assertion is true, the semantics of the program are not changed; if it is false, the program is not HPF conforming and has no defined meaning.

Apart from the INDEPENDENT directive, HPF introduces a number of directives that allow the programmer to suggest the distribution of data among available processors to the compiler. Like the INDEPENDENT directive, the *data distribution directives* are structured comments of the form

```
!HPF$  directive-body
```

These directives may affect the efficiency of the computation performed, but they do not change the value computed by the program. Therefore, when properly written, an HPF program may be compiled by Fortran compilers that do not support HPF and be executed serially.

Two basic data distribution directives are the PROCESSORS directive and the DISTRIBUTE directive.

HPF provides a logical view of the parallel machine as a rectilinear arrangement of abstract processors in one or more dimensions. The PROCESSOR directive allows the programmer to declare such a rectilinear processor arrangement, specifying its name, its rank (number of dimensions), and the extent in each dimension. For example, the directive

```
!HPF$  PROCESSORS p(4,8)
```

specifies a logical 4 × 8 grid of abstract processors p.

The intrinsic functions NUMBER_OF_PROCESSORS and PROCESSORS_ SHAPE may be used to inquire about the total number of physical processors actually used to execute the program. This information may then be used to calculate appropriate sizes for the declared abstract processor arrangements. The values returned by these functions remain constant for the duration of one program execution. Therefore the values may be used in data distribution directives. For example, the directive

```
!HPF$  PROCESSORS  q(4,  NUMBER_OF_PROCESSORS()/4)
```

may be used to specify a logical grid of abstract processors q, each abstract processor of which is supposed to be mapped to a separate physical processor.

Several processors arrangements may be declared in the same program. If two processor arrangements have the same shape, then the corresponding elements of the two arrangements are understood to refer the same abstract processor. Therefore, if function NUMBER_OF_PROCESSORS returns 32, then elements p(2,3) and q(2,3) of the arrangements above will refer the same abstract processor.

The DISTRIBUTE directive specifies a mapping of data objects (mainly arrays) to abstract processors in a processor arrangement. There are two basic distribution types: block and cyclic.

For example, the code fragment

```
     REAL A(10000)
!HPF$ DISTRIBUTE A(BLOCK)
```

specifies that array A should be distributed across some set of abstract processors by partitioning it uniformly into blocks of contiguous elements. If there are 50 processors, the array would be divided into groups of 200 elements, with A(1:200) mapped to the first processor, A(201:400) mapped to the second processors, and so on. If there is only one processor, the entire array is mapped to that processor as a single block of 10,000 elements.

The block size may be specified explicitly:

```
     REAL A(10000)
!HPF$ DISTRIBUTE A(BLOCK(256)).
```

This specifies that groups of exactly 256 elements should be mapped to successive abstract processors. There must be at least 40 abstract processors if the directive is to be satisfied. The fortieth processor will contain a partial block of only 16 elements.

The code fragment

```
     INTEGER D(52)
!HPF$ DISTRIBUTE D(CYCLIC(2))
```

specifies a cyclic distribution of array D. Successive two-element blocks of the array are mapped to successive abstract processors in a round-robin fashion.

Thus, if there are four abstract processors, the first processor will contain D(1),
D(2), D(9), D(10), ..., D(45), D(46); the second processor will contain
D(3), D(4), D(11), D(12), ..., D(47), D(48); the third processor will
contain D(5), D(6), D(13), D(14), ..., D(49), D(50); and the fourth
processor will contain D(7), D(8), D(19), D(16), ..., D(51), D(52).

CYCLIC by definition means the same as CYCLIC(1). Therefore the code
fragment

```
      INTEGER DECK_OF_CARDS(52)
!HPF$ PROCESSORS PLAYERS(4)
!HPF$ DISTRIBUTE DECK_OF_CARDS(CYCLIC) ONTO PLAYERS
```

specifies that the first processor of processor arrangement PLAYERS
will contain DECK_OF_CARDS[1:49:4], the second processor will
contain DECK_OF_CARDS[2:50:4], the third processor will contain
DECK_OF_CARDS[3:51:4], and the fourth processor will contain
DECK_OF_CARDS[4:52:4].

Distributions are specified independently for each dimension of a multidimensional array:

```
      INTEGER CHESS_BOARD(8,8), GO_BOARD(19,19)
!HPF$ DISTRIBUTE CHESS_BOARD(BLOCK, BLOCK)
!HPF$ DISTRIBUTE GO_BOARD(CYCLIC,*)
```

The CHESS_BOARD array will be partitioned into contiguous rectangular
patches that will be distributed onto a two-dimensional arrangement of
abstract processors. The GO_BOARD array will have its rows distributed cycli-
cally over a one-dimensional arrangement of abstract processors. The asterisk
(*) specifies that GO_BOARD is not to be distributed along the second axis; thus
an entire row is to be distributed as one object.

Consider the following simple HPF program:

```
      PROGRAM SIMPLE
      REAL, DIMENSION(1000,1000):: A, B, C
!HPF$ PROCESSORS p(4,4)
!HPF$ DISTRIBUTE (BLOCK,BLOCK) ONTO p:: A, B, C
!HPF$ INDEPENDENT
      DO J=1,1000
!HPF$     INDEPENDENT
          DO I=1,1000
              A(I,J)=1.0
              B(I,J)=2.0
          END DO
      END DO
!HPF$ INDEPENDENT
      DO J=1,1000
```

```
!HPF$        INDEPENDENT
             DO I=1,1000
                    C(I,J)=0.0
                    DO K=1,1000
                            C(I,J)=C(I,J)+A(I,K)*B(K,J)
                    END DO
             END DO
       END DO
       END
```

The program implements matrix operation $C = A \times B$ on a 16-processor MPP, where A, B are dense square 1000×1000 matrices.

The PROCESSORS directive specifies a logical 4×4 grid of abstract processors, p. The DISTRIBUTE directive recommends the compiler to partition each of the arrays A, B, and C into equal-sized blocks along each of its dimension. This will result in a 4×4 configuration of blocks, each containing 250×250 elements with one block per processor. The corresponding blocks of arrays A, B, and C will be mapped to the same abstract processor and, hence, to the same physical processor.

Each of the four INDEPENDENT directives in the program is applied to a DO loop. They advise the compiler that the loop does not carry any dependences, and therefore its different iterations may be executed in parallel.

Altogether the directives give the compiler enough information in order to generate a target message-passing program. Additional information is given by a general HPF rule saying that evaluation of an expression should be performed on the processor in the memory of which its result will be stored. Actually the HPF program above specifies the parallel matrix-matrix multiplication algorithm based on a two-dimensional matrix decomposition, as was presented in Section 4.1. Thus, a clever HPF compiler should be able to generate an SPMD message-passing code such as the following:

```
PROGRAM SIMPLE
REAL, DIMENSION(250,250):: A, B, C
REAL, DIMENSION(250,1000):: Arows, Bcols
INTEGER colcom, rowcom, col, row
INTEGER rank, colrank, rowrank
INTEGER err
CALL MPI_INIT(ierr)
CALL MPI_COMM_RANK(MPI_COMM_WORLD, rank);
row = rank/4
col = rank-row*4
DO J=1,250
        DO I=1,250
                A(I,J)=1.0
                B(I,J)=2.0
```

```
        END DO
END DO
CALL MPI_COMM_SPLIT(MPI_COMM_WORLD, row, rank, rowcom, err)
CALL MPI_COMM_SPLIT(MPI_COMM_WORLD, col, rank, colcom, err)
CALL MPI_ALLGATHER(A, 40000, MPI_REAL, Arows, 62500,
&MPI_REAL, rowcom, err)
CALL MPI_ALLGATHER(B, 40000, MPI_REAL, Bcols, 62500,
&MPI_REAL, colcom, err)
DO J=1,250
    DO I=1,250
            C(I,J)=0.0
            ind1=1
            ind2=J
        DO K=1,1000
                C(I,J)=C(I,J)+Arows(I,K)*Bcols
                (ind1,ind2)
                IF(ind1.LT.250) THEN
                        ind1=ind1+1
                ELSE
                        ind1=1
                        ind2=ind2+250
                END IF
            END DO
        END DO
END DO
CALL MPI_COMM_FREE(rowcom, err)
CALL MPI_COMM_FREE(colcom, err)
CALL MPI_FINALIZE(err)
END
```

The preceding code is in Fortran 77 with calls to MPI routines. It is supposed to be executed by all 16 processes making up the parallel program. Each process locally contains one 250×250 block of global arrays A, B, and C of the source HPF program. A logical 4×4 process grid is formed from the 16 participating processes, and each process gets its coordinates row and col in the grid. In order to compute its block of the resulting matrix C, the process needs blocks of matrix A from its horizontal neighbours in the 4×4 process grid, and blocks of matrix B from its vertical neighbors (see Figure 4.3). The necessary communication is achieved as we show next.

First, communicators are created for horizontal communication, one for each row of the 4×4 process grid. The MPI_COMM_SPLIT routine performs this operation, returning the new communicators in rowcom. Then a call to MPI_COMM_SPLIT creates communicators for columns of the process grid and returns them in colcom.

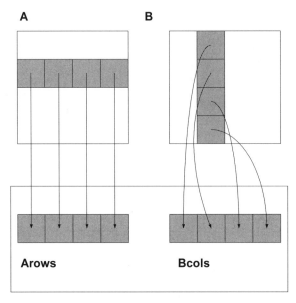

Figure 4.6. Storage schemes used in the target message-passing program to store a row of blocks of matrix A and a column of blocks of matrix B in local arrays Arows and Bcols, respectively.

Now all processes call the MPI_ALLGATHER routine supplying rowcom as a communicator argument. This call performs, in parallel, four collective gather-to-all communication operations, each on its row of the process grid. As a result each process has in its local array Arows a copy of the corresponding row of blocks of matrix A.

The next call to MPI_ALLGATHER with colcom as a communicator argument also performs, in parallel, four collective gather-to-all communication operations but on columns of the process grid. During the execution of this call, each process gathers in local array Bcols copies of blocks of the corresponding column of blocks of matrix B. Note that array Bcols stores the blocks horizontally, as a row of blocks, and not in the form of columns of blocks as they are normally stored (see Figure 4.6). Therefore the inner DO loop, which computes an element of the resulting matrix C, must recalculate indexes of Bcols elements to make successive iterations of the loop refer to successive elements of the corresponding column of matrix B.

The main optimization performed by an HPF compiler is the minimization of the cost of the interprocessor communication. This is not a trivial problem. It requires full analysis of both the source code and the executing MPP. HPF provides no specific constructs nor directives to help the compiler solve the problem. This is why HPF is considered a difficult language to compile.

For example, many real HPF compilers (i.e., the ADAPTOR HPF compiler from GMD) will translate the HPF program above into a message-passing program, whose processes each send its blocks of matrices *A* and *B* to *all* the other processes. That straightforward communication scheme guarantees that each process receives all of the elements of global arrays A and B that it needs to compute its elements of global array C. However, in many cases, including ours, this universal scheme involves a good deal of redundant communications, sending and receiving data that are never used in computation. The better a compiler is, the more accurate communication patterns it generates to avoid redundant communications as much as possible. The message-passing program above is generated by an imaginary clever HPF compiler and performs no redundant communication. Each process of the program sends its blocks of matrices *A* and *B* only to 3 other processes, and not to 15 as each process of the straightforward program does.

The PROCESSORS, DISTRIBUTE, and INDEPENDENT directives make up the core of HPF. There are two more HPF directives introduced mainly to facilitate the specification of the coordinated distribution of a group of interrelated arrays and other data objects. These two are the TEMPLATE and ALIGN data distribution directives. The directives provide a two-level mapping of data objects to abstract processors. Data objects are first *aligned* relative to some template, which is simply an abstract space of indexed positions (an array of nothings). The template is then distributed with the DISTRIBUTE directive implying that all array elements and scalar objects aligned with the same position in the template will be mapped to the same abstract processor. For example, the code fragment

```
REAL, DIMENSION(10000,10000) :: NW, NE, SW, SE
!HPF$  TEMPLATE EARTH(10001,10001)
!HPF$  ALIGN NW(I,J) WITH EARTH(I,J)
!HPF$  ALIGN NE(I,J) WITH EARTH(I,J+1)
!HPF$  ALIGN SW(I,J) WITH EARTH(I+1,J)
!HPF$  ALIGN SE(I,J) WITH EARTH(I+1,J+1)
!HPF$  DISTRIBUTE EARTH(BLOCK, BLOCK)
```

aligns four 10000×10000 arrays NW, NE, SW, and SE to the four corners of template EARTH of size 10001×10001.

The presented model of data parallel programming MPPs, which is supported by the PROCESSORS, TEMPLATE, ALIGN, DISTRIBUTE, and INDEPENDENT directives, is the fundamental model provided by HPF 1.1. HPF 2.0 extends this model in three directions.

The first set of extensions provides the programmer with greater control over the mapping of the data. These include directives for dynamic remapping of data: DYNAMIC, REDISTRIBUTE, and REALIGN. The DYNAMIC directive

```
!HPF$  DYNAMIC alignee-or-distributee-list
```

specifies that objects in *alignee-or-distributee-list* may be dynamically realigned or redistributed.

The REDISTRIBUTE directive is similar to the DISTRIBUTE directive but is considered executable. An array or template may be redistributed at any time if it has been declared DYNAMIC. Any other objects currently ultimately aligned with the array (or template) when it is redistributed are also remapped to preserve alignment relationships in the new distribution.

The REALIGN directive is similar to the ALIGN directive but is considered executable. An array or template may be realigned at any time if it has been declared DYNAMIC. Unlike redistribution, realigning a data object does not cause any other object to be remapped. However, realignment of even a single object, if it is large, can require a lot of computational and communication effort at runtime.

The ONTO clause used in the DISTRIBUTE directive is extended to allow direct distribution to subsets of processors. Explicit mapping of pointers and components of derived types are also introduced.

The second set of extensions allows the programmer to provide the compiler with information useful for generating efficient code. The programmer can use the RANGE directive to specify the range of distributions that a dynamically distributed array or a pointer may have. The SHADOW directive allows the programmer to specify the amount of additional space required on a processor to accommodate nonlocal elements in a nearest-neighbor computation.

The third set of extensions provides some basic support for *task parallelism*, that is, parallelism implied by computation partitioning rather than data partitioning. These include the ON directive, the RESIDENT directive, and the TASK_REGION construct. The ON directive partitions computations among the processors of a parallel machine (much as the DISTRIBUTE directive partitions the data among the processors). The RESIDENT directive asserts that certain data access do not require interprocessor data movement for their implementation. The TASK_REGION construct provides the means to create independent coarse-grain tasks, each of which can itself execute a data-parallel (or nested task parallel) computation. These extensions make HPF a multiparadigm parallel programming language rather than a pure data parallel programming language as it was originally designed.

4.4. SUMMARY

The MPP architecture provides much more parallelism than the SMP architecture. Moreover, unlike all other parallel architectures, the MPP architecture is scalable. It means that the speedup provided by this architecture is potentially infinite. This is due to the absence of principle bottlenecks that might limit the number of efficiently interacting processors.

Message passing is the dominant programming model for the MPP architecture. As the MPP architecture is much far away from the serial scalar architecture than the vector, superscalar and even SMP architectures, it is very difficult to automatically generate efficient message-passing code for a serial source code written in C or Fortran 77. In fact optimizing C or Fortran 77 compilers for MPPs would have to solve the problem of automatic synthesis of an efficient message-passing program using the source serial code as a specification of its functional semantics. This problem is still a research challenge. Therefore no industrial optimizing C or Fortran 77 compiler for the MPP architecture is now available.

Basic programming tools for MPPs are message-passing libraries and high-level parallel languages. Message-passing libraries directly implement the message-passing paradigm and allow the programmers to explicitly write efficient parallel programs for MPPs. MPI is a standard message-passing interface supporting efficiently portable parallel programming MPPs. Unlike the other popular message-passing library, PVM, MPI supports modular parallel programming and hence can be used for development of parallel libraries.

MPI is a powerful programming tool that allows the programmers to implement a wide range of parallel algorithms on MPPs in the form of highly efficient and portable message-passing applications. However, scientific programmers find the explicit message passing provided by MPI tedious and error-prone. They use data parallel programming languages, mainly HPF, to write programs for MPPs. When programming in HPF, the programmer specifies the strategy for parallelization and data partitioning at a higher level of abstraction, based on the single-threaded data parallel model with a global name space. The tedious low-level details of translating from an abstract global name space to the local memories of individual processors and the management of explicit interprocessor communication are left to the compiler.

Data parallel programs are easy to write and debug. At the same time, data parallel programming model allows the programmer to express only a limited class of parallel algorithms. HPF 2.0 addresses the problem by extending purely data parallel HPF 1.1 with some task parallel features. The resulting multiparadigm language is more complicated and not as easy-to-use as pure data parallel languages.

Data parallel languages (i.e., HPF) are difficult to compile. Therefore it is hard to get top performance via data parallel programming. The efficiency of data parallel programs strongly depends on the quality of the compiler.

## CHAPTER 5

Networks of Computers: Architecture and Programming Challenges

Local networks of computers (NoCs) are the most common and available parallel architecture. Nowadays not only big businesses and organizations but practically any medium or small enterprize has several computers interconnected in a local network.

Generally, a local network of computers consists of PCs, workstations, SMP servers, and even MPP supercomputers and clusters interconnected via mixed network equipment (see Figure 5.1). At a first glance this architecture is very similar to the MPP architecture. Like the latter it provides a number of processors not sharing global main memory and interconnected via a communication network. Therefore the most natural model of program for NoCs is also a set of parallel processes, each running on a separate processor and using message passing to communicate with the others. That is, message passing is the basic programming model for this architecture.

Because of this similarity between MPPs and NoCs, it might be expected that NoCs would be as widely used as MPPs for high-performance parallel computing. In reality, NoCs are hardly used for parallel computing. The reason is why the huge performance potential of millions NoCs around the world is so underutilized is that parallel programming for NoCs is a lot more difficult than parallel programming for MPPs.

Unlike MPPs, which are designed and manufactured specifically for high-performance parallel computing, a typical NoC is a naturally developed computer system. A NoC is a general-purpose computer system that is developed incrementally over a relatively long period of time. As a result NoCs are not nicely regular nor balanced for high-performance computing. On the contrary, irregularity, heterogeneity, and instability are their inherent features unlike the architecture of MPPs. These very features make parallel programming for NoCs particularly challenging.

There are three sources of difficulties. The first one is the heterogeneity of processors. Generally speaking, in a NoC, different processors are of the different architecture.

Parallel Computing on Heterogeneous Networks, by Alexey Lastovetsky
ISBN 0-471-22982-2   Copyright © 2003 by John Wiley & Sons, Inc.

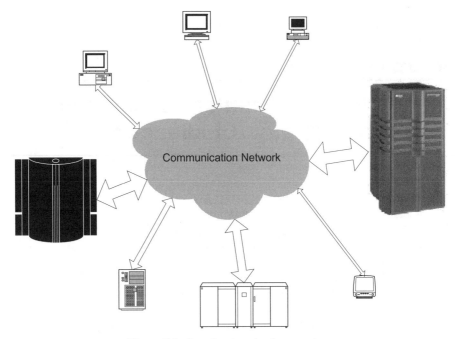

Figure 5.1. Local network of computers.

The second source is the communication network. As we noted above, it is not designed for high-performance parallel computing.

The third source is the multiple-user capacity of NoCs. A NoC is not a strongly centralized computer system. It consists of relatively autonomous computers, each of which may be used and administered independently by its users. In NoCs different components are not as strongly integrated and controlled as in MPPs.

In the chapter we discuss the sources and analyze the programming challenges coming from each of these sources.

5.1. PROCESSORS HETEROGENEITY

5.1.1. Different Processor Speeds

An immediate implication from the fact that an NoC uses processors of different architectures is that the processors run at different speeds. Let us see what happens when a parallel application, which provides a good performance while running on homogeneous MPPs, runs on the cluster of heterogeneous processors.

A good parallel application for MPPs tries to evenly distribute computations over available processors. This even distribution ensures the maximal speedup on MPPs, which consist of identical processors. On the cluster of processors running at different speeds, faster processors will quickly perform their part of computations and wait for slower ones at points of synchronization. Therefore the total time of computations will be determined by the time elapsed on the slowest processor. In other words, when executing parallel applications that evenly distribute computations among available processors, the heterogeneous cluster is equivalent to a homogeneous cluster that is composed of the same number but the slowest processors.

The following simple experiment corroborates the statement. Two subnetworks of the same local network were used, each consisting of four Sun workstations. The first subnetwork included identical workstations of the same model, and was thus homogeneous. The second one included workstations of three different models. Their relative speeds, demonstrated while executing a LAPACK Cholesky factorization routine, were 1.9, 2.8, 2.8, and 7.1. As the slowest workstation (relative performance 1.9) was shared by both clusters, the total power of the heterogeneous cluster was almost twice that of the homogeneous one.

It might be expected that a parallel ScaLAPACK Cholesky solver would be executed on the more powerful cluster almost twice as fast as on the weaker one. But in reality it ran practically at the same speed (~2% speedup for a 1800×1800 dense matrix).

Thus a good parallel application for a NoC must distribute computations unevenly, taking into account the difference in processor speed. The faster processor is, the more computations it must perform. Ideally the volume of computation performed by a processor should be proportional to its speed.

For example, a simple parallel algorithm implementing the matrix operation $C = A \times B$ on a p-processor heterogeneous cluster, where A, B are dense square $n \times n$ matrices, can be summarized as follows:

- Each element c_{ij} in C is computed as $c_{ij} = \sum_{k=0}^{n-1} a_{ik} \times b_{kj}$.
- The A, B, and C matrices are identically partitioned into p vertical slices. There is one-to-one mapping between these slices and the processors. Each processor is responsible for computing its C slice.
- Because all C elements require the same amount of arithmetic operations, each processor executes an amount of work proportional to the number of elements that are allocated to it, and hence proportional to the area of its slice. Therefore, to balance the load of the processors, the area of the slice mapped to each processor is proportional to its speed (see Figure 5.2).
- To compute elements of its C slice, each processor requires all elements of the A matrix. Therefore, during the execution of the algorithm, each processor receives from $p - 1$ other processors all elements of their slices (shown gray in Figure 5.2).

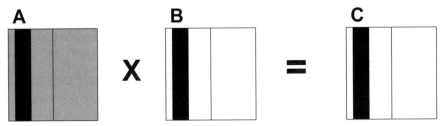

Figure 5.2. Matrix-matrix multiplication with matrices *A*, *B*, and *C* unevenly partitioned in one dimension. The area of the slice mapped to each processor is proportional to its speed. The slices mapped onto a single processor are shaded black. During execution this processor requires all of matrix *A* (shown shaded gray).

This heterogeneous parallel algorithm cannot be implemented in HPF 1.1, since the latter provides no way to specify a heterogeneous distribution of arrays across abstract processors. But HPF 2.0 addresses the problem by extending BLOCK distribution with the ability to explicitly specify the size of each individual block (GEN_BLOCK distribution).

For example, the following HPF program implements the parallel algorithm above to multiply two dense square 1000×1000 matrices on a four-processor heterogeneous cluster, whose processors have the relative speeds 2, 3, 5, and 10:

```
        PROGRAM HETEROGENEOUS
        INTEGER, DIMENSION(4), PARAMETER:: M=(/100, 150,
        250, 500/)
        REAL, DIMENSION(1000,1000):: A, B, C
!HPF$   PROCESSORS p(4)
!HPF$   DISTRIBUTE (*, GEN_BLOCK(M)) ONTO p:: A, B, C
!HPF$   INDEPENDENT
        DO J=1,1000
!HPF$          INDEPENDENT
               DO I=1,1000
                     A(I,J)=1.0
                     B(I,J)=2.0
               END DO
        END DO
!HPF$   INDEPENDENT
        DO J=1,1000
!HPF$          INDEPENDENT
               DO I=1,1000
                     C(I,J)=0.0
                     DO K=1,1000
                        C(I,J)=C(I,J)+A(I,K)*B(K,J)
```

           END DO

        END DO

    END DO

    END

In the preceding program the "generalized" block distribution, GEN_BLOCK, is used to map contiguous segments of arrays A, B, and C of unequal sizes onto processors. The sizes of the segments are specified by values of the user-defined integer mapping array M, one value per target processor of the mapping. That is, the ith element of the mapping array specifies the size of the block to be stored on the ith processor of the target processor arrangement p. The asterisk (*) in the DISTRIBUTE directive specifies that arrays A, B, and C are not to be distributed along the first axis; thus an entire column is to be distributed as one object. So array elements A(:,1:100), B(:,1:100), and C(:,1:100) are mapped on p(1); A(:,101:250), B(:,101:250), and C(:,101:250) are mapped on p(2); A(:,251:500), B(:,251:500), and C(:,251:500) are mapped on p(3); and A(:,501:1000), B(:,501:1000); and C(:,501:1000) are mapped on p(4).

That distribution of matrices A, B, and C across processors ensures that the area of the vertical slice mapped to each processor is proportional to the speed of the processor. Note that the responsibility of the programmer is to explicitly specify the exact distribution of the arrays across processors. The specification is based on the knowledge of both the parallel algorithm and the executing heterogeneous cluster.

HPF 2.0 also allows the programmer to distribute the arrays with the REDISTRIBUTE directive based on a mapping array whose values are computed at runtime. This allows a more portable application to be written. But again, either the programmer or the user must explicitly specify the data distribution, which ensures the best performance of this particular parallel algorithm on each heterogeneous cluster.

Apparently the algorithm above can be implemented in MPI as well. The corresponding MPI program, however, will be not as simple as HPF because of the much lower level of the MPI's programming model. Actually MPI is a programming tool of the assembler level for message-passing programming. Therefore practically all message-passing algorithms can be implemented in MPI.

Whatever programming tool is used to implement the parallel algorithm above, the efficiency of the corresponding application depends on the accuracy of estimation of the relative speed of processors of the executing heterogeneous cluster. The distribution of arrays, and hence, distribution of computations across the processors, is determined by an estimation of the relative speeds of the processors. If this estimation is not accurate enough, the load of processors will be unbalanced, resulting in poor performance.

The problem of making an accurate estimation of the relative speed of processors is not easy. For two processors of the same architecture that differ only in clock rate, it is not difficult to accurately estimate their relative speed. The relative speed will be the same for every application.

But for processors of different architectures the situation changes drastically. Everything in the processors may be different: the set of instructions, number of instruction execution units, number of registers, structure of memory hierarchy, size of each memory level, and so on and on. Therefore the processors will demonstrate different relative speeds for different applications. Moreover processors of the same architecture but different models or configurations may also demonstrate different relative speeds in different applications.

Even different applications of the same narrow class may be executed by two different processors at significantly different relative speeds. To avoid speculation, consider the following experiment. Three slightly different implementations of Cholesky factorization of a 500×500 matrix were used to estimate the relative speed of a SPARCstation-5 and a SPARCstation-20. Code

```
for(k=0; k<500; k++) {
    for(i=k, lkk=sqrt(a[k][k]); i<500; i++)
      a[i][k] /= lkk;
    for(j=k+1; j<500; j++)
      for(i=j; i<500; i++)
        a[i][j] -= a[i][k]*a[j][k];
}
```

estimated their relative speed as $10:9$, meanwhile code

```
for(k=0; k<500; k++) {
    for(i=k, lkk=sqrt(a[k][k]); i<500; i++)
      a[i][k] /= lkk;
    for(i=k+1; i<500; i++)
      for(j=i; j<500; j++)
        a[i][j] -= a[k][j]*a[k][i];
}
```

as $10:14$. Routine `dptof2` from the LAPACK package, solving the same problem, estimated their relative speed as $10:10$.

5.1.2. Heterogeneity of Machine Arithmetic

Since processors of an NoC may do floating-point arithmetic differently, there are special challenges associated with writing numerical software on NoCs. In particular, two basic issues potentially affect the behavior of a numerical parallel application running on a heterogeneous NoC.

First, different processors do not guarantee the same storage representation and the same results for operations on floating point numbers. Second, if a floating-point number is communicated among processors, the communication layer does not guarantee the exact transmittal of the floating-point value. Normally transferring a floating point number in a heterogeneous environment includes two conversions of its binary representation: the representation of the number on the sender site is first converted into a machine-independent representation, which is then converted into the representation for floating-point numbers on the receiver site. The two successive conversions may change the original value; that is, the value received by the receiver may differ from the value sent by the sender.

To see better the potential problems, consider the iterative solution of a system of linear equations where the stopping criterion depends on the value of some function, f, of the relative machine precision, ε. A common definition of the relative machine precision, or unit roundoff, is the smallest positive floating-point value, ε, such that $fl(1 + \varepsilon) > 1$, where $fl(x)$ is the floating-point representation of x. The test for convergence might well include a test of the form

if $\left(\dfrac{\|e_r\|_2}{\|x_r\|_2} < f(\varepsilon) \right)$ **goto** converged;

In a heterogeneous setting the value of f may be different on different processors and e_r and x_r may depend on data of different accuracies. Thus one or more processes may converge in a fewer number of iterations. Indeed, the stopping criterion used by the most accurate processor may never be satisfied if it depends on data computed less accurately by other processors. If the code contains communication between processors within an iteration, it may not complete if one processor converges before the others. In a heterogeneous environment, the only way to guarantee termination is to have one processor make the convergence decision and broadcast that decision.

Another problem is that overflow and underflow exceptions may occur during floating-point representation conversions, resulting in a failure of the communication.

5.2. AD HOC COMMUNICATION NETWORK

One can imagine a local network of heterogeneous computers whose communication layer is almost as good as the communication layer of the MPP architecture. Parallel programming for such networks, called in this book *heterogeneous clusters*, faces no specific communication-related challenges. Heterogeneous clusters are normally designed specifically for high-performance distributed computing.

However, the topology and structure of the communication network in a typical common local network of computers is determined by many different factors, among which high-performance computing is far away from being a primary factor if considered at all. The primary factors include the structure of the organization, the tasks that are solved on computers of the NoC, the security requirements, the construction restrictions, the budget limitations, the qualification of technical personnel, and so on.

An additional important factor is that the communication network is constantly developing rather than being fixed once and forever. The development is normally occasional and incremental. Therefore the structure of the communication network reflects the evolution of the organization rather than its current snapshot.

All the factors make the common communication network far away from the ideal MPP communication network, which is homogeneous with communication speedup and bandwidth being balanced with the number and speed of processors.

First of all, the common communication network is heterogeneous. The speed and bandwidth of communication links between different pairs of processors may differ significantly. Second, some of the communication links may be of low speed and/or narrow bandwidth. This makes the problem of optimal distribution of computations and communications across an NoC more difficult than across a cluster of heterogeneous processors interconnected with a homogeneous high-performance communication network. The additional difficulty comes from the larger size of the problem, which is now $O(n^2)$, where n is the total number of processors (respectively, n^2 is the total number of interprocessor communication links).

Apart from that, due to low performance of some communication links, the optimal distribution of computations and communications may be across some subnetwork of the NoC, and not across the entire NoC. This substantially extends the space of possible solutions and increases the complexity of the distribution problem even further.

To take an example, consider a network of p homogeneous processors interconnected by a plain Ethernet network. The bandwidth of the Ethernet-based communication network is equal to 1 because the network cannot simultaneously carry more than one data package.

Let us estimate the time of execution of the simplest parallel algorithm of matrix-matrix multiplication from Section 4.1 on this network. Remember that the algorithm has been proved scalable when executing on an MPP. The contribution of computation in the total execution time of the parallel algorithm above will be the same:

$$t_{comp} = \frac{t_{proc} \times n^3}{p}.$$

The per-processor communication cost will also be the same:

$$t_{comm} = (p-1) \times t_{slice} \approx t_s \times p + t_e \times n^2.$$

However, as all of the communications are performed serially, and not in parallel, the total execution time of the parallel algorithm on the network will be

$$t_{total} \approx t_{proc} \times \frac{n^3}{p} + t_s \times p^2 + t_e \times n^2 \times p.$$

The execution of the algorithm is still accelerated while upgrading the network from the one-processor to the two-processor configuration, if n is large enough (typically, if $n > 200$). But the algorithm is no longer scalable. Indeed, the algorithm would be scalable, if and only if t_{total} were a monotonically decreasing function of p, that is, if

$$\frac{\partial t_{total}}{\partial p} = 2 \times t_s \times p + t_e \times n^2 - t_{proc} \times \frac{n^3}{p^2} < 0,$$

or

$$2 \times \frac{t_s}{t_{proc}} \times \left(\frac{p}{n}\right)^3 + \frac{t_e}{t_{proc}} \times \left(\frac{p}{n}\right) \times p < 1.$$

This inequality will be true only if p is small enough, whatever n and the ratio between p and n are. It means that the algorithm is not scalable on the network, and there is some optimal number of processors that solves the problem the fastest. This number is very likely to be less than the total number of available processors.

But it could be just a wrong algorithm. Perhaps the improved algorithm, which is based on two-dimensional matrix decomposition, is scalable on the network. Then the total execution time of the improved algorithm on the network would be

$$t_{total} \approx t_{proc} \times \frac{n^3}{p} + 2 \times t_s \times p \times \sqrt{p} + 2 \times t_e \times n^2 \times \sqrt{p}.$$

So the algorithm would be scalable, if and only if

$$\frac{\partial t_{total}}{\partial p} = 3 \times t_s \times \sqrt{p} + t_e \times n^2 \times \frac{1}{\sqrt{p}} - t_{proc} \times \frac{n^3}{p^2} < 0,$$

that is, if

$$3 \times \frac{t_s}{t_{proc}} \times \left(\frac{p}{n}\right)^3 \times \frac{1}{\sqrt{p}} + \frac{t_e}{t_{proc}} \times \left(\frac{p}{n}\right) \times \sqrt{p} < 1.$$

This inequality will also be true only if p is small enough, whatever n and the ratio between p and n are. Therefore the improved algorithm is also not scalable on the network.

Further improvements of the algorithm cannot change the situation and result in a matrix-matrix multiplication algorithm that would be scalable on the network. The point is that there is nothing wrong with the algorithm. It is the network that has a problem, and the problem is its narrow bandwidth. The bandwidth puts limits on speedup and makes "normal" message-passing applications nonscalable on the network. In terms of scalability, this network is very similar to the SMP architecture, where the bandwidth of the memory bus is also a bottleneck limiting speedup (see Section 3.1).

5.3. MULTIPLE-USER DECENTRALIZED COMPUTER SYSTEM

Unlike MPPs, NoCs are not strongly centralized computer systems. A typical NoC consists of relatively autonomous computers, each of which may be used and administered independently by its users.

5.3.1. Unstable Performance Characteristics

The first implication from the multiple-user decentralized nature of NoCs is that computers that execute a parallel program may be also used for other computations and be involved in other communications. In this case the real performance of processors and communication links can dynamically change depending on the external computations and communications.

Therefore a good parallel program for a NoC must be sensitive to such dynamic variations of its workload. In such a program, computations and communications are distributed across the NoC in accordance to the actual performance at the moment of execution of the program.

5.3.2. High Probability of Resource Failures

Fault tolerance is not a primary problem for parallel applications running on MPPs. The probability of unexpected resource failures in a centralized dedicated parallel computer system is quite small. But this probability reaches much higher figures for NoCs. First, any single computer in an NoC may be switched off or rebooted unexpectedly for other users in the NoC. The same may happen with any other resource in the NoC. Second, not all building elements of the common NoC as well as interaction between different elements are equally reliable. These characteristics make fault tolerance a desirable feature for parallel applications that run on NoCs, and the longer the execution time of the application is, the more important the feature becomes.

The basic programming tool for distributed memory parallel architectures, MPI, does not address the problem. This is because a fault-tolerant parallel program assumes a dynamic process model. Failure of one or more processes of the program does not necessarily lead to failure of the entire program. The program may continue running even after its set of processes has changed.

The MPI 1.1 process model is fully static. MPI 2.0 does include some support for dynamic process control, although this is limited to the creation of new MPI process groups with separate communicators. These new processes cannot be merged with previously existing communicators to form intracommunicators needed for a seamless single application model; they are limited to a special set of extended collective communications.

To date, there is no industrial fault-tolerant implementation of MPI. However, there are a few research versions of MPI that suggest different approaches to the problem of fault-tolerant parallel programming.

The first approach to making MPI applications fault tolerant is through the use of checkpointing and rollback. This approach is that all processes of the MPI program will flush their message queues to avoid in flight messages getting lost, and then they will all synchronously checkpoint. If any error occurs at some later stage, the entire MPI program will be rolled back to the last complete checkpoint and be re-started. This approach needs the entire application to checkpoint synchronously, which depending on the application, and its size may become expensive in terms of time (with potential scaling problems).

The second approach is to use "spare" processes that are utilized when there is a failure. For example, MPI-FT supports several master/slave models where all communicators are built from grids that contain "spare" processes. To avoid loss of message data between the master and slaves, all messages are copied to an observer process that can reproduce lost messages in the event of a failure. This system has a high overhead for every message and considerable memory needs for the observer process during long-running applications. This system is not a full checkpoint system in that it assumes any data (or state) can be rebuilt using just the knowledge of any passed messages, which might not be the case for nondeterministic unstable solvers.

MPI-FT is an example of an implicit fault-tolerant MPI. Such implementations of MPI do not extend to the MPI interface. No specific design is needed for an application that uses an implicit fault-tolerant MPI. The system takes full responsibility over fault-tolerant features of the application. The drawback of such an approach is that the programmer cannot control fault-tolerant features of the application and fine-tune for better balance between fault tolerance and performance as system and application conditions may dictate.

Unlike MPI-FT, FT-MPI is an explicit fault-tolerant MPI that extends the standard MPI's interface and semantics. An application using FT-MPI has to be designed to take advantage of its fault-tolerant features.

First of all, FT-MPI extends MPI communicator and process states. Standard semantics of MPI indicate that a failure of an MPI process or communication causes all communicators associated with them to become *invalid*. As the standard provides no method to reinstate them (and it is unclear if they can be freed), this causes MPI_COMM_WORLD itself to become *invalid* and thus the entire MPI application will be brought to a halt.

FT-MPI extends the MPI communicator states from {*valid, invalid*}, or {*ok, failed*}, to a range {*ok, problem, failed*}.

The MPI process states are also extended from typical states of {*ok, failed*} to {*ok, unavailable, joining, failed*}. The unavailable state includes *unknown, unreachable,* or *"we have not voted to remove it yet"* states. A communicator changes its state when either an MPI process changes its state or a communication within that communicator fails for some reason.

The typical MPI semantics is from *ok* to *failed,* which then causes an application to abort. Allowing the communicator to be in an intermediate state gives the application the ability to determine how to alter the communicator, and its state, as well as how communication within the intermediate state behaves.

On detecting a failure within a communicator, that communicator is marked as having a probable error. As soon as this occurs, the underlying system sends a state update to all other processes involved in that communicator. If the error was a communication error, not all communicators are forced to be updated. If it was a process exit, then all communicators that include this process are changed.

Once a communicator has an error state, it can only recover by rebuilding it, using a modified version of one of the MPI communicator build functions such as MPI_Comm_create, MPI_Comm_dup, or MPI_Comm_split. Under these functions the new communicator will follow one of the following semantics depending on its failure mode:

- SHRINK: The communicator is reduced so that the data structure is contiguous. The ranks of the processes are changed, forcing the application to recall MPI_COMM_RANK.
- BLANK: The same as the SHRINK mode, except that the communicator can now contain gaps to be filled later. Communicating with a gap will cause an invalid rank error. Calling MPI_COMM_SIZE will return the extent of communicator, and not the number of valid processes within it.
- REBUILD: Most complex mode that forces the creation of new processes to fill any gaps until the size is the same as the extent. The new processes can either be placed into the empty ranks or the communicator can be shrunk, and the remaining processes placed at the end.
- ABORT: A mode that effects the application immediately on detection of an error and forces a graceful abort. The user is unable to trap this. If the application needs to avoid this mode, it must set all communicators to one of the communicator modes above.

Communications within the communicator are controlled by a message mode for the communicator, which can take one of two forms:

- NOP: No operation on error. That is, no user-level message operations are allowed, and all simply return an error code. This is used to allow an application to return from any point in the code to a state where it can take appropriate action as soon as possible.
- CONT: All communication that is not to the affected/failed process can continue as normal. Attempts to communicate with a failed process will return errors until the communicator state is reset.

The user discovers errors from the return code of MPI calls, with a new fault indicated by MPI_ERR_OTHER. Details as to the nature and specifics of an error are available through the cached attributes interface of MPI.

FT-MPI takes extra care in implementation of collective operations. When an error occurs during an operation, the result of the operation will be the same as if there had been no error, or else the operation is aborted. In broadcast, even if there is a failure of a receiving process, the receiving processes still receive the same data, that is, the same end result for the surviving processes. Gather and all-gather are different in that the result depends on whether or not the problematic processes sent data to the gatherer/root. In the case of gather, the root may or may not have gaps in the result. For the all-to-all operation, which typically uses a ring algorithm, it is possible that some processes may have complete information and others incomplete. Thus for operations that require multiple process input as in gather/reduce type of operations, any failure causes all processes to return an error code, rather than possibly invalid data.

Typical usage of FT-MPI would be in the form of an error check and then some corrective action such as a communicator rebuild. For example, in the following code fragment the communicator is simply rebuilt and reused on an error:

```
rc = MPI_Send(..., comm)
if(rc== MPI_ERR_OTHER)
  MPI_Comm_dup(comm, newcomm);
comm = newcomm;
// Continue...
```

Some types of parallel programs such as SPMD master/worker codes only need the error checking in the master code if the user is willing to accept the master as the only point of failure. The next example shows how complex a master code can become:

```
rc = MPI_Bcast(..., comm); // Initial work
if(rc == MPI_ERR_OTHER)
  reclaim_lost_work(...);
while(!all_work_done)
{
```

```
if(work_allocated)
{
    rc = MPI_Recv(buf, ans_size, result_dt,
                  MPI_ANY_SOURCE, MPI_ANY_TAG, comm,
                  &status);
    if(rc == MPI_SUCCESS)
    {
        handle_work(buf);
        free_worker(status.MPI_SOURCE);
        all_work_done--;
    }
    else
    {
        reclaim_lost_work(status.MPI_SOURCE);
        if(no_surviving_workers)
    {
        // Do something
    }
    }
}
// Get a new worker as we must have received a result or a death
rank = get_free_worker_and_allocate_work();
if(rank)
{
    rc = MPI_Send(...,rank,...);
    if(rc == MPI_OTHER_ERR)
        reclaim_lost_work(rank);
    if(no_surviving_workers)
    {
        // Do something
    }
    }
}
```

In this example the communicator mode is BLANK and communications mode is CONT. The master keeps track of work allocated, and on an error just reallocates the work to any "free" surviving processes. Note that the code has to check if there is any surviving worker process left after each death is detected.

5.4. SUMMARY

In summarizing challenges associated with parallel programming for NoCs, let us recall main features of an ideal parallel program running on a NoC.

Such a program distributes computations and communications unevenly across processors and communications links, taking into account their actual performance during the execution of the code of the program. The distribution is not static and may be different not only for different NoCs but also for different executions of the program on the same NoC, depending on the workload of its elements. The program may find profitable to involve in computations not all available computers. This way the program will be efficiently portable.

The program keeps running even if some resources in the executing network fail. In the case of a resource failure, it is able to reconfigure itself and resume computations from some point in the past.

The program takes into account differences in machine arithmetic on different computers and avoids erroneous behavior of the program that might be caused by the differences.

This book focuses on the issue of portable efficiency of parallel programs for NoCs. The challenges associated with fault tolerance and machine arithmetic are beyond the scope of our discussion.

HPF provides some basic support for programming heterogeneous algorithms. It allows the programmer to specify uneven distribution of data across abstract HPF processors. Still it is the responsibility of the programmer to provide a code that analyses the implemented parallel algorithm and the executing NoC, and calculates the best distribution. Another problem is that the programmer cannot influence the mapping of abstract HPF processors to computers of the NoC. HPF provides no language constructs allowing the programmer to better control the mapping of heterogeneous algorithms to heterogeneous clusters. The HPF programmer should rely on some default mapping provided by the HPF compiler. The mapping cannot be sensitive to peculiarities of each individual algorithm just because the HPF compiler has no information about the peculiarities. Therefore, to control the mapping and account for both the peculiarities of the implemented parallel algorithm and the peculiarities of the executing heterogeneous environment, the HPF programmer needs to additionally write a good piece of complex code. HPF does not address fault tolerance at all.

As a general-purpose message-passing tool of the assembler level, MPI allows the programmer to write efficiently portable programs for NoCs. However, it provides no support to facilitate such programming. It is the responsibility of the programmer to write all the code that makes the application efficiently portable among NoCs. In other words, when programming for NoCs, a programmer must solve the extremely difficult problem of portable efficiency every time from scratch. Standard MPI also does not address the problem of fault tolerance.

We use in this book a high-level language, mpC, to introduce into parallel programming for NoCs. The language is designed to facilitate parallel programming for the common heterogeneous networks of computers. It addresses all the challenges associated with writing efficiently portable programs for NoCs.

Part II presents the main mpC language constructs and explains how they can be used for programming NoCs. It also introduces basic models underlying the language and the principles of its implementation.

PARALLEL PROGRAMMING FOR NETWORKS OF COMPUTERS WITH MPC AND HMPI

The mpC programming language is an extension of the ANSI C language designed specially for programming parallel computations on common networks of heterogeneous computers. HMPI (Heterogeneous MPI) is an extension of MPI obtained by applying the mpC parallel programming model to the message-passing library.

The main goal of parallel computing is to speed up the solution of a single problem. Just this differentiates parallel computing from distributed computing, where the main goal is to make software inherently distributed over different computers work together. In parallel computing the partitioning of the entire program into components running on different computers is a way to accelerate the program rather than an inherent property. Therefore in mpC the primary focus is on how to facilitate the development of highly efficient (and portable) applications that solve problems on common networks of computers.

## CHAPTER 6

Introduction to mpC

6.1. FIRST MPC PROGRAMS

A parallel mpC program is a set of parallel processes interacting (i.e., synchronizing their work and transferring data) by means of message passing. The mpC programmer cannot determine how many processes make up the program and which computers execute which processes. This is specified by some means external to the mpC language. The source mpC code determines only which process of the program performs which computations.

To begin, consider a simple program that does the same thing as the most famous C program, namely which is to output the text "Hello, world!" to the user's terminal:

```
#include <stdio.h>
int [*]main()
{
    [host]printf("Hello, world.\n");
}
```

The code of this mpC program differs very little from the code of the C program. The first difference is the [*] construct before the name main in the definition of the main function. This specifies the kind of the function and shows that code of this function will be executed by all processes of the parallel program. Functions similar to the function main are called *basic* functions in mpC. A basic function works correctly only if all processes of the parallel program call it. The mpC compiler controls the correctness of the basic function calls.

The second difference is construct [host] before the function name printf in the expression where this standard C library function is called. Unlike function main, function printf does not need to be called in parallel by all processes of the parallel program in order to work correctly.

Parallel Computing on Heterogeneous Networks, by Alexey Lastovetsky
ISBN 0-471-22982-2   Copyright © 2003 by John Wiley & Sons, Inc.

Moreover a call to the function in any single process of the parallel program makes sense and is correct. Such functions are called *nodal* in mpC.

The mpC language allows any single process of the parallel program to call a nodal function. Any group of processes is allowed to call a nodal function in parallel. In the program above, a call to function `printf` is only executed by a single process of the parallel program. Namely it is executed by a process that is associated with the user's terminal, which is the terminal from which the program was started. The mpC keyword `host` is always associated with this very process. So, in the execution of the program, all processes do nothing except that the host-process calls function `printf`.

The syntax of the next program

```
#include <stdio.h>
int [*]main()
{
  printf("Hello, world.\n");
}
```

differs even less from the syntax of the C "Hello, world!" program. Nevertheless, it describes more parallel computations than the previous mpC program. Namely, in its execution, *all* processes of the parallel program call function `printf`.

The result of this program depends on the operating environment. In some environments, the standard output of all the parallel processes will go to the user's terminal, from which the program was started. Then the user will see as many greetings "Hello, world!" on the terminal as many parallel processes will constitute the program—one greeting from each process. In other environments, the user will only see the greetings from the processes, running on the same computer as the host-process, or even a single greeting from the host-process.

Thus the program above may produce different results in different environments. This means that the program is not portable. This is a serious disadvantage of the program.

The next program outputs the greeting "Hello, world!" to the user's terminal from all processes of the parallel program:

```
#include <mpc.h>
int [*]main()
{
  MPC_Printf("Hello, world.\n");
}
```

Unlike the previous program, this program is portable. The mpC library function `MPC_Printf` guarantees that each process that calls this function outputs "Hello, world!" right to the user's terminal.

The third mpC program only differs from our first one by a richer content message, which the host-process sends to the user's terminal. Again, all of the other processes do nothing:

```
#include <stdio.h>
#include <sys/utsname.h>

int [*]main()
{
    struct utsname [host]un;

    [host]uname(&un);
    [host]printf("Hello world! Host-process runs on \"%s\".\n",
            un.nodename);
}
```

Note that, in addition to "Hello, world!" the host-process outputs the name of the computer that runs that process. To initiate this, we define variable un, which is allocated in the memory of the host-process (specified by the construct [host] before the name of this variable in the definition). After the host-process calls the nodal library function uname, member nodename of structure un will contain a pointer to the name of the computer running the process.

The next program sends messages with richer content to the user's terminal from all processes of the parallel program:

```
#include <mpc.h>
#include <sys/utsname.h>

int [*]main()
{
    struct utsname un;
    uname(&un);
    MPC_Printf("Hello world! I'm on \"%s\".\n",
            un.nodename);
}
```

In addition to greeting "Hello, world!" each process informs of the name of the computer that runs the process. This is because the *distributed* variable un is defined in the program. The variable is called distributed because each process of the parallel program holds a copy of this variable in its memory. Therefore the region of storage, represented by this variable, is distributed over the processes. Actually the distributed variable un is nothing more than a set of normal (undistributed) variables, each of which is called a *projection* of this distributed variable onto the corresponding process.

After each process of this parallel program calls function uname, member nodename of the corresponding projection of the distributed structure un will provide a pointer to the name of the computer, which runs the process. The value of a distributed variable or distributed expression, such as un.nodename or &un, is distributed over processes of the parallel program in natural way, and is called a *distributed* value.

The preceding mpC program depends on the Unix utsname library in obtaining the names of the computing nodes in the network. Therefore the program can be compiled and executed only on networks consisting of Unix computers. The next mpC program has the same functionality but provides more portability:

```c
#include <mpc.h>
#include <stdlib.h>

int [*]main()
{
  char *nodename;
  int namelen;

  MPC_Processor_name(&nodename, &namelen);
  MPC_Printf("Hello world! I'm on \"%s\".\n",
             nodename);
  free(nodename);
}
```

The program uses the mpC nodal library function MPC_Processor_name to get the name of the processor on which it is called. The name is returned as a character string. The function also returns the number of characters in the string. This program can be compiled and executed on networks of computers running different operating systems, and not only different clones of Unix. The function MPC_Processor_name allocates memory for the name of the processor, and it is the responsibility of the programmer to free the memory as soon as the name is no longer needed.

The next program extends the output of the preceding program with information about the total number of processes of the parallel program:

```c
#include <mpc.h>
#include <stdlib.h>

int [*]main()
{
  char *nodename;
  int namelen;
  repl int one;
  repl int number_of_processes;
```

```
MPC_Processor_name(&nodename, &namelen);
one = 1;
number_of_processes = one[+];
MPC_Printf("Hello world! I'm one of %d processes"
           "and run on \"%s\".\n", number_of_processes,
           nodename);
free(nodename);
}
```

The program defines two integer distributed variables, one and number_of_processes. All projections of variable one are assigned 1 as a result of evaluation of assignment one=1.

The result of applying the postfix reduction operator [+] to variable one will be a *distributed value* whose projection to any process will be equal to the sum of values of all projections of variable one. In other words, the projection of the value of expression one[+] to any process of the parallel program will be equal to the total number of processes. After the distributed value is assigned to the distributed variable number_of_processes, all of the projections of this variable will hold that value, which is the total number of processes of the parallel program.

The definition of the distributed variable one contains the mpC keyword repl (a short form of *replicated*). It informs the compiler that all projections of the value of the variable should be equal to each other in any expression of the program. Such distributed variables are called *replicated* in mpC (correspondingly, the value of a replicated variable is called a replicated value).

Replicated variables and expressions play an important role in mpC. The mpC compiler checks the property "to be replicated" declared by the programmer and warns about its possible violations.

Note that a simpler program,

```
#include <mpc.h>
#include <stdlib.h>

int [*]main()
{
  char *nodename;
  int namelen;

  MPC_Processor_name(&nodename, &namelen);
  MPC_Printf("Hello world! I'm one of %d processes"
             "and run on \"%s\".\n", MPC_Total_nodes(),
             nodename);
  free(nodename);
}
```

enables the same result as the previous program by using the mpC library function `MPC_Total_nodes`, which just returns the total number of processes of the parallel program. Besides, this program is more efficient because, unlike the evaluation of expression `one[+]`, a parallel call to function `MPC_Total_nodes` does not need data transfer between processes of the program.

In comparison the next program is less efficient:

```
#include <mpc.h>
#include <stdlib.h>

int [*]main()
{
  char *nodename;
  int namelen;
  int [host]local_one;
  repl int one;
  repl int number_of_processes;

  MPC_Processor_name(&nodename, &namelen);
  local_one = 1;
  one = local_one;
  number_of_processes = one[+];
  MPC_Printf("Hello world! I'm one of %d processes"
             "and run on \"%s\".\n", number_of_processes,
             nodename);
  free(nodename);
}
```

However, this program does demonstrate how assignment can be used to specify transferring data between processes of the mpC program. Variable `local_one` is allocated in memory of the host-process and initialized by 1. Variable `one` is replicated across processes of the parallel program. Execution of assignment `one=local_one` first broadcasts the value of variable `local_one` to all processes of the program, and then locally assigns the value to each projection of variable `one`.

6.2. NETWORKS

So far we considered mpC programs that involve in computations either all processes or only the host-process. However, the number of processes involved in parallel solution of a problem often depends on the problem itself and/or on the parallel algorithm of its solution. Moreover the number is often determined by input data.

To see this, consider a parallel algorithm that simulates the evolution of *N* groups of bodies under the influence of Newtonian gravitational attraction, using a single process for a single group of bodies. In the corresponding parallel computations exactly *N* processes will have to be involved independent of the total number of processes that would constitute the parallel mpC program implementing the algorithm. Recall that an mpC program is started by mechanisms external to the mpC language. The mpC programmer cannot specify the total number of processes of the program; the programmer can only obtain this number.

The following program gives a first introduction to such a language means that allows the programmer to describe the parallel computations on the necessary number of processes:

```
#include <mpc.h>
#define N 3

int [*]main()
{
   net SimpleNet(N) mynet;
   [mynet]MPC_Printf("Hello, world!\n");
}
```

The computations themselves are quite simple: each participating process just outputs "Hello, world!" to the user's terminal. But the number of participating processes, N=3, is defined by the programmer and does not depend on the total number of processes of the parallel program.

In mpC the notion of *network* corresponds to a group of processes jointly performing some parallel computations. An mpC network is an abstraction facilitating the work with actual processes of the parallel program (like the notion of data object and variable in programming languages facilitate the work with memory).

In the simplest case an mpC network is just a set of *abstract processors*. In order to program parallel computations, which must be executed by a given number of processes of the program, the programmer must first define a network consisting of this number of abstract processors, and then describe the parallel computations on this network.

The definition of an mpC network causes the creation of a group of processes that represent the network, whereby each abstract processor of the network is represented by a single process of the parallel program. The programmer's description of the parallel computations on the network leads to the execution of these parallel computations by exactly those processes, that represent the abstract processors of this network.

An important difference in the actual processes of the mpC program that separates them from the abstract mpC processors is that at different times of program execution the same process can represent different abstract processors of different mpC networks. In other words, the definition of an mpC network causes mapping of the abstract processors of this network to the actual processes of the parallel program, and this mapping is constant during the lifetime of this network.

The preceding program first defines the network mynet of N abstract processors, and then calls the nodal library function MPC_Printf on this network. The execution of this program consists in a parallel call of function MPC_Printf by those N processes of the program to which abstract processors of network mynet has been mapped. This mapping is performed at runtime. If the mapping cannot be performed (e.g., if N is greater than the total number of processes of the program), the program will terminate abnormally with corresponding diagnostics.

Note the similarity of language constructs [mynet] and [host]. Indeed, keyword host can be considered as the name of a pre-defined mpC network consisting of exactly one abstract processor that is always mapped to the host-process associated with the user's terminal.

The next program outputs messages from those processes of the parallel program to which abstract processors of network mynet are mapped:

```
#include <mpc.h>
#include <stdlib.h>
#define N 3

int [*]main()
{
  net SimpleNet(N) mynet;
  char *[mynet]nodename;
  int [mynet]namelen;

  [mynet]MPC_Processor_name(&nodename, &namelen);
  [mynet]MPC_Printf("Hello world! I'm on \"%s\".\n",
                    nodename);
  [mynet]free(nodename);
}
```

In addition to "Hello, world!" each involved process outputs the name of the computer that executes the process. In so doing, the program defines variables nodename and namelen, both *distributed over network* mynet. Only a process that represents one of abstract processors of network mynet holds in its memory a copy of variables nodename and namelen. Only those processes call function MPC_Processor_name that are specified with construct [mynet] before the function name. After this call each projection of the distributed variable nodename will point to the name of the computer running the corresponding process.

The semantics of the next mpC program is completely equivalent to that of the previous program:

```
#include <mpc.h>
#include <stdlib.h>
#define N 3

int [*]main()
{
  net SimpleNet(N) mynet;
  char *[mynet]nodename;
  int [mynet]namelen;

  [mynet]:
    {
      MPC_Processor_name(&nodename, &namelen);
      MPC_Printf("Hello world! I'm on \"%s\".\n",
                 nodename);
      free(nodename);
    }
}
```

However, because of the use of a special *distributed label*, [mynet], this program has a simpler syntax. Any statement labeled with a distributed label (here it is a compound statement) will be executed only by the abstract processors of the network, whose name is used in the label.

The next mpC program demonstrates that the number of abstract processors of an mpC network can be specified dynamically, that is, at runtime:

```
#include <stdlib.h>
#include <mpc.h>

int [*]main(int [host]argc, char **[host]argv)
{
 repl n;

 if(argc<2)
   n=1;
 else
   n=[host]atoi(argv[1]);

 if(n<1)
   [host]printf("Wrong input (%d processes required).\n", [host]n);
 else if(n>MPC_Total_nodes())
```

```
[host]printf("Too many processes required (%d against %d available).\n",
          [host]n,
          [host]MPC_Total_nodes());
else
{
  net SimpleNet(n) mynet;
  char *[mynet]nodename;
  int [mynet]namelen;

  [mynet]MPC_Processor_name(&nodename, &namelen);
  [mynet]MPC_Printf("Hello world! I'm on \"%s\".\n",
                nodename);
  [mynet]free(nodename);
}
MPC_Printf("* ");
}
```

This program treats its only external argument as a processor number. The user specifies the argument when starting up the program. This argument is accessible to the host-process.

The expression [host]atoi(argv[1]) is evaluated on the host-process, and its value is then assigned to the integer variable n, which is replicated over all processes of the parallel program. The execution of this assignment consists in broadcasting this value to all processes of the program, where it is assigned to the corresponding projection of variable n.

Before the program defines (creates) a network of the user-specified number of abstract processors and executes the described computations on the network, it checks the correctness of input data. If the specified number of abstract processors is incorrect (less than 1 or greater than the total number of processes of the parallel program), the program outputs to the corresponding diagnostics.

Otherwise, the program defines network mynet consisting of n abstract processors as well as variables nodename and namelen distributed over this network. Then the nodal function MPC_Processor_name is called on network mynet, resulting in each projection of the distributed variable nodename pointing to the name of the computer where the corresponding abstract processor has been placed. Next a call to the nodal function MPC_Printf on network mynet outputs from each abstract processor the greeting "Hello, world!" together with the name of the computer hosting this abstract processor. Finally, a call to the nodal function free on network mynet releases the memory allocated for the computer name on each of abstract processors of this network.

The lifetimes of both network mynet and variables nodename and namelen are limited by the block in which they are defined. When the execution of the block ends, all processes of the program, which have been taken for abstract processors of network mynet, are freed and can be used for other networks. Such mpC networks are called *automatic*.

The lifetimes of *static* networks are only limited by the time of program execution. The next two mpC programs demonstrate the difference between static and automatic networks. The programs look almost identical. Both consist in a cyclic execution of the block that defines a network and executes already familiar computations on the network. The only essential difference is that the first program defines an automatic network, whereas the second defines a static network.

The first program is as follows:

```
#include <mpc.h>
#define Nmin 3
#define Nmax 5


int  [*]main()
{
 repl n;

 for(n=Nmin; n<=Nmax; n++)
 {
   auto net SimpleNet(n) mynet;
   char *[mynet]nodename;
   int [mynet]namelen;

   [mynet]MPC_Processor_name(&nodename, &namelen);
   [mynet]MPC_Printf("I'm from a %d-processor automatic network"
                  " on\"%s\".\n",
                  [mynet]n,nodename);
   [mynet]free(nodename);
 }
}
```

During execution of this program, at the first loop iteration (n=Nmin=3) a network of three abstract processors is created on the entry into the block, and this network is destructed when execution of the block ends. At the second loop iteration (n=4) a new network of four abstract processors is created on the entry into the block, and that network is also destructed when execution of the block ends. So at the time of the repeated initialization of the loop (evaluation of expression n++), the four-processor network no longer exists. Finally, at the last iteration an automatic network of five virtual processors (n=Nmax=5) is created on the entry into the block.

The mpC program demonstrating the use of static networks is as follows:

```
#include <mpc.h>
#define Nmin 3
#define Nmax 5
```

```
int [*]main()
{
  repl n;

  for(n=Nmin; n<=Nmax; n++)
  {
    static net SimpleNet(n) mynet;
    char *[mynet]nodename;
    int [mynet]namelen;

    [mynet]MPC_Processor_name(&nodename, &namelen);
    [mynet]MPC_Printf("I'm from the %d-processor static network"
                " on \"%s\".\n",
                [mynet]n, nodename);
    [mynet]free(nodename);
  }
}
```

During execution of the program, at the first loop iteration a network of three virtual processors is also created on the entry into the block, but this network is not deconstructed when the execution of the block ends. It simply becomes invisible. Thus here the block is not a region where the network exists but a region of its visibility. Now, at the time of the repeated initialization of the loop and evaluation of the loop condition, the static three-processor network exists but is not available because these points of the program are out of scope of the network name mynet. On the next entries into the block at subsequent loop iterations, no new networks are created, but the static network, which was created on the first entry into the block, becomes visible.

Thus, whereas in the first program the same name mynet denotes absolutely different networks at different loop iterations, in the second program this name denotes a unique network existing from the first entry in the block, in which it is defined, until the end of program execution.

If the kind of mpC network is not specified explicitly by using keyword auto or static in its definition, the network will be considered either automatic, when declared inside a function, or static, when declared out of any function. So all networks in mpC programs in this section, except the last two programs, are implicitly declared automatic.

6.3. NETWORK TYPE

By now in our mpC programs all abstract processors of the same network have performed the same computations. Therefore there was no need to separate the different abstract processors inside the network. But, if a parallel algorithm needs different processes to execute differrent computations, means to separate abstract processors inside the network are needed.

The mpC language provides the programmer with such means. In particular, it allows the programmer to associate abstract processors of any network with a coordinate system and identify a single abstract processor by specifying its coordinates in this coordinate system.

Generally speaking, in mpC one cannot simply define a network but only a network of a type. *Type* is the most important attribute of a network. In particular, it determines how to access separate abstract processors of the network.

The type specification is a mandatory part of any network definition. Therefore any network definition should be preceded by a definition of the corresponding network type. In all of the mpC programs considered so far, the network type SimpleNet was used in the network definitions. A definition of this network type is in the header file mpc.h among other standard definitions of the mpC language, and it was included in these programs with the include directive. This definition appears as follows:

```
nettype SimpleNet(int n)
{
   coord I=n;
};
```

It introduces name SimpleNet of the network, whose type is parameterized with the integer parameter n. The body of the definition declares the *coordinate variable* I ranging from 0 to n-1. Type SimpleNet is the simplest parameterized network type that describes networks consisting of n abstract processors well-ordered by their positions on the coordinate line.

The next application demonstrates how different computations on different abstract processors of the same network can be specified in mpC:

```
#include <mpc.h>
#define N 5

int [*]main()
{
 net SimpleNet(N) mynet;
 int [mynet]my_coordinate;

 my_coordinate = I coordof mynet;
 if(my_coordinate%2==0)
    [mynet]MPC_Printf("Hello, even world! My coordinate is %d.\n",
                my_coordinate);
 else
```

```
[mynet]MPC_Printf("Hello, odd world! My coordinate is %d.\n",
                 my_coordinate);
}
```

This program uses the binary operator `coordof` with the coordinate variable
`I` and network `mynet` as its left and right operands respectively. The result is
an integer value distributed over network `mynet`. The projection of this value
to each abstract processor of this network will be equal to the value of coordinate `I` of this abstract processor in network `mynet`.

After evaluation of assignment

```
my_coordinate = I coordof mynet,
```

each projection of variable `my_coordinate` will hold the coordinate of the
corresponding abstract processor of network `mynet`. As a result abstract
processors with even coordinates will output messages beginning with greeting "Hello, even world!" while processors with odd coordinates will output
messages that begin with "Hello, odd world!"

The order in which messages from different abstract processors of `mynet`
will appear on the user's terminal is not defined. It may depend, for example,
on the order in which the mesages arrive at the host-computer.

The next mpC program defines a network whose abstract processors are
associated with a two-dimensional coordinate system:

```
#include <mpc.h>

nettype Mesh(int m, int n)
{
  coord I=m, J=n;
};

#define M 2
#define N 3

int [*]main()
{
  net Mesh(M,N) mynet;

  [mynet]:
    {
      char *nodename;
      int namelen;

      MPC_Processor_name(&nodename, &namelen);
      MPC_Printf("I'm on \"%s\". My coordinates are (%d, %d).\n",
```

```
            nodename,
        I coordof nodename,
        J coordof nodename);
    free(nodename);
    }
}
```

Each abstract processor of network `mynet` outputs its coordinates and the name of the computer hosting the abstract processor. Note that in this program variable `nodename` is used as the second operand of operator `coordof`, and not network `mynet`. In general, the second operand of operator `coordof` may be either an expression or a network. If it is an expression, then the expression is not evaluated. It is only used to determine the network over which this expression is distributed. And then the operator will be executed as if that network is its second operand.

6.4. NETWORK PARENT

We just saw that the lifetime of an automatic network is limited by the block in which the network is defined. When the execution of the block ends, the network ceases to exist, and all processes taken for virtual processors of the network are freed and can be used for other networks.

The question is how the computational result on an automatic network can be saved and used in further computations. Our previous programs did not raise this issue because the only result of parallel computations on networks is output of the some messages to the user's terminal.

Actually the mpC networks are not entirely independent of each other. A newly created network has one abstract processor that is shared with an already existing network (or with several already existing networks). That abstract processor is called a *parent* of this newly created network. The parent is the very connecting link through which the computational results are passed if the network ceases to exist.

The parent of a network is always specified by its definition, explicitly or implicitly. So far no network was defined with explicit specification of its parent. The parent was specified implicitly, and the parent was nothing other than the abstract host-processor. The solution is obvious, for at any time of program execution the existence of only one network can be guaranteed. This network is the network `host`, that is, a pre-defined network consisting of only the abstract processor, which is always mapped onto the host-process associated with the user's terminal.

The next mpC application implements almost the same functionality as does the first program in Section 6.3, but it does this without the help of the `MPC_Printf` function:

```
#include <mpc.h>
#include <stdio.h>
#define N 5
#define MAX_MSG_LEN 64

int [*]main()
{
  net SimpleNet(N) mynet;
  int [mynet]my_coordinate;
  repl [mynet]j;
  char [mynet]my_message[MAX_MSG_LEN];
  char [host]msg_buffer[MAX_MSG_LEN];

  my_coordinate = I coordof mynet;
  if(my_coordinate%2==0)
    [mynet]sprintf(my_message, "Hello, even world! "
                   "My coordinate is %d.\n",
                   my_coordinate);
  else
    [mynet]sprintf(my_message, "Hello, odd world! "
                   "My coordinate is %d.\n",
                   my_coordinate);
  for(j=0; j<N; j++)
  {
    msg_buffer[] = [mynet:I==j]my_message[];
    [host]printf("%s", msg_buffer);
  }
}
```

First each abstract processor of network mynet locally forms a message that will be output to the user's terminal. The processor stores the message in its projection (a local copy) of the distributed character array my_message. Abstract processors of mynet do it in parallel by calling the nodal library function sprintf. Then all of the abstract processors of network mynet execute in parallel a for loop.

At the very first iteration of the loop (j=0) all processors, except the abstract host-processor, do nothing. Indeed, the parent of any network of type SimpleNet has coordinate 0 in the network. The parent of network mynet is the host-processor. Therefore specifiers [mynet:I==0] and [host] designate the same abstract processor. Array msg_buffer is also located on this abstract processor. As a result all data processed at the first iteration are located on the abstract host-processor. At this iteration the host-processor executes the following computations:

```
msg_buffer[] = my_message[];
printf("%s", msg_buffer);
```

Recall that the mpC language is a superset of the C[ ] language that allows the programmer to explicitly describe operations on arrays (see Section 2.6.2). In particular, C[ ] code

```
msg_buffer[] = my_message[]
```

assigns the value of the *i*th element of array my_message to the *i*th element of array msg_buffer ($i = 0, \ldots,$ MAX_MSG_LEN-1).

The second iteration of this loop (j=1) involves the host-processor and abstract processor with coordinate 1. All other processors of mynet just do nothing. During execution of statement

```
msg_buffer[] = [mynet:I==1]my_message[];
```

the value of array my_message (a vector of MAX_MSG_LEN characters) is first sent from processor 1 to the host-processor, where it is assigned to array msg_buffer. Statement

```
[host]printf("%s", msg_buffer);
```

is then executed on the host-processor and outputs msg_buffer to the user's terminal. Similarly the third iteration (j=2) is executed by the host-processor and abstract processor 2, and so on.

Unlike the mpC program using MPC_Printf, this program defines the order in which messages from different abstract processors of network mynet will appear on the user's terminal. The order is determined by the order of execution of iterations of the for loop by the host-processor, that is, by the very abstract processor that outputs the messages to the user's terminal. Therefore a message from processor 0 (the host-processor) always appears first, a message from processor 1 appears second, and so on.

The next mpC program is completely equivalent to the second program in Section 6.3, except that the parent of network mynet is specified explicitly:

```
#include <mpc.h>

nettype Mesh(int m, int n)
{
    coord I=m, J=n;
    parent [0,0];
};

#define M 2
#define N 3

int [*]main()
{
```

```
net Mesh(M,N) [host]mynet;

[mynet]:
  {
    char *nodename;
    int namelen;

    MPC_Processor_name(&nodename, &namelen);
    MPC_Printf("I'm on \"%s\". My coordinates are (%d, %d).\n",
            nodename,
            I coordof nodename,
            J coordof nodename);
  free(nodename);
  }
}
```

One more difference can be found in the definition of network type Mesh. Line

parent [0,0];

has been added, which explicitly specifies coordinates of the parent in a network of the type Mesh. By default, the coordinates are also set to zeros. Should for any reason we need the parent of network mynet to have not the least but the greatest coordinates, line

parent [m-1,n-1];

has to be used in the definition of network type Mesh instead of line

parent [0,0]; .

By now at most one network has existed at any time of the mpC program execution. This is not a restriction of the mpC language. The mpC language allows the programmer to write programs with an arbitrary number of simultaneously existing (and visible) networks. The only limitation is the total number of processes of the parallel program.

The next program defines three networks net1, net2, and net3 that exist simultaneously:

```
#include <mpc.h>


nettype TrivialNet(int n, int m)
{
```

```
   coord I=n;
   parent [m];
};


int [*]main()
{
   [host]MPC_Printf("I'm host. I'll be a parent of net1.\n\n");
   {
     net TrivialNet(3,0) net1;
     int [net1]mycoordinnet1;

     mycoordinnet1 = I coordof net1;
     [net1]:
       if(mycoordinnet1)
          MPC_Printf("I'm a regular member of net1. "
                     "My coordinate in net1 is %d.\n"
                     " I'll be a parent of net%d.\n\n",
                     mycoordinnet1, mycoordinnet1+1);
       else
          MPC_Printf("I'm a parent of net1. "
                     "My coordinate in net1 is %d.\n\n",
                     mycoordinnet1);
       {
          net TrivialNet(3,1) [net1:I==1]net2;
          net TrivialNet(3,2) [net1:I==2]net3;

          [net2]:
            {
               int mycoordinnet2;

               mycoordinnet2 = I coordof net2;
               if(mycoordinnet2!=1)
                  MPC Printf("I'm a regular member of net2."
                             "My coordinate in net2 is %d.\n\n",
                             mycoordinnet2);
       else
          MPC_Printf("I'm a parent of net2. "
                     "My coordinate in net2 is %d.\n\n",
                     mycoordinnet2);
   }
   [net3]:
       {
       int mycoordinnet3;
```

```
        mycoordinnet3 = I coordof net3;
      if(mycoordinnet3!=2)
         MPC_Printf("I'm a regular member of net3. "
                    "My coordinate in net3 is %d.\n\n",
                    mycoordinnet3);
      else
         MPC_Printf("I'm a parent of net3. "
                    "My coordinate in net3 is %d.\n\n",
                    mycoordinnet3);
    }
  }
  [net1]:
      if(mycoordinnet1)
         MPC_Printf("I'm a regular member of net1. "
                    "My coordinate in net1 is %d.\n"
                    " I was a parent of net%d.\n\n",
                    mycoordinnet1, mycoordinnet1+1);
  }
  [host]MPC_Printf("I'm host. I was a parent of
                    net1.\n\n");
}
```

The parent of network net1 is the abstract host-processor. This is specified implicitly by the definition of this network. The parent of network net2 is the abstract processor of network net1 with coordinate 1. This is specified explicitly by using construct [net1:I==1] in the definition of network net2. The parent of network net3 is the abstract processor of network net1 with coordinate 2, which is also specified explicitly in the definition of network net3.

6.5. SYNCHRONIZATION OF PROCESSES

We mentioned earlier that an mpC parallel program is a set of parallel processes synchronizing their work and transferring data by message passing. The small subset of the mpC language, as was introduced, allows the programmer to specify the number of processes involved in the parallel computations and to distribute the computations among the processes. In principle, this subset of mpC is sufficient for synchronization of the processes during execution of the parallel program.

The basic synchronization mechanism for parallel processes interacting via message passing is a *barrier*. A barrier is a section of the parallel program where processes synchronizing their work wait for each other. The processes that do the synchronizing may leave the barrier and resume their computations only after all processes have entered this section. If for some reason one of the processes does not enter the barrier, all other processes will "hang" in this section of the program, and the program itself will never terminate normally.

Some barriers in the mpC applications are implicit. They are generated by the mpC compiler. However, mpC programmers can explicitly put barriers in their applications.

Consider, for example, the first program in Section 6.3 that outputs to the user's terminal different messages from abstract processors with even and odd coordinates. This program does not define an order in which messages from different abstract processors of mynet appear on the user's terminal. The order is not defined even under the assumption that a call to MPC_Printf is *synchronous* and thus can complete successfully only if the corresponding message has appeared on the user's terminal. However, messages directed to the host-computer may not arrive in the same order as parallel processes calling function MPC_Printf have sent them.

Let us slightly modify this program to guarantee that if a call to MPC_Printf is synchronous, then messages from abstract processors with odd coordinates come to the user's terminal only after messages from abstract processors with even coordinates. The modified mpC program is as follows:

```
#include <mpc.h>
#define N 5

int [*]main()
{
  net SimpleNet(N) mynet;
  int [mynet]my_coordinate;

  my_coordinate = I coordof mynet;
  if(my_coordinate%2==0)
    [mynet]MPC_Printf("Hello, even world! My coordinate is %d.\n",
                  my_coordinate);
  Barrier:
  {
    int [host]bs[N], [mynet]b=1;

    bs[]=b;
    b=bs[];

  }
  if(my_coordinate%2==1)
    [mynet]MPC_Printf("Hello, odd world! My coordinate is %d.\n",
                  my_coordinate);
}
```

To achive this result, a barrier section is inserted between calls to MPC_Printf made by the abstract processors of network mynet with even and odd coordinates.

The barrier section has the form of a block labeled `Barrier`. This block defines array bs located on the virtual host-process and variable b distributed over the network `mynet`. The number of elements in array bs is equal to the number of abstract processors in network `mynet`.

Assignment

```
bs[] = b
```

is evaluated by all abstract processors of network `mynet` as follows: Processor with coordinate I=i sends the value of its projection of variable b to the abstract host-processor, where this value is assigned to bs[i] (i=0,..., N−1). Assignment

```
b = bs[]
```

is also evaluated by all abstract processors of network `mynet`. The host-processor sends the value of bs[i] to abstract processor with coordinate I=i, where this value is assigned to b (i=0,...,N−1).

Assume that the abstract host-processor has not entered the block. In that case no other abstract processor of network `mynet` can complete the second assignment and leave the block, because it must receive a value from the host-processor in order to complete the operation.

Assume now that some abstract processor of network `mynet` different from the host-processor has not entered the block. Here the host-processor cannot complete the first assignment because it must receive a value from this abstract processor in order to complete this operation.

Thus no abstract processor of `mynet` can leave the block until all processors of this network enter it. This shows that the barrier block is nothing more than a means of synchronizing the abstract processors of network `mynet`.

The mpC language does not specify whether a call to `MPC_Printf` is synchronous or not. If it is asynchronous, then the barrier cannot guarantee that messages from even abstract processors appear first on the user's terminal. In that case it can only guarantee that messages from even processors start the race first, but it cannot guarantee that they finish first. In general, the properties of communication operations in mpC are the same as those in MPI.

The next mpC program implements explicit barrier synchronization in a simpler and more concise way:

```
#include <mpc.h>
#define N 5

int [*]main()
{
```

```
net SimpleNet(N) mynet;
int [mynet]my_coordinate;

my_coordinate = I coordof mynet;
if(my_coordinate%2==0)
   [mynet]MPC_Printf("Hello, even world! My coordinate is %d.\n",
                     my_coordinate);
Barrier:
{
  int [mynet]b=1;
  b[+];
}
  if(my_coordinate%2==1)
   [mynet]MPC_Printf("Hello, odd world! My coordinate is %d.\n",
                     my_coordinate);
}
```

The efficiency of this barrier section could hardly be made worse. The most obvious implementation of operator [+] only differs from the barrier in the preceding program by an additional summation on the host-processor. The execution time of the summation is too short compared to the time of data transfer.

Actually mpC programmers do not need to invent different ways to implement barriers. The mpC language provides two library functions that efficiently implement the barrier synchronization for the operating environment of the parallel program. First, the basic function MPC_Global_barrier synchronizes all processes of the parallel program. Its declaration is in header mpc.h and is stated as follows:

```
int [*]MPC_Global_barrier(void);.
```

Next the program demonstrates the use of this function:

```
#include <mpc.h>
#define N 5

int [*]main()
{
  net SimpleNet(N) mynet;
  int [mynet]my_coordinate;

  my_coordinate = I coordof mynet;
  if(my_coordinate%2==0)
     [mynet]MPC_Printf("Hello, even world! My coordinate is %d.\n",
                       my_coordinate);
```

```
MPC_Global_barrier();
if(my_coordinate%2==1)
   [mynet]MPC_Printf("Hello, odd world! My coordinate is %d.\n",
                     my_coordinate);
}
```

Unlike the two previous programs, all processes of this program, and not only those implementing network `mynet`, participate in the barrier synchronization. Naturally this implies a greater number of messages transferring during the execution of the barrier and hence some deceleration of the process.

6.6. NETWORK FUNCTIONS

The library function `MPC_Barrier` allows the synchronization of the abstract processors of the specified mpC network. The next program demonstrates how this function is used:

```
#include <mpc.h>
#define N 5

int [*]main()
{
 net SimpleNet(N) mynet;
 int [mynet]my_coordinate;

 my_coordinate = I coordof mynet;
 if(my_coordinate%2==0)
   [mynet]MPC_Printf("Hello, even world! My coordinate is %d.\n",
                     my_coordinate);
 ([(N)mynet])MPC_Barrier();
 if(my_coordinate%2==1)
   [mynet]MPC_Printf("Hello, odd world! My coordinate is %d.\n",
                     my_coordinate);
 }
```

Note that in this program only the processes that implement network `mynet` participate in the barrier synchronization. A call to function `MPC_Barrier` looks unusual in that it differs from all functions we have dealt with before. It is an example of a *network* function.

Unlike the basic functions, which are always executed by all processes of the parallel program, a network function is executed on a network. Therefore network functions can be executed in parallel with other network or nodal functions.

Unlike the nodal functions, which can also be executed in parallel by abstract processors of a network, the network function can in its execution include data transfer between abstract processors. This makes the network functions somewhat similar to the basic functions.

Function MPC_Barrier is declared in the header file mpc.h as

```
int [net SimpleNet(n) w] MPC_Barrier(void);
```

The network function has a special *network* parameter that represents the network executing the function. In the declaration of the network function, the specification of its network parameter is in brackets just before the name of the function. This specification looks like a network definition.

In the declaration of function MPC_Barrier, the network parameter is specified as

```
net SimpleNet(n) w
```

In addition to formal network w executing function MPC_Barrier, this declaration introduces parameter n of this network. Like "normal" function parameters, this parameter is available in the body of the function as if it were declared with the specifiers repl and const. Since in the definition of the network type SimpleNet, parameter n is declared of type int, it is treated in the body of function MPC_Barrier as if it were a normal parameter of this function declared as follows:

```
repl int const n
```

All "normal" parameters of a network function are considered distributed over the network specified by its special network parameter. Thus the integer constant parameter n replicated over network w determines the number of abstract processors of this network.

If function MPC_Barrier were not a library function, it might be defined as in the following mpC application:

```
#include <mpc.h>
#define N 5

int [net SimpleNet(n) w] MPC_Barrier(void)
  {
  int [w:parent]bs[n], [w]b=1;
  bs[]=b;
  b=bs[];
  }
```

```
int [*]main()
{
  net SimpleNet(N) mynet;
  int [mynet]my_coordinate;

  my_coordinate = I coordof mynet;
  if(my_coordinate%2==0)
    [mynet]MPC_Printf("Hello, even world! My coordinate is %d.\n",
                       my_coordinate);
  ([(N)mynet])MPC_Barrier();
  if(my_coordinate%2==1)
    [mynet]MPC_Printf("Hello, odd world! My coordinate is %d.\n",
                       my_coordinate);
}
```

The body of the function MPC_Barrier defines array bs of n elements and variable b. Array bs is located on the parent of network w, which is specified with construct [w:parent] before the name of this array. Variable b is distributed over network w. The two statements that follow the definition implement a barrier for abstract processors of network w.

In the program above, a call to function MPC_Barrier passes network mynet as an argument for network parameter w. It also passes a value for parameter n of network type SimpleNet. At a first glance the latter may look redundant, since a data structure that represents network mynet is supposed to keep all essential information about this network, including its parameters. Therefore one could presume that a value for parameter n is available in function MPC_Barrier via the data structure assigned to its network parameter. But the fact is that a network of any type, not only of type SimpleNet, may be passed to this function as a network argument. The next mpC program demonstrates this possibility:

```
#include <mpc.h>
nettype Mesh(int m, int n) {
  coord I=m, J=n;
  parent [0,0];
};

#define M 2
# define N 3

int [*]main()
{
  net Mesh(M,N) [host]mynet;
  [mynet]:
  {
```

```
char *nodename;
int namelen;

MPC_Processor_name(&nodename, &namelen);
if(I coordof mynet == 0)
  MPC_Printf("I'm on \"%s\" and have coordinates (%d, %d).\n",
             nodename, I coordof mynet,
             J coordof mynet);

([(M*N)mynet])MPC_Barrier();
if(I coordof mynet != 0)
  MPC_Printf("I'm on \"%s\" and have coordinates (%d, %d).\n",
             nodename, I coordof mynet,
             J coordof mynet);
}
}
```

Network `mynet` of type `Mesh` is used in this program as a network argument in a call to function `MPC_Barrier`. However, function `MPC_Barrier` only *treats* the group of processes, on which it is called, as representing an mpC network of type `SimpleNet`. Data passed to function `MPC_Barrier` with network argument `mynet`, such as values for parameters m and n of network type `Mesh`, cannot help to calculate the value for parameter n of this function. Therefore this value must be explicitly provided as a part of the function call.

In general, a network argument in a call to a network function may be an mpC network of any network type that is different from the network type T_p of the network parameter of this function. There may be many different ways to interpret abstract processors passed via the network argument as a network of type T_p. Explicit provision in the function call values of the T_p parameters specifies how exactly these abstract processors are interpreted as abstract processors constituting a network of type T_p.

The next program demonstrates a situation where different values for network-type parameters in a call to a network function interpret differently the abstract processors of the passed network argument in this function:

```
#include <mpc.h>
#define N 6

nettype Mesh(int m, int n)
{
  coord I=m, J=n;
```

```
  parent [0,0];
};

int [net Mesh(m,n) w] My_Barrier( void )
{
  int [w:parent]bs[m*n], [w]b=1;

  MPC_Printf("Regards from My_Barrier. "
             "My coordinates here are (%d, %d).\n",
             I coordof w, J coordof w);
  bs[]=b;
  b=bs[];
}

int [*]main()
{
  net SimpleNet(N) mynet;
  int [mynet]my_coordinate;

  my_coordinate = I coordof mynet;

  ([(1,N)mynet])My_Barrier();
  if(my_coordinate%2==0)
    mynet]MPC_Printf("Hello, even world!\n");

  ([(3,N/3)mynet])My_Barrier();
  if(my_coordinate%2==1)
    [mynet]MPC_Printf("Hello, odd world!\n");
}
```

The abstract processors of network mynet will be arranged differently inside function My_Barrier during two calls to this network function. During the first call, they are interpreted as a 1 × 6 processor arrangement. During the second call, they are interpreted as a 3 × 2 processor arrangement. Therefore these two calls will result in different messages coming to the user's terminal from the same abstract processor.

In general, different values for network-type parameters of a network function will result in different computations performed by the function.

6.7. SUBNETWORKS

Let us recall once more the fact that a parallel mpC program is a set of parallel processes synchronizing work and interchanging data by means of message passing. The mpC language as it has been introduced allows the programmer to specify the number of processes necessary for parallel solution of the problem, to distribute computations among the processes, and to synchronize their work during the execution of the parallel program. But these means obviously are not sufficient for the specification of data transfer between processes.

So far either all processes of the parallel program or all abstract processors of one or another network took part in the data transfer. The data transfer mainly consisted in broadcasting some value to all participating processes or in gathering values from all participating processes on one of them.

More complicated data transfer, such as that between groups of abstract processors of an mpC network or a parallel exchange between neighboring abstract processors of the network, cannot be specified in the mpC language as it has been presented so far.

The basic mpC device for describing complicated communications is the *subnetwork*. Any subset of the total set of abstract processors of a network constitutes a subnetwork of this network. For example, any row or column of a network of type Mesh(m,n) is a subnetwork of the network.

Consider the following mpC program:

```
#include <mpc.h>
#include <string.h>
#include <mpc.h>

nettype Mesh(int m, int n)
{
   coord I=m, J=n;
   parent [0,0];
};

#define MAXLEN 256

int [*]main()
{
   net Mesh(2,3) [host]mynet;

   [mynet]:
   {
      char *nodename, me[MAXLEN], neighbor[MAXLEN];
      int namelen;
      subnet [mynet:I==0]row0, [mynet:I==1]row1;

      MPC_Processor_name(&nodename, &namelen);
      strcpy(me, nodename);
      free(nodename);
      [row0]neighbor[] = [row1]me[];
```

```
       [row1]neighbor[] = [row0]me[];
       MPC_Printf("I'm on \"%s\" and have coordinates (%d, %d),\n"
                  "My neighbor with coordinates"
                  "(%d, %d) is on \"%s\".\n\n",
                  me, I coordof mynet, J coordof mynet,
                  (I coordof mynet + 1)%2,
                  J coordof mynet, neighbor);
   }
}
```

In this program each abstract processor of network `mynet` of type `Mesh(2,3)` outputs to the user's terminal not only the name of the computer hosting this abstract processor but also the name of the computer that hosts its closest neighbor from other row of abstract processors. In so doing, the program defines two subnetworks `row0` and `row1` of network `mynet`. Subnetwork `row0` consists of all abstract processors of network `mynet` whose coordinate `I` is equal to zero, that is, corresponds to the zeroth processor row of network `mynet`. This fact is specified with construct `[mynet:I==0]` before the name of this subnetwork in its definition. Similarly subnetwork `row1` corresponds to the first processor row of network `mynet`.

In general, logical expressions describing abstract processors of subnetworks can be complex leading to the specification of very sophisticated subnetworks. For example, the expression

```
I<J && J%2==0
```

specifies abstract processors of a network of type `Mesh(m,n)` that are over the main diagonal of the $m \times n$ processor arrangement in even columns.

Assignment

```
[row0]neighbor[] = [row1]me[]
```

is evaluated in parallel by abstract processors of network `mynet`. During this evaluation each abstract processor of row `row1` sends the value of its projection of distributed array `me` (a vector of `MAXLEN` characters) to the abstract processor of row `row0` with the same coordinate `J`, where the vector is assigned to the projection of distributed array `neighbor` (`j=0,1,2`).

Similarly, during evaluation of assignment

```
[row1]neighbor[] = [row0]me[]
```

abstract processors of row `row0` send in parallel the value of their projection of distributed array `me` to abstract processors of row `row1` with the same

coordinate J, where it is assigned to the projection of the distributed array
neighbor.

As a result, on the abstract processor with coordinates (0,j), array
neighbor will contain the name of the computer, which hosts the abstract
processor with coordinates (1,j). On the abstract processor with coordinates
(1,j), this array will contain the name of the computer hosting the abstract
processor with coordinates (0,j).

The next mpC program demonstrates that the subnetwork can be defined
implicitly:

```
#include <stdlib.h>
#include <string.h>
#include <mpc.h>


nettype Mesh(int m, int n)
{
   coord I=m, J=n;
   parent [0,0];
};


#define MAXLEN 256


int [*]main()
{
   net Mesh(2,3) [host]mynet;

   [mynet]:
   {
      char *nodename, me[MAXLEN], neighbor[MAXLEN];
      int namelen;
      MPC_Processor_name(&nodename, &namelen);
      strcpy(me, nodename);
      free(nodename);
      [mynet:I==0]neighbor[] = [mynet:I==1]me[];
      [mynet:I==1]neighbor[] = [mynet:I==0]me[];
      MPC_Printf("I'm on \"%s\" and have coordinates (%d, %d),\n"
                 "My neighbor with coordinates"
                 "(%d, %d) is on \"%s\".\n\n",
                 me, I coordof mynet, J coordof mynet,
                 (I coordof mynet + 1)%2,
                 J coordof mynet, neighbor);
   }
}
```

The only difference of this program from the previous one is that the row sub-networks are not defined explicitly. In this particular case, usage of implicitly defined subnetworks is justified because it simplifies the program code without a loss of the program efficiency or functionality. But there may be situations where explicit definition of subnetworks cannot be avoided. For example, network functions cannot be called on implicitly defined subnetworks but only on explicitly defined ones.

6.8. A SIMPLE HETEROGENEOUS ALGORITHM SOLVING AN IRREGULAR PROBLEM

In Section 6.2 we saw that the definition of an mpC network causes mapping of abstract processors of this network to processes of the parallel program, and that this mapping is constant during the lifetime of this network. But we did not discuss how the programming system performs this mapping, and how the programmer can control it.

It has been multiply emphasized in this book that the main goal of parallel computing is to accelerate the solution of a single problem on the available computer resources. Therefore it is quite natural that the mapping of abstract processors of the mpC network to parallel processes of the mpC program should be performed in such a way that minimizes the execution time of this program.

The mapping is performed by the mpC programming system based on two types of information. On the one hand, this is information about the network of computers that executes the program. Relative speeds of processors of this network are an example of that type of information.

On the other hand, this is information about the parallel algorithm, which is performed by the mpC network. Relative volumes of computations, which must be performed by abstract processors of the network, are an example of algorithmic information that can be provided by the mpC programmer.

We have not yet specified the volumes of computations in our programs. Therefore the mpC programming system assumed that all abstract processors of the network performed the same volume of computation.

Under this assumption, the programming system performed the mapping trying to keep the number of abstract processors mapped to each physical processor approximately proportional to its performance (naturally, taking into account the maximum number of abstract processors that could be hosted by this physical processor). Such a mapping ensures that the parallel processes, which represent abstract processors of the network, will execute computations approximately at the same speed. Therefore, if the volume of computation, which is performed by different abstract processors between points of synchronization or data transfer, is approximately the same, then the parallel program will be balanced; that is, its processes will not wait for each other at these communication points of the program.

This mapping appeared acceptable in all of our programs because different abstract processors of the network performed practically the same computation, which was, in addition, a very small volume. But if volumes of computations performed by different abstract processors vary substantionally, this mapping may lead to a very low speed of program execution.

Indeed, in this case the computations are executed by all involved processes at the same speed, and this implies that processes performing smaller volume computations will wait at communication points for processes executing computations of bigger volume. A mapping making the speed of each process proportional to the volume of computation that a process peforms would lead to a more balanced and faster parallel program.

The mpC language provides means for specification of relative volumes of computations performed by different abstract processors of the same mpC network. The mpC programming system uses this information to map abstract processors of the mpC network to processes of the parallel program in such a way that ensures each abstract processor to perform computations at the speed proportional to the volume of computation it performs.

The next program introduces these means:

```
#include <stdio.h>
#include <stdlib.h>
#include <math.h>
#include <mpc.h>

#define DELTA (0.5)
typedef struct
        {
            double len;    /* length of rail */
            double wid;    /* width of rail */
            double hei;    /* height of rail */
            double mass;   /* mass of rail */
        } rail;
nettype HeteroNet(int n, double v[n])
{
  coord I=n;
  node { I>=0: v[I]; };
  parent [0];
};

double Density(double x, double y, double z)
{
  return 6.0*sqrt(exp(sin(sqrt(x*y*z))));
}

int [*]main(int [host]argc, char **[host]argv)
```

```
{
  repl N=3;

  if(argc>1)
    N=[host]atoi(argv[1]);
  if(N<=0)
  {
    [host]printf("Wrong input (N=%d)\n", [host]N);
    MPC_Exit(-1);
  }
  else
  {
    static rail [host]steel_hedgehog[[host]N];
    repl double volumes[N];
    double [host]start;
    int [host]i;
    repl j;
/* Initialize geometry of "hedgehog" on host-processor */
for(i=0; i<[host]N; i++)
{
  steel_hedgehog[i].len = 200.0*(i+1);
  steel_hedgehog[i].wid = 5.0*(i+1);
  steel_hedgehog[i].hei = 10.0*(i+1);
}


/* Set the time on host-processor */
start = [host]MPC_Wtime();


/* Compute the volume of each j-th rail on host-processor, */
/* broadcast it to all processes of the program, where */
/* store it in j-th element of local copy of array volumes */
for(j=0; j<N; j++)
  volumes[j] = steel_hedgehog[j].len *
               steel_hedgehog[j].wid *
               steel_hedgehog[j].hei;
{
  net HeteroNet(N, volumes) mynet;
  rail [mynet]myrail;
  double [mynet]x, [mynet]y, [mynet]z;


  /* Broadcast "hedgehog" from host processor to all */
  /* processors of mynet, where store it in a local copy */
```

```
/* (projection) of distributed structure myrail */
myrail = steel_hedgehog[];

/* Each abstract processor of mynet compute */
/* the mass of its rail of "hedgehog" */
for(myrail.mass=0., x=0.; x<myrail.len; x+=DELTA)
  for(y=0.; y<myrail.wid; y+=DELTA)
  for(z=0.; z<myrail.hei; z+=DELTA)
    myrail.mass += [mynet]Density(x,y,z);
myrail.mass *= DELTA*DELTA*DELTA;

[mynet]MPC_Printf("Rail #%d is %gcm x %gcm x%gcm "
                  "and weights %g kg\n", I coordof myrail.len,
                  myrail.wid, myrail.hei,
                  myrail.mass/1000.0);

/* Compute the sum of all projections of distributed */
/* variable myrail.mass and output a local copy of */
/* the result from host-processor */
[host]printf("The steel hedgehog weights %g kg\n",
             [host]((myrail.mass)[+])/1000.0);
}
[host]printf("\nIt took %.1f seconds to run the program.\n",
             [host]MPC_Wtime()-start);
}
```

This program defines network type HeteroNet, which is parameterized by two parameters. The integer scalar parameter n determines the number of abstract processors in a network of this type. Vector parameter v consists of n elements of type double and is used for specification of relative volumes of computations performed by different abstract processors of the network.

The definition of network type HeteroNet contains an unusual declaration,

node { I>=0: v[I]; },

saying the following: *for any **I>=0** the relative volume of computation performed by the abstract processor with coordinate **I** is equal to **v[I]**.*

The mpC program above calculates the mass of a metallic construction welded from N heterogeneous rails. For parallel computation of the total mass of the metallic "hedgehog," it defines network mynet consisting of N abstract processors, each calculating the mass of one of the rails.

The calculation is performed by numerical three-dimensional integration of the density function `Density` with a constant integration step. Obviously the volume of computation to calculate the mass of a rail is proportional to the volume of the rail. Therefore the replicated array `volumes`, whose ith element just contains the volume of the ith rail, is used as the second actual parameter of network type `HeteroNet` in the definition of network `mynet`. The program thus specifies that the volume of computations performed by the ith abstract processor of network `mynet` is proportional to the volume of the rail, whose mass is computed by this abstract processor.

Besides the calculations, the program outputs the wall time elapsed to execute the calculations. To do this, the program uses the library nodal function `MPC_Wtime`. This function returns the astronomical time in seconds elapsed from some moment in the past not specified but fixed for the process calling the function.

We will not go into philosophical speculations about the relativity of time passing on different processes. We just briefly note that despite its seeming simplicity, this is the wall time that has elapsed in solving the problem, starting from data input and until output of results and measured on the host-process. This time is the most objective and interesting for the end-user temporal metrics of the program. Minimization of this characteristic is actually the main goal of parallel computing.

The next mpC program is equivalent to the previous one except that it does not specify explicitly the relative volumes of computations performed by different abstract processors of network `mynet`:

```
#include <stdio.h>
#include <stdlib.h>
#include <math.h>
#include <mpc.h>

#define DELTA (0.5)
typedef struct
        {
            double len;
            double wid;
            double hei;
            double mass;
        } rail;

double Density(double x, double y, double z)
{
    return 6.0*sqrt(exp(sin(sqrt(x*y*z))));
}

int [*]main(int [host]argc, char **[host]argv)
```

```
{
  repl N=3;

  if(argc>1)
    N=[host]atoi(argv[1]);
  if(N<=0)
  {
    [host]printf("Wrong input (N=%d)\n", [host]N);
    MPC_Exit(-1);
  }
  else
  {
static rail [host]steel_hedgehog[[host]N];
repl double volumes[N];
double [host]start;
int [host]i;
repl j;

for(i=0; i<[host]N; i++)
{
  steel_hedgehog[i].len = 200.0*(i+1);
  steel_hedgehog[i].wid = 5.0*(i+1);
  steel_hedgehog[i].hei = 10.0*(i+1);
}
start = [host]MPC_Wtime();
for(j=0; j<N; j++)
  volumes[j] = steel_hedgehog[j].len *
               steel_hedgehog[j].wid *
               steel_hedgehog[j].hei;
{
  net SimpleNet(N) mynet;
  rail [mynet]myrail;
  double [mynet]x, [mynet]y, [mynet]z;

  myrail = steel_hedgehog[];
  for(myrail.mass=0., x=0.; x<myrail.len; x+=DELTA)
    for(y=0.; y<myrail.wid; y+=DELTA)
      for(z=0.; z<myrail.hei; z+=DELTA)
        myrail.mass += [mynet]Density(x,y,z);
  myrail.mass *= DELTA*DELTA*DELTA;
  [mynet]MPC_Printf("Rail #%d is %gcm x %gcm x%gcm "
                    "and weights %g kg\n", I coordof mynet,
                    myrail.len, myrail.wid,
                    myrail.hei, myrail.mass/1000.0);
```

```
[host]printf("The steel hedgehog weights %g kg\n",
          [host]((myrail.mass)[+])/1000.0);
}
[host]printf("\nIt took %.1f seconds to run the program.\n",
          [host]MPC_Wtime()-start);
}
```

Therefore, while mapping the abstract processors of mynet to the processes of the program, the mpC programming system regards them as performing equal volumes of computations. In this case it leads to suboptimal mapping and hence to a longer time period of solving the problem as compared to the previous program.

The deceleration is visible if the program runs on a heterogeneous network that includes processors significantly differing in performance. In that case the mass of the biggest rail will likely be calculated on the slowest processor, resulting in a multi-fold deceleration as compared to the execution of the same calculations by the previous program, where we ensured that the fastest processor would compute the mass of the biggest rail.

6.9. THE RECON STATEMENT: A LANGUAGE CONSTRUCT TO CONTROL THE ACCURACY OF THE UNDERLYING MODEL OF COMPUTER NETWORK

The mapping of abstract processors of an mpC network to parallel processes of the program is based on the information about the speed at which the processes run on the physical processors of the executing network. By default, the mpC programming system uses the same estimation of speeds of the physical processors that was obtained earlier by the execution of a special parallel test program during the initialization of the mpC system on the network of computers.

In Chapter 5 of this book we mentioned that the estimation is not sufficiently accurate in parallel computing on common networks of computers because of the processors' heterogeneity and their multiple users. An estimate may be far off from the actual speeds of processors during program execution if

- the executed code essentially differs from the code of this special test program, or
- the workload of computers substantially differs from their workload during the execution of the special parallel test program.

The mpC language provides the means for programmers to change at runtime the default estimation of the processor speed by tuning it to the computations that will actually be executed. The next program demonstrates this effect:

```c
#include <stdio.h>
#include <stdlib.h>
#include <math.h>
#include <mpc.h>

#define DELTA (0.5)
typedef struct
        {
            double len;
            double wid;
            double hei;
            double mass;
        } rail;

nettype HeteroNet(int n, double v[n])
{
  coord I=n;
  node { I>=0: v[I]; };
  parent [0];
};

double Density(double x, double y, double z)
{
  return 6.0*sqrt(exp(sin(sqrt(x*y*z))));
}

double RailMass(double len, double wid, double hei,
double delta) {
  double mass, x, y, z;
  for(mass=0., x=0.; x<len; x+=delta)
    for(y=0.; y<wid; y+=delta)
      for(z=0.; z<hei; z+=delta)
        mass+=Density(x,y,z);
  return mass*delta*delta*delta;
}

int [*]main(int [host]argc, char **[host]argv)
{
  repl N=3;

  if(argc>1)
    N=[host]atoi(argv[1]);
```

```
if(N<=0)
{
   [host]printf("Wrong input (N=%d)\n", [host]N);
   MPC_Exit(-1);
}
else
{
   static rail [host]steel_hedgehog[[host]N];
   repl double volumes[N];
   double [host]start;
   int [host]i;
   repl j;

   for(i=0; i<[host]N; i++)
   {
      steel_hedgehog[i].len = 200.0*(i+1);
      steel_hedgehog[i].wid = 5.0*(i+1);
      steel_hedgehog[i].hei = 10.0*(i+1);
   }
   start = [host]MPC_Wtime();
   for(j=0; j<N; j++)
      volumes[j] = steel_hedgehog[j].len *
                   steel_hedgehog[j].wid *
                   steel_hedgehog[j].hei;

   recon RailMass(20., 4., 5., 0.5);
   {
      net HeteroNet(N,volumes) mynet;
      rail [mynet]myrail;
      double [mynet]x, [mynet]y, [mynet]z;

      myrail = steel_hedgehog[];
      myrail.mass = [mynet] RailMass(myrail.len,
                                     myrail.wid,
                                     myrail.hei, DELTA);
   [mynet]MPC_Printf("Rail #%d is %gcm x %gcm x%gcm "
                     "and weights %g kg\n",
                     I coordof mynet, myrail.len,
                     myrail.wid,myrail.hei, myrail.mass/ 1000.0);
   [host]printf("The steel hedgehog weights %g kg\n",
      [host]((myrail.mass)[+])/1000.0);
   }
   [host]printf("\nIt took %.1f seconds to run the program.\n",
                [host]MPC_Wtime()-start);
}
```

The program differs from the first program in Section 6.8 mainly by its introduction of a statement `recon`, which is executed just before the definition of the network `mynet`. All physical processors running the program are thus instructed to execute in parallel a piece of code provided by the statement, and the time elapsed by each of the processors to execute the piece of code is used to refresh the estimation of its speed.

In our case the piece of code is a call to function `RailMass` with arguments `20.0`, `4.0`, `5.0`, and `0.5`. The main part of the volume of computations performed by each abstract processor of network `mynet` falls exactly into the execution of calls to function `RailMass`. Therefore, while mapping abstract processors of network `mynet`, the mpC programming system will use such an estimation of speeds of physical processors that will be very close to their actual performance during the execution of this program.

It is important that the `recon` statement allow the programmer to refresh the estimation of processor speeds dynamically, at runtime, just before this estimation is used, and in particular, if the network of computers that executes the mpC program is used for other compuatations as well. The real speed of processors can dynamically change depending on their load by other computations external to the mpC program. Use of the `recon` statement allows the programmer to write parallel programs that are sensitive to such dynamic variation of the workload of the executing network. In such programs the computations are distributed over the physical processors in accordance with their actual computational performances.

6.10. A SIMPLE HETEROGENEOUS ALGORITHM SOLVING A REGULAR PROBLEM

An *irregular* problem is characterized by some inherent coarse-grained or large-grained structure. This structure implies a quite deterministic decomposition of the whole problem into a relatively small number of subtasks, which are of different size and can be solved in parallel. Correspondingly a natural way of decomposing the whole program, which solves the irregular problem on a network of computers, is by a set of parallel processes solving the subtasks and altogether interacting via message passing. As sizes of these subtasks differ, the processes perform different volumes of computation. Calculation of the mass of a metallic construction welded from N heterogeneous rails is an example of an irregular problem.

The most natural decomposition of a *regular* problem is a large number of small identical subtasks that can be solved in parallel. As those subtasks are identical, they are all of the same size. Multiplication of two $n \times n$ dense matrices is an example of a regular problem. This problem is naturally decomposed into n^2 identical subtasks, each of which is to compute one element of the resulting matrix.

An efficient solution on a heterogeneous network of computers would transform the problem into an irregular problem, whose structure is determined by the structure of the executing network rather than the structure of the regular problem itself. This way the whole regular problem is decomposed into a set of relatively large subproblems, each made of a number of small identical subtasks stuck together. The size of each subproblem, that is, the number of elementary identical subtasks constituting the subproblem, depends on the speed of the processor, on which the subproblem will be solved.

Correspondingly the parallel program that solves the problem on the heterogeneous network of computers is a set of parallel processes, each handling one subproblem on a separate physical processor and altogether interacting via message passing. The volume of computations performed by each of these processes should be proportional to its speed.

In Section 5.1 we considered a simple heterogeneous parallel algorithm of matrix-matrix multiplication on a heterogeneous network of computers as well as its implementation in HPF 2.0. Let us now consider a much similar algorithm of parallel multiplication on a heterogeneous network of matrix A and the transposition of matrix B, performing matrix operation $C = A \times B^T$, where A, B are dense square $n \times n$ matrices.

This algorithm can be summarized as follows:

- Each element in C is a square $r \times r$ block and the unit of computation is the computation of one block, that is, a multiplication of $r \times n$ and $n \times r$ matrices. For simplicity we assume that n is a multiple of r.
- The A, B, and C matrices are identically partitioned into p horizontal slices, where p is the number of processors performing the operation. There is one-to-one mapping between these slices and the processors. Each processor is responsible for computing its C slice.
- Because all C blocks require the same amount of arithmetic operations, each processor executes work proportional to the number of blocks that are allocated to it, hence, proportional to the area of its slice. To balance the load of the processors, the area of the slice mapped to each processor is proportional to its speed (see Figure 6.1).
- At each step a row of blocks (the pivot row) of matrix B, representing a column of blocks of matrix B^T, is communicated (broadcast) vertically, and all processors compute the corresponding column of blocks of matrix C in parallel (see Figure 6.2).

The following mpC program implements this algorithm:

```
#include <stdio.h>
```

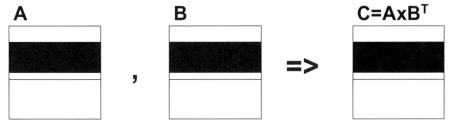

Figure 6.1. Matrix operation $C = A \times B^T$ with matrices A, B, and C unevenly partitioned in one dimension. The slices mapped onto a single processor are shaded in black.

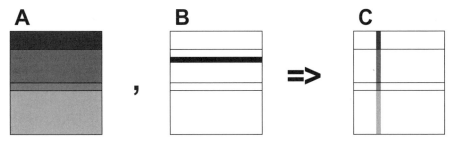

Figure 6.2. One step of parallel multiplication of matrices A and B^T. The pivot row of blocks of matrix B (shown slashed) is first broadcast to all processors. Then each processor computes, in parallel with the others, its part of the corresponding column of blocks of the resulting matrix C.

```
#include <stdlib.h>
#include <mpc.h>


void Partition(), SerialAxBT();


nettype ParallelAxBT(int p, int d[p])
{
   coord I = p;
   node { I>=0: d[I]; };
   parent [0];
};


int [*]main(int [host]argc, char **[host]argv)
{
   repl int n, r, p, *d;
   repl double *speeds;
```

```
n = [host]atoi(argv[1]);
r = [host]atoi(argv[2]);

/* Run a test code in parallel by all physical processors */
/* to refresh information about their speeds */
{
    repl double a[r][n], b[r][n], c[r][n];
    repl int i, j;

    for(i=0; i<r; i++)
        for(j=0; j<n; j++)
        {
            a[i][j] = 1.0;
            b[i][j] = 1.0;
        }
    recon SerialAxBT((void*)a, (void*)b, (void*)c, r, n);
}

/* Detect the total number of physical processors */
p = MPC_Get_number_of_processors();

speeds = calloc(p, sizeof(double));
d = calloc(p, sizeof(int));

/* Detect the speed of the physical processors */
MPC_Get_processors_info(NULL, speeds);

/* Calculate the number of rows of the resulting matrix */
/* to be computed by each processor */
Partition(p, speeds, d, n, r);
{
    net ParallelAxBT(p, d) w;
    int [w]myn;

    myn = ([w]d)[I coordof w];
    [w]:
    {
        double A [myn/r][r][n], B[myn/r][r][n],
        C[myn/r][r][n];
        repl double Brow[r][n];
        int i, j, k;

        for(i=0; i<myn/r; i++)
            for(j=0; j<r; j++)
                for(k=0; k<n; k++)
                {
```

```
                 A[i][j][k]  = 1.0;
                 B[i][j][k]  = 1.0;
              }
{
   repl int PivotNode=0, RelPivotRow, AbsPivotRow;

   for (AbsPivotRow=0, RelPivotRow=0, PivotNode=0;
        AbsPivotRow < n;
        RelPivotRow += r, AbsPivotRow += r)
   {
     if(RelPivotRow >= d[PivotNode])
     {
        PivotNode++;
        RelPivotRow = 0;
     }
     Brow[] = [w:I==PivotNode]B[RelPivotRow/r][];
     for(j=0; j<myn/r; j++)
        SerialAxBT((void*)A[j][0], (void*)Brow[0],
                 (void*)(C[j][0]+AbsPivotRow), r, n);
      }
    }
   }
  }
  free(speeds);
  free(d);
}

void SerialAxBT(double *a, double *b, double *c, int r, int n)
{
   int i, j, k;
   double s;

   for(i=0; i<r; i++)
   for(j=0; j<r; j++)
   {
      for(k=0, s=0.0; k<n; k++)
         s += a[i*n+k]*b[j*n+k];
      c[i*n+j]=s;
   }
}

void Partition(int p, double *weight, int *d, int n, int r)
{
   int rows, distributed_rows, i;
   double total_weight;
```

```
rows = n/r;
for(i=0, total_weight=0.0; i<p; i++)
   total_weight += weight[i];
for(i=0, distributed_rows=0; i<p; i++)
{
   d[i] = (int)(weight[i]/total_weight*rows);
   distributed_rows += d[i];
}
   for(i=0; i<p && distributed_rows!=rows; i++, distributed_rows++)
   d[i]++;
if(distributed_rows!=rows)
   d[0] += rows-distributed_rows;
for(i=0; i<p; i++)
   d[i] *= r;
}
```

In this program the network type `ParallelAxBT` describes two features of the implemented algorithm of parallel matrix multiplication:

- The number of involved parallel processes.
- The relative volume of computations to be performed by each of the processes.

The definition of `ParallelAxBT` declares that an mpC network of p abstract processors will perform the algorithm. It is supposed that the ith element of vector parameter d is just the number of rows in the C slice mapped to the ith abstract processor of the mpC network. Thus the node declaration specifies relative volumes of computations to be performed by the abstract processors.

Network w is defined so that

- one-to-one mapping would occur between its abstract processors and physical processors of the executing network, and
- the volume of computation to be performed by each abstract processor would be proportional to the speed of the physical processor running the abstract processor.

To achieve this, the program first detects the number of physical processors that execute the program. This is achieved by calling the nodal library function `MPC_Get_number_of_processors`. The function is called by all processes of the program in parallel. So after this call the value of all projections of replicated variable p will be equal to the total number of physical processors executing the program.

Then the program detects the speeds of the physical processors by calling the nodal library function `MPC_Get_processors_info`. The function returns in array `speeds` the latest information about the speed of processors, which the programming system has received. In this case it will be the speed demonstrated by the processors during execution of the code specified in the `recon` statement. The code just multiplies the test $r \times n$ and $n \times r$ matrices with a call to function `SerialAxBT`.

Note that computations performed in this program mainly fall into calls to function `SerialAxBT`, each of which multiplies two $r \times n$ and $n \times r$ matrices. Therefore, after the call to function `MPC_Get_processors_info`, the value of `speeds [i]` will be very close to the speed of the ith physical processors demonstrated during the execution of the program ($i = 0, \ldots, $p-1).

The test code used to estimate the speed of processors must match well the computations performed by the program. For example, if we used mutiplication of two 200×200 matrices in the program above for estimation of the speed of processors, the resulting estimation would typically be much less accurate. The reason is that multiplication of 10×4000 and 4000×10 matrices causes more intensive data swapping between different levels of the memory hierarchy than multiplication of two 200×200 matrices. As a result, despite these two matrix operations performing the same amount of arithmetic operations, the amount of memory access operations will be different. So the underlying computations will be different as well.

After detecting the number of physical processors and their speeds, the program calculates how many rows of the resulting matrix each physical processor should compute. It calls the nodal function `Partition`, which distributes the total number of rows, `n`, between p processors in such a way that the number of rows mapped to each processor would be proportional to its speed. The distribution is returned in array `d` so that $d[i]$ is the number of rows that should be mapped to the ith processor and $d[i]/d[j] \approx speeds[i]/speeds[j]$ ($i,j = 0, \ldots, $p-1) and $\Sigma_{i=0}^{p-1}d[i] = n$.

Finally, the program defines an mpC network, w, which consists of as many abstract processors as many the physical processors are involved in the execution of the program. The relative volume of computations to be performed by the ith abstract processor of network w is specified to be proportional to the speed of the ith physical processor. Therefore any conforming implementation of mpC will map the ith abstract processor of w to a process running on the ith physical processor, just because this is the very mapping that makes the speed of each abstract processor proportional to the volume of computation that the abstract processor performs.

The rest of the program code describes the parallel matrix multiplication on network w itself. First of all, each abstract processor of w computes the number of rows in the C slice to be computed by the processor, and stores this number in variable `myn`. Then the program defines the distributed arrays A, B, and C to store matrices A, B, and C respectively. The horizontal slice of matrix A mapped to each abstract processor of network w will be stored in its projection of array A. Note that projections of the distributed array A are of different shapes depending on the size of the A slice mapped to one or another processor. The same is true for distributed arrays B and C.

The program also defines a replicated array, Brow, to store the pivot row of matrix B. All projections of array Brow are of the same shape. After that, a nested for-loop executed by all abstract processors of network w in parallel initializes distributed arrays A and B.

Finally, the main for-loop of the program describes n/r steps of the matrix multiplication algorithm. At each step, assignment

```
Brow[] = [w:I==PivotNode]B[RelPivotRow/r][]
```

broadcasts a row of blocks (the pivot row) of matrix B, representing a column of blocks of matrix B^T, to all abstract processors of network w, where it is stored in array Brow. Then all of the abstract processors compute the corresponding column of blocks of matrix C in parallel.

6.11. PRINCIPLES OF IMPLEMENTATION

This section introduces the basic implementation principles of the subset of the mpC language presented above. The discussion is addressed not only to implementers of parallel programming systems, knowledge of these principles allows mpC users to write more efficient programs. The primary components of the mpC programming system are the compiler, the runtime support system, the library, and the command-line user interface.

The mpC compiler translates a source mpC program into the ANSI C program with calls to functions of the mpC runtime system. It normally uses the SPMD model of the target code, when all processes constituting the target message-passing program run the identical code. Optionally, it can translate a source mpC file into two separate target files: one for the host-process and the other for the remaining processes.

The mpC runtime system is an internal library that is not available to the mpC programmer. Its functions are only used by the mpC compiler in the generated target code. It provides both operations on parallel processes of the mpC program and interprocess communication operations. The mpC runtime system has a precisely specified interface and encapsulates a particular communication package such as MPI. It ensures platform-independence of the mpC compiler.

The mpC library provides some definitions and operations that can be used by programmers in their mpC programs. The definition of network SimpleNet is an example of an mpC library definition. Operations are provided in the form of a basic, nodal, or network function. MPC_Global_barrier is an example of an mpC basic library function.

MPC_Wtime is an example of an mpC nodal library function. MPC_Barrier is an example of an mpC network library function. All mpC library definitions and prototypes of the mpC library functions are made available via the header file mpc.h.

The mpC command-line user interface consists of a number of utilities that allow the user to initialize the mpC programming system on the network of computers, and to compile, link, and run parallel mpC programs on the network.

6.11.1. Model of a Target Message-Passing Program

We have noted that the mpC compiler translates each mpC program into a message-passing program that uses the mpC runtime system for process management and interprocess communication. The parallel processes that constitute the target program are divided into two groups.

The first group consists of common *working* processes that perform computations and communications specified in the source mpC program and can play the role of abstract processors of one or another mpC network.

The second group consists of exactly one process that plays the role of the manager of the working processes. This specific process is called *dispatcher*. The dispatcher works as a server. It receives requests from the working processes and sends them commands to be performed.

In the target program each network of the source mpC program is represented by a group of working processes called a *team*. Definition of the mpC network causes creation of the team, whose processes play the role of abstract processors of this network.

At any time of program execution, each working process is either free (i.e., not a member of any team) or a member of one or more teams. This is the dispatcher who assigns processes into a newly created team and dismisses them on the destruction of the team. The only exception is a pre-assigned *host-process* representing the mpC pre-defined abstract host-processor. Thus, immediately after initialization of the target program, its working processes consist of the host-process and a set of temporarily free processes.

Two main operations on working processes performed during execution of the target program are creation and destruction of teams of processes representing mpC networks of the source program. Implementation of these operations determines both the whole structure of the target code and the functionality of the mpC runtime system.

To create a team, the process that plays the role of the parent of the corresponding mpC network computes the actual parameters of this network and sends a creation request to the dispatcher. The request contains information about the team to be created, including the number of processes and the relative volume of computation the processes should perform.

The dispatcher has information about the executing network of computers that includes

- the number of physical processors,
- the relative speed of the processors, and
- the mapping of working processes onto the physical processors.

Based on this information, the dispatcher selects those free working processes that are the most appropriate to be assigned to the newly created team.

After that, the dispatcher sends to each free working process a message saying whether or not the process is assigned into the team. Each process assigned to the team also receives comprehensive information about the team and its identification in this team as part of the message from the dispatcher, and stores the data in its memory.

To destruct a team, its parent process sends a destruction request to the dispatcher. Note that the parent process of the team retains its membership in all those teams that have existed from the time this team was created. The other members of the destructed team become free and await commands from the dispatcher.

Any working process can detect whether or not it is free. It is not free if a call to function `MPC_Is_busy` of the mpC runtime system returns 1. If such a call returns 0, the process is free.

Any working process can also detect whether or not it is a member of any existing team. A team of working processes is accessed via its *descriptor*. If descriptor `td` is associated with the team, then a working process belongs to this team if and only if a function call `MPC_Is_member(&td)` returns 1. In this case descriptor `td` allows the process to access comprehensive information about the team and to identify itself in this team. Remember that these data are received from the dispatcher and stored in the memory of the process during the creation of the team. A team descriptor has the same scope and duration class (automatic or static) in the generated code as the corresponding mpC network in the source mpC code.

Creation of a team involves its parent process, all free processes and the dispatcher. The mpC compiler inserts in the target code all of the necessary synchronization operations in order to guarantee coordinated arrival of all interested working processes in the code section that performs the team creation operation.

The parent process first computes the data that specify the team to be created and then composes a creation request, which includes these data and a transferable ID of the team. The ID is used by processes to locally identify the correct team descriptor. As during creation of the team all participating working processes execute a code located in the same file, the team ID does not have to be globally unique. It is enough for the ID to be unique in the scope of the file so that there is one-to-one mapping between the team descriptors defined in this file and the IDs. The IDs can be generated at compile time. For example, the ordinal number of the mpC network in the source mpC file may be used as such an ID.

The parent process next sends the creation request to the dispatcher and begins to wait for a message from the dispatcher confirming the creation of the team. Upon receipt of the confirmation message, the parent process enters a barrier section that completes the team creation operation.

Meantime each free process waits for a message from the dispatcher. Upon receipt of the message, the process acts according to what the message says. If this message says that the process is not selected for the team, it awaits the next message from the dispatcher.

Otherwise, the received message contains data specifying the team and identifying the process in the team. The process stores the data in its memory and associates the stored data with the team descriptor, which is identified by the received team ID. Then it leaves the set of free processes and enters the barrier section, completing the team creation operation.

A free process leaves the waiting point either after it becomes a member of a team or after the dispatcher sends to all free processes a message commanding them to leave the point. The dispatcher sends such a message after all the teams have been created by this team creation operation. Upon receipt of this command, each free process also enters the barrier section, completing the team creation operation.

The barrier section completing the creation operation finalizes the creation of the teams. For example, if the mpC runtime system is built on top of MPI, the finalization may mean the creation of a communcator for each team of processes.

6.11.2. Mapping of the Parallel Algorithm to the Processors of a Heterogeneous Network

The preceding subset of the mpC language introduced an abstraction of the heterogeneous parallel algorithm in the form of an mpC network. This abstraction can be used by the mpC programmer to advise the mpC compiler of some features of the implemented parallel algorithm that might have an impact on its performance. This model of parallel algorithm ignores communication operations and is quite simple. In fact the implemented parallel algorithm is characterized by only two main attributes:

- The number of abstract processors to perform the algorithm.
- The relative volume of computations to be executed by each processor.

As we have discussed, the dispatcher uses this information to map the parallel algorithm to the physical processors of the executing network of computers. In this section we explain how the dispatcher performs the mapping.

Technically the dispatcher maps abstract processors of the mpC network to physical processes of the parallel program running on the heterogeneous network of computers. To perform the mapping, the dispatcher uses

- the mpC model of the parallel algorithm that should be executed,
- the model of the executing network of computers that reflects the network's state just before the execution of the algorithm,
- a map of working processes of the parallel program. For each computer of the executing network, the map displays the number of working processes running on the computer, and the number of currently free ones.

This model of a network of computers matches the model of a parallel algorithm that ignores communication operations. Correspondingly the model of a heterogeneous network ignores the network communication layer and is quite simplistic. The model considers the network as a set of heterogeneous multiprocessors.

Each computer is characterized by two attributes:

- The relative speed s of execution of a (serial) test code on the computer.
- The number of physical processors, or *scalability*, of the computer.

The first attribute is a function of time, $s(t)$, and can vary even during the execution of the same mpC application (if the application uses the `recon` statement). Relative speeds of computers are normalized so that the computer running the host-process is always of unit speed ($s = 1$). The second attribute is a constant, n. It determines the number of noninteracting processes that can run in parallel on the computer without a loss of speed.

The algorithm of mapping of abstract processors of the mpC network to working processes of the program can be summarized as follows: The dispatcher first computes the relative volume of computations to be performed by each abstract processor so that the parent abstract processor gets the same relative volume that it had in the existing mpC network(s). The dispatcher does not need to map the parent abstract processor because it has been mapped before. The remaining abstract processors are mapped successively, starting from the most loaded abstract processor. It is mapped to the fastest remaining free process. Then the second most loaded abstract processor is mapped to the fastest of the remaining free processes, and so on.

At each step of the procedure, the speed of free processes is estimated as follows: Let v be the relative volume of computations associated with abstract processor a that should be mapped at this step. Let s be the speed associated with computer C in the model of the executing network. Let n be the scalability of C. Let A be a set of the mpC program's abstract processors that are currently mapped to working processes running on C. Let A be divided into n nonintersecting subsets $A_1, \ldots, A_n$, where the abstract processors from each subset are supposed to be mapped on processes running on the same physical processor of computer C. Let v_{ij} be the relative volume of computations to be performed by the ith abstract processor from subset A_j.

Then the speed of free working processes running on computer C is estimated as follows:

$$\max_i \left\{ \frac{s}{v + \Sigma_{j=1}^{n} v_{ij}} \right\}.$$

The dispatcher maps abstract processor a to the computer, whose free processes have the highest estimated speed. Let C be this computer. Then abstract processor a will be added to subset A_k such that

$$\frac{s}{v + \Sigma_{j=1}^{n} v_{kj}} = \max_i \left\{ \frac{s}{v + \Sigma_{j=1}^{n} v_{ij}} \right\}.$$

The algorithm above is based on the obvious observation that the smaller things are, the easier they can be evenly distributed. Hence bigger things should be distributed under weaker constraints than smaller ones.

For example, to distribute a number of balls of different size over a number of baskets of different size, we would start from the biggest ball and put it into the biggest basket, then put the second biggest ball into the basket having the biggest free space, and so on. That algorithm keeps the balance between ball sizes and free basket space and guarantees that if at some step there is not enough space for the next ball, there is no way to put all the balls in the baskets.

Similarly, if the algorithm above cannot balance the load of physical processors, this simply means that there is no way to balance them at all.

6.12. SUMMARY

The subset of the mpC language presented in this chapter addresses some primary challenges of heterogeneous parallel computing. Namely it focuses on the uneven distribution of computations in heterogeneous parallel algorithms and heterogeneity of physical processors of the executing network.

The programmers can explicitly specify the uneven distribution of computations across parallel processes dictated by the implemented heterogeneous parallel algorithm. The mpC compiler will use the provided information to map the parallel processes to the executing network of computers.

A simple model of the executing network is used when parallel processes of the mpC program are mapped to physical processors of the network. The relative speed of the physical processors is a key parameter in the model. In heterogeneous environments the parameter is very sensitive to both the particular code executed by the processors and their current workload by external computations. The programmers can control the accuracy of this model at runtime, and adjust its parameters to their particular applications by using the `recon` statement. This statement

- provides a test code that should be used to estimate the relative speed of physical processors, and
- specifies the exact point in the program where the test code should be executed to modify parameters the underlying model of the network of computers.

Now we briefly discuss some important topics regarding the mpC language. These are topics that are not presented in detail in this chapter but that should be addressed.

The first is the kind of applications for which the mpC language is suited. The language is most suitable for the parallel solution of irregular problems, such calculating the mass of a building construction frame welded from heterogeneous metal rails, on both homogeneous and heterogeneous distributed-memory computer systems.

The mpC language is also suitable for solving in heterogeneous environments regular problems such as dense linear algebra. There are two approaches to solving regular problems on heterogeneous clusters using mpC:

- Irregularization of the problem in accordance with the irregularity of the executing hardware.
- Distribution of a relatively large number of homogeneous parallel processes over physical processors of the heterogeneous cluster in accordance with their speed.

The mpC language provides natural implementation in a portable form of these two approaches. The first approach was demonstrated in Section 6.10 for parallel matrix-matrix multiplication. The second approach is demonstrated in Section 9.1.3.

Another interesting issue involves deciding on the number of processes of the mpC program. How many processes should be allocated to each participating computer when the user starts up the program? Obviously the more processes one has, the better load balancing that can be achieved. On the other hand, more processes consume more resources and cause more interprocess communications, and so can significantly increase the total overhead.

Some basic rules of making a choice are the following: First, the number of processes running a computer should not be less than the number of processors of the computer that are capable handling all the available processor resources.

At its upper bound, the number is limited by the underlying operating system and/or the communication platform. For example, LAM MPI version 5.2 installed under Solaris 2.3 does not allow more than 15 MPI processes to run on an individual workstation.

If the mpC application does not define a sufficient amount of static data, then all the processes not selected for the abstract processors of the mpC network subside and do not consume much in terms of processor cycles or memory. The only overhead is the additional communications with the processes that include initialization of the underlying communication platform and the mpC specific communications during execution of the application. The latter mainly fall into the creation of a network. The time elapsed by this operation does not keep up with the rapid growth of the number of processes.

For example, the use of six processes instead of one process per workstation on a network of nine uniprocessor workstations caused only a 30% increase of the time of the network creation. This is because the operation includes some relatively significant calculations, and the calculations are more sensitive to the number of computers than to the number of processes running on each of the computers.

Some applications are designed to run as not more than one process per processor. The matrix multiplication in Section 6.10 is an example of such an application.

Apart from data parallelism, the mpC language also supports *task parallelism*, mainly via the mechanism of nodal and, especially, networks functions. Different nodal and network functions can be called in parallel, each having its own control flow.

Network functions also enable *modular parallel programming* in mpC. One programmer can implement a parallel algorithm in the form of a network function, and the other programmers can safely use that program unit in parallel with other computations in their applications without any knowledge of its code.

The next topic concerns applications where different parallel algorithms are coupled. There are many ways of programming such applications in mpC. If two algorithms are loosely coupled, two different mpC networks of the different type executing the algorithms *in parallel* can be defined. The mpC programming system will try to map the algorithms to the executing network of computers so as to ensure the best execution time.

Alternatively, two different mpC networks executing the algorithms can be defined *serially* (especially, if there is strong data dependency). In this case the first mpC network should be destructed before the second one is created in order to make all processes of the program available when mapping each of the algorithms on the underlying hardware. If two algorithms are tightly coupled, they can be described in the framework of the same network type and performed by the same mpC network.

## CHAPTER 7

Advanced Heterogeneous Parallel Programming in mpC

7.1. INTERPROCESS COMMUNICATION

The subset of the mpC language presented in Chapter 6 allows the programmers not only to describe computations and communications implementing the heterogeneous parallel algorithm but also to specify its performance model. The performance model reflects the following basic features of the implemented algorithm having an impact on its execution time:

- The number of parallel processes executing the algorithm.
- The relative volume of computations performed by each of the processes.

The compiler uses this information to map the parallel processes of the algorithm to the network of computers in order to minimize its execution time.

The perfomance model provided by the mpC subset fully ignores communication operations. In other words, the model presumes that the communication operations' contribution to the total execution time of the algorithm is negligibly small compared to that of the computations.

This assumption is acceptable for "normal" message-passing parallel algorithms if the communication layer of the executing network of computers is of the quality of the MPP communication layer, that is, homogeneous, fast, and balanced in the number and speed of processors (see Section 4.1 for more detail). In other words, the assumption is acceptable for "normal" parallel algorithms running on *heterogeneous clusters* as they are defined in Section 5.2.

The assumption is also acceptable for message-passing algorithms whose parallel processes do not communicate frequently sending each other relatively short messages, even if they run on the network of computers whose communication layer is far removed from the ideal MPP communication network.

Parallel Computing on Heterogeneous Networks, by Alexey Lastovetsky
ISBN 0-471-22982-2   Copyright © 2003 by John Wiley & Sons, Inc.

However, this assumption is too far removed from the reality of what happens during "normal" message-passing parallel algorithms running on common heterogeneous networks of computers. In Section 5.2 we have showed that the low speeds and narrow bandwidths of some communication links can cause communication operations to raise the total execution time of a "normal" parallel algorithm to an even more significant extent than the computations. The mapping of the parallel algorithm to the executing common network of computers, which does not take into account the material nature of communication operations, will therefore not be accurate. These may even result a parallel program that is slower than the corresponding serial program solving the same problem.

Thus, in order to support parallel programming for common networks of computers, the mpC language should additionally allow the programmers to explicitly specify the volume of data that should be transferred between different parallel processes during execution of the algorithm. Unfortunately, such an advanced performance model of a heterogeneous parallel algorithm that can take into account the costs of computations and communications cannot be obtained by a straightforward extension of the simplified basic model. As soon as communication operations are brought into the model, the algorithm should provide more information about computations than just their relative volume performed by different parallel processes. Otherwise, specification of communication operations will be useless.

To see this point, consider two parallel algorithms that are equivalent in terms of the total number of parallel processes, relative volumes of computation, and volumes of transferred data. During execution of any of the algorithms, all processes perform the same volume of computation and transfer in total about 10 Mbyte.

Let us assume the following:

- The algorithms differ in *absolute* volumes of computation performed by the parallel processes so that the first algorithm performs about 100 times as much computation compared to the second one.
- All processors of the executing network of computers are identical.
- The per-processor cost of computation of the first algorithm on the network is around 10^3 seconds, while that of the second algorithm is around 10 seconds.
- The executing network consists of two communication segments, one based on plain 10 Mbit Ethernet and the other using 1 Gigabit Ethernet.
- The number of processors in each of the segments is greater than the total number of processes of the algorithms.

Then any one-to-one mapping of processes of the first algorithm to processors of the network will be approximately equivalent in terms of the execution time. Even if the algorithm is entirely executed by processors of the slower segment, its execution will still take nearly 10^3 seconds since the communications will add to the total execution time about 1 second.

However, the execution time of the second algorithm may differ significantly depending on the mapping of its processes to the executing network. If processors of the faster segment execute the algorithm, it will take about 10 seconds as in this case the cost of communications will be close to 10^{-1} second. If it is executed by processors of the slower segment, it will take more than 20 seconds as the cost of communications will be no less than 10 seconds. Thus the two algorithms, which are equivalent in terms of relative volumes of computation and volumes of transferred data but not equivalent in terms of absolute volumes of computation, should be mapped differently to achieve a better execution time.

For the compiler to optimally map parallel algorithms with substantial contribution of communication operations into the execution time, the programmers should specify absolute volumes of computation to be performed by different processes and volumes of data transferred between the processes. The mpC language provides the programmers with such facilities. The key issue in specification of absolute volumes of computation and communication is how to measure these volumes. The specification should provide the compiler with information sufficient for it to estimate the computation and communication portions of the total execution time.

Specification of the volume of communication is not a big problem. The *byte* is a natural unit of mesurement for data transferred between processes of the parallel algorithm. Given the size in bytes of data transferred between a pair of processes and the speed and bandwidth of the corresponding communication link, the compiler can estimate the time elapsed by the communication operation.

Specification of the volume of computation is not as easy. What is the natural unit of computation to measure the volume of computations performed by a process? The main requirement is that if given the volume of the computation measured in those units, the compiler should be able to accurately esimate the time of execution of the corresponding computations by any process of the program.

The solution proposed in the mpC language is that the very code that was used to estimate the speed of physical processors of the executing network can also serve as a unit of measure for the volume of computation performed by processes of the parallel algorithm. Recall that the code is commonly provided by the programmer as a part of the `recon` statement (see Section 6.9).

To introduce the advanced mpC model of a heterogeneous parallel algorithm and the language constructs supporting the model, let us consider two typical mpC applications. The first simulates the evolution of a system of bodies under the influence of Newtonian gravitational attraction. It is supposed that the system consists of a number of large groups of bodies, with different groups at a good distance from each other (see Figure 7.1).

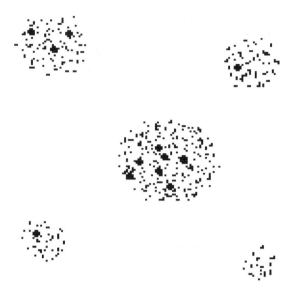

Figure 7.1. The system of bodies consists of large groups of bodies, with different groups at a good distance from each other. The bodies move under the influence of Newtonian gravitational attraction.

Since the magnitude of interaction among the bodies falls off rapidly with distance, the effect of a large group of bodies may be approximated by a single equivalent body, if the group of bodies is far enough away from the point where the effect is being evaluated. This way we can effect a paralleling of the problem. The parallel algorithm simulating the evolution of the system of bodies can be summarized as follows:

- Each body is characterized by several variables, including its position x, y, and z (the Cartesian x, y, and z coordinates); its velocity v_x, v_y, and v_z (the x, y and z components of velocity); and its mass m.
- *Newton's law of gravitation* is used to calculate the strength of the gravitational force between two bodies: the strength is given by the product of their masses divided by the square of the distance between them, scaled by the gravitational constant G,

$$F = \frac{G \times m_1 \times m_2}{r^2}.$$

- To calculate the total force acting on one body, the gravitational force between this body and every other body in the system should be accumulated. The *principle of superposition* says that the net force acting on a body is the sum of the individual pairwise forces. Therefore the total forces in the x, y, and z directions are obtained by adding up the forces in the x, y, and z directions.

- *Newton's second law of motion*, $F = m \times a$, is used to get the x, y, and z components of the body's acceleration is implied by these forces.
- Time is discretized, and the time variable t is increased in increments of the time quantum dt. The simulation is more accurate when dt is very small. At each discrete time interval dt, the force on each body is computed, and this information is used to update the position and velocity of each body:

  1. The position at time t is used to compute the gravitational force F and acceleration a.
  2. Velocity v and acceleration a at time t are used to compute velocity v' at time $t + dt$ as $v' = v + a \times dt$.
  3. Position p, velocity v, and acceleration a at time t as well as velocity v' at time $t + dt$ are used to compute position p' at time $t + dt$ as $p' = p + (\alpha \times v' + \beta \times v) \times dt + a \times (dt^2/2)$. In this formula, α, $\beta \geq 0$ and $\alpha + \beta = 1$ (usually $\alpha = \beta = \frac{1}{2}$) are used.
  4. After the position and velocity of each body are updated, all bodies whose distances between each other are small enough compared to their masses are merged into a single body. The mass of the resulting single body is the sum of the individual masses of the merged bodies, $m = \Sigma_i m_i$. The position of the resulting body is the center of mass of the collection of merged bodies. The velocity of the resulting body is computed so that the momentum of the resulting body is equal to the total momentum of the collection of merged bodies, $v = \Sigma_i m_i \times v_i/m$.

- There is one-to-one mapping between groups of bodies and parallel processes of the algorithm. Each process has in its memory all data characterizing bodies of its group, and is responsible for updating it.
- The effect of each remote group of bodies is approximated by a single equivalent body. This means that in order to update the position and velocity of bodies, each process requires the total mass and the position of center of mass of the remote group (see Figure 7.2).
- The total mass of a group of bodies is constant during the simulation. Therefore it is calculated once in the very beginning of the execution of the algorithm. Each process receives from the other processes their calculated total masses, and stores all these values in its memory.
- The position of the center of mass of a group is a function of time. Therefore, at each step of the simulation, a process computes the center of mass of its group and sends it to other processes. Each process receives from the other processes their calculated center, of mass and stores all the centers in its memory.
- It is presumed that at every step of the simulation the updated system of bodies is displayed on the computer. For this reason all groups of bodies

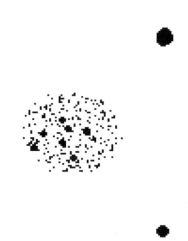

Figure 7.2. The point of view of each individual process. The system of bodies includes all bodies of its group while each remote group is approximated by a single equivalent body.

are gathered by the process responsible for effecting the visualization which is the *host-process*.

In general, since different groups of the system of bodies have different sizes, different processes perform different volumes of computation, and different volumes of data are transferred between different pairs of processes. Like the parallel algorithm of Section 6.8 for calculating the mass of a metallic construction welded from N heterogeneous rails, the heterogeneity of the algorithm above is induced by the irregularity of the problem being solved by the algorithm. Schematically this algorithm can be expressed by the following pseudocode:

```
Initialize groups of bodies on the host-process
Visualize the groups of bodies
Scatter the groups across processes
Compute masses of the groups in parallel
Communicate to share the masses among processes
while(1) {
  Compute centers of mass of the groups in parallel
  Communicate to share the centers among processes
  Update the state of the groups in parallel
  Gather the groups to the host-process
  Visualize the groups of bodies
}
```

The core of the mpC application, implementing the preceding algorithm, is the specification of its performance model:

```
nettype Nbody(int m, int k, int n[m])
{
    coord I=m;
    node { I>=0: bench*((n[I]/k)*(n[I]/k)); };
    link { I>0 : length*(n[I]*sizeof(Body)) [I]->[0]; };
    parent [0];
};
```

Informally, it looks like a description of an abstract network of computers (which execute the algorithm) complemented by a description of the workload of each processor and each communication link of this abstract network.

From the mpC language point of view, the description defines a parameterized type of abstract networks. The first line of this network type of definition introduces the name Nbody of the network type and a list of parameters, including the integer scalar parameters m and k, and the vector parameter n of m integers. The next line declares the coordinate system with which the abstract processors will be associated. It introduces the coordinate variable I, which ranges from 0 to m-1. The following line associates the abstract processors with this coordinate system, and describes the (absolute) volume of computation to be performed by each processor.

As a unit of measure, the volume of computation performed by some benchmark code is used. In this particular case it is assumed that the benchmark code updates the position and velocity of bodies of a single group of k bodies. It is also assumed that the ith element of vector n is just equal to the number of bodies in the group updated by the ith abstract processor.

The number of operations to update the position and velocity of bodies of one group is proportional to the number of bodies in this group squared. Therefore the volume of computations to be performed by the I-th abstract processor is $(n[I]/k)^2$ times bigger than the volume of computations performed by the benchmark code. This line just says it.

The following line specifies the volume of data in bytes to be transferred between the abstract processors during execution of the algorithm. This line simply says that the ith abstract processor $(i = 1, . . .)$ will send data characterizing all of its bodies to the host-processor, where they should be visualized.

Note that the definition of the Nbody network type actually specifies the volume of computation and communication during a single iteration of the main loop of the algorithm. This is a good approximation because practically all computations and communications concentrate in this loop. Therefore the total execution time of this algorithm is approximately equal to the execution time of a single iteration multiplied by the total number of iterations.

In general, the mpC code implementing the heterogeneous parallel algorithm takes the following form:

```c
#include <stdio.h>
#include <stdlib.h>
#include <mpc.h>
typedef double Triplet[3];
typedef struct
        {
           Triplet p; // Position
           Triplet v; // Velocity
           double m; // Mass
        } Body;

nettype Nbody(int m, int k, int n[m])
{
  coord I=m;
  node { I>=0: bench*((n[I]/k)*(n[I]/k)); };
  link { I>0: length*(n[I]*sizeof(Body)) [I]->[0]; };
  parent [0];
};

repl M;          // The number of groups
double [host]t;  // The time variable
repl int tgsize; // The number of bodies in a test group

#include "serial_code.h"

void [net Nbody(m, 1, n[m]) g] ShareMasses (void *masses)
{
  double mass;
  repl i, j;
  typedef double (*pArray)[m];

  mass = (*(pArray)masses)[I coordof i];
  for(i=0; i<m; i++)
    for(j=0; j<m; j++)
      [g:I==i](*(pArray)masses)[j] = [g:I==j]mass;
}
void [net Nbody(m, 1, n[m]) g] ShareCenters(void *centers)
{
  Triplet center;
  repl i, j;
  typedef Triplet (*pArray)[m];

  center[] = (*(pArray)centers)[I coordof i][];
  for(i=0; i<m; i++)
    for(j=0; j<m; j++)
```

```
        [g:I==i](*(pArray)centers)[j][] = [g:I==j]center[];
}


void [*]main(int [host]argc, char **[host]argv)
{
  // Get the number of groups on the host-process
  // and broadcast it to all processes
  M = [host]GetNumberOfGroups(argv[1]);

{

  repl N[M]; // Array of group sizes
  Body *[host]Groups[[host]M];

  // Initialize N and Groups on the abstract host-processor
  [host]: InputGroups(argv[1], M, &N, &Groups);

  // Broadcast the group sizes across all processes
  N[] = [host]N[];

  // Set the size of test group to the size of the smallest
  // group in the system of bodies
  tgsize = [?<]N[];

// Update performance characteristics of the executing
// physical processors
{
  Body OldTestGroup[tgsize], TestGroup[tgsize];
  typedef Body (*pTestGroup)[tgsize];

  // Make the test group consist of first tgsize bodies
  // of the very first group of the system of bodies
  OldTestGroup[] = (*(pTestGroup)Groups[0])[];

  recon UpdateGroup(tgsize, &OldTestGroup, &TestGroup,
                    1, NULL, NULL, 0);
}


// Define an abstract mpC network, g, and specify
// computations and communications on the network
// implementing the heterogeneous parallel algorithm
{
  net Nbody(M, tgsize, N) g;
```

```
int [g]myN, // Size of my group
    [g]mycoord; // My coordinate in network g

mycoord = I coordof g;
myN = ([g]N)[mycoord];
{
  double [g]Masses[[g]M]; // Masses of all groups
  Triplet [g]Centers[[g]M]; // Centers of mass of all groups
  Body [g]OldGroup[myN], // State of my group at time t
       [g]Group[myN]; // State of my group at time t+DELTA

repl [g]gc, // Counter of groups in the system of bodies
     [g]bc, // Counter of bodies in group
     [g]gsize; // Size of group

//Scatter groups
for(gc=0; gc<[g]M; gc++)
{
  [host]: gsize = N[gc];
  {
    typedef Body (*pGroup)[[host]gsize];
    [g:I==gc]Group[] = (*(pGroup)Groups[gc])[];
  }
}

// Visualize the system of bodies on the computer display
// associated with the abstract host-processor
[host]: FirstDrawGroups(argc, argv, M, N, Groups);

// Compute masses of the groups in parallel
for(bc=0, Masses[mycoord]=0.0; bc<myN; bc++)
  Masses[mycoord] += Group[bc].m;

// Communicate to share the masses among abstract
// processors of network g
([[([g]M, [g]tgsize, [g]N)g])ShareMasses(Masses);

// Main loop of the parallel algorithm
do
{
  OldGroup[] = Group[];

// Compute centers of masses of the groups in parallel
Centers[] = 0.0;
for(bc=0; bc<myN; bc++)
```

```
Centers[mycoord][] +=
   (Group[bc].m/Masses[mycoord])*(Group[bc].p)[];

// Communicate to share the centers among abstract
// processors of network g
([([g]M, [g]tgsize, [g]N)g])ShareCenters(Centers);

// Update the groups of bodies in parallel. OldGroup
// contains the state of each group at time t.
// Group will contain the state of each group
// at time t+DELTA.
([g]UpdateGroup)(myN, &OldGroup, &Group, [g]M,
                 &Centers, &Masses, mycoord);

// Increment the time variable t
t += DELTA;

// Gather all groups to the abstract host-processor
for(gc=0; gc<[g]M; gc++)
{
   gsize = [host]N[[host]gc];
   {
      typedef Body (*pGroup)[gsize];
      (*(pGroup)Groups[gc])[] = [g:I==gc]Group[];
   }
}

// Visualise the groups on the computer display
// associated with the abstract host-processor
if(DrawGroups([host]M, [host]N, Groups)<0)
   MPC_Exit(-1);
}
while(1);
[host]: DrawBye(M, N, Groups);
}
}
}
}
```

The code presented here does not contain the source code of the mpC program, which specifies the routine serial computations peformed by a single process to update the state of a group of bodies or to visualize the system of bodies. It only contains the mpC-specific parallel code. The serial routine code is contained in the file `source_code.h`, and it is included in the program with an `include` directive. The full code of the mpC application can be found in Appendix A.

In the preceding code there are three key components that control the mapping of the heterogeneous parallel algorithm to the executing network of computers:

- The definition of the network type `Nbody`.
- The `recon` statement updating performance characteristics of physical processors.
- The definition of the abstract mpC network `g`.

The `recon` statement uses a call to function `UpdateGroup` that updates the state of a test group of `tgsize` bodies, in order to estimate the speeds of the physical processors. The total volume of computations performed by each abstract processor of network `g` mainly falls into execution of calls to function `UpdateGroup`. Therefore the obtained speed estimations of the physical processors will be very close to their actual speeds in executing the program.

The `recon` statement not only updates the performance characteristics of the physical processors but also specifies a unit of measure for the absolute volume of the computation. It is assumed that after the execution of the `recon` statement and before the execution of the next `recon` statement, the absolute volume of computation is measured in calls to function `Update-Group`, which updates the state of a group of `tgsize` bodies. Thus, if some computations are specified to be of volume v in this time slot, the execution time of the computations will be considered equal to the execution time of the call to function `UpdateGroup` updating the state of a test group of `tgsize` bodies multiplied by v, $t_{comp} = t_{unit} \times v$.

The `recon` statement is executed right before definition of network `g`. The definition causes the creation of an mpC network of type `Nbody` with the following actual parameters:

- Integer variable `M` specifying the actual number of groups of bodies.
- Integer variable `tgsize` specifying the actual size of the group, whose bodies' position and velocity are updated by the benchmark code.
- Array `N` of `M` integers containing actual sizes of the groups of bodies of the modeled system.

These parameters in concert with the definition of the network type `Nbody` and the test code provided by the `recon` statement specify that

- network g will consist of M abstract processors,
- the absolute volume of computation performed by the ith abstract processor will be $(\mathtt{N[i]/tgsize})^2$ times bigger than the volume of computation performed by a call to function UpdateGroup updating the state of a group of tgsize bodies, and
- the ith abstract processor will send N[i]*sizeof(Body) bytes to the abstract host-processor.

In effect the volume of computations and communications performed by a single iteration of the main loop of the program is specified in the program with high accuracy. This information, along with information about the performance characteristics of the physical processors and communication links, is used to map the abstract processors of network g to the parallel processes of the parallel program.

The mapping is performed at runtime to minimize the execution time of a single iteration of the main loop. Note that the performance characteristics of the physical processors are refreshed by the recon statement directly before the mapping is performed. Therefore the mapping is based on the actual speeds of the physical processors demonstrated during the execution of the program. By all these means the mpC programming system can accurately estimate the execution time of a single iteration of the main loop for any particular mapping of abstract processors to parallel processes of the program, and then select mapping leading to faster execution.

Note that the mpC program implicitly assumes that the size of type Body is the same on all abstract processors. Because of this condition the communications time element can be accurately estimated. In heterogeneous environments this condition may not be satisfied. The following slight modification of the definition of the Nbody network type makes the program independent of this condition:

```
nettype Nbody(int m, int k, int n[m])
{
   coord I=m;
   node { I>=0: bench*((n[I]/k)*(n[I]/k));};
   link { I>0: length(Body)*n[I] [I]->[0];};
   parent [0];
};
```

By default, a link declaration uses *byte* as a unit of measure and so specifies the volume of communication data in bytes. The link declaration in the network type above defines a unit of measure different from byte. It specifies that the volume of data transferred between abstract processors be measured in Bodys. This means that the data units are now equal in size to that of type Body on the abstract processor sending the data.

The next mpC application implements an algorithm of parallel multiplication of matrix A and the transposition of matrix B on a heterogeneous network; that is, it performs matrix operation $C = A \times B^T$, where A, B are dense square $n \times n$ matrices. The algorithm is a result of slight modification of the algorithm presented in Section 6.10.

The modification is aimed at taking into account the contribution of communication operations into the execution time of the algorithm. As communication overheads may exceed gains due to the parallel execution of computations, the distribution of computations across all available physical processors does not always result in the fastest execution of the matrix-matrix multiplication. Sometimes certain subnetworks of the computers better execute the algorithm.

In general, there is some optimal subset of the available physical processors that will perform the matrix-matrix multiplication. The modified algorithm includes such an optimal subset in the computations. The main problem that must be solved by the modified algorithm of parallel matrix-matrix multiplication is that of finding a subset of physical processors to execute the algorithm faster than the other subsets.

Suppose that there are, in total, p physical processors available and that we can estimate the execution time of the algorithm on each given subset. Then, to arrive at an accurate solution, we should examine as many as 2^p possible subsets to find the optimal one. Obviously that computational complexity is not acceptable for a practical algorithm. Therefore the algorithm will search for an approximate solution that can be found in some reasonable time. Namely, instead of 2^p subsets, only p subsets $\{s_i\}_{i=1}^p$ will be examined. The subsets are defined as follows:

- Subset s_1 consists of the processor running the host-process.
- Subset s_i consists of all processors of subset s_{i-1} and the fastest of the remaining processors $(i = 2, \ldots, p)$.

This scheme assumes that among subsets with the same number of processors, the fastest execution of the algorithm is provided by the subset having the highest total speed of processors. An obvious case when this approach may not work well is when a very slow communication link connects the fastest processor with other processors. The following mpC code implements this modified algorithm:

```
#include <stdio.h>
#include <stdlib.h>
#include <mpc.h>
#include <float.h>

void Partition(), SerialAxBT();
```

```
nettype ParallelAxBT(int p, int n, int r, int d[p])
{
   coord I=p;
   node { I>=0: bench*((d[I]*n)/(r*r)); };
   link (J=p) { I!=J: length*(d[I]*n*sizeof(double))
   [J]->[I]; };
   parent [0];
};


int compar(const void *px, const void *py)
{
   if(*(double*)px > *(double*)py)
     return -1;
   else if(*(double*)px < *(double*)py)
     return 1;
   else
     return 0;
}


int [*]main(int [host]argc, char **[host]argv)
{
   repl int n, r, p, *d;
   repl double *speeds;

   n = [host]atoi(argv[1]);
   r = [host]atoi(argv[2]);

// Run a test code in parallel by all physical processors
// to refresh the estimation of their speeds
{
   repl double a[r][n], b[r][n], c[r][n];
   repl int i, j;

   for(i=0; i<r; i++)
     for(j=0; j<n; j++)
     {
        a[i][j] = 1.0;
        b[i][j] = 1.0;
     }
   recon SerialAxBT((void*)a, (void*)b, (void*)c, r, n);
}

// Detect the total number of physical processors
p = MPC_Get_number_of_processors();

speeds = calloc(p, sizeof(double));
```

```
d = calloc(p, sizeof(int));

// Detect the speed of the physical processors
MPC_Get_processors_info(NULL, speeds);

// Sort the speeds in descending order
qsort(speeds+1, p-1, sizeof(double), compar);

// Calculate on the abstract host-processor the optimal number
// of physical processors to perform the matrix operation
[host]:
   {
     int m;
     struct {int p; double t;} min;
     double t;

     min.p = 0;
     min.t = DBL_MAX;
     for(m=1; m<=p; m++)
     {
       // Calculate the size of C slice to be computed by
       // each of m involved physical processors
       Partition(m, speeds, d, n, r);

       // Estimate the execution time of matrix-matrix
       // multiplication on m physical processors
       t = timeof(net ParallelAxBT(m, n, r, d) w);

       if(t<min.t)
       {
         min.p = m;
         min.t = t;
       }
     }
     p = min.p;
   }

// Broadcast the optimal number of involved processors to all
// parallel processes of the program
p = [host]p;

// Calculate the size of C slice to be computed by
// each of p involved physical processors
Partition(p, speeds, d, n, r);
{
```

```
net ParallelAxBT(p, n, r, d) w;
int [w]myn;


myn = ([w]d)[I coordof w];
[w]:
{
  double A[myn/r][r][n], B[myn/r][r][n],
  C[myn/r][r][n];
  repl double Brow[r][n];
  int i, j, k;

  for(i=0; i<myn/r; i++)
    for(j=0; j<r; j++)
    for(k=0; k<n; k++)
{
      A[i][j][k] = 1.0;
      B[i][j][k] = 1.0;
    }
  {

  repl int PivotNode=0, RelPivotRow, AbsPivotRow;

  for(AbsPivotRow=0, RelPivotRow=0, PivotNode=0;
      AbsPivotRow < n;
      RelPivotRow += r, AbsPivotRow += r)
  {
    if(RelPivotRow >= d[PivotNode])
    {
      PivotNode++;
      RelPivotRow = 0;
    }
    Brow[] = [w:I==PivotNode]B[RelPivotRow/r][];
    for(j=0; j<myn/r; j++)
      SerialAxBT((void*)A[j][0], (void*)Brow[0],
              (void*)(C[j][0]+AbsPivotRow), r, n);
      }
    }
  }
}
free(speeds);
free(d);
}
```

The preceding code does not contain the source code of functions `Partition` and `SerialAxBT`, which is identical to that presented in Section 6.10. It is presumed that there is one-to-one mapping between processes of the parallel program and physical processors of the executing network of computers. That is, the total number of processes of the mpC program is assumed to be equal to the total number of available physical processors with each processor running exactly one process.

Major changes are made in the definition of the network type `Parallel1AxBT`. Recall that this network type describes the performance model of the implemented algorithm of parallel matrix-matrix multiplication. Now this performance model includes the absolute volume of computation performed by each abstract processor and the volume of data transferred between each pair of abstract processors.

It is presumed that the test code, which is used for estimation of the speed of physical processors, multiplies rxn and nxr matrices, where r is small enough compared to n and supposed to be a multiple of n. It is also presumed that *i*th element of vector parameter d is just the number of rows in the C slice mapped to the *i*th abstract processor of the mpC network performing the algorithm.

Correspondingly the `node` declaration specifies that the volume of computation to be performed by the *i*th abstract processor is `d[i]*n/(r*r)` times bigger than the volume of computation performed by the test code. The `link` declaration specifies that each abstract processor will send its B slice to each of other abstract processors.

The `recon` statement updates the estimation of the speed of the physical processors of the executing network by using serial multiplication of test rxn and nxr matrices with the function `SerialAxBT`. The computations performed by each abstract processor will mainly fall into the execution of calls to `SerialAxBT`. Therefore the speed of the physical processors returned in array `speeds` by function `MPC_Get_processors_info` will be an accurate approximation of the real speed demonstrated by the physical processors during execution of the program. The `recon` statement also specifies that a call to function `SerialAxBT` multiplying rxn and nxr matrices will be used as a unit of measure of the absolute volume of computation in this program.

There is a brand new block in this program executed by the abstract host-processor. The block calculates the number of physical processors that will perform the parallel matrix-matrix multiplication. In this block the operator `timeof` estimates the execution time of the parallel algorithm, which is specified by its operand, without its real execution.

The only operand of the `timeof` operator looks like a definition of the mpC network. The definition specifies the performance model of a parallel algorithm providing the following information:

- The number of abstract processors performing the algorithm.
- The volume of computation performed by each abstract processor measured in units specified by the most recently executed `recon` statement.

In our program the volume will be measured in calls to function `Seri-alAxBT` multiplying `rxn` and `nxr` matrices.

- The volume of communication between each pair of the abstract processors measured in bytes.

Based on this information and the most recent performance characteristics of physical processors and communication links, the operator does not really create an mpC network specified by its operand. Instead, it calculates the time of execution of the corresponding parallel algorithm on such a network as if it were created at this point of the program. The operator returns the calculated time in seconds.

Thus, at each iteration of the `for` loop in the block, the `timeof` operator returns the calculated time of execution of the matrix-matrix multiplication on an mpC network of m abstract processors (m = 1, . . . , p). As there is one-to-one mapping between abstract processors of the mpC network and physical processors, the mpC network represents the subset of physical processors consisting of the host-processor and m-1 fastest processors. After execution of this block, the value of variable p on the host-processor will be equal to the number of processors in the subset providing the fastest execution of the algorithm.

The definition of network w specifies exactly this optimal number of processors. Therefore the parallel matrix-matrix multiplication itself will be performed by the very subset of physical processors that is found to provide the fastest execution of the algorithm.

Note, again, that the mpC program above implicitly assumes that the size of `double` is the same on all abstract processors. The following slight modification of the definition of the `ParallelAxB` network type makes the program independent of the condition:

```
nettype ParallelAxBT(int p, int n, int r, int d[p])
{
   coord I=p;
   node { I>=0: bench*((d[I]*n)/(r*r)); };
   link (J=p) { I!=J: length(double)*(d[I]*n) [J]->[I]; };
   parent [0];
};
```

7.2. COMMUNICATION PATTERNS

In the mpC programs presented in Section 7.1, we used the `link` declaration to describe the contribution of communication operations in the execution of the parallel algorithm. More specifically, the `link` declaration in a network type definition specifies:

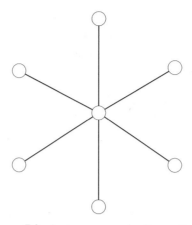

Figure 7.3. A star communication pattern.

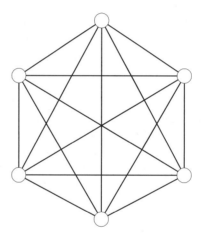

Figure 7.4. A fully connected network.

- the pattern of communication among the abstract processors, meaning a set of communication links over which the abstract processors communicate with each other, and
- the volume of data transferred via each of the communication links.

The communication pattern can be graphically depicted with nodes representing the abstract processors and arcs representing the communication links. The communication pattern described by the link declaration in the definition of the Nbody network type is known as a *star* (see Figure 7.3). The communication pattern described by the link declaration in the definition of the ParallelAxBT network type is known as a *fully connected network* (see Figure 7.4).

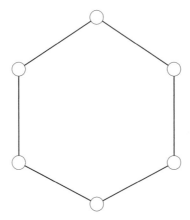

Figure 7.5. A ring communication pattern.

While the communication patterns are very simple, they are widely used in many parallel algorithms. Yet another simple communication pattern is a *ring* (see Figure 7.5). The next mpC program implements a parallel algorithm using this pattern:

```
#include <stdio.h>
#include <stdlib.h>
#include <mpc.h>

#define M 100

nettype Ring(int p, double comp, int comm) {
  coord I=p;
  node { I>=0: bench*comp; };
  link
  {
    I>=0: length*(comm*sizeof(int)) [I]->[(I+1)%p];
  };
  parent [0];
};
void [net Ring(n, comp, comm) r] shift(void *a)
{
  int me, right, left, (*b)[comm];

  b=a;
  me = I coordof r;
  right = (me+1)%n;
  left = (me+n -1)%n;
```

```
    [r:I==right](*b)[]  =  [r:I==me](*b)[];
    [r:I==me](*b)[]  =  [r:I==left](*b)[];
}


int [*]main(int [host]argc, char **[host]argv)
{
  repl int n;
  n = [host]atoi(argv[1]);
  {
    net Ring(n, 0.000001, M) r;
    int [r]a[M];

    a[] = I coordof r;
    [host]: printf("[+]a[]=%d\n", [+]a[]);
    ([([r]n, [r]0.000001, [r]M)r])shift(a);
    [host]: printf("[+]a[]=%d\n", [+]a[]);
  }
}
```

The abstract processors of network r are logically connected into a communication ring. During the program's execution each abstract processor sends its copy of array a to the neighbor at the right in this ring while receiving its copy of this array from the neighbor at the left. In other words, the program shifts clockwise the distributed array a in this ring.

The network function shift, which performs the shift operation, is not a good programming style example. It is given here only to demonstrate that the mpC language allows the programmer to split a single communication operation into two suboperations, one of which sends data and the other receives it.

For example, execution by each abstract processor of the assignment

```
[r:I==right](*b)[]  =  [r:I==me](*b)[];
```

only results in *sending* an array pointed by b from this abstract processor to its neighbor at the right. The reason is that variables me and right are not replicated and have different values on different abstract processors. The logical expression I==me will be true on each abstract processor. Therefore all abstract processors will send data during execution of the assignment. The logical expression I==right will be false on each abstract processor, and therefore none of them will receive data during execution of the operation. Similarly execution of assignment

```
[r:I==me](*b)[]  =  [r:I==left](*b)[];
```

by each abstract processor only results in *receiving* data from its neighbor at the left and storing the data in an array pointed by b.

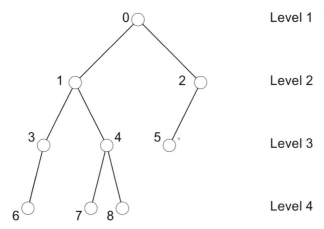

Figure 7.6. A four-level binary tree. Node 0 is a *root*. Nodes 5, 6, 7, and 8 are *leaves*. Nodes 1, 2, 3, and 4 are *interior*.

Although this style of parallel programming can sometimes lead to a more concise and efficient code, it is unsafe and not easy to understand. It is therefore not recommended.

The volume of computation performed by the abstract processors of network r is specified because the contribution of computations into the total execution time is negligibly small compared to that of communications. This informs the compiler to optimize data transfer rather than the computations during the mapping of the abstract processors of network r to the parallel processes of the program.

The next mpC program uses a more complex communication pattern known as a *binary tree*, meaning a tree with at most two children for each node (see Figure 7.6). In this program the root node of the tree computes some data and broadcasts the data to all other nodes:

```
#include <stdio.h>
#include <stdlib.h>
#include <mpc.h>

#define M 100

nettype Tree(int p, double comp, int comm) {
  coord I=p;
  node
  {
    I==0: bench*comp;
    I>0: bench*0.;
  };
```

```
link
{
    I>=0: length*(comm*sizeof(int))  [I]->[2*I+1],
                                     [I]->[2*I+2];
};
parent [0];
};


int [*]main(int [host]argc, char **[host]argv)
{
    repl n; //Number of levels in a binary tree
    repl p; //Number of nodes in an n-level perfect binary tree
    repl i, j;

    n = [host]atoi(argv[1]);
    for(i=1, j=2, p=1; i<n; i++, j*=2)
        p+=2*i;
    {
        net Tree(p, 0.000001, M) t;
        int [t]a[M];
        repl [t]i;

        [host]: a[] = p;
        [host]: printf("[+]a[]=%d\n", [+]a[]);
        for(i=0; i<[t]p/2; i++)
        {
            [t:I==2*i+1]a[] = [t:I==i]a[];
            [t:I==2*i+2]a[] = [t:I==i]a[];
        }
        [t:I==p-1]: MPC_Printf("[+]a[]=%d\n", [+]a[]);
    }
}
```

In the program the `Tree` network type specifies a communication pattern that forms a *complete binary tree*, that is, an n-level binary tree in which all leaf nodes are at level n or $n-1$, level $n-1$ is full, and all leaves at level n are toward the left (see Figure 7.7).

Network t of type `Tree` is defined in the program so that its communication pattern forms a *perfect binary tree*. This is a particular case of the complete binary tree in which all levels are full (see Figure 7.8).

The program computes the value of array a for the parent of network t and broadcasts the array to all other abstract processors of this network as follows:

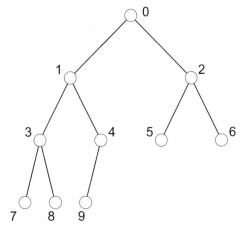

Figure 7.7. A four-level complete binary tree. Level 3 is full.

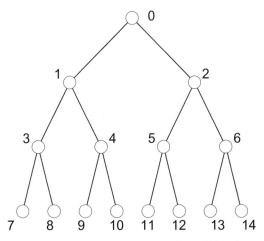

Figure 7.8. A four-level perfect binary tree, since all levels are full. An n-level perfect binary tree has $2^n - 1$ nodes.

- First the parent, which is the root of the broadcast tree, sends array a to its children.
- Then each interior node of the tree sends array a to its children after it has received this array from its parent.

So far all the communication patterns specified in our programs were *static* in that while the quantitive characteristics of the communication pattern (e.g., number of nodes and links) could be specified at runtime, the shape of the pattern was always the same. For example, the pattern of communications between the abstract processors of any mpC network of the Nbody type will always form a star no matter what parameters are specified. In general, the mpC language allows dynamic communication patterns.

There are several ways to describe dynamic patterns in mpC. One simple approach is demonstrated by the following network type definition:

```
nettype Dynamic(int p, int comp, int comm, int pattern)
{
  coord I=p;
  node { I>=0: bench*comp; };
  link
  {
    pattern==STAR: length*comm [0]->[I];
    pattern==RING: length*comm [I]->[(I+1)%p];
  };
  parent [0];
};
```

The link declaration in this definition describes the star or ring communication pattern depending on the parameter pattern.

The mpC language allows the programmer to specify not only regular but also irregular communication patterns. The following example demonstrates how an artibrary irregular coomunication pattern might be specified in mpC:

```
nettype Irregular(int p, int comp, int comm, int pattern[p][p])
{
  coord I=p;
  node { I>=0: bench*comp; };
  link (J=p)
  {
    I!=J: length*(comm*pattern[I][J]) [I]->[J];
  };
  parent [0];
};
```

In the definition above, an array parameter pattern is used to specify the presence or absence of communcation between pairs of abstract processors. It is supposed that the value of elements of the array is either 0 or 1. If pattern[I][J] is equal to 0, the link declaration will specify no data transfer from abstract processor I to abstract processor J. If pattern[I][J] is equal to 1, the transfer of comm bytes from abstract processor I to abstract processor J will be specified. Note that as information about the volume of data transfer between abstract processors is calculated and used at runtime, regular communication patterns have no advantage over irregular ones in terms of efficiency.

7.3. ALGORITHMIC PATTERNS

The performance model of the parallel algorithm presented in Section 7.1 takes into account the contribution of communication operations to the total execution time. This characteristic makes it much more realistic compared to the basic model presented in Chapter 6. The main parameters of this model are as follows:

- The number of parallel processes executing the algorithm.
- The absolute volume of computations performed by each process.
- The absolute volume of data transferred between each pair of processes during the execution of the algorithm.

However, one more important feature of the parallel algorithm that has a significant impact on its execution time is still not reflected in this model. That feature is the order of execution of computations and communications by the parallel processes of the algorithm.

The model says nothing about how exactly parallel processes are interacting during the execution of the algorithm. Therefore the mpC compiler must make some assumptions about the interaction in order to calculate the execution time of the algorithm. Namely, to calculate the execution time, the compiler assumes that

- each process executes all its computations in parallel with other processes,
- the processes execute all the communications in parallel, and
- a synchronization barrier exists between the execution of the computations and the communications.

This assumption is satisfactory only for a restricted class of parallel algorithms. In many parallel algorithms there are data dependencies among computations performed by different processes. One process may need data computed by other processes in order to start its computations, which serializes certain computations performed by different parallel processes. As a result the real execution time of the algorithm will be longer than the execution time calculated proceeding from the assumption about strictly parallel execution of computations.

On the other hand, some parallel algorithms can overlap computations and communications to achieve better performance. The real execution time of those algorithms will be shorter than the execution time proceeding from the assumption that computations and communications do not overlap.

Thus, when calculation of the execution time of different parallel algorithms is based on the same scenario of interactions of parallel processes during execution of the algorithm, the calculated execution time may be not accurate. This may lead to the mapping of the algorithms to the executing network of computers, which is far removed from optimal mapping. An obvious example is an algorithm with fully serialized computations performed by different processes. The optimal mapping should always assign all the processes to the fastest physical processor. Nevertheless, the assumption above could lead, as it often does, to mapping that involves all available processors.

The mpC language allows the programmer to specify the interactions of the parallel processes during execution of the parallel algorithm. This specification is a part of the network type's definition. A new type of declaration, a scheme declaration, is introduced. It describes the interactions of abstract processors during the execution of the specified algorithm.

For example, the network type definition

```
nettype Nbody(int m, int k, int n[m])
{
  coord I=m;
  node { I>=0: bench*((n[I]/k)*(n[I]/k));};
  link { I>0: length*(n[I]*sizeof(Body)) [I]->[0];};
  parent [0];
  scheme
  {
    int i;
    par (i=0; i<m; i++) 100%%[i];
    par (i=1; i<m; i++) 100%%[i]->[0];
  };
};
```

includes a scheme declaration. The definition describes a performance model of the parallel N-body simulation algorithm presented in Section 7.1. The scheme declaration just says to the mpC compiler that first all abstract processors perform in parallel 100 percent of computations that should be performed, and then all the processors, except the host-processor, send in parallel 100 percent of data that should be sent to the host-processor.

In this case the scheme declaration is redundant because the scenario it describes is identical to the default scenario used by the mpC compiler. The next network type definition describes the algorithm of parallel multiplication on a heterogeneous network of matrix A and the transposition of matrix B also presented in Section 7.1:

```
nettype ParallelAxBT(int p, int n, int r, int d[p]) {
  coord I=p;
```

```
node { I>=0: bench*((d[I]*n)/(r*r)); };
link (J=p) { I!=J: length*(d[I]*n*sizeof(double)) [J]->[I]; };
parent [0];
scheme
{
    int i, j, PivotProcessor=0, PivotRow=0;
    for(i=0; i<n/r; i++, PivotRow+=r)
    {
        if(PivotRow>=d[PivotProcessor])
        {
            PivotProcessor++;
            PivotRow=0;
        }
        for(j=0; j<p; j++)
            if(j!=PivotProcessor)
                (100.*r/d[PivotProcessor])%%[PivotProcessor]->[j];
        par(j=0; j<p; j++)
            (100.*r/n)%%[j];
    }
};
};
```

This definition of the network type `ParallelAxBT` also includes a scheme declaration. The scheme declaration simply says that

- the algorithm consists of n/r successive steps, and
- at each step a row of blocks (the pivot row) of matrix B, representing a column of blocks of matrix B^T, is communicated (broadcast) vertically, and all abstract processors compute the corresponding column of blocks of matrix C in parallel.

Note that this algorithm was defined exactly the same way in Section 6.10 (see also Figure 6.2). The mpC compiler uses this information to estimate with higher accuracy the execution time of this algoirhtm. The rest of the code of the corresponding mpC program is entirely the same as it is given in Section 7.1.

The scheme declarations in the two examples above are relatively simple. They just reflect the relative simplicity of the underlying parallel algorithms. In general, the mpC language allows the programmer to describe quite sophisticated heterogeneous parallel algorithms by a wide use of parameters, locally declared variables, expressions, and statements.

7.4. UNDERLYING MODELS AND THE MAPPING ALGORITHM

Thus in mpC the programmer can specify a performance model of the implemented parallel algorithm, including

- the number of parallel processes executing the algorithm,
- the absolute volume of computations performed by each process,
- the absolute volume of data transferred between each pair of processes, and
- the scenario of interaction between the parallel processes during the algorithm execution.

This model is used to map the algorithm to the physical processors of the executing network of computers. As we saw earlier, the mapping is performed by a component of the programming system called a *dispatcher* (see Section 6.11). Apart from the performance model of the algorithm, the dispatcher also uses a model of the executing network of computers to perform the mapping.

This section introduces a model of a heterogeneous network of computers that matches the advanced performance model of the parallel algorithm and takes into account the communication layer of network. It also introduces an algorithm that maps the abstract processors of an mpC network to processes of the parallel program running on a heterogeneous network of computers.

7.4.1. Model of a Heterogeneous Network of Computers

The basic model of a heterogeneous network of computers does not allow for communication links between computers, and treats the network as a set of heterogeneous multiprocessors. Each computer is characterized by two attributes:

- The time of execution of a (serial) test code on the computer;
- The number of physical processors.

The first attribute is a function of time, $s(t)$, and it can vary even during the execution of the same mpC application (if the application uses the recon statement). Relative speeds of computers are normalized so that the computer running the host-process is always of unit speed ($s = 1$). The second attribute is a constant, n, and it determines how many noninteracting processes can run in parallel on the computer without a loss of speed.

There is a new advanced model, however, that is more sophisticated and allows for the material nature of communication links and their heterogeneity. This model considers a heterogeneous network to be a multilevel hierarchy of interconnected sets of heterogeneous multiprocessors. The hierarchy reflects the heterogeneity of the communication links, and it may be represented in the form of an attributed tree.

Each node of the tree represents a homogeneous communication space of the heterogeneous network. The first attribute associated with an internal node is a set of computers that communicate over the space, and this set is just a union of all computers which are descendents of the node.

The second attribute is the speed of data transfer between two computers from different sets associated with its children. This attribute characterizes the point-to-point communication at this communication layer and is a function of size of the transferred data block, $q(d)$. Note that $q(0)$ may be nonzero and equal to the start-up time of point-to-point communication at this layer.

The third attribute indicates whether the communication layer allows parallel point-to-point communications between different pairs of computers without a loss of data transfer speed, or whether the layer serializes all of the communications. This attribute can have two values—*serial* and *parallel*. A pure Ethernet network is serial. However, the use of switches can make it parallel.

The next group of attributes is only applicable to a parallel communication layer. It characterizes collective communication operations such as broadcast, scatter, gather, and reduction. The point is that in general, a collective communication operation cannot be considered as a set of independent point-to-point communications. It normally has some special process, called a *root*, that is involved in more communications than other participating processes.

The level of parallelism of each collective communication operation depends on its implementation, and this is reflected in the model by a corresponding attribute. For example, the attribute f_b characterizes the level of parallelism of a broadcast. It is presumed that the execution time t of this operation can be calculated as follows:

$$t = f_b \times t_p + (1 - f_b) \times t_s,$$

where t_s is the time of a purely serial execution of the operation, and t_p is the time of an ideally parallel execution of this operation ($0 \le f_b \le 1$).

Each leaf node of this tree represents a single (homogeneous) multiprocessor computer. In addition to the attributes inherited from the basic model, each node is also characterized by the attributes of the communication layer provided by the computer.

Figure 7.9 depicts the model for a local network of five computers, labeled $A, B, C, D,$ and E. Computer A is a distributed memory eight-processor computer, D is a shared memory two-processor server. Computers $B, C,$ and E are uniprocessor workstations. The local network consists of two segments with $A, B,$ and C belonging to the first segment. Computers D and E belong to the second segment.

The speed of transfer of a data block of k bytes from a process running on computer C to a process running on computer D is estimated by $q_0(k)$, while

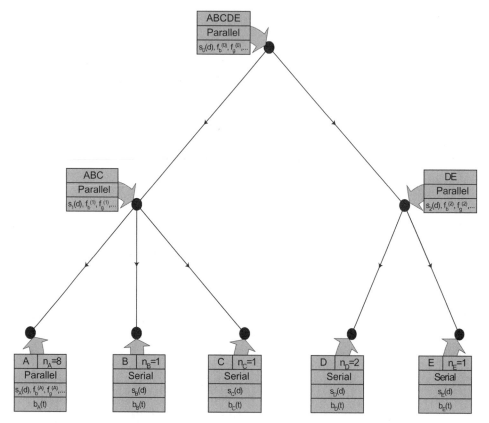

Figure 7.9. Hierarchical model of a heterogeneous network of five computers.

the speed of transfer of the same data block from a process running on computer C to the one running on computer A is estimated by $q_1(k)$. The level of parallelism of a broadcast operation involving processes running on computers B, C, and E is $f_b^{(0)}$, while that of a broadcast involving processes running on computer A is $f_b^{(A)}$.

This communication model is simple but rough. It is used at runtime by the mpC programming system to predict the execution time of the implemented parallel algorithm. It uses a small number of integral attributes presenting some average characteristics rather then a detailed and fine-structured description.

The main reason of this simplicity is that the target architecture for the mpC language is the common network of computers, which normally consists of a multiple-user environment whose structure is irregular and not very stable. Therefore fine-grained communication effects can hardly be reliably predicted for that architecture.

Second, the mpC language is aimed at programming applications in which computations prevail over communications; that is, the contribution of computations in the total execution time is more sunstantial than that of communications. Where that is not the case, it normally means that the main goal of the application is not to speed up the solution of some individual problem, and the distribution of its components over different computers is its intrinsic feature; in other words, the application is actually not parallel but *distributed*.

Thus the mpC language needs an efficient communication model of common heterogeneous networks of computers suitable for prediction of the execution time of data transfer operations involving the transfer of relatively big volumes of data. The accuracy of the prediction does not need to be particularly high because the contribution of communications in the total execution time is supposed to be relatively small. Actually the accuracy cannot be high because of the nature of the modeled hardware.

This communication model is designed to satisfy the primary necessities of the mpC language. Its main disadvantage is that it is static. If an efficient way were found to update its parameters at runtime to reflect the current situation, that could improve its accuracy.

The model of parallel communication layer and collective communication operations also has room for improvement. Multiple experiments with different network configurations could make the model more useful for a wide range of common networks.

7.4.2. The Mapping Algorithm

Any mpC program running on a network of computers is nothing more than a number of processes interacting via message passing. The total number of processes, and the number of processes running on each computer of the network, are determined by the user during the start-up of the program. This information is available to the dipatcher responsible for mapping the abstract mpC networks to these processes.

Each definition of an mpC network creates a group of processes that will act as abstract processors of the network. The main criterion in the selection of the processes for this group is minimization of the execution time of the parallel algorithm whose performance model is described by this mpC network, on a particular network of computers.

Thus at runtime the dispatcher solves the problem of optimally mapping the abstract processors of the mpC network to a set of processes running on different computers of the heterogeneous network. In solving the problem, the dispatcher considers the following:

- The performance model of the parallel algorithm to be executed.
- The model of the executing network of computers, which normally reflects the state of this network right before the execution of the algorithm.

- A map of processes of the parallel program. For each computer the map displays both the total number of running processes and the number of free processes, meaning those processes available to act as the abstract processor of the mpC network.

Each mapping, $\mu:I \to C$, where I is a set of coordinates of the abstract processors of the mpC network and C is a set of computers of the executing network, is characterized by the estimation of the execution time of the algorithm on the network of computers. The estimation is calculated based on the performance models of the parallel algorithm and the executed network.

The execution time of each computation unit in the scheme declaration of the form `e%%[i]` is calculated as follows:

timeof`(e%%[i])` $= (e/100)\,{}^*v_i{}^*b_{\mu(i)}(t_0)$,

where v_i is the total volume of computations to be performed by the abstract processor with coordinate i, and $b_{\mu(i)}(t_0)$ is the execution time of the test code on the computer $\mu(i)$ obtained as a result of execution of the corresponding recon statement (t_0 denotes time when this execution took place). The execution time of each communication unit of the form `e%%[i]->[j]` is calculated as follows:

timeof`(e%%[i]->[j])` $= (e/100)\,{}^*w_{i\text{->}j}{}^*s_{\mu(i)\text{->}\mu(j)}(w_{i\text{->}j})$,

where $w_{i\text{->}j}$ is the total volume of data to be transferred from the abstract processor with the coordinates i to the abstract processor with the coordinates j, and $s_{\mu(i)\text{->}\mu(j)}(w_{i\text{->}j})$ is the speed of transfer of data block of $w_{i\text{->}j}$ bytes between computers $\mu(i)$ and $\mu(j)$.

A simple rule of calculation of the execution time is associated with each sequential algorithmic pattern in the scheme declaration. For example, the execution time **T** of the pattern

for`(e1;e2;e3)a`

is calculated as

```
for(T=0, e1; e2; e3)
   T += timeof(a);
```

The execution time **T** of the pattern

if`(e)` `a1` **else** `a2`

is calculated as

```
if (e)
   T = timeof (a1);
else
   T = timeof (a2);
```

These rules just reflect semantics of the corresponding serial algorithmic patterns. The rule for calculation of the execution time of the parallel algorithmic pattern

```
par (e1; e2; e3) a
```

is more complicated. Informally, this pattern describes parallel execution of some actions (mixtures of computations and communications) on the corresponding abstract mpC network.

Let $A = \{a_0, a_1, \ldots, a_{N-1}\}$ be a set of the actions ordered in accordance with the estimation of their execution time, namely

```
timeof (a0) >=timeof (a1) >= . . . >=timeof (aN-1) .
```

Let B be a subset of A consisting of all actions that only perform communications, $B = \{b_0, b_1, \ldots, b_{Q-1}\}$. Let $C = \{c_0, c_1, \ldots, c_{M-1}\}$. Finally, let m_i be the number of abstract processors of the mpC network mapped on computer c_i, and let n_i be the total number of physical processors of this computer. Then the rule for calculation of the execution time **T** of this pattern is as follows:

```
for (j=0, T=0; j<M; j++) {
   for (i=0, T0=0, k=0; k<Upper (mj, nj) && i<N; i++) {
      if (ai performs some computations on cj) {
         T0 += timeof (ai);
         k++;
      }
   }
   T = max (T, T0);
}
T = max (T, timeof (B) );
```

Here the function **Upper** is defined as

```
Upper (x, y) = if (x/y<=1)
               then 1
               else if ((x/y)*y == x)
                     then x/y
                     else x/y+1
```

Informally, the preceding system of loops first computes for each computer the estimation time T_0 of its parallel execution activity for some computations. The estimate is obtained by the assumption that if the number of parallel actions on one computer exceeds the number of its physical processors, then

- the actions are distributed evenly over the physical processors—that is, the number of actions executed by different physical processors differs by at most one; and
- the most computationally intensive actions are executed on the same physical processor.

The parallel actions that do not involve computation (i.e., perform pure communications) are separated into set B. Let $1(B)$ be the lowest communication layer covering all communication links in B, and let f_b, f_g be the parallel levels of broadcast and gather correspondingly for this layer. Then the rule for calculation of time **T** of the parallel execution of the communication operations from set B is as follows:

```
if(1(B) is serial)
   for(i=0, T=0; i<Q; i++)
   T += timeof(bᵢ);
else if(B matches broadcast/scatter) {
   for(i=0, Tserial=0, Tparallel=0; i<Q; i++) {
     Tserial += timeof(bᵢ);
     Tparallel = max(T₂, timeof(bᵢ));
   }
   T = f_b*Tparallel+(1-f_b) *Tserial
}
else if(B matches gather) {
   for(i=0, Tserial=0, Tparallel=0; i<Q; i++) {
     Tserial += timeof(bᵢ);
     Tparallel = max(T₂, timeof(bᵢ));
   }
   T = f_g*Tparallel+(1-f_g) *Tserial
}
else
   for(i=0, T=0; i<Q; i++)
     T += max(T, timeof(bᵢ));
```

This rule just sums the execution time of the parallel communication operations if the underlying communication layer serializes all data packages. Otherwise, we have a parallel communication layer. Thus, if set B of the communication operations indicates that it is about to broadcast or scatter (i.e., one abstract processor sends data to other involved abstract processors), then the time of parallel execution of the communication operations is calculated as if the broadcast were performed. Similarly, if B indicates that it is about to gather (i.e., one abstract processor receives data from other involved abstract processors), then the time of parallel execution of the communication operations is calculated as if the gather was performed.

In all other instances, it is assumed that B is a set of independent point-to-point communications. Note that it is the responsibility of the programmer not to specify different communication operations sharing the same communication link as the parallel ones.

The rule for estimating the execution time of the parallel algorithmic pattern determes the accuracy and efficiency of the entire mapping algorithm. The rule takes into account the material nature and heterogeneity of the processors and the network equipment.

The rule depends on fair allocation of the processes to the physical processors in the shared memory multiprocessors that are normally implemented by the operating systems for processes of the same priority (e.g., mpC processes). However, the rule takes a pessimistic point of view where the workloads of different processors of that multiprocessor must be estimated.

The communication cost is sensitive to the scalability of the underlying communication network technology. The rule treats differently the communication layers serializing data packages from those supporting their parallel transfer. The most typical and widely used collective communication operations also must be treated individually to provide more accurate estimates of their execution time.

An important feature of the rule nevertheless is its relative simplicity and efficiency, and its efficiency is a crucial consideration because the algorithm is intended to be multiply executed at runtime. A disadvantage of the rule is just the reverse of its simplicity and its efficiency. Except for some common collective communication operations, the rule is not sensitive to different collective communication patterns such as ring data shifting, and tree reduction; rather it treats them all as independent point-to-point communications. The problem is that recognition of different patterns is very costly. One way around this maybe is to introduce into the mpC language explicit constructs that specify all possible important collective communication patterns.

Another disadvantage of the rule in regard to estimation accuracy is that any parallel communications are treated as if they occur within the same communication layer in a hierarchy, namely at the lowest communication layer that encompasses all of the involved processors. In reality some communications will use different communication layers. The task of incorporate multilayer parallel communications in this algorithm without significant loss of efficiency poses a very difficult research problem.

Ideally, the mpC dispatcher should find the mapping that has been proved to provide the fastest execution of the parallel algorithm. In reality, for accurate mapping as many as M^K possible mappings have to be examined in order to find the best one (here K is the power of the set I of coordinates of abstract processors). Obviously such computational complexity is not acceptable for a practical algorithm that must be performed at runtime. Therefore the dispatcher must search for an approximate solution that can be found in some reasonable time frame, namely after examination of $M \times K$ possible mappings instead of M^K.

The underlying algorithm can be summarized as follows: At a preliminary step, set I is re-ordered in accordance with the volume of computations to be performed by the abstract processors so that the most loaded abstract processor will come first. Let $P = \{p_k\}$ $(k=0, \dots, K-1)$ be this well-ordered set.

Let Q_j be a subnetwork of the mpC network formed by the set $P_j = \{p_i\}$ $(i=0, \dots, j)$ of abstract processors. By definition, a subnetwork is a result of projection of the mpC network onto some subset of its abstract processors. Essentially the subnetwork is equivalent to its supernetwork, which is modified as follows:

- Zero volume computations are set for each abstract processor not included in the subnetwork.
- A zero volume of communications is set for each pair of abstract processors where at least one is not included in the subnetwork.

Finally, we let c_j denote the jth computer from set C. Then the main loop of the algorithm can be described by the following pseudocode:

```
for(k=0; k<K; k++) {
    for(j=0, t_best=MAXTIME, c_best=c_0; j<M; j++) {
        if(p_k is not a parent of the mpC network) {
            Map p_k to c_j
            Estimate execution time t for this mapping of Q_k to C
            if(t<t_best) {
                t_best=t;
                c_best=c_j;
            }
            Unmap p_k
        }
    }
    Map p_k to c_best
}
```

The algorithm above reflects the fact that the mpC language is designed to focus on applications with computations prevailing over communications. Therefore abstract processors rather than communication links drive the algorithm. Another argument for this approach is that the maximal number of abstract communication links is equal to the total number of abstract processors squared. Therefore, in general, an algorithm driven by communication links can be quite expensive to execute.

Informally, the algorithm first maps the most loaded abstract processor, ignoring the other abstract processors and communications. After the first abstract processor is mapped, it maps the second most loaded abstract processor only regarding the communications between these two processors, and so on. At the ith step, it maps the ith most loaded abstract processor only regarding data transfer between these i abstract processors. This algorithm exploits the principle that smaller things can be the more evenly distributed than, bigger things. It may be useful to recall here the analogy of balls and baskets in Section 6.11. In distributing balls of different sizes among the baskets of different sizes, it makes sense to start with the biggest ball and put it into the biggest basket, then the second biggest ball into the basket with the biggest free space left, and so on. This algorithm keeps the balance between the ball sizes and the free basket space, and guarantees that if at some step there is no more space left for the next ball, it simply means that there is no way to put all the balls in the baskets.

Similarly, if the algorithm cannot balance the load of physical processors in the case of a low communication cost, it simply means that there is no way to balance the load at all. This algorithm could work as well if the data transfer between the more loaded abstract processors is more significant than that between the less loaded processors. Then the more loaded abstract communication links must be accounted for at earlier stages of the algorithm.

An obvious situation where this mapping algorithm may not work well is when the least loaded abstract processor is involved in a transfer of a much bigger volume of data than more loaded processors, and the contribution of communications to the total execution time is significant. But common sense shows us that this is not what occurs in most parallel algorithms.

7.5. SUMMARY

Besides allowing the user to program computations and communications of the heterogeneous parallel algorithm, the mpC language allows the user to specify the performance model of the algorithm. This performance model takes into account the main features of the algorithm having an impact on its execution time, including

- the number of parallel processes executing the algorithm,
- the absolute volume of computations performed by each process,
- the absolute volume of data transferred between each pair of processes, and
- the scenario of interaction between the parallel processes during the execution of the algorithm.

This information is used at runtime to map the algorithm to the physical processors of the computer network. When perfoming the mapping, the mpC programming system tries to minimize the execution time of the algorithm.

The mpC language is designed with a common network of computers as the target parallel architecture. In such networks the performance of communication links and processors is rarely balanced for high-performance computing. Normally the ratio of the speed of data transfer to the speed of processors is significantly lower than that of specialized parallel computer systems. In addition the performance characteristics of common networks are usually not stable; indeed, performance can vary greatly because many independent users have access to their resources.

As a result it is very difficult—if at all possible—to make portable and efficient implementations of parallel algorithms using a fine and sophisticated structure of communications, or making communications prevail over computations, on common networks of computers. The mpC language is mainly suitable for programming parallel algorithms with a relatively simple and coarse-grained structure of communications, and allowing computations to prevail over communications.

## CHAPTER 8

Toward a Message-Passing Library for Heterogeneous Networks of Computers

8.1. MPI AND HETEROGENEOUS NETWORKS OF COMPUTERS

In Section 4.2 we presented MPI as the standard message-passing library used for parallel programming a homogeneous distributed memory architecture. In practice, MPI is very often used for parallel programming NoCs as well. There are a number of reasons behind the popularity of MPI among the programmers developing parallel applications for NoCs:

1. There are two free high-quality implementations of MPI, LAM MPI and MPICH, that support cross-platform MPI applications. For example, if an NoC consists of computers running different clones of Unix such as Linux, Solaris, HP/UX, and IRIX, then having installed such an MPI implementation on each computer of the network, the users can develop and execute MPI program running across the computers of the heterogeneous NoC.

2. The standard MPI encapsulates the problem of different data representations in processors of different architectures. The MPI can properly convert data communicated between processors of different architectures. On the sender side, MPI will convert the data to a machine-independent form. The data will be transferred to the receiver in this machine-independent form, where the data will be converted to the receiver's machine-specific form.

3. While very well designed and easy to understand, the MPI communication model is of a low enough level to write efficient code for any NoC.

However, the standard MPI does not address additional challenges posed by heterogeneous NoCs. We analyzed some of the challenges in Chapter 5. We repeat these challenges here:

Parallel Computing on Heterogeneous Networks, by Alexey Lastovetsky
ISBN 0-471-22982-2   Copyright © 2003 by John Wiley & Sons, Inc.

- *Heterogeneity of processors.* A good parallel application for heterogeneous NoCs must distribute computations unevenly in accord with the speeds of the processors. The efficiency of the parallel application also depends on the accuracy of estimation of the processors speeds. Estimating a processors speed is a difficult task because the processor may run at different speeds for different applications because of differences in instructions, the number of instruction execution units, the number of registers, the structure of its memory's hierarchy, and so on.

- *Ad hoc communication network.* The common communication network is heterogeneous, so the speed and bandwidth of communication links between different pairs of processors may differ significantly. This makes the problem of optimal distribution of computations and communications across the heterogeneous NoC more difficult than across a dedicated cluster of workstations interconnected with a homogeneous high-performance communication network. The other issue is that a common communication network can use multiple network protocols for communication between different pairs of processors. A good parallel application should be able to use multiple network protocols between different pairs of processors within the same application for faster execution of communication operations.

- *Multiple-user decentralized computer system.* Unlike dedicated clusters and supercomputers, NoCs are not strongly centralized computer systems. A typical NoC consists of relatively autonomous computers, where each computer may be used and administered independently by its user. The first implication of the multiple user decentralized nature of NoCs is unstable performance during the execution of a parallel program as the computers may be used for other computations and communications. The second implication is the much higher probability of resource failures in NoCs compared to dedicated clusters of workstations, and this makes fault tolerance a desired feature for parallel applications running on NoCs.

These three main challenges posed by NoCs are not addressed by a standard MPI library. First, the standard MPI library does not employ multiple network protocols between different pairs of processors for efficient communication in the same MPI application. The only exception is the use of shared memory and TCP/IP in the MPICH implementation of MPI. Namely, if two processes of the MPI program run on the same SMP computer, they will communicate by shared memory. If the processes run on different computers, they will communicate by the TCP/IP protocol. There has been some effort made to address this challenge, such as the Nexus research implementation of MPI.

Second, the standard MPI library does not allow programmers to write fault-tolerant parallel applications for NoCs. In Section 5.3.2 we outlined the research efforts made to add the feature of fault tolerance to MPI applications. The most recent research result is FT-MPI, which is an explicit fault-tolerant MPI that extends the standard MPI's interface and semantics. FT-MPI provides application programmers with different methods of dealing with failures within an MPI application than just checkpoint and restart. FT-MPI allows the semantics and associated modes of failures to be explicitly controlled by an application via the modified MPI API. FT-MPI allows for atomic communications, and the level of correctness can be varied for individual communicators. This enables users to fine-tune for coherency or performance as system and application conditions may dictate.

Third, the standard MPI library does not provide features that facilitate the writing of parallel programs that distribute computations and communications unevenly, taking into account the processor speeds and the speeds and bandwidths of communication links. In this chapter we present a research effort in this direction—a small set of extensions to MPI, called HMPI (Heterogeneous MPI), aimed at efficient parallel computing on heterogeneous NoCs. Actually HMPI is an of adaptation of mpC language to the MPI programming level.

8.2. HMPI: HETEROGENEOUS MPI

The standard MPI specification provides communicator and group constructors that allow the application programmers to create a group of processes that execute together some parallel computations to solve a logical unit of a parallel algorithm. The participating processes in the group are explicitly chosen from an ordered set of processes. This approach to the group creation is quite acceptable if the MPI application runs on homogeneous distributed memory computer systems as one process per processor. Then the explicitly created group will execute the parallel algorithm typically with the same execution time as any other group with the same number of processes, because the processors have the same computing power, and the speed and the bandwidth of communication links between different pairs of processors are the same. However, on heterogeneous NoCs, a group of processes optimally selected by their speeds, and the speeds and the bandwidths of the communication links between them, will execute the parallel algorithm faster than any other group of processes. The selection of such a group is usually very difficult. The programmers must write a lot of complex code to detect the actual speeds of the processors and the speeds of the communication links between them, and then use this information to select the optimal set of processes running on different computers of the heterogeneous network.

The main idea of HMPI is to automate the selection of such a group of processes that executes the heterogeneous algorithm faster than any other group. HMPI allows the application programmers to describe a performance model of their implemented heterogeneous algorithm. This model is essentially the same as the one used in the mpC language and presented in Chapters 6 and 7. It allows for all the main features of the underlying parallel algorithm that have an essential impact on application execution performance on heterogeneous NoCs:

- The total number of processes executing the algorithm.
- The total volume of computations to be performed by each process in the group during the execution of the algorithm.
- The total volume of data to be transferred between each pair of processes in the group during the execution of the algorithm.
- The order of execution of the computations and communications by the involved parallel processes in the group, that is, how exactly the processes interact during the execution of the algorithm.

HMPI provides a small and dedicated model definition language for specifying this performance model. This language is practically a subset of the mpC language used to specify mpC network types. A compiler compiles the description of this performance model to generate a set of functions. The functions make up an algorithm-specific part of the HMPI runtime system.

Having provided such a description of the performance model, application programmers can use a new operation, whose interface is shown below, to create a group that will execute the heterogeneous algorithm faster than any other group of processes,

```
int HMPI_Group_create(HMPI_Group* gid,
                      const HMPI_Model* perf_model,
                      const void* model_parameters,
                      int param_count);
```

where

- `perf_model` is a handle that encapsulates all the features of the performance model in the form of a set of functions generated by the compiler from the description of the performance model,
- `model_parameters` are the parameters of the performance model (see the example below), and
- `param_count` is the number of parameters of the performance model.

This function returns an HMPI handle to the group of MPI processes in `gid`.

In HMPI the groups are not entirely independent of each other. Every newly created group has exactly one process shared with already existing groups. That process is called a *parent* of the newly created group, and it is the connecting link through which the computation results are passed if the group ceases to exist. `HMPI_Group_create` is a collective operation, and it must be called by the parent and all the processes, that are not members of any HMPI group.

During the creation of the process group, the HMPI runtime system solves the problem of selecting the optimal set of processes running on different computers of the heterogeneous network. The solution to the problem is based on the following:

- The performance model of the parallel algorithm in the form of the set of functions generated by the compiler from the description of the performance model.
- The model of the executing network of computers, which reflects the state of this network just before the execution of the parallel algorithm.

The algorithms used to solve the problem of process selection are essentially the same as those used in the mpC compiler, as were discussed in Section 7.6. The accuracy of the model of the executing network of computers depends on the accuracy of the estimation of the processor speeds. HMPI provides an operation to dynamically update the estimation of processor speeds at runtime. It is especially important to consider if the computers executing the target program are used for other computations as well. In that case the actual speeds of processors can dynamically change depending on the external computations. The use of this operation, whose interface is shown below, allows the application programmers to write parallel programs that are sensitive to such dynamic variation of the workload in the underlying computer system,

```
int HMPI_Recon(HMPI_Benchmark_function func,
               const void* input_p, int num_of_parameters,
               void* output_p)
```

This operation causes all of the processors to execute a benchmark function `func` in parallel, and the time elapsed by each processor in executing the code is used to update its speed estimate. This is a collective operation that must be called by all of the processes in the group associated with the predefined communication universe `HMPI_COMM_WORLD` of HMPI.

Another principal operation provided by HMPI allows application programmers to predict the total execution time of the algorithm on the underlying hardware. Its interface is written as

```
double HMPI_Timeof(const HMPI_Model* perf_model,
                   const void* model_parameters,
                   int param_count)
```

This function allows the application programmers to write such a parallel application that can follow different parallel algorithms to solve the same problem, making the choice at runtime depending on the particular executing network and its actual performance. This is a local operation that can be called by any process that is a member of the group associated with the predefined communication universe HMPI_COMM_WORLD of HMPI.

A typical HMPI application starts with the initialization of the HMPI runtime system using the operation

```
int HMPI_Init (int argc, char** argv)
```

where argc and argv are the same arguments, passed into the application, as the arguments to main. This routine must be called before any other HMPI routine, and must be called once. This routine must be called by all the processes running in the HMPI application.

After the initialization the application can call any other HMPI routines. In addition MPI users can use normal MPI routines, with the exception of MPI initialization and finalization, including the standard group management and communicator management routines to create and free groups of MPI processes. However, they must use the predefined communication universe HMPI_COMM_WORLD of HMPI instead of MPI_COMM_WORLD of MPI.

We recommend that application programmers avoid using groups created with the MPI group constructor operations to perform computations and communications in parallel with HMPI groups, as this may not result in the best execution performance of the application. The point is that the HMPI runtime system is not aware of any group of the MPI processes that is not created under its control. Therefore the HMPI runtime system cannot guarantee that an HMPI group will execute its parallel algorithm faster than any other group of MPI processes if some groups of MPI processes other than HMPI groups, are active during the algorithm execution.

The only group constructor operation provided by HMPI is the creation of the group using HMPI_Group_create, and the only group destructor operation provided by HMPI is

```
int HMPI_Group_free(HMPI_Group* gid)
```

where gid is the HMPI handle to the group of MPI processes. This is a collective operation that must be called by all the members of this group. There are no analogues of the other group constructors of MPI such as the setlike operations on groups and the range operations on groups in HMPI. This is because

- First, HMPI does not guarantee that groups composed using these operations can execute a logical unit of parallel algorithm faster than any other group of processes, and
- Then, it is relatively straightforward for application programmers to perform such group operations by obtaining the groups associated with

the MPI communicator given by the `HMPI_Get_comm` operation (see the interface shown below).

The other additional group management operations provided by HMPI, apart from the group constructor and destructor, are the following group accessors:

- `HMPI_Group_rank` to get the rank of the process in the HMPI group.
- `HMPI_Group_size` to get the number of processes in this group.

The initialization of HMPI runtime system is typically followed by:

- Updating of the estimation of the speeds of processors with `HMPI_Recon`.
- Finding the optimal values of the parameters of the parallel algorithm with `HMPI_Timeof`.
- Creation of a group of processes, which will perform the parallel algorithm, by using `HMPI_Group_create`.
- Execution of the parallel algorithm by the members of the group. At this point, control is handed over to MPI. MPI and HMPI are interconnected by operation

```
const MPI_Comm* HMPI_Get_comm (const HMPI_Group* gid)
```

which returns an MPI communicator with communication group of MPI processes defined by `gid`. This is a local operation not requiring interprocess communication. Application programmers can use this communicator to call the standard MPI communication routines during the execution of the parallel algorithm. This communicator can safely be used in other MPI routines.

- Freeing the HMPI groups with `HMPI_Group_free`.
- Finalizing the HMPI runtime system by using operation

```
Int HMPI_Finalize (int exitcode).
```

8.3. SUMMARY

The standard message-passing library, MPI, is generally used for parallel programming common heterogeneous NoCs. However MPI does not address some key challenges posed by NoCs. In particular, it does not support fault-tolerant parallel computing, and does not facilitate optimal distribution of computations and communications across heterogeneous NoCs. While some primary research has been carried out to improve MPI, further effort is needed to obtain a good version of MPI for heterogeneous NoCs. The future ideal hetrerogeneous MPI should combine the features separately provided by the Nexus implementation of MPI (mutliprotocol communications), FT-MPI (fault tolerance), and HMPI (optimal heterogeneous distribution computations and communications).

## PART III

APPLICATIONS OF HETEROGENEOUS PARALLEL COMPUTING

## CHAPTER 9

Scientific Applications

9.1. LINEAR ALGEBRA

9.1.1. Matrix Multiplication

Matrix multiplication is widely used in a variety of applications and is often one of the core components of many scientific computations. It is a simple but very important linear algebra kernel. We have widely used matrix multiplication in this book. We used it to analyze the scalability of different parallel architectures, including shared memory multiprocessors (Section 3.1), distributed memory multiprocessors (Section 4.1), and computer networks (Section 5.2). We used matrix multiplication to illustrate parallel programming languages and tools such as MPI 1.1 (Section 4.2.6), HPF 1.1 (Section 4.3), HPF 2.0 (Section 5.1.1), and mpC (Sections 6.10 and 7.1).

In this section we start by introducing a more realistic parallel algorithm for matrix multiplication on homogeneous distributed memory multiprocessors than those given in Section 4.1. Then we give a modification of this algorithm for heterogeneous computer networks, its implementation in the mpC language, and some experimental results.

9.1.1.1. Block Cyclic Algorithm of Parallel Matrix Multiplication on Homogeneous Platforms. The way in which matrices are distributed over the processors has a major impact on the performance and scalability of the parallel algorithm. In Section 4.1 we considered two distributions, both known as *block* distributions. We demonstrated that they are equivalent in terms of computation cost. We also demonstrated that the communication cost of the parallel algorithm based on the two-dimensional block distribution is considerably less than that of the parallel algorithm based on the one-dimensional distribution. Therefore we take this two-dimensional algorithm as a basis for further improvements.

In our performance analysis we proceeded from the assumption that the parallel algorithm consists of two basic steps:

Parallel Computing on Heterogeneous Networks, by Alexey Lastovetsky
ISBN 0-471-22982-2 Copyright © 2003 by John Wiley & Sons, Inc.

- First all processors communicate so that each processor receives all data necessary to compute its block of the resulting matrix (shown shaded in gray in Figure 4.3);
- Then, all processors compute the resulting matrix in parallel.

The scalability of this large-grained parallel algorithm in terms of per-processor computation cost is actually far from the ideal situation presented in Section 4.1. Recall that we assumed that the per-processor computation cost of the parallel multiplication of two dense square $n \times n$ matrices A and B on a p-processor MPP is

$$t_{\text{comp}} = \frac{t_{\text{proc}} \times n^3}{p},$$

where t_{proc} is a constant representing the speed of a single processor and does not depend on n and p.

In reality, t_{proc} is not constant. It depends on the size of data simultaneously stored in the memory of each individual processor and used by the processor in computations. The memory typically has a hierarchical structure with levels of fixed sizes (see Section 2.7 for more detail). Therefore, as more processed data are stored in the memory, the more levels of the memory hierarchy they fill. As a result more data become stored in slow memory. This increases the average execution time of a single arithmetic operation. Thus t_{proc} is an increasing function of the size of stored (and processed) data.

In our case each processor receives $2 \times (\sqrt{p} - 1) \times (n^2/p)$ matrix elements, and hence stores in total $2 \times (n^2/\sqrt{p})$ elements of matrices A and B in its memory. This means that if the size of problem n increases k times, the number of processors executing the algorithm must be increased k^4 times to avoid degradation in average speed of processors.

To improve the scalability and per-processor computation cost of the basic two-dimensional block algorithm, we modify it as follows:

- Matrices A, B, and C are still identically partitioned into p equal $(n/\sqrt{p}) \times (n/\sqrt{p})$ squares, so that each row and each column contain $\sqrt{p}$ squares (for simplicity, we assume that p is a square number, and n is a multiple of $\sqrt{p}$). There is one-to-one mapping between these squares and the processors. Each processor is responsible for computing its C square (see Figure 9.1).
- Each element in A, B, and C is a square $r \times r$ block and the unit of computation is the updating of one block, meaning a matrix multiplication of size r. For simplicity, we assume that $\sqrt{p}$ is a multiple of r.
- The algorithm consists of n/r steps. At each step k,
    - a column of blocks (the pivot column) of matrix A is communicated (broadcast) horizontally (see Figure 9.1),

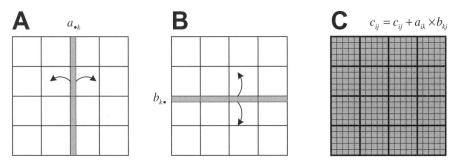

Figure 9.1. One step of the modified algorithm of parallel matrix-matrix multiplication based on two-dimensional block distribution of matrices A, B, and C. First, the pivot column $a_{\bullet k}$ of $r \times r$ blocks of matrix A (shown shaded in gray) is broadcast horizontally, and the pivot row $b_{k \bullet}$ of $r \times r$ blocks of matrix B (shown shaded in gray) is broadcast vertically. Then each $r \times r$ block c_{ij} of matrix C (also shown shaded in gray) is updated, $c_{ij} = c_{ij} + a_{ik} \times b_{kj}$.

- a row of blocks (the pivot row) of matrix B is communicated (broadcast) vertically (see Figure 9.1), and
- each processor updates each block in its C square with one block from the pivot column and one block from the pivot row so that each block $c_{ij}(i, j \in \{1, \ldots, n/r\})$ of matrix C will be updated, $c_{ij} = c_{ij} + a_{ik} \times b_{kj}$ (see Figure 9.1).

Thus, after n/r steps of the algorithm, each block c_{ij} of matrix C will be

$$c_{ij} = \sum_{k=1}^{n/r} a_{ik} \times b_{kj},$$

that is, $C = A \times B$.

As during the execution of this algorithm each processor in total receives from each of its $\sqrt{p} - 1$ horizontal and $\sqrt{p} - 1$ vertical neighbors n^2/p matrix elements, its per-processor communication cost will be the same as that of the basic two-dimensional algorithm. However, at each step of the modified algorithm, each processor receives from the other processors and stores in its memory only $2 \times r \times (n/\sqrt{p})$ elements of matrices A and B. Therefore at any time of execution of the algorithm, each processor stores in total only

$$3 \times \frac{n^2}{p} + 2 \times r \times \frac{n}{\sqrt{p}}$$

elements of matrices A, B, and C in its memory, while at any execution time of the basic two-dimensional algorithm, each processor stores

$$2 \times \frac{n^2}{\sqrt{p}} + \frac{n^2}{p}$$

elements of these matrices. The significant decrease in the amount of data, which are simultaneously stored and processed by each individual processor, leads to a lower per-processor computation cost and better scalability of the algorithm. Now, if the size of the problem increases k times, then we will need to increase the number of processors executing the algorithm only k^2 times instead of k^4 times in order to avoid degradation in the average speed of processors. Optimal values of r depend on the memory hierarchy. Usually r is much smaller than p, $r \ll p$.

The modified two-dimensional block algorithm still has room for improvements. Let us take a closer look at the algorithm from the processors' point of view. The processors of the MPP executing the algorithm are arranged into a two-dimensional $m \times m$ grid $\{P_{ij}\}$, where $m = \sqrt{p}$ and $i, j \in \{1, \ldots, m\}$. Each step k of the algorithm takes the following form:

- The pivot column $a_{\bullet k}$ is owned by the column of processors $\{P_{iK}\}_{i=1}^{m}$ and the pivot row $b_{k \bullet}$ is owned by the row of processors $\{P_{Ki}\}_{i=1}^{m}$, where

$$K = \left[\frac{r \times k}{n/m} \right].$$

- Each processor P_{iK} (for all $i \in \{1, \ldots, m\}$) horizontally broadcasts its part of the pivot column $a_{\bullet k}$ to processors $P_{i \bullet}$.
- Each processor P_{Kj} (for all $j \in \{1, \ldots, m\}$) vertically broadcasts its part of the pivot row $b_{k \bullet}$ to processors $P_{\bullet j}$.
- Each processor P_{ij} receives the corresponding part of the pivot column and pivot row and uses them to update each $r \times r$ block of its C square.

Note that at each step k, each processor P_{ij} participates in two collective communication operations: a broadcast involving the row of processors $P_{i \bullet}$ and a broadcast involving the column of processors $P_{\bullet j}$. Processor P_{iK} is the *root* for the first broadcast, and processor P_{Kj} is the root for the second. As r is usually much less than m, in most cases at the next step $k + 1$ of the algorithm, processor P_{iK} will be again the root of the broadcast involving the row of processors $P_{i \bullet}$, and processor P_{Kj} will be the root of the broadcast involving the column of processors $P_{\bullet j}$. Therefore, at step $k + 1$, the broadcast involving the row of processors $P_{\bullet j}$ cannot start until processor P_{iK} completes this broadcast at step k. Similarly the broadcast involving the column of processors $P_{\bullet j}$ cannot start until processor P_{Kj} completes that broadcast at step k. The root of the broadcast communication operation completes when its communication buffer can be re-used. Typically the completion means that the root has sent out the contents of the communication buffer to all receiving processors.

The strong dependence between the successive steps of the parallel algorithm hinders a parallel execution of the steps. If at the successive steps of the algorithm the broadcast operations involving the same set of processors had different roots, they could be executed in parallel. As a result more communications will be executed in parallel, and more computations and communications will be overlapped.

To break the dependence between the successive steps of the algorithm, we modify the way in which matrices A, B, and C are distributed over the processors. The modified distribution is called a *two-dimensional block cyclic distribution*. It can be summarized as follows:

- Each element in A, B, and C is a square $r \times r$ *block*.
- The blocks are scattered in a cyclic fashion along both dimensions of the $m \times m$ processor grid so that for all $i, j \in \{1, \ldots, n/r\}$, blocks a_{ij}, b_{ij}, c_{ij} will be mapped to processor P_{IJ} where $I = (i - 1) \bmod m + 1$ and $J = (j - 1) \bmod m + 1$.

Figure 9.2a illustrates the distribution from the matrix's point of view. The matrix is now partitioned into $n^2/(r^2 \times m^2)$ equal squares so that each row and each column contain $n/(r \times m)$ squares. All of the squares are identically partitioned into m^2 equal $r \times r$ blocks, so that each row and each column contain m blocks. There is one-to-one mapping between these blocks and the processors. Thus all of the $m \times m$ squares are identically distributed over the $m \times m$ processor grid in a two-dimensional block fashion. Figure 9.2b shows this distribution from the processor's point of view. Each square represents the total area of blocks allocated to a single processor.

The two-dimensional block cyclic distribution is a general-purpose basic decomposition in parallel dense linear algebra libraries for MPPs such as ScaLAPACK. The block cyclic distribution has been also incorporated in the HPF language (see Section 4.3).

9.1.1.2. Block Cyclic Algorithm of Parallel Matrix Multiplication on Heterogeneous Platforms. In Section 9.1.1.1 we focused on the fine structure of the algorithm of matrix multiplication. We tried to improve its performance and scalability on MPPs by better using the memory hierarchy and wider overlapping computations and communications.

In this section we modify this algorithm for heterogeneous clusters. The modification returns us to a fundamental design issue of parallel algorithms that can greatly affect performance and scalability—*load balancing*.

In an MPP all processors are identical. The load of the processors will be perfectly balanced if each processor performs the same amount of work. As all $r \times r$ blocks of the C matrix require the same amount of arithmetics, each processor executes an amount of work that is proportional to the number of $r \times r$ blocks allocated to it and, hence, proportional to the area of its rectangle (see Figure 9.2b). Therefore, to equally load all processors of the MPP, a rectangle of the same area must be allocated to each processor.

	1	2	3	4	5	6	7	8	9	10	11	12	13	14	15	16	17	18
1	P_{11}	P_{12}	P_{13}	P_{11}	P_{12}	P_{13}	P_{11}	P_{12}	P_{13}	P_{11}	P_{12}	P_{13}	P_{11}	P_{12}	P_{13}	P_{11}	P_{12}	P_{13}
2	P_{21}	P_{22}	P_{23}	P_{21}	P_{22}	P_{23}	P_{21}	P_{22}	P_{23}	P_{21}	P_{22}	P_{23}	P_{21}	P_{22}	P_{23}	P_{21}	P_{22}	P_{23}
3	P_{31}	P_{32}	P_{33}	P_{31}	P_{32}	P_{33}	P_{31}	P_{32}	P_{33}	P_{31}	P_{32}	P_{33}	P_{31}	P_{32}	P_{33}	P_{31}	P_{32}	P_{33}
4	P_{11}	P_{12}	P_{13}	P_{11}	P_{12}	P_{13}	P_{11}	P_{12}	P_{13}	P_{11}	P_{12}	P_{13}	P_{11}	P_{12}	P_{13}	P_{11}	P_{12}	P_{13}
5	P_{21}	P_{22}	P_{23}	P_{21}	P_{22}	P_{23}	P_{21}	P_{22}	P_{23}	P_{21}	P_{22}	P_{23}	P_{21}	P_{22}	P_{23}	P_{21}	P_{22}	P_{23}
6	P_{31}	P_{32}	P_{33}	P_{31}	P_{32}	P_{33}	P_{31}	P_{32}	P_{33}	P_{31}	P_{32}	P_{33}	P_{31}	P_{32}	P_{33}	P_{31}	P_{32}	P_{33}
7	P_{11}	P_{12}	P_{13}	P_{11}	P_{12}	P_{13}	P_{11}	P_{12}	P_{13}	P_{11}	P_{12}	P_{13}	P_{11}	P_{12}	P_{13}	P_{11}	P_{12}	P_{13}
8	P_{21}	P_{22}	P_{23}	P_{21}	P_{22}	P_{23}	P_{21}	P_{22}	P_{23}	P_{21}	P_{22}	P_{23}	P_{21}	P_{22}	P_{23}	P_{21}	P_{22}	P_{23}
9	P_{31}	P_{32}	P_{33}	P_{31}	P_{32}	P_{33}	P_{31}	P_{32}	P_{33}	P_{31}	P_{32}	P_{33}	P_{31}	P_{32}	P_{33}	P_{31}	P_{32}	P_{33}
10	P_{11}	P_{12}	P_{13}	P_{11}	P_{12}	P_{13}	P_{11}	P_{12}	P_{13}	P_{11}	P_{12}	P_{13}	P_{11}	P_{12}	P_{13}	P_{11}	P_{12}	P_{13}
11	P_{21}	P_{22}	P_{23}	P_{21}	P_{22}	P_{23}	P_{21}	P_{22}	P_{23}	P_{21}	P_{22}	P_{23}	P_{21}	P_{22}	P_{23}	P_{21}	P_{22}	P_{23}
12	P_{31}	P_{32}	P_{33}	P_{31}	P_{32}	P_{33}	P_{31}	P_{32}	P_{33}	P_{31}	P_{32}	P_{33}	P_{31}	P_{32}	P_{33}	P_{31}	P_{32}	P_{33}
13	P_{11}	P_{12}	P_{13}	P_{11}	P_{12}	P_{13}	P_{11}	P_{12}	P_{13}	P_{11}	P_{12}	P_{13}	P_{11}	P_{12}	P_{13}	P_{11}	P_{12}	P_{13}
14	P_{21}	P_{22}	P_{23}	P_{21}	P_{22}	P_{23}	P_{21}	P_{22}	P_{23}	P_{21}	P_{22}	P_{23}	P_{21}	P_{22}	P_{23}	P_{21}	P_{22}	P_{23}
15	P_{31}	P_{32}	P_{33}	P_{31}	P_{32}	P_{33}	P_{31}	P_{32}	P_{33}	P_{31}	P_{32}	P_{33}	P_{31}	P_{32}	P_{33}	P_{31}	P_{32}	P_{33}
16	P_{11}	P_{12}	P_{13}	P_{11}	P_{12}	P_{13}	P_{11}	P_{12}	P_{13}	P_{11}	P_{12}	P_{13}	P_{11}	P_{12}	P_{13}	P_{11}	P_{12}	P_{13}
17	P_{21}	P_{22}	P_{23}	P_{21}	P_{22}	P_{23}	P_{21}	P_{22}	P_{23}	P_{21}	P_{22}	P_{23}	P_{21}	P_{22}	P_{23}	P_{21}	P_{22}	P_{23}
18	P_{31}	P_{32}	P_{33}	P_{31}	P_{32}	P_{33}	P_{31}	P_{32}	P_{33}	P_{31}	P_{32}	P_{33}	P_{31}	P_{32}	P_{33}	P_{31}	P_{32}	P_{33}

(a) Block cyclic distribution over 3×3 grid

Figure 9.2. A matrix with 18×18 blocks is distributed over a 3×3 processor grid. The numbers at the left and at the top of the matrix represent indexes of a row of blocks and a column of blocks, respectively. (*a*) The labeled squares represent blocks of elements, and the label indicates at which location in the processor grid the block is stored—all blocks labeled with the same name are stored in the same processor. Each shaded and unshaded area represents different generalized blocks. (*b*) Each processor has 6×6 blocks.

In a heterogeneous cluster the processors perform computations at different speeds. To balance the load of the processors, each processor should execute an amount of work that is proportional to its speed. In matrix multiplication this means that the number of $r \times r$ blocks allocated to each processor should be proportional to its speed. Let us modify the two-dimensional block cyclic distribution to satisfy the requirement.

Suppose that the relative speed of each processor P_{ij} is characterized by a real positive number, s_{ij}, so that $\Sigma_{i=1}^{m}\Sigma_{j=1}^{m}s_{ij} = 1$. Then the area of the rectangle allocated to processor P_{ij} should be $s_{ij} \times n^2$.

The homogeneous two-dimensional block cyclic distribution partitions the matrix into *generalized blocks* of size $(r \times m) \times (r \times m)$, each partitioned into $m \times m$ blocks of the same size $r \times r$, going to separate processors (see Figure

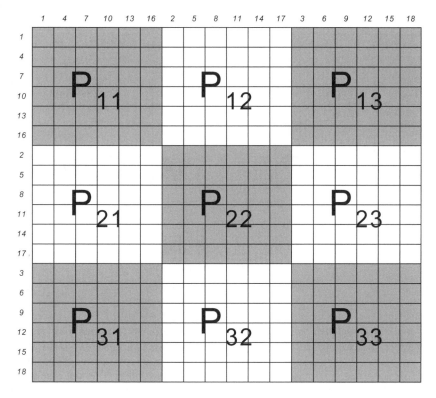

(b) Data distribution from processor point of view

Figure 9.2. *Continued.*

9.2*a*). The modified, *heterogeneous*, distribution also partitions the matrix into generalized blocks of the same size, $(r \times l) \times (r \times l)$, where $m \leq l \leq n/r$. The generalized blocks are identically partitioned into m^2 rectangles, each assigned to a different processor. The main difference is that the generalized blocks are partitioned into unequal rectangles. The area of each rectangle is proportional to the speed of the processor that stores the rectangle.

The partitioning of a generalized block can be summarized as follows:

- Each element in the generalized block is a square $r \times r$ block of matrix elements. The generalized block is a $l \times l$ square of $r \times r$ blocks.
- The $l \times l$ square is first partitioned into m vertical slices so that the area of the jth slice is proportional to $\sum_{i=1}^{m} s_{ij}$ (see Figure 9.3*a*). It is supposed that blocks of the jth slice will be assigned to processors of the jth column in the $m \times m$ processor grid. Thus, at this step, we balance the load *between* processor columns in the $m \times m$ processor grid so that each processor column will store a vertical slice whose area is proportional to the total speed of its processors.

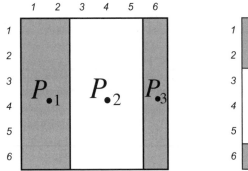
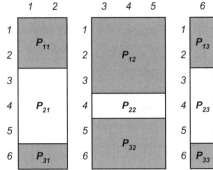

(a) Partition between processor columns   (b) Partition inside each processor column

Figure 9.3. Example of two-step distribution of a 6×6 generalized block over a 3×3 processor grid. The relative speed of processors is given by matrix

$$s = \begin{pmatrix} 0.11 & 0.25 & 0.05 \\ 0.17 & 0.09 & 0.08 \\ 0.05 & 0.17 & 0.03 \end{pmatrix}.$$

(*a*) At the first step, the 6×6 square is distributed in a one-dimensional block fashion over processors columns of the 3×3 processor grid in proportion $0.33:0.51:0.16 \approx 2:3:1$. (*b*) At the second step, each vertical rectangle is distributed independently in a one-dimensional block fashion over processors of its column. The first rectangle is distributed in proportion $0.11:0.17:0.05 \approx 2:3:1$. The second one is distributed in proportion $0.25:0.09:0.17 \approx 3:1:2$. The third one is distributed in proportion $0.05:0.08:0.03 \approx 2:3:1$.

- Each vertical slice is then partitioned independently into m horizontal slices, so that the area of the i-th horizontal slice in the jth vertical slice is proportional to s_{ij} (see Figure 9.3b). It is supposed that blocks of the ith horizontal slice in the jth vertical slice will be assigned to processor P_{ij}. Thus, at this step, we balance the load of processors *within* each processor column independently.

Figure 9.4a illustrates the heterogeneous two-dimensional block cyclic distribution from the matrix point of view. Figure 9.4b shows this distribution from the processor point of view. Each rectangle represents the total area of blocks allocated to a single processor.

Figure 9.5 depicts one step of the algorithm of parallel matrix-matrix multiplication on a heterogeneous $m \times m$ processor grid. Note that the total volume of communications during execution of this algorithm is exactly the same as that for a homogeneous $m \times m$ processor grid. Indeed, at each step k of both algorithms,

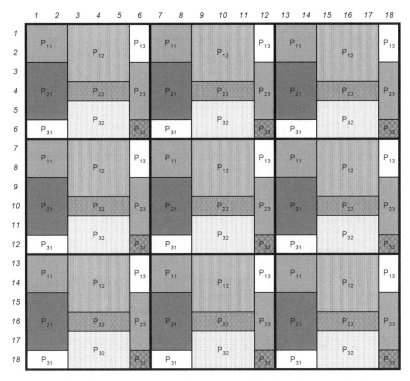

(a) Heterogeneous block cyclic distribution over 3x3 grid.

Figure 9.4. A matrix with 18×18 blocks is distributed over a 3×3 processor grid. The relative speed of processors is given by matrix $\begin{pmatrix} 0.11 & 0.25 & 0.05 \\ 0.17 & 0.09 & 0.08 \\ 0.05 & 0.17 & 0.03 \end{pmatrix}$. The numbers on the left and on the top of the matrix represent indices of a row of blocks and a column of blocks, respectively. (*a*) Each labeled (shaded and unshaded) area represents different rectangles of blocks, and the label indicates at which location in the processor grid the rectangle is stored—all rectangles labeled with the same name are stored in the same processor. Each square in a bold frame represents different generalized blocks. (*b*) Each processor has the number of blocks approximately proportional to its relative speed,

$$\begin{pmatrix} 6 \times 6 & 9 \times 9 & 6 \times 3 \\ 9 \times 6 & 3 \times 9 & 9 \times 3 \\ 3 \times 6 & 6 \times 9 & 3 \times 3 \end{pmatrix} \approx \begin{pmatrix} 0.11 & 0.25 & 0.05 \\ 0.17 & 0.09 & 0.08 \\ 0.05 & 0.17 & 0.03 \end{pmatrix}.$$

- each $r \times r$ block a_{ik} of the pivot column of matrix A is sent horizontally from the processor, which stores this block, to $m - 1$ processors, and
- each $r \times r$ block b_{kj} of the pivot row of matrix B is sent vertically from the processor, which stores this block, to $m - 1$ processors.

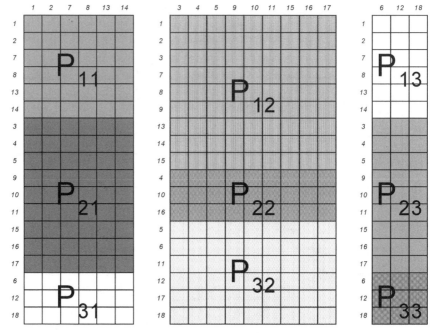

(b) Data distribution from processor point-of-view.

Figure 9.4. *Continued.*

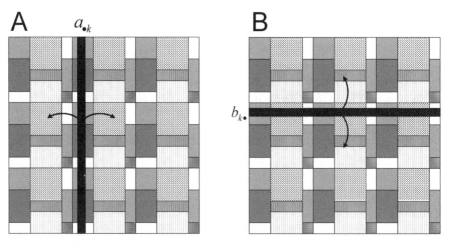

Figure 9.5. One step of the algorithm of parallel matrix-matrix multiplication based on heterogeneous two-dimensional block distribution of matrices A, B, and C. First each $r \times r$ block of the pivot column $a_{\bullet k}$ of matrix A (shown shaded in dark gray) is broadcast horizontally, and each $r \times r$ block of the pivot row $b_{k\bullet}$ of matrix B (shown shaded in dark gray) is broadcast vertically. Then each $r \times r$ block c_{ij} of matrix C is updated, $c_{ij} = c_{ij} + a_{ik} \times b_{kj}$.

The size l of a generalized block is an additional parameter of the heterogeneous algorithm. The range of the parameter is $[m, n/r]$. The parameter controls two conflicting aspects of the algorithm:

- The accuracy of load-balancing.
- The level of potential parallelism in execution of successive steps of the algorithm.

The greater is this parameter, the greater is the total number of $r \times r$ blocks in a generalized block, and hence the more accurately this number can be partitioned in a proportion given by positive real numbers. Therefore, the greater is this parameter, the better the load of processors is balanced. However, the greater is this parameter, the stronger is the dependence between successive steps of the parallel algorithm, which hinders parallel execution of the steps.

Consider two extreme cases. If $l = n/r$, the distribution provides the best possible balance of the processors' load. However, the distribution turns into a pure two-dimensional block distribution resulting in the lowest possible level of parallel execution of successive steps of the algorithm. If $l = m$, then the distribution is identical to the homogeneous distribution, which does not bother with load-balancing. However, it provides the highest possible level of parallel execution of successive steps of the algorithm. Thus the optimal value of this parameter lies in between these two, being a result of a trade-off between load-balancing and parallel execution of successive steps of the algorithm.

The algorithms are easily generalized for an arbitrary two-dimensional processor arrangement.

9.1.1.3. Implementation of the Heterogeneous Algorithm in mpC.

Consider an mpC implementation of the heterogeneous algorithm of parallel matrix multiplication presented in Section 9.1.1.2. One process per physical processor is the assumed configuration of this mpC program. The core of the mpC application is the following definition, which describes the performance model of the algorithm:

```
typedef struct {int I; int J;} Processor;
nettype ParallelAxB(int m, int r, int N, int l, int w[m],
                    int h[m][m][m][m])
{
    coord I=m, J=m;
    node
    {
        I>=0 && J>=0: bench*(w[J]*h[I][J][I][J]*(N/l)*(N/l)*N);
    };
    link (K=m, L=m)
    {
        I>=0 && J>=0 && J!=L && h[I][J][K][L]>0 :
```

```
        length*(w[J]*h[I][J][K][L]*(N/l)*(N/l)*(r*r)* sizeof(double))
            [I, J]->[K, L];

    I>=0 && J>=0 && I!=K :
        length*(w[I]*h[I][J][I][J]*(N/l)*(N/l)*(r*r)* sizeof(double))
            [I, J] -> [K, J];
};
parent[0,0];
scheme
{
int k;
Block Ablock, Bblock;
Processor Root, Receiver, Current;

for(k = 0; k < N; k++)
{
    int Acolumn = k%l, Arow;
    int Brow = k%l, Bcolumn;

    // Broadcast a B row vertically
    par(Bcolumn = 0; Bcolumn < l; )
    {
        GetProcessor(Brow, Bcolumn, &Root);
        par(Receiver.I = 0; Receiver.I < m; Receiver.I++)
            if(Root.I != Receiver.I)
                (100/(h[Root.I][Root.J][Root.I][Root.J]*(N/l))) %%
                    [Root.I, Root.J]->[Receiver.I, Root.J];
        Bcolumn += w[Root.J];
    }

    // Brodcast an A column horizontally
    par(Arow = 0; Arow < l; )
    {
        GetProcessor(Arow, Acolumn, &Root);
        par(Receiver.I = 0; Receiver.I < m; Receiver.I++)
            par(Receiver.J = 0; Receiver.J < m; Receiver.J++)
                if((Root.I != Receiver.I || Root.J !=
                    Receiver.J) && Root.J != Receiver.J)
                if(h[Root.I][Root.J][Receiver.I][Receiver.J])
                (100/(w[Root.J]*(N/l)))%%
                        [Root.I, Root.J]->[Receiver.I, Receiver.J];
    Arow += h[Root.I][Root.J][Root.I][ Root.J];
    }
    // Update C matrix
    par(Current.I = 0; Current.I < m; Current.I++)
```

```
    par(Current.J = 0; Current.J < m; Current.J++)
      (100/N) %% [Current.I, Current.J];
  }
 };
};
```

The network type `ParallelAxB` describing the algorithm has six parameters. Parameter m specifies the number of abstract processors along the row and along the column of the processor grid executing the algorithm. Parameter r specifies the size of a square block of matrix elements, the updating of which is the unit of computation of the algorithm. Parameter N is the size of square matrices A, B, and C measured in $r \times r$ blocks. Parameter l is the size of a generalized block also measured in $r \times r$ block.

Vector parameter w specifies the widths of the rectangles of a generalized block assigned to different abstract processors of the $m \times m$ grid. The width of the rectangle assigned to processor P_{IJ} is given by element w[J] of the parameter (see Figures 9.3b and 9.4b). All widths are measured in $r \times r$ blocks.

Parameter h specifies the heights of rectangle areas of a generalized block of matrix A, which are horizontally communicated between different pairs of abstract processors. Let R_{IJ} and R_{KL} be the rectangles of a generalized block of matrix A assigned to processors P_{IJ} and P_{KL} respectively. Then h[I][J][K][L] gives the height of the rectangle area of R_{IJ}, which is required by processor P_{KL} to perform its computations. All heights are measured in $r \times r$ blocks.

Figure 9.6 illustrates possible combinations of rectangles R_{IJ} and R_{KL} in a generalized block. Let us call a $r \times r$ block of R_{IJ} a *horizontal neighbor* of R_{KL} if the row of $r \times r$ blocks that contains this $r \times r$ block will also contain a $r \times r$ block of R_{KL}. Then the rectangle area of R_{IJ}, which is required by processor P_{KL} to perform its computations, comprises all horizontal neighbors of R_{KL}.

Figure 9.6a shows the situation where rectangles R_{IJ} and R_{KL} have no horizontal neighbors. Correspondingly h[I][J][K][L] is zero. Figure 9.6b shows the situation where all $r \times r$ blocks of R_{IJ} are horizontal neighbors of R_{KL}. In this case both h[I][J][K][L] are equal to the height of R_{IJ}. Figures 9.6c and 9.6d show the situation where only some of $r \times r$ blocks of R_{IJ} are horizontal neighbors of R_{KL}. In this case h[I][J][K][L] is equal to the height of the rectangle subarea of R_{IJ} comprising the horizontal neighbors of R_{KL}. Note that h[I][J][I][J] specifies the height of R_{IJ}, and h[I][J][K][L] will be always equal to h[K][L][I][J].

The `coord` declaration introduces two coordinate variables, I and J, both ranging from 0 to m − 1. The `node` declaration associates abstract processors with this coordinate system to form a $m \times m$ grid. It also describes the absolute volume of computation to be performed by each of the processors. As a unit

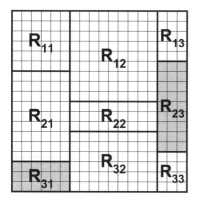

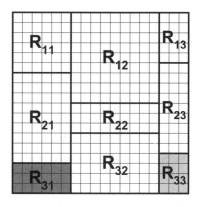

(a) R_{31} has no horizontal neighbors of R_{23}

(b) All $r \times r$ blocks of R_{31} are horizontal neighbors of R_{33}

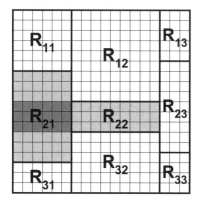

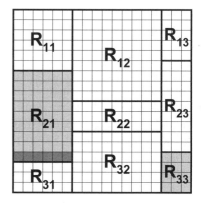

(c) In R_{21}, horizonatal neighbors of R_{22} constitute a 3×6 rectangle subarea

(d) Last row of R_{21} consists of horizontal neighbors of R_{33}

Figure 9.6. Different combinations of rectangles in a generalized block. (a) No $r \times r$ block of rectangle R_{31} is a horizontal neighbor of rectangle R_{23}; therefore h[3][1][2][3] = 0. (b) All $r \times r$ blocks of rectangle R_{31} are horizontal neighbors of rectangle R_{33}; h[3][1][3][3] = 3. (c) Neighbors of rectangle R_{22} in rectangle R_{21} make up a 3×6 rectangle area (shaded in dark gray); h[2][1][2][2] = 3. (d) Neighbors of rectangle R_{33} in rectangle R_{21} make up the last row of this rectangle (shaded in dark gray); h[2][1][3][3] = 1.

of measure, the volume of computation performed by the code multiplying two $r \times r$ matrices is used. At each step of the algorithm, abstract processor P_{IJ} updates $(w_{IJ} \times h_{IJ}) \times n_g$ $r \times r$ blocks, where w_{IJ}, h_{IJ} are the width and height of the rectangle of a generalized block assigned to processor P_{IJ}, and n_g is the total number of generalized blocks. As computations during the updating of one $r \times r$ block mainly fall into the multiplication of two $r \times r$ blocks, the volume of computations performed by the processor P_{IJ} at each step of the algorithm will be approximately $(w_{IJ} \times h_{IJ}) \times n_g$ times larger than the volume of computations performed to multiply two $r \times r$ matrices. As w_{IJ} is given by w[J], h_{IJ} is given by h[I][J][I][J], n_g is given by (N/l)*(N/l), and the total number of steps of the algorithm is given by N, the total volume of computation performed by abstract processor P_{IJ} will be w[J]*h[I][J][I][J]* (N/l)*(N/l)*N times bigger than the volume of computation performed by the code multiplying two $r \times r$ matrices.

The link declaration specifies the volumes of data to be transferred between the abstract processors during the execution of the algorithm. The first statement in this declaration describes communications related to matrix A. Obviously abstract processors from the same column of the processor grid do not send each other elements of matrix A. Abstract processor P_{IJ} will send elements of matrix A to processor P_{KL} only if its rectangle R_{IJ} in a generalized block has horizontal neighbors of the rectangle R_{KL} assigned to processor P_{KL}. In this case processor P_{IJ} will send all such neighbors to processor P_{KL}. Thus, in total, processor P_{IJ} will send $N_{IJKL} \times n_g$ $r \times r$ blocks of matrix A to processor P_{KL}, where N_{IJKL} is the number of horizontal neighbors of rectangle R_{KL} in rectangle R_{IJ} and n_g is the total number generalised blocks. As N_{IJKL} is given by w[J]*h[I][J][K][L], n_g is given by (N/l)*(N/l), and the volume of data in one $r \times r$ block is given by (r*r)*sizeof(double), the total volume of data transferred from processor P_{IJ} to processor P_{KL} will be given by w[J]*h[I][J][K][L]*(N/l)*(N/l)*(r*r)*sizeof(double).

The second statement in the link declaration describes communications related to matrix B. Obviously only abstract processors from the same column of the processor grid send each other elements of matrix B. In particular, processor P_{IJ} will send all of its $r \times r$ blocks of matrix B to all other processors from column J of the processor grid. The total number of $r \times r$ blocks of matrix B assigned to processor P_{IJ} is given by w[J]*h[I][J][I][J]*(N/l)* (N/l).

The scheme declaration describes n successive steps of the algorithm. At each step k:

- A row of $r \times r$ blocks of matrix B is communicated vertically. For each pair of abstract processors P_{IJ} and P_{KJ} involved in this communication, P_{IJ} sends a part of this row to P_{KJ}. The number of $r \times r$ blocks transferred from P_{IJ} to P_{KJ} will be $w_{IJ} \times \sqrt{n_g}$, where $\sqrt{n_g}$ is the number of generalized blocks along the row of $r \times r$ blocks. The total number of $r \times r$ blocks of matrix B, which processor P_{IJ} sends to processor P_{KJ}, is $(w_{IJ} \times h_{IJ}) \times n_g$. Therefore

$$\frac{w_{IJ} \times \sqrt{n_g}}{(w_{IJ} \times h_{IJ}) \times n_g} \times 100 = \frac{1}{h_{IJ} \times \sqrt{n_g}} \times 100$$

percent of data that should be in total sent from processor P_{IJ} to processor P_{KJ} will be sent at this step. The first nested `par` statement in the main `for` loop of the `scheme` declaration just specifies it. The `par` algorithmic patterns are used to specify that during the execution of this communication, data transfer between different pairs of processors is carried out in parallel.

- A column of $r \times r$ blocks of matrix A is communicated horizontally. If processors P_{IJ} and P_{KL} are involved in this communication so that P_{IJ} sends a part of this column to P_{KL}, then the number of $r \times r$ blocks transferred from P_{IJ} to P_{KL} will be $H_{IJKL} \times \sqrt{n_g}$, where H_{IJKL} is the height of the rectangle area in a generalized block, which is communicated from P_{IJ} to P_{KL}, and $\sqrt{n_g}$ is the number of generalized blocks along the column of $r \times r$ blocks. The total number of $r \times r$ blocks of matrix A that processor P_{IJ} sends to processor P_{KL}, is $N_{IJKL} \times n_g$. Therefore

$$\frac{H_{IJKL} \times \sqrt{n_g}}{N_{IJKL} \times n_g} \times 100 = \frac{H_{IJKL} \times \sqrt{n_g}}{(H_{IJKL} \times w_{IJ}) \times \sqrt{n_g}} \times 100 = \frac{1}{w_{IJ} \times \sqrt{n_g}} \times 100$$

percent of data that should be in total sent from processor P_{IJ} to processor P_{KL} will be sent at this step. The second nested `par` statement in the main `for` loop of the `scheme` declaration specifies this fact. Again, we use the `par` algorithmic patterns in this specification to stress that during the execution of this communication, data transfer between different pairs of processors is carried out in parallel.

- Each abstract processor updates each its $r \times r$ block of matrix C with one block from the pivot column and one block from the pivot row so that each block c_{ij} $(i, j \in \{1, \ldots, N\})$ of matrix C is updated, $c_{ij} = c_{ij} + a_{ik} \times b_{kj}$. The processor performs the same volume of computation at each step of the algorithm. Therefore at each of N steps of the algorithm the processor will perform $100/N\%$ of the volume of computations it performs during the execution of the algorithm. The third nested `par` statement in the main `for` loop of the `scheme` declaration just says so. The `par` algorithmic patterns are used here to specify that all abstract processors perform their computations in parallel.

Function `GetProcessor` is used in the `scheme` declaration to iterate over abstract processors that store the pivot row and the pivot column of $r \times r$ blocks. It returns in its third parameter the grid coordinates of the abstract processor storing the $r \times r$ block, whose coordinates in a generalized block of a matrix are specified by its first two parameters.

The main function of this application appears as follows:

```
#define H(a, b, c, d, m) h[(a*m*m*m+b*m*m+c*m+d)]
int [*] main(int [host] argc, char** [host] argv)
```

```
{
  repl int m, r, N, l, *w, *h, *trow, *lcol;
  repl double* speeds;
  int [host] opt_l;
  double [host] time_i, Elapsed_time;

  m = [host]atoi(argv[1]);
  r = [host]atoi(argv[2]);
  N = [host]atoi(argv[3]);

  // Update the estimation of the processors speed
  {
    repl int i, j;
    repl double x[r*r], y[r*r], z[r*r];
    for(i = 0; i < r; i++)
      for(j = 0; j < r; j++) {
        x[i*r+j] = 2.;
        y[i*r+j] = 2.;
        z[i*r+j] = 0.;
      }
    recon rMxM(x, y, z, r);
  }
    // Detect the speed of the physical processors
    speeds = (double*)malloc(sizeof(double)*m*m);
    MPC_Get_processors_info(NULL, speeds);

    // w --- widths of rectangular areas in generalized block
    // h --- heights of 'horizontal-neighbors' subrectangles
    // trow --- Top rows of rectangular areas in generalized block
    // lcol --- Left columns of these rectangular areas
    w = (int*)malloc(sizeof(int)*m);
    h = (int*)malloc(sizeof(int)*(m*m*m*m));
    trow = (int*)malloc(sizeof(int)*m*m);
    lcol = (int*)malloc(sizeof(int)*m);

    // Determine the optimal generalized block size
    [host]:
    {
      int i;
      double algo_time, min_algo_time = DBL_MAX;
      for(i = m; i < N; i++) {
        DistributeLoad(m, speeds, i, w, h, trow, lcol);
        algo_time = timeof(net ParallelAxB(m, r, N, i, w, h) paxb);
        if(algo_time < min_algo_time) {
          opt_l = i;
```

```
                 min_algo_time = algo_time;
             }
         }
    }
    // Start timing the algorithm
    time_i = [host]MPC_Wtime();


    // Broadcast the optimal generalized block size
    l = opt_l;
    // Determine widths, top rows, top columns of the rectangular
    // areas in generalized block, and the heights of their
    // 'horizontal-neighbors' subrectangles
    DistributeLoad(m, speeds, l, w, h, trow, lcol);
    free(speeds);
    {
       // Create the mpC network
       net ParallelAxB(m, r, N, l, w, h) g;
       int [g] icrd, [g] jcrd;

       // Initialize the matrix elements and execute the algorithm
       [g]:
       {
       int x, y, i, j, s, t, MyTopRow, MyLeftColumn;
       double *a, *b, *c;

       a = (double*)malloc(sizeof(double)*(N*r)*(N*r));
       b = (double*)malloc(sizeof(double)*(N*r)*(N*r));
       c = (double*)malloc(sizeof(double)*(N*r)*(N*r));

       icrd = I coordof g;
       jcrd = J coordof g;


       MyTopRow = trow[icrd*m + jcrd];
       MyLeftColumn = lcol[jcrd];

       for(x = MyTopRow; x < N; x+=l)
         for(y = MyLeftColumn; y < N; y+=l)
           for(i = 0; i < H(icrd,jcrd,icrd,jcrd,m); i++)
             for(j = 0; j < w[jcrd]; j++)
               for(s = 0; s < r; s++)
                 for(t = 0; t < r; t++) {
                   a[(x*r*N*r)+y*r+(i*r*N*r)+j*r+(s*r*N)+t] = 2.;
                   b[(x*r*N*r)+y*r+(i*r*N*r)+j*r+(s*r*N)+t] = 2.;
                   c[(x*r*N*r)+y*r+(i*r*N*r)+j*r+(s*r*N)+t] = 0.;
```

```
                }
        ([(m,r,N,l,w,h)g])ComputeAxB(icrd,jcrd,a,b,c,trow,lcol);
        free(w); free(h); free(trow); free(lcol);
        free(a); free(b); free(c);
        ([(0)g])MPC_Barrier();
    }
}
// Print the algorithm execution time
[host]:
{
    Elapsed_time = MPC_Wtime() - time_i;
    printf("Problem size=%d, time(sec)=%0.6f, time(min)=%0.6f\n",
            N*r, Elapsed_time,
            Elapsed_time/60.);
}
}
```

This code specifies the following sequence of steps performed by the mpC program:

- First, it gets the inputs to the mpC application. These inputs are
  - the size of block stored in the replicated variable r,
  - the problem size stored in the replicated variable N, and measured in $r \times r$ blocks, and
  - the number of processors along a row or column stored in the replicated variable m.
- Then, the actual speeds of the processors are estimated with the help of the recon statement. This recon statement uses a call to function rMxM, which multiplies two $r \times r$ matrices, as a test code.
- Then, function MPC_Get_processors_info is used to obtain the actual processors speeds and store them in the replicated array speeds.
- Then, the optimal generalized block size is computed on the host-process with the help of the timeof operator.
- Then, the optimal generalized block size is broadcast from the host-process to all the other processes of the parallel program.
- Then, the parameters of the heterogeneous parallel algorithm are computed in parallel by all processes of the mpC program, using function DistributeLoad. This function calculates the parameters of the heterogeneous block distribution of a generalized $l \times l$ block across an $m \times m$ grid of processors in proportion to their speeds given by elements of array speeds.

- Then, mpC network g of type `ParallelAxB` is created using the computed parameters of the heterogeneous algorithm. Abstract processors of this mpC network are mapped to the processes of the program so as to minimize the algorithm execution time. As one process per physical processor is supposed, there will be one-to-one mapping between the abstract processors of the mpC network g and the physical processors of the executing network.
- Then, the matrix elements are initialized on the abstract processors of network g.
- Then, all the abstract processors of network g call the network function `ComputeAxB` to perform the core computations and communications of the algorithm.
- Then, the elapsed execution time is printed on the console associated with the host-processor.

The full text of the mpC program is given in Appendix B. In particular, it includes the source code for functions `DistributeLoad` and `GetProcessor`. Actually mpC provides the library functions for an optimal distribution of datasets and workloads in heterogeneous environments for a wide range of applications, and we could use calls to some of the functions instead of calls to `DistributeLoad` and `GetProcessor`. The reason behind our using home-made functions is to give an idea of how the mpC distribution library functions are implemented.

9.1.1.4. Experimental Results. We will assess the heterogeneous algorithm by comparing with its homogeneous prototype. Thus we will assess the heterogeneous modification rather than analyze the algorithm as an isolated entity. Our basic postulate is that the heterogeneous algorithm cannot be more efficient than its homogeneous prototype. By this we mean that the heterogeneous algorithm cannot be executed on the heterogeneous network faster than its homogeneous prototype on the *equivalent* homogeneous network. A homogeneous network of computers is equivalent to the heterogeneous network if

- its communication characteristics are the same,
- it has the same number of processors, and
- the speed of each processor is equal to the average speed of processors of the heterogeneous network.

The heterogeneous algorithm is considered optimal if its efficiency is the same as that of its homogeneous prototype. To compare the heterogeneous algorithm of matrix multiplication with its homogeneous prototype, we assume that parameters n, m, and r are the same. Then both algorithms consist of n/r successive steps.

At each step, equivalent communication operations are performed by each of the algorithms:

- Each $r \times r$ block of the pivot column of matrix A is sent horizontally from the processor that stores this block to $m - 1$ processors.
- Each $r \times r$ block of the pivot row of matrix B is sent vertically from the processor stores this block to $m - 1$ processors.

Thus the per-step communication cost is the same for both algorithms.

If l is large enough, then at each step each processor of the heterogeneous network will perform the volume of computation approximately proportional to its speed. In this case the per-processor computation cost will be approximately the same for both algorithms.

Thus the per-step cost of the heterogeneous algorithm will be approximately the same as that of the homogeneous one. So the only reason for the heterogeneous algorithm to be less efficient than its homogeneous prototype is a lower level of potential overlapping of communication operations at successive steps of the algorithm. Obviously the bigger the ratio between the maximal and minimal processor speed, the lower is this level. Note that if the communication layer serializes data packages (e.g., plain Ethernet), then the heterogeneous algorithm has approximately the same efficiency as the homogeneous one. Therefore in this case the presented heterogeneous algorithm is the optimal modification of its homogeneous prototype.

In this section we present some experimental results that allow us to estimate the significance of the additional dependence between the successive steps of the algorithm if the communication layer allows multiple data packages. Now we look at some results of experiments with this mpC application. All the results are obtained for $r=8$ and generalized block size $l=9$, which seem to be optimal for both homogeneous and heterogeneous block cyclic distributions.

A small heterogeneous local network of nine different Solaris and Linux workstations is used in the experiments presented in Figure 9.7. The relative speed of the workstations demonstrated on the core computation of the algorithms (updating of a matrix) is as follows: 46, 46, 46, 46, 46, 46, 46, 84, and 9. The network is based on 100 Mbit Ethernet with a switch enabling parallel communications among the computers.

For the experiments presented in Figure 9.8 we use the same heterogeneous network and a homogeneous local network of nine Solaris workstations with the following relative speeds: 46, 46, 46, 46, 46, 46, 46, 46, 46. The two sets of workstations share the same network equipment. Note that the total perfor-

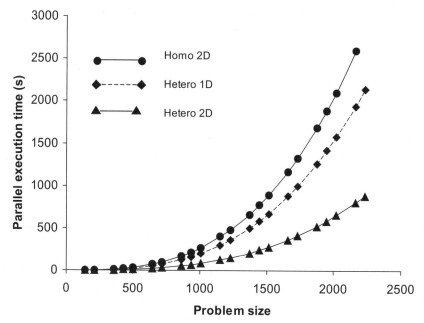

Figure 9.7. Execution times of the heterogeneous and homogeneous 2D algorithms and the heterogeneous 1D algorithm. All algorithms are performed on the same heterogeneous network.

mance of the processors of the heterogeneous network is practically the same as that of the homogeneous one.

Figure 9.7 shows the comparison of the execution times of three parallel algorithms of matrix multiplication:

- The algorithm based on 2D heterogeneous block cyclic distribution.
- The algorithm based on 1D heterogeneous block cyclic distribution.
- The algorithm based on 2D homogeneous block cyclic distribution.

Clearly, the 2D heterogeneous algorithm is almost twice as fast as the 1D heterogeneous algorithm and almost three times as fast as the 2D homogeneous one. Figure 9.8 compares the speedups by the heterogeneous and the homogeneous algorithms. Figure 9.9 compares the execution times of the 2D heterogeneous block cyclic algorithm performed on the heterogeneous network and the 2D homogeneous block cyclic algorithm performed on the homogeneous network.

We can see that the algorithms demonstrate practically the same speed but each on its own network. As the two networks are practically of the same

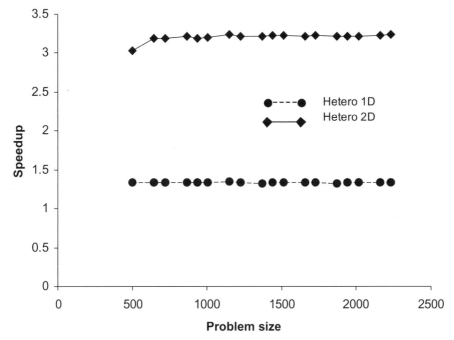

Figure 9.8. Speedups of the heterogeneous 1D and 2D algorithms compared with that of the homogeneous 2D block cyclic algorithm. All algorithms are performed on the same heterogeneous network.

power, we can conclude that the heterogeneous algorithm is very close to the optimal heterogeneous modification of the basic homogeneous algorithm. The experiment shows that the additional dependence between successive steps introduced by the heterogeneous modification has practically no impact on the efficiency of the algorithm. This may be explained by the following two facts:

- The speedup due to the overlapping of communication operations performed at successive steps of the algorithm is not particularly significant.
- The speeds of processors in the heterogeneous network do not differ much. Actually the network is moderately heterogeneous. Therefore, for this particular network, the additional dependence between steps is very weak.

Thus, for reasonably heterogeneous networks, the presented heterogeneous algorithm has proved to be very close to the optimal one by significantly accelerating matrix multiplication on such platforms compared to its homogeneous prototype.

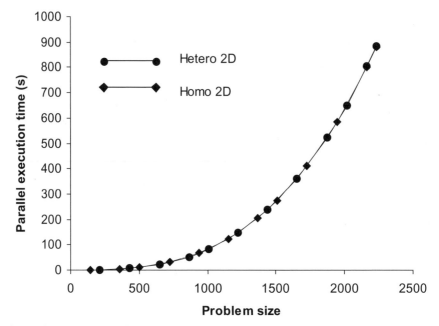

Figure 9.9. Execution times of the 2D heterogeneous block cyclic algorithm on a heterogeneous network and of the 2D homogeneous block cyclic algorithm on a homogeneous network. The networks have approximately the same total power of processors and share the same communication network.

9.1.2. Matrix Factorization

Many complex scientific and engineering problems involve solutions of large linear systems of equations as the key computational steps. LU, QR, and Cholesky factorizations are the most widely used methods for solving dense linear systems of equations, and they have been extensively studied and implemented on serial and parallel computers.

In this section we first introduce Cholesky factorization and a parallel algorithm for Cholesky factorization on homogeneous distributed memory multiprocessors. Then we give a modification of this algorithm for heterogeneous networks of computers, outline its implementation in the mpC language, and present some experimental results.

9.1.2.1. The Cholesky Factorization. We start introducing the Cholesky factorisation from some basic definitions. A real $n \times n$ matrix A is *symmetric* if $A = A^T$. A *quadratic form* is a function $f: \Re^n \to \Re$ that can be expressed as

$$f(x) = x^T A x = \sum_{i=1}^{n} \sum_{j=1}^{n} a_{ij} x_i x_j,$$

where $A = A^T$. A is *positive definite* if $x^T A x > 0$ for all $x \neq 0$.

Now we can formulate main properties of positive definite matrices. Let A be a real, $n \times n$, symmetric, positive definite matrix.

Property 1. A is nonsingular, namely $Ax \neq 0$ for all nonzero x.

Proof. By definition, $x^T A x > 0$ for all nonzero x; hence $Ax \neq 0$. ∎

Property 2. $a_{ii} > 0$ for all i.

Proof. Let all elements of a real vector e_i except for the ith element be 0. Let the i th element of e_i be 1. Then $e_i \neq 0$ We also have $x^T A x > 0$ for all $x \neq 0$. Therefore $a_{ii} = e_i^T A e_i > 0$. ∎

Property 3. If A is partitioned as

$$A = \begin{pmatrix} a_{11} & A_{21}^T \\ A_{21} & A_{22} \end{pmatrix},$$

where $a_{11} \in \Re$, then $C = A_{22} - A_{21} A_{21}^T / a_{11}$ is positive definite.

Proof. Take any $v \neq 0$ and $w = -A_{21}^T v / a_{11}$. Then

$$v^T C v = (w \; v^T) \begin{pmatrix} a_{11} & A_{21}^T \\ A_{21} & A_{22} \end{pmatrix} \begin{pmatrix} w \\ v \end{pmatrix} > 0.$$

Thus, if A is a real, symmetric, positive definite matrix, then it can be factorized as $A = LL^T$, where L is lower triangular with positive diagonal elements. This factorization is called the *Cholesky factorization* of A. ∎

The recursive algorithm for implementing the factorization is derived from the obvious equations:

$$A = \begin{pmatrix} a_{11} & A_{21}^T \\ A_{21} & A_{22} \end{pmatrix} = \begin{pmatrix} l_{11} & 0 \\ L_{21} & L_{22} \end{pmatrix} \begin{pmatrix} l_{11} & L_{21}^T \\ 0 & L_{22}^T \end{pmatrix} = \begin{pmatrix} l_{11}^2 & l_{11} L_{21}^T \\ l_{11} L_{21} & L_{21} L_{21}^T + L_{22} L_{22}^T \end{pmatrix},$$

where a_{11} and l_{11} are scalars, A_{21} and L_{21} are vectors of length $n - 1$, and A_{22} and L_{22} are matrices of size $(n - 1) \times (n - 1)$. From this we derive the equations

$$l_{11} = \sqrt{a_{11}},$$

$$L_{21} = \frac{1}{l_{11}} A_{21},$$

$$A_{22} - L_{21} L_{21}^T = L_{22} L_{22}^T.$$

The algorithm for computing the Cholesky factorization can be summarized as follows:

- Partition $A = \begin{pmatrix} a_{11} & A_{21}^T \\ A_{21} & A_{22} \end{pmatrix}$.
- Compute $a_{11} \leftarrow l_{11} = \sqrt{a_{11}}$.
- Compute $A_{21} \leftarrow L_{21} = \dfrac{1}{l_{11}} A_{21}$.
- Compute $A_{22} \leftarrow A_{22} - L_{21}L_{21}^T$.
- Continue recursively with A_{22}.

This recursive algorithm works for any symmetric, definite positive matrix $A \in \Re^{n \times n}$. Indeed, if A is positive definite, then $a_{11} > 0$ and $A_{22} - A_{21}A_{21}^T/a_{11}$ is positive definite. Hence the algorithm works for $n = m + 1$ if it works for $n = m$. Obviously it works for $n = 1$, and hence it works for all n.

Solving a positive-definite linear system of equations

$$Ax = b,$$

where $A = A^T \in \Re^{n \times n}$ and positive definite, can be carried out as follows:

- First, A is factorized as $A = LL^T$.
- Then, $LL^Tx = b$ is solved in two steps:
  - First, by forward substitution $Lz = b$.
  - Second, by backward substitution $L^Tx = z$.

9.1.2.2. Block Cyclic Algorithm of Parallel Cholesky Factorization on Homogeneous Platforms.
The serial algorithm of Cholesky factorization presented in Section 9.1.2.1 factors a $n \times n$ matrix A into the product of a lower triangular matrix L and its transpose in n successive steps. At each step the column $\begin{pmatrix} l_{11} \\ L_{21} \end{pmatrix}$ is computed and the trailing submatrix A_{22} is updated. It is assumed that the computed elements of L overwrite the given elements of A.

A block-partitioned form of this algorithm allows for more effective use of a memory hierarchy. Each element in A is now a square $r \times r$ block. For simplicity we assume that n is a multiple of r. The block Cholesky factorization algorithm takes n/r steps and is derived from the following equations:

$$A = \begin{pmatrix} a_{11} & A_{21}^T \\ A_{21} & A_{22} \end{pmatrix} = \begin{pmatrix} l_{11} & 0 \\ L_{21} & L_{22} \end{pmatrix}\begin{pmatrix} l_{11}^T & L_{21}^T \\ 0 & L_{22}^T \end{pmatrix} = \begin{pmatrix} l_{11}l_{11}^T & l_{11}L_{21}^T \\ l_{21}l_{11}^T & L_{21}L_{21}^T + L_{22}L_{22}^T \end{pmatrix},$$

where a_{11} and l_{11} are $r \times r$ blocks, A_{21} and L_{21} are of size $(n - r) \times r$, and A_{22} and L_{22} are matrices of size $(n - r) \times (n - r)$. L_{22} and l_{11} are lower triangular.

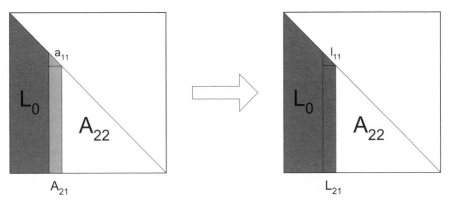

Figure 9.10. One step of the block Cholesky factorization algorithm: the column panel $L = \begin{pmatrix} l_{11} \\ L_{21} \end{pmatrix}$ is computed and the trailing submatrix A_{22} is updated.

If we assume that l_{11}, the lower triangular Cholesky factor of a_{11}, is known, we can compute L_{21},

$$L_{21} = A_{21}(l_{11}^T)^{-1},$$

and update A_{22},

$$A_{22} \leftarrow A_{22} - L_{21}L_{21}^T = L_{22}L_{22}^T.$$

Thus the block Cholesky factorization algorithm can be summarized as follows:

- Partition $A = \begin{pmatrix} a_{11} & A_{21}^T \\ A_{21} & A_{22} \end{pmatrix}$, where a_{11} is an $r \times r$ block.
- Compute l_{11}, the lower Cholesky factor of a_{11}.
- Compute $a_{11} \leftarrow l_{11}$.
- Compute $A_{21} \leftarrow L_{21} = A_{21}(l_{11}^l)^{-1}$.
- Compute $A_{22} \leftarrow A_{22} - L_{21}L_{21}^T$.
- Continue recursively with A_{22}.

Figure 9.10 shows one step of this algorithm. At each step the column panel $L = \begin{pmatrix} l_{11} \\ L_{21} \end{pmatrix}$ is computed, and the trailing submatrix A_{22} is updated.

The parallel algorithm of Cholesky factorization of an $n \times n$, symmetric, positive definite matrix A on a p-processor MPP is based on the two-dimensional block cyclic data distribution presented in Section 9.1.1.1. Let the processors of the MPP be arranged into a two-dimensional $m \times m$ grid $\{P_{ij}\}$, where $m = \sqrt{p}$ and $i, j \in \{1, \ldots, m\}$. Then the two-dimensional block cyclic distribution of matrix A can be summarized as follows:

- Each element in A is a square $r \times r$ block.
- The blocks are scattered in a cyclic fashion along both dimensions of the $m \times m$ processor grid, so that for each $i, j \in \{1, \ldots, n/r\}$ block a_{ij} will be mapped to processor P_{IJ} so that $I = (i - 1)$ mod $m + 1$ and $J = (j - 1)$ mod $m + 1$ (see Figure 9.2).

One step of the parallel Cholesky factorization algorithm proceeds as follows:

- First a processor that has the $r \times r$ diagonal block a_{11} performs the Cholesky factorization of a_{11} computing its lower triangular factor l_{11}.
- Then l_{11} is broadcast vertically along a column of blocks A_{21} on the processors that have this column.
- The processors of this grid column compute a column of blocks L_{21}.
- The column of blocks L_{21} is broadcast horizontally so that each $r \times r$ block of this column is broadcast along a row of the processor grid. Now each processor has its own portion of L_{21}.
- For processors to have portions of L_{21}^T, the row of blocks L_{21}^T should be first computed and then broadcast vertically so that each $r \times r$ block of this row is broadcast along a column of the processor grid. This operation is performed more efficiently if each $r \times r$ block L_{21} is broadcast to all processors of the corresponding grid column, and then locally transposed. Now each processors has its own portions of L_{21} and L_{21}^T.
- Finally all processors update their local portions of the matrix A_{22}.

Cholesky factorization demonstrates the advantage of the block cyclic data distribution over the block data distribution more explicitly than matrix multiplication. Indeed, at each next step of the Cholesky factorization, a matrix of smaller size is processed (see Figure 9.10). At the first step, we process a matrix of size $n \times n$. At the second step, it is a matrix of size $(n - r) \times (n - r)$. At the step k, a matrix of size $(n - (k - 1) \times r) \times (n - (k - 1) \times r)$ is processed. Therefore, if matrix A is block distributed, then the number of processors involved in the execution of the algorithm will decrease with the algorithm's progression. Namely the first $n/(m \times r)$ steps of the two-dimensional block algorithm will be executed by all processors of the $m \times m$ grid. The next $n/(m \times r)$ steps will not involve the first row and first column of the processor grid. The next $n/(m \times r)$ steps will not involve the processors of the first two rows and first two columns of this grid, and so on. This results in an unbalanced load of processors during the algorithm's execution. In contrast, the two-dimensional block cyclic distribution allows all processors of the grid to evenly load through most of the algorithm's execution.

9.1.2.3. Block Cyclic Cholesky Factorization on Heterogeneous Platforms.

The algorithm of Cholesky factorization on a heterogeneous cluster is obtained from the parallel Cholesky factorization algorithm presented in Section 9.1.2.2 by using a heterogeneous block cyclic distribution of matrix A (see Section 9.1.1.2) instead of a homogeneous one. Both homogeneous and heterogeneous block cyclic algorithms are easily generalized for an arbitrary two-dimensional processor arrangement.

The heterogeneous parallel algorithm of Cholesky factorization was implemented in mpC. The key fragments of the parallel mpC code are as follows:

```
nettype HeteroGrid (int P, int Q, double grid[P*Q])
{
   coord I=P, J=Q;
   node {I>=0 && J>=0: grid[I*Q+J];};
};
...
repl P, Q, PxQ;
repl double *speeds;
...
{
   int n=100, info;
   double a[n][n];
   Initialize(a, n);
   recon dpotf2_("U", &n, a, &n, &info);
}
MPC_Get_processors_info(&PxQ, speeds);
MakeGrid(PxQ, &P, &Q);
{
   net HeteroGrid (P, Q, speeds) phf;
   ...
}
```

In this mpC code the network type definition supplies a simple performance model of the implemented parallel algorithm. It introduces

- The name HeteroGrid of the network type.
- A list of parameters, including integer scalar parameters P, Q, and vector parameter grid of P*Q floating-point elements.
- Coordinate variables, I, ranging from 0 to P-1, and J, ranging from 0 to Q-1.
- The abstract processors performing the algorithm are associated with this coordinate system, and the relative volume of computations to be performed by each processor is declared. The abstract processors are arranged into a $P \times Q$ grid. The relative area of $r \times r$ blocks mapped to the (I, J)-th processor of this grid is given by grid[I*Q+J].

**TABLE 9.1. Relative speeds of workstations
demonstrated on serial Cholesky factorization**

Workstation's Number	Relative Speed
1–4	1.9
5	1.0
6–7	2.8
8	7.1

It is assumed that the program is executed by a heterogeneous cluster with one process per processor running, so that there is always one-to-one mapping between abstract and physical processors. The `recon` statement uses the LAPACK routine `dpotf2` performing serial Cholesky factorization of a 100 × 100 dense matrix to update the speed estimation of each physical processor.

The library function `MPC_Get_processors_info` returns the number of available physical processors (in the variable `PxQ`) and their relative speeds (in the array `speeds`). Function `MakeGrid` suggests a two-dimensional arrangement of the processors returning the number of processor rows in variable `P`, and the number of processor columns in variable `Q`.

The next key line of this code defines the abstract network `phf` of the type `HeteroGrid`, with the actual parameters `P` and `Q` specifying the actual size of the physical processor grid, and `speeds`, an array of the relative speeds of the physical processors. The remaining computations and communications will be performed on this abstract network.

The mpC programming system maps abstract processors of network `phf` to physical processors so that the total area of blocks of matrix A mapped to each physical processor will be proportional to its relative speed. Therefore the load of processors will be balanced during the program execution.

Now we turn to the results of some experiments with Cholesky factorization on a local network of eight Sun workstations interconnected via plain 10 Mbit Ethernet. Table 9.1 gives the relative speeds demonstrated by the workstations upon execution of a serial Cholesky factorization of a 100 × 100 dense matrix with the LAPACK routine `dpotf2`.

In the experiments the homogeneous and heterogeneous block cyclic parallel algorithms of the Cholesky factorization were compared. The workstations were logically arranged into a 2 × 4 grid. The homogeneous algorithm was executed with block size $r = 6$, and the heterogeneous algorithm with block size $r = 20$. Block sizes were found that experimentally provided the best execution time for each algorithm.

Figure 9.11 shows that the heterogeneous algorithm speeds up the Cholesky factorization on the heterogeneous network of workstations compared to its homogeneous counterpart. This speedup is mainly due to better load balancing. Note that the speedup is relatively low compared with the experimental results for matrix multiplication in Section 9.1.14. It is explained by the larger

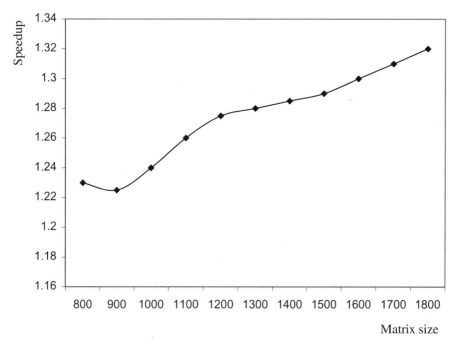

Figure 9.11. Speedup achieved by the heterogeneous block cyclic Cholesky factorization compared to its homogeneous counterpart on a heterogeneous network of eight workstations.

contribution of communication operations into the total execution time: due to the nature of Cholesky factorization, on the one hand, and the low performance of the network, on the other.

9.1.3. Heterogeneous Distribution of Data and Heterogeneous Distribution of Processes Compared

In Sections 9.1.1 and 9.1.2 we designed parallel algorithms that solve regular problems such as dense linear algebra problems on heterogeneous networks. This approach can be summarized as follows:

- Start with a parallel algorithm that solves the problem on MPPs. This algorithm should evenly distribute data and, hence, computations across parallel processes, with one process per processor running.
- Then modify this homogeneous algorithm by unevenly distributing data across processes so that each process performs the volume of computations proportional to the speed of the processor running this process. One process is to run per processor.

In this section we present another approach in our design of parallel algorithms for regular problems on heterogeneous networks. We again start with a homogeneous parallel algorithm that solves the problem on MPPs. The modified algorithm distributes data across parallel processes exactly in the same fashion as its homogeneous prototype. However, this algorithm is modified to allow: more than one process involved in its execution to be run on each processor so that the number of processes running on the processor is proportional to its speed. In other words, while distributed evenly across parallel processes, data and computations are distributed unevenly over processors of the heterogeneous network, and this way each processor performs the volume of computations proportional to its speed.

The mpC language provides natural implementation in a portable form of heterogeneous algorithms of this type. Consider how the corresponding algorithm of the Cholesky factorization can be implemented in mpC:

```
nettype Grid(int P, int Q)
{
   coord I=P, J=Q;
};
int [net Grid(int p, int q) w]mpC2Cblacs_gridinit(int*, char*);
void [*]Cholesky(repl int P, repl int Q)
{
   {
      int n=100, info;
      double a[n][n];
      Initialize(a, n);
      recon dpotf2_("U", &n, a, &n, &info);
   }
   {
      net Grid (P, Q) phf;
      [phf]:
      {
         int ConTxt;
         ([(P,Q)phf])mpC2Cblacs_gridinit(&ConTxt, "R");
         pdlltdriver1_(&ConTxt);
         mpC2Cblacs_gridexit(ConTxt);
      }
   }
}
```

In this code, the definition of the network type Grid describes the simplest performance model of the implemented parallel algorithm when all abstract processors perform the same volume of computations.

It is assumed that the program is executed by a heterogeneous cluster, with each processor running several processes. The `recon` statement uses the LAPACK routine `dpotf2` performing serial Cholesky factorization of a 100 × 100 dense matrix to update the speed estimation of each physical processor.

The mpC network `phf` executing the parallel algorithm is then defined as consisting of `P*Q` abstract processors each performing the same volume of computations. The abstract processors will be mapped to the parallel processes of the program so that the number of abstract processors mapped to each physical processor is proportional to the processor's speed.

The parallel Cholesky factorization is actually performed on this mpC network by calls to ScaLAPACK routines. ScaLAPACK is a well-known library for solving linear algebra problems on MPPs. The BLACS (Basic Linear Algebra Communication Subprograms) is a communication layer of ScaLAPACK providing a linear algebra oriented message-passing interface.

In the BLACS there are two routines, `Cblacs_gridinit` and `Cblacs_gridmap`, that create a process grid and its enclosing context. The context is an analogue of the MPI's communicator. These routines return context handles that are simple integers. Subsequent BLACS routines will be passed these handles, which allow the BLACS to determine what grid a routine is being called from. The routine `Cblacs_gridexit` releases contexts. The mpC network function

```
int [net Grid(int p, int q) w]mpC2Cblacs gridinit(int *pConTxt,
                                                  char *order)
```

is a wrapper for the BLACS routine

```
int Cblacs_gridinit(int * pConTxt, char * order,
                    int p, int q) ,
```

where `pConTxt` is a pointer to the context to be created, p and q are numbers of rows and columns in the process grid associated with the context, and `order` indicates how to map processes to the BLACS grid. Thus the mpC function `mpC2Cblacs_gridinit` creates the BLACS grid and associated context from processes representing abstract processors of the mpC network w. The created context can be used to call ScaLAPACK routines. The mpC function `mpC2Cblacs_gridexit` is an mpC wrapper for the ScaLAPACK function `Cblacs_gridexit`.

Thus, in the mpC code above, a call to function `mpC2Cblacs_gridinit` creates the BLACS context associated with abstract processors of the mpC network `phf`. In this context the ScaLAPACK test driver for Cholesky factorization is called on the network `phf`. This driver reads problem parameters (matrix and block sizes) from a file, forms a test matrix, and performs its Cholesky factorization.

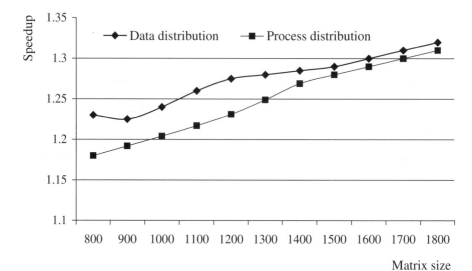

Figure 9.12. Speedups achieved by the heterogeneous Cholesky factorizations based on the data distribution and process distribution compared to their homogeneous prototype on a heterogeneous network of eight workstations.

The presented approach has the advantage of allowing us to easily utilize parallel software that has been developed for MPPs. The disadvantage is that it requires a larger number of processes, so more resources are consumed and more inter-process communications created. This will increase the overhead, although, in many instances the additional overhead has not been significant. Figure 9.12 compares two such mpC applications performing Cholesky factorization on the same heterogeneous network of eight workstations as are described in Section 9.1.2. The first application (presented in Section 9.1.2) is based on a heterogeneous distribution of data across processes with one process per processor running; the second (presented in this section) is based on heterogeneous distribution of a larger number of evenly loaded processes across the processors. As can be seen the first application is faster, but the difference is not very big and it lessens with growth of matrix size.

9.2. *N*-BODY PROBLEM

In this section we look at some experimental results of the mpC *N*-body application presented in Section 7.1. The run time of the mpC program was compared to a carefully written MPI counterpart. Three workstations — SPARCstation 5 (hostname gamma), SPARCclassic (omega), and SPARCstation 20 (alpha), connected via 10Mbits Ethernet — were used as the NoC. There were 23 other computers in the same segment of the local network. LAM MPI version 5.2 [12] was used as the communication platform.

The computing space of the mpC programming environment consisted of 15 processes, 5 processes running on each workstation. The dispatcher ran on gamma and used the following relative performances of the workstations obtained automatically upon the creation of the virtual parallel machine: 1150 (gamma), 331 (omega), and 1662 (alpha).

The MPI program was written in a way that would minimize communication overhead. All our experiments dealt with nine groups of bodies. Three MPI processes were mapped to gamma, 1 process to omega, and 5 processes to alpha, providing the optimal mapping if the numbers of bodies in these groups were equal to each other.

The first experiment compared the mpC and MPI programs for homogeneous input data where all groups consisted of the same number of bodies. In effect, it showed how much time is lost in using mpC instead of pure MPI. It turned out that the run time of the MPI program consisted of about 95% to 97% of the run time of the mpC program. The loss in performance was 3% to 5%.

The second experiment compared these programs for heterogeneous input data. The groups consisted of 10, 10, 10, 100, 100, 100, 600, 600, and 600 bodies correspondingly.

The run time of the mpC program did not depend on the order of the numbers. The dispatcher selected three different groups of numbers:

- Four processes on gamma for virtual processors of network g computing two 10-body groups, one 100-body group, and one 600-body group.
- Three processes on omega for virtual processors computing one 10-body group and two 100-body groups.
- Two processes on alpha for virtual processors computing two 600-body groups.

The mpC program took 94 seconds to simulate 15 hours of the galaxy evolution.

The run time of the MPI program essentially depended on the order of the selected numbers. It took from 88 to 391 seconds to simulate 15 hours of the galaxy evolution dependent on the particular order. Figure 9.13 shows the relative runtime of the MPI and mpC programs for different permutations of these numbers. All possible permutations can be broken down into 24 disjoint subsets of the same power in such a way that if two permutations belong to the same subset, the corresponding run times are equal to each other. We let these subsets be numerated so that as the number of the subset has became greater, the MPI program took longer to run. In Figure 9.13 we represent each such a subset by a bar, whose height is equal to the corresponding value t_{MPI}/t_{mpC}. As can be seen in the figure, for almost all input data the runtime of the MPI program exceeds (and often, essentially) the run time of the mpC program.

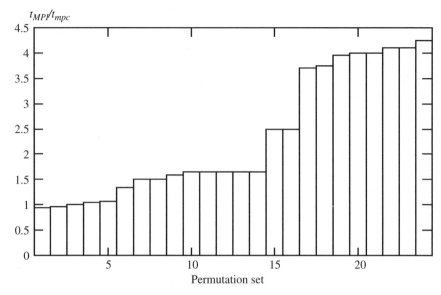

Figure 9.13. Speedups for different permutations of the numbers of bodies in groups.

9.3. NUMERICAL INTEGRATION

In this section we extend the problem of numerical approximation to definite integrals on heterogeneous networks of computers. First, we briefly introduce numerical integration, following the excellent book *Computer Methods for Mathematical Computations* by Forsythe, Malcolm, and Moler (1977). Then we give a parallel algorithm of numerical integration on heterogeneous networks as well as its mpC implementation.

To avoid confusion with numerical *integration* of ordinary differential equations, the term *quadrature* is commonly used for numerical approximation of definite integrals. Let $[a,b]$ be a finite interval on the x axis that is partitioned into n subintervals called *panels*, $[x_i, x_{i+1}]$, $i = 0, \ldots, n - 1$. Assume $x_0 = a, x_n = b$, and $x_0 < x_1 < \ldots < x_n$. Let $h_i = x_{i+1} - x_i$ be the panel widths.

Let $f(x)$ be a function defined on $[a,b]$. Suppose that an approximation is desired to the definite integral

$$I(f) = \int_a^b f(x)dx.$$

Clearly, $I(f)$ can be expressed as a sum of integrals over the panels

$$I(f) = \sum_{i=0}^{n-1} I_i,$$

where

$$I_i = I_i(f) = \int_{x_i}^{x_{i+1}} f(x)dx.$$

A *quadrature rule* is a simple formula for approximating the individual I_i. A *composite quadrature rule* is a formula giving an approximation to $I(f)$ as a sum of the quadrature rule approximations to the individual I_i. Two of the simplest quadrature rules are the rectangle rule and the trapezoid rule.

9.3.1. Basic Quadrature Rules

The rectangle rule uses function values in the midpoints of the panels

$$y_i = \frac{x_i + x_{i+1}}{2} \quad i = 0,\ldots,n-1.$$

It approximates each I_i by the area of the rectangle with base h_i and height $f(y_i)$. This gives

$$I_i \approx h_i f(y_i),$$

and hence we have the *composite rectangle rule*:

$$R(f) = \sum_{i=0}^{n-1} h_i f(y_i).$$

The trapezoid rule uses function values at the end points of the panels. It approximates I_i by the area of the trapezoid with base h_i and height that varies linearly from $f(x_i)$ on the left to $f(x_{i+1})$ on the right. This leads to

$$I_i \approx h_i \frac{f(x_i) + f(x_{i+1})}{2},$$

and hence we have the *composite trapezoid rule*:

$$T(f) = \sum_{i=0}^{n-1} h_i \frac{f(x_i) + f(x_{i+1})}{2}.$$

It is easily shown that if $f(x)$ is continuous (or even merely Riemann integrable) on $[a,b]$ and $h = \max_i h_i$, then

$$\lim_{h \to 0} R(f) = I(f)$$

and

$$\lim_{h \to 0} T(f) = I(f).$$

That is, both rules converge as the lengths of the subintervals decrease.

The rectangle rule is based on piecewise constant interpolation, while the trapezoid rule is based on piecewise linear interpolation. One might therefore expect the trapezoid rule to be more accurate that the rectangle rule. But this natural expectation does not always prove true.

Indeed, assume that f has five continuous derivatives and that the values of these derivatives are not too large. Consider a panel $[x_i, x_{i+1}]$. The Taylor series expansion of $f(x)$ about y_i, the center of this panel, is

$$f(x) = f(y_i) + (x - y_i)f'(y_i) + \frac{1}{2}(x - y_i)^2 f''(y_i) + \frac{1}{6}(x - y_i)^3 f'''(y_i)$$
$$+ \frac{1}{24}(x - y_i)^4 f^{IV}(y_i) + \dots.$$

These assumptions about f imply that the remainder term denoted by ellipses (...) is less significant than the terms explicitly shown.

To integrate this series over $[x_i, x_{i+1}]$, observe that

$$\int_{x_i}^{x_{i+1}} (x - y_i)^p \, dx = \begin{cases} h_i, & p = 0, \\ 0, & p = 1, \\ \dfrac{h_i^3}{12}, & p = 2, \\ 0, & p = 3, \\ \dfrac{h_i^5}{80}, & p = 4. \end{cases}$$

Note that the odd powers integrate to zero. Consequently

$$\int_{x_i}^{x_{i+1}} f(x)dx = h_i f(y_i) + \frac{1}{24} h_i^3 f''(y_i) + \frac{1}{1920} h_i^5 f^{IV}(y_i) + \dots.$$

This shows that when h_i is small, the error for the rectangle rule on one panel is $h_i^3 f''(y_i)/24$ plus some less significant terms.

Returning to the Taylor series and substituting $x = x_i$ and $x = x_{i+1}$, we obtain

$$\frac{f(x_i) + f(x_{i+1})}{2} = f(y_i) + \frac{1}{8} h_i^2 f''(y_i) + \frac{1}{384} h_i^4 f^{IV}(y_i) + \dots.$$

Combining this with the expansion for the integral gives

$$\int_{x_i}^{x_{i+1}} f(x)dx = h_i \frac{f(x_i) + f(x_{i+1})}{2} - \frac{1}{12} h_i^3 f''(y_i) - \frac{1}{480} h_i^5 f^{IV}(y_i) + \ldots.$$

This shows that when h_i is small, the error for the trapezoid rule on one panel is $-h_i^3 f''(y_i)/12$ plus some less significant terms.

The total error for either rule is the sum of the errors on the individual panels. Let

$$E = \frac{1}{24} \sum_{i=0}^{n-1} h_i^3 f''(y_i),$$

$$F = \frac{1}{1920} \sum_{i=0}^{n-1} h_i^5 f^{IV}(y_i).$$

Then

$$I(f) = R(f) + E + F + \ldots = T(f) - 2E - 4F + \ldots.$$

If the h_i are sufficiently small, then $h_i^5 \ll h_i^3$; so if f^{IV} is not too badly behaved, then $F \ll E$.

The first conclusion from these results is that for many functions $f(x)$, the rectangle rule is about twice as accurate as the trapezoid rule. The second conclusion is that the difference between the values obtained by the rectangle and trapezoid rules can be used to estimate the error in either one of them. The third conclusion is that, for functions $f(x)$ having continuous, bounded second derivatives, *doubling* the number of panels by bisecting them in either the rectangle or trapezoid rule can be expected to roughly *quadruple* the accuracy. The difference in the results of either of these rules before and after doubling the number of panels can be used to estimate the error or improve the computed result.

The technique of repeatedly doubling the number of panels and estimating the error can be programmed to produce a method that automatically determines the panels so that the approximate integral is computed to within some prescribed error tolerance. Combining the rectangle and trapezoid rules in the proper way can produce a new rule, for which the error formula no longer contains E. Indeed, the error in the combined quadrature rule

$$S(f) = \frac{2}{3} R(f) + \frac{1}{3} T(f)$$

is given by the formula

$$I(f) - S(f) = \frac{2}{3}[I(f) - R(f)] + \frac{1}{3}[I(f) - T(f)] = -\frac{2}{3}F + \ldots$$

$$= -\frac{1}{2880}\sum_{i=0}^{n-1} h_i^5 f^{IV}(y_i) + \ldots.$$

This rule is called the *composite Simpson's rule*. Notice that even though $S(f)$ is based on second-degree interpolation, the error term involves the fourth derivative, and hence Simpson's rule is exact for cubic functions. In other words, like the rectangle rule, Simpson's rule obtains an "extra" order of accuracy.

If the length of each panel is halved, then each h_i^5 term in the error formula is decreased by a factor of 1/32. The total number of terms is increased by a factor of 2, so the overall error is decreased by a factor close to 1/16. This fact is important for programs that automatically choose the number and size of the panels.

9.3.2. Adaptive Quadrature Routines

An *adaptive quadrature routine* is a numerical quadrature algorithm that uses one or two basic quadrature rules and automatically determines the subinterval sizes so that the computed result meets some prescribed accuracy requirement. Different mesh sizes may be used in different parts of the interval. Relatively large meshes are used where the integrand is smooth, and slowly varying and relatively small meshes are used in regions where the integration becomes difficult. This way an attempt is made to provide a result with the prescribed accuracy at as small a cost in computer time as possible.

An adaptive quadrature routine normally requires that the user specify a finite interval $[a,b]$, provide a subroutine that computes $f(x)$ for any x in the interval, and choose an error tolerance ε. The routine attempts to compute a quantity Q so that

$$\left| Q - \int_a^b f(x)dx \right| \le \varepsilon.$$

The routine may decide that the prescribed accuracy is not attainable, do the best it can, and return an estimate of the accuracy actually achieved.

In assessing the efficiency of any quadrature routine, it is generally assumed that the major portion of the computation cost lies in evaluation of the integrand $f(x)$. So, if two subroutines are given the same function to integrate and both produce answers of about the same accuracy, the subroutine that requires the smaller number of function evaluations is regarded as the more efficient in that particular problem.

It is always possible to invent integrands $f(x)$ that "fool" the routine into producing a completely wrong result. However, for good adaptive routines the class of such examples has been made as small as possible without unduly complicating the logic of the routine or making it inefficient in handling reasonable problems.

During the computation the interval $[a, b]$ is broken down into subintervals $[x_i, x_{i+1}]$. Each subinterval is obtained by bisecting a subinterval obtained earlier in the computation. The actual number of subintervals, as well as their locations and lengths, depends on the integrand $f(x)$ and the accuracy requirement ε. The numbering is arranged so that $x_0 = a$, and the routine determines an n so that $x_n = b$. We let $h_i = x_{i+1} - x_i$ be the subinterval width.

A typical scheme applies two different quadrature rules to each subinterval. Let us denote the results by P_i and Q_i. Both P_i and Q_i are approximations to

$$I_i = \int_{x_i}^{x_{i+1}} f(x)dx.$$

The basic idea of adaptive quadrature is to compare the two approximations P_i and Q_i and thereby obtain an estimate of their accuracy. If the accuracy is acceptable, one of them is taken as the value of the integral over the subinterval. If the accuracy is not acceptable, the subinterval is divided into two parts and the process repeated on the smaller subintervals.

To reduce the total number of function evaluations, it is usually arranged that the two rules producing P_i and Q_i require integrand values at some of the same points. Consequently processing a new subinterval normally requires about the same number of new function evaluations.

For simplicity we assume that Q_i is obtained simply by applying the rule for P_i twice, once to each half of the interval. Let us also assume that the rule for P_i gives the exact answer if the integrand is a polynomial of degree $p - 1$, or equivalently, if the p-th derivative $f^{(p)}(x)$ is identically zero. By expanding the integrand in a Taylor series about the midpoint of the subinterval, we can then show that there is a constant c so that

$$I_i - P_i = ch_i^{p+1} f^{(p)}\left(x_i + \frac{h_i}{2}\right) + \dots.$$

The exponent of h_i is $p + 1$ rather than p because the subinterval is of length h_i. From the assumption that Q_i is the sum of two P's from two subintervals of length $h_i/2$, it follows that

$$I_i - Q_i = c\left(\frac{h_i}{2}\right)^{p+1}\left[f^{(p)}\left(x_i + \frac{h_i}{4}\right) + f^{(p)}\left(x_i + \frac{3h_i}{4}\right)\right] + \dots.$$

Since

$$f^{(p)}\!\left(x_i+\frac{h_i}{4}\right)+f^{(p)}\!\left(x_i+\frac{3h_i}{4}\right)=2f^{(p)}\!\left(x_i+\frac{h_i}{2}\right)+\dots$$

and the two errors are related by

$$I_i-Q_i=\frac{2}{2^{p+1}}(I_i-P_i)+\dots=\frac{1}{2^p}(I_i-P_i)+\dots.$$

This indicates that bisecting the subinterval decreases the error by a factor of about 2^p. Solving for the unknown I_i and rearranging terms, we obtain

$$Q_i-I_i=\frac{1}{2^p-1}(P_i-Q_i)+\dots.$$

In other words, the error in the more accurate approximation Q_i is about $1/2^p-1$ times the difference between the two approximations.

The basic task of a typical routine is to bisect each subinterval until the following inequality is satisfied:

$$\frac{1}{2^p-1}|P_i-Q_i|\le\frac{h_i}{b-a}\varepsilon,$$

where ε is the user-supplied accuracy tolerance. If the entire interval $[a, b]$ can be covered by n subintervals, on which this is valid, then the routine would return

$$Q=\sum_{i=0}^{n-1}Q_i.$$

Combining the above and ignoring the higher-order terms, we find that

$$\left|Q-\int_a^b f(x)dx\right|=\left|\sum_{i=0}^{n-1}(Q_i-I_i)\right|\le\sum_{i=0}^{n-1}|Q_i-I_i|\le\frac{1}{2^p-1}\sum_{i=0}^{n-1}|P_i-Q_i|$$

$$\le\frac{1}{2^p-1}\times\frac{2^p-1}{b-a}\varepsilon\sum_{i=0}^{n-1}h_i=\varepsilon,$$

which is the desired goal.

This analysis requires the assumptions that $f^{(p)}(x)$ be continuous and that the error be proportional to $h_i^{p+1}f^{(p)}(x)$. Even when these conditions are not exactly satisfied, the routine may perform well, and the final result may be within the desired tolerance. However, the detailed behavior will be different.

For simplicity we have also assumed that the routine is using an absolute error criterion, that is,

$$|Q - \int f| \le \varepsilon.$$

In many situations the preferred error tolerance is the relative kind, which is independent of the scale factors in f. The pure relative criterion

$$\frac{|Q - \int f|}{|\int f|} \le \varepsilon$$

is complicated by several factors. The denominator $\int f$ might be zero. Even if the denominator is merely close to zero because the positive values of f at one part of the interval nearly cancel the negative values of f at another part, the criterion may be impossible to satisfy in practice. Furthermore a good approximation to the value of the denominator is not available until the end of the computation

Some routines use a criterion involving $\int |f|$,

$$\frac{|Q - \int f|}{\int |f|} \le \varepsilon.$$

The denominator cannot be zero unless f is identically zero and does not suffer the cancellation difficulties associated with oscillatory integrands. However, this route does involve more computation, although no more function evaluations, and does require a more elaborate explanation.

9.3.3. The quanc8 Adaptive Quadrature Routine

One of the most popular adaptive quadrature routines is a routine called quanc8. The user of the routine must supply a function fun for the integrand $f(x)$; the lower and upper limits of integration, a and b; and the absolute and relative error tolerances, abserr and relerr. The routine returns the approximation of the integral; an estimate of the absolute error, errest; the number of function evaluations required, nofun; and a reliability indicator, flag. If flag is zero, then the approximation likely has the desired accuracy. If flag is large, then some unacceptable integrand has been encountered.

The name quanc8 is derived from *qu*adrature, *a*daptive, *N*ewton-*C*otes's 8-panel. The *Newton-Cotes formulas* are a family of quadrature rules that are obtained by integrating interpolating polynomials over equally spaced evaluation points. The rectangle, trapezoid, and Simpson's rules are obtained by integrating zeroth-, first-, and second-degree polynomials, and they constitute the first three members of the family. The eigth-panel formula is obtained by integrating an eighth-degree polynomial, but just as by the rectangle and Simpson's rules, an "extra" degree is acquired, so the formula gives the exact result for polynomials of degree 9.

For integration over the interval $[0, 1]$ the rule is

$$\int_0^1 f(x)\,dx \approx \sum_{k=0}^{8} w_k f\left(\frac{k}{8}\right).$$

Rational expressions for the weights w_k (multiplied by 8) are included in the routine itself. Since the rule is exact for $f(x) \equiv 1$, the weights satisfy

$$\sum_{k=0}^{8} w_k = 1.$$

However, some of the weights are negative, and

$$\sum_{k=0}^{8} |w_k| = 1.4512.$$

This factor is important in error analysis. For example, suppose that function $f(x) \equiv 1$ is contaminated by some error factor so that $f(x) = 0.99$ at $x = \frac{2}{8}, \frac{4}{8}, \frac{6}{8}$, and $f(x) = 1.01$ at all other nodes. The eight-panel rule would give 1.014512 as the value of the integral. The error in the function values is slightly magnified in the result. The magnification is inconsequential in this rule, but for the Newton-Cotes formulas involving higher polynomials, this sort of error is unacceptable.

A rule with eight panels has been chosen so that each panel width is the basic interval width, $b - a$, divided by a power of 2. Consequently there are usually no round-off errors in computing the nodes x_i on a computer.

The eight-panel rule is used in quanc8 to obtain the quantity P_i. The quantity Q_i is obtained by applying the same rule to the two halves of the interval, thereby using 16 panels. In the program, variables qprev and qnow are used for P_i and Q_i. Variables qleft and qright are used for the results on the two halves of the interval.

Since the basic rule is exact for ninth-degree polynomials, the error in Q_i will be about $1/(2^{10} - 1) = 1/1023$ times the error in P_i whenever the integrand is smooth and higher-order terms can be ignored. Thus the results for a particular subinterval are acceptable if

$$\frac{1}{1023}|P_i - Q_i| \le \frac{h_i}{b - a}\varepsilon.$$

In quanc8 this test is made by comparing two quantities

```
esterr = fabs(qnow-qprev)/1023.
```

and

`tollerr = fmax(abserr, relerr*fabs(area))*(step/stone).`

The ratio `step/stone` is equal to $h_i/(b-a)$, and area is an estimate of the integral over the entire interval, so ε is the maximum of `abserr` and `relerr*`|∫f|. The subinterval is acceptable if `esterr<=tolerr`.

When the subinterval is accepted, qnow is added to `result`, and esterr is added to `errest`. Then the quantity (qnow-qprev)/1023 is added to variable `corr11` because $Q_i + (Q_i - P_i)/1023$ is usually a more accurate estimate of I_i than simply Q_i. The final value of `corr11` is added to `result` just before its value is returned.

Each time a subinterval is bisected, the nodes and function values for the right half are saved for later use. Limit `levmax=30` is set on the level of bisection. When this maximum is reached, the subinterval is accepted even if the estimated error is too large, but a count of the number of such subintervals is kept and returned as the integer part of flag. The length of each of these subintervals is quite small, $(b-a)/2^{30}$, so for most integrands a few of subintervals can be included in the final result without affecting accuracy much.

However, if the integrand has discontinuities or unbounded derivatives, or if it is contaminated by round-off error, the bisection level maximum will be frequently reached. Consequently another limit, nomax, is set on the number of function evaluations. When it appears that this limit may be exceeded, `levmax` is reduced to `levout` so that the remainder of the interval can be processed with fewer than nomax function evaluations. Furthermore the point x0 where the trouble is encountered is noted and the quantity (b-x0)/(b-a) is returned as the fractional part of flag. This is the portion of the interval that remains to be processed with the lower bisection limit.

As based on piecewise polynomial approximation, quanc8 is not designed to handle certain kinds of integrals. Roughly these are integrals of functions $f(x)$ for which some derivative $f^{(k)}(x)$ with $k \le 10$ is unbounded or fails to exist.

The C code of quanc8 is as follows:

```
#define fmax(a,b) ((a)>(b)?(a):(b))

// Quanc8 estimates the integral of fun(x) from a to b to a user
// provided tolerance (a relative error tolerance, relerr, and/or
// an absolute error tolerance, abserr). Quanc8 is an automatic
// adaptive routine based on the 8-panel Newton-Cotes rule.
// It returns an approximation to the integral hopefully
// satisfying the least stringent of the two error tolerances.
// An estimate of the magnitude of the actual error is returned
// in variable pointed by errest. The number of function values
// used in calculation of the result is returned in variable
// pointed by nofun. A reliability indicator is returned in
// variable pointed by flag. If it is zero, then the result
```

```
// probably satisfies the error tolerance. If it is x.y, then x
// is the number of intervals that have not converged and 0.y
// is the fraction of the interval left to do when the limit on
// nofun was approached.
double quanc8(double (*fun)(double), double a, double b,
              double abserr, double relerr, double *errest,
              int *nofun, double *flag)
{
    static double w[] = {3956.0/14175.0, 23552.0/14175.0,
                         -3712.0/14175.0, 41984.0/14175.0,
                         -18160.0/14175.0};
    double area=0., result=0., stone, step, cor11=0.0,
    temp;
    double qprev=0.0, qnow, qdiff, qleft, esterr, tollerr;
    double qright[31], f[17], x[17], fsave[30][8], xsave[30][8];
    int levmin=1, levmax=30, levout=6, nomax=5000, nofin,
    lev=0,nim=1, i, j;


    if(a==b)
        return result;
        // Initialization
        nofin = nomax-8*(levmax-levout+(int)pow(2,
        levout+1));
        *flag=0;
        *errest=0.0;
        *nofun=0;
        x[0] = a;
        x[16] = b;
        f[0] = (*fun)(x[0]);
        stone = (b-a)/16.0;
        x[8] = (x[0]+x[16])/2.0;
        x[4] = (x[0]+x[8])/2.0;
        x[12] = (x[8]+x[16])/2.0;
        x[2] = (x[0]+x[4])/2.0;
        x[6] = (x[4]+x[8])/2.0;
        x[10] = (x[8]+x[12])/2.0;
        x[14] = (x[12]+x[16])/2.0;
        for(j=2; j<17; j+=2)
            f[j] = (*fun)(x[j]);
        *nofun = 9;

        // Central calculation
    m30:
```

```
for (j=1; j<16; j+=2)
{
   x[j] = (x[j-1]+x[j+1])/2.0;
   f[j] = (*fun)(x[j]);
}
*nofun += 8;
step = (x[16]-x[0])/16.0;
qleft = (w[0]*(f[0]+f[8])+
          w[1]*(f[1]+f[7])+
          w[2]*(f[2]+f[6])+
          w[3]*(f[3]+f[5])+
          w[4]*f[4]
         )*step;
qright[lev] = (w[0]*(f[8]+f[16])+
               w[1]*(f[9]+f[15])+
               w[2]*(f[10]+f[14])+
               w[3]*(f[11]+f[13])+
               w[4]*f[12]
              )*step;
qnow = qleft+qright[lev];
qdiff = qnow-qprev;
area = area+qdiff;


// Interval convergence test
esterr = fabs(qdiff)/1023.0;
tollerr = fmax(abserr, relerr*fabs(area))*(step/stone);
if(lev<levmin)
   goto m50;
if(lev>=levmax)
   goto m62;
if(*nofun>nofin)
   goto m60;
if(esterr<=tollerr)
   goto m70;


// Locate next interval and save right-hand elements for future
// use
m50:
   nim *= 2;
   for(i=0; i<8; i++)
   {
      fsave[lev][i] = f[i+9];
      xsave[lev][i] = x[i+9];
```

```
   }
   lev++;


   // Assemble left-hand elements for immediate use
   qprev = qleft;
   for(i=-1; i>-9; i--)
   {
      f[2*i+18] = f[i+9];
      x[2*i+18] = x[i+9];
   }
   goto m30;


   // Trouble: number of function values is about to exceed limit.
m60:
   nofin *= 2;
   levmax = levout;
   *flag += (b-x[0])/(b-a);
   goto m70;


   // Trouble: current level is levmax.
m62:
   *flag += 1.0;


   // Interval converged: add contributions into running sums.
m70:
   result += qnow;
   *errest += esterr;
   cor11 += qdiff/1023.0;


   // Locate next interval.
m72:
   if(nim==2*(nim/2))
      goto m75;
   nim/=2;
   lev--;
   goto m72;
m75:
   nim++;
   if(lev<=0)
      goto m80;


   // Assemble elements required for the next interval.
   qprev = qright[lev-1];
   x[0] = x[16];
   f[0] = f[16];
```

```
for(i=1; i<9; i++)
{
    f[2*i] = fsave[lev-1][i-1];
    x[2*i] = xsave[lev-1][i-1];
}
goto m30;

// Finalize and return: make sure that errest not less than
// round-off level.
m80:
    result+=cor11;
    if(!*errest)
        return result;
m82:
    temp = fabs(result)+*errest;
    if(temp!=fabs(result))
        return result;
    *errest*=2.0;
    goto m82;
}
```

9.3.4. Parallel Adaptive Quadrature Routine for Heterogeneous Clusters

The best adaptive quadrature routines are designed to provide an approximation to definite integrals with the prescribed accuracy in the fastest possible computer time. The large portion of the computation cost lies in evaluation of the integrand $f(x)$. Therefore, to achieve the best efficiency on serial computers, the programmer should minimize the total number of function evaluations.

If the evaluation of integrand $f(x)$ is prohibitively expensive, the speedup may be achieved via parallel computing of the integrand values. To do this, we let $t_p(f)$ be the time of evaluation of $f(x)$ at a single point on a processor p. We let $t_{p \to q}$ be the time of transfer of a single floating-point value from the processor p to a processor q. Say we have a cluster of heterogeneous processors, and the time of evaluation of $f(x)$ on a single processor exceeds the time of transfer of a single floating-point value between any pair of the processors doubled,

$$\min_{p}\{t_p(f)\} > 2 \times \max_{p,q}\{t_{p \to q}\}.$$

We can write an algorithm of parallel evaluation of integrand $f(x)$ at n different points on two processors p and q. We let n points be stored in the memory of processor p, and resulting integrand values be stored in the memory of this processor. Let $s_p(f)$ and $s_q(f)$ be the relative speed of processors p and q respectively, demonstrated on the evaluation of integrand $f(x)$:

$$n_p = n \times \frac{s_p(f)}{s_p(f) + s_q(f)},$$

$$n_q = n \times \frac{s_q(f)}{s_p(f) + s_q(f)}, \quad \text{and}$$

$$n = n_p + n_q.$$

- At the first step of the algorithm, processor p sends n_q points to processor q.
- At the second step, processor p evaluates $f(x)$ at n_p points, while processor q evaluates $f(x)$ at the n_q points received from processor p. Note that the number of function evaluations performed by each processor will be proportional to its relative speed, $n_p/n_q = s_p(f)/s_q(f)$. From the assumption that the relative speed is demonstrated on the evaluation of the integrand $f(x)$, it follows that $s_p(f)/s_q(f) = t_q(f)/t_p(f)$. Therefore $n_p \times t_p(f) = n_q \times t_q(f)$.
- Finally processor p receives n_q integrand values from processor q and stores them in its memory.

The total time of serial evaluation of $f(x)$ at n different points on the processor p will exceed the time of the parallel evaluation on a cluster of two processors, p and q:

$$
\begin{aligned}
t_{\text{serial}} &= n \times t_p(f) = (n_q + n_p) \times t_p(f) \\
&= n_q \times t_p(f) + n_p \times t_p(f) \\
&= n_q \times t_p(f) + \max\{n_p \times t_p(f), n_p \times t_p(f)\} \\
&= n_q \times t_p(f) + \max\{n_p \times t_p(f), n_q \times t_q(f)\} \\
&> n_q \times (2 \times \max\{t_{p \to q}, t_{q \to p}\}) + \max\{n_p \times t_p(f), n_q \times t_q(f)\} \\
&\geq n_q \times (t_{p \to q} + t_{q \to p}) + \max\{n_p \times t_p(f), n_q \times t_q(f) \\
&= n_q \times t_{p \to q} + \max\{n_p \times t_p(f), n_q \times t_q(f)\} + n_q \times t_{q \to p} \\
&= t_{\text{parallel}}.
\end{aligned}
$$

The result can be easily generalized to a heterogeneous cluster consisting of an arbitrary number of processors.

There are different ways of designing parallel adaptive quadrature routines for a heterogeneous cluster of p processors. One simple way is to break up the interval $[a, b]$ into p subintervals, with each subinterval assigned to a separate processor. The desired integral over the entire interval $[a, b]$ is obtained as a sum of integrals over these subintervals. Each processor computes an estimate of the integral over its subinterval following the same serial adaptive quadrature routine. To balance the load of processors, one would make the length of the kth interval proportional to the relative speed of the kth processor.

This algorithm is quite simple and straightforward to implement. However, it balances the load of processors only if the same mesh size is used in all parts of the interval $[a, b]$. If different mesh sizes are used in different parts of this interval, the number of function evaluations performed by each processor will be no longer proportional to its relative speed, resulting in unbalanced loads processor.

This algorithm will not be efficient if integrand $f(x)$ is smooth and slowly varying in some regions of interval $[a, b]$ and has high peaks in other regions. If the same interval spacing required near the peaks to obtain the desired accuracy, is used throughout the entire interval $[a, b]$, then many more function evaluations will be performed than is necessary (although the load of the processors will be balanced). If larger meshes are used in regions where the integrand is smooth and slowly varying, and smaller meshes are used in regions where the integration becomes difficult, then the balance between the loads of different processors will be broken. In both situations the actual computing time will be far longer from the optimal one. This is when we turn to a parallel adaptive quadrature routine, pquanc8, that tries to keep balance between loads of processors while minimizing the total number of function evaluations required to provide a result with the prescribed accuracy.

As it might be clear from its name, the pquonc8 routine is a parallel version of the quanc8 adaptive quadrature routine. The algorithm of parallel numerical integration on a cluster of p heterogeneous processors can be summarized as follows:

- The algorithm uses a master worker parallel programming paradigm. All computations, except for function evaluations, are performed serially by a *host-processor.*
- The host-processor keeps a list of subintervals of the entire interval $[a, b]$, whose contributions to the integral are still to be estimated. Each subinterval $[l, r]$ is represented by a data structure that consists of
  - an array x to contain a set of points $x_0, x_1, \ldots, x_{16}$ so that $x_0 = l, x_{16} = r$, $x_0 < x_1 < \ldots < x_{16}$, and $x_{i+1} - x_i = (l - r)/16$;
  - an array f to contain a set of integrand values $f(x)$ at these points; and

- a variable `qprev` to contain an estimate of the integral over the interval $[l, r]$ obtained by using the eight-panel rule, that is, by using values $f(x_0), f(x_2), f(x_4), f(x_6), f(x_{10}), f(x_{12}), f(x_{14}), f(x_{16})$.

Initially the list consists of interval $[a, b]$ and the host-processor computes the integrand values at even points $x_0, x_2, \ldots, x_{16}$ associated with the interval.

- At each iteration of the main loop of the algorithm, an estimate of the integral over each subinterval in the current list of subintervals is calculated. The estimate is obtained from the integrand values at all 17 points associated with the subinterval. If the subinterval is acceptable, its contribution is added to the result. If the subinterval is not acceptable, the interval is bisected into two new subintervals that are added to a list of subintervals to be processed at next iteration of the main loop. In other words, one step of routine `quanc8` is applied to each subinterval in the current list. Note that at the beginning of the iteration all subintervals in the current list are of the same length.

- In order to estimate the integral over each subinterval in the current list, the host-processor needs integrand $f(x)$ to be evaluated at odd points x_1, $x_3, \ldots, x_{15}$ of the subinterval. The estimation involves all processors of the cluster and is performed as follows:

  - First the host-processor forms a set of all odd points associated with subintervals in the current list.

  - Then it scatters the set across p processors of the cluster. The number of points received by each processor is proportional to the current estimation of its relative speed.

  - Each processor estimates integrand $f(x)$ at the points received form the host-processor. Besides making the estimation, the processor measures the time taken to do the estimation. Then it sends to the host-processor both the integrand values and the time taken to compute the values.

  - The host-processor uses the computation time received from each processor to calculate their relative speeds demonstrated during this integrand evaluation. This fresh estimation of the relative speeds of processors will be used at the next iteration of the main loop. Note that this approach makes `pquanc8` adaptive to possible changes in the speeds of the individual processors even during the execution of the program (i.e., due to some external applications).

The mpC implementation of routine `pquanc8` takes the following form:

```
#include <stdio.h>
#include <stdlib.h>
#include <mpc.h>
#include <math.h>
```

```
#include "quanc8.h"
#include "partition.h"


typedef struct Interval
{
   double *x, *f;
   double qprev;
   struct Interval *next;
} *IntervalList;


#include "interval.h"


double [*]pquanc8(double (*fun)(double), double
         [host]a, double [host]b, double
         [host]abserr, double [host]relerr,
            double *[host]errest, int *[host]nofun, int
            *[host]flag, double *[host]badpoint)
{
   double [host]area=0., [*]result=0., [host]absarea,
            [host]stone, [host]step, [host]minstep,
            [host]cor11=0., [host]esterr,
            [host]tollerr, [host]qleft, [host]qright,
            [host]qnow, [host]qdiff, [host]prevleft=0.;
   int [host]repeat=0, [host]maxrepeat=2;
   double *[host]f, *[host]x;
   IntervalList [host]ints, [host]nextints;
   repl int p;
   repl double *speeds;


   if(a==b)
      return result;


   // Initialization for first interval
   [host]:
   {
      *flag = 0;
      *errest = 0.;
      *nofun = 0;
      stone = (b-a)/16.;
      minstep = stone*relerr+abserr;
      InitFirstInterval(fun, a, b, &x, &f);
      *nofun=9;
   }
```

```
MPC_Processors_static_info(&p, &speeds);
{
   net SimpleNet(p) s;
   int [s]myn;
   repl [s]nints, *[s]ns, *[s]dsp, [s]src=0;
   double *[s]nodes, *[host]times;
   double *[s]mynodes, *[s]myvalues, [s]mytime;
   [s]:
   {
      ns = malloc(p*sizeof(int));
      dsp = malloc(p*sizeof(int));
   }
   [host]: times = malloc(p*sizeof(double));


   ints = ([host]CreateInterval)(x, f, 0., NULL);
   nints = 1;


   // Main loop of the algorithm
   for(step=stone; ints!=NULL; ints=nextints,
      step/=2.0)
   {
      // Calculate points, where integrand should be evaluated
      // at this iteration, proceeding from list ints of nints
      // subintervals of width step, whose contribution into
      // the integral is still to be estimated. Store the points
      // in array nodes.
      [host]:
      {
         int j, k;
         struct Interval *i;

         nodes = malloc(nints*8*sizeof(double));
         for(i=ints, k=0; i!=NULL; i=i->next)
            for (j=1; j<16; j+=2, k++)
               nodes[k] = i->x[j] = (i->x[j-1]+i->x[j+1])/2.;
      }
      nints = [host]nints;


      // Become alert if the left end point of left subinterval
      // does not change from iteration to iteration
      [host]:
         if(fabs(prevleft-nodes[0])<relerr*fabs(prevleft) ||
```

```
        fabs(prevleft-nodes[0])<abserr)
        repeat++;
    else
    {
        prevleft = nodes[0];
        repeat = 0;
    }
// Convergence test
if(repeat>maxrepeat && step<minstep)
{
    *flag = 1;
    *badpoint = [host]nodes[0];
    [s]: break;
}
[s]:
{
    int k;

    // Calculate the number of points assigned to each
    // processor and store it in array ns; the number is
    // proportional to the processor's relative speed
    Partition(p, speeds, ns, nints*8);

    // Distribute the points across processors
    myn = ns[I coordof myn];
    mynodes = malloc(myn*sizeof(double));
    myvalues = malloc(myn*sizeof(double));
    for(k=1, dsp[0]=0; k < p; k++)
        dsp[k] = ns[k-1]+dsp[k-1];
    ([[(p)s]]MPC_Scatter(&src, nodes, dsp, ns, myn, mynodes);

    // Evaluate the integrand at the points in parallel and
    // measure the time taken by each processor
    if(myn)
    {
        mytime = MPC_Wtime();
        for(k=0; k<myn; k++)
            myvalues[k] = (*fun)(mynodes[k]);
            mytime = MPC_Wtime()-mytime;
    }
    else
        mytime = 0.;
}
```

```
// Calculate the actual relative speed of processors
// and store it in array speeds
times[] = mytime;
[host]:
{
    int j;
    double temp;

    for(j=0, temp=0.; j<p; j++)
        if(ns[j] && times[j] > temp*ns[j])
            temp = times[j]/ns[j];
    for(j=0; j<p; j++)
        if(ns[j])
            speeds[j] = temp/times[j]*1000.*ns[j];
}
[s]: ([(p)s])MPC_Bcast(&src, speeds, 1, p, speeds, 1);


// Gather the function values to host-processor storing
// them in array nodes
([([s]p)s])MPC_Gather(&src, nodes, dsp, ns, myn, myvalues);


// Complete computation of all elements of list ints that
// represents a set of subintervals of width step,whose
// contribution into the integral is still to be estimated
[host]:
{
    int j, k;
    struct Interval *i;

    for(i=ints, k=0; i!=NULL; i=i->next)
        for (j=1; j<16; j+=2, k++)
            i->f[j] = nodes[k];
}


// Increase number of function values
*nofun += ([host]nints)*8;


[s]free(mynodes);
[s]free(myvalues);
[host]: free(nodes);


// Calculate an estimate of the integral over each
```

```
// interval in list ints. If the interval is acceptable,
// add its contribution to the result. If not, bisect it
// and add 2 new subintervals to a list of subintervals to
// be processed at next iteration of the main loop
[host]:
{
    struct Interval *i;


    for(i=ints, nextints=NULL, nints=0; i!=NULL;
        i=i->next)
    {
      CentralQuanc8Calculation(i, step, &qleft, &qright);
      qnow = qleft+qright;
      qdiff = qnow - i->qprev;
      area = area+qdiff;
      esterr = fabs(qdiff)/1023.0;
      absarea = fabs(area);
      tollerr = fmax(abserr, relerr*absarea)*(step/stone);


      if(esterr <= tollerr) //Interval convergence test
      { // Interval converged. Add contributions into sums.
        result += qnow;
        *errest += esterr;
        cor11 += qdiff/1023.0;
        free(i->x);
        free(i->f);
      }
      else
      {// No convergence. Bisect interval i and add its
         // subintervals to list nextints of intervals to be
         // processed at next iteration of the main loop
         nextints = BisectInterval(i, nextints,
         qleft, qright);
         nints += 2;
      }
    }
  }
  [host]FreeList(ints);
}
}
[host]:
{
  double temp;
```

```
      result += cor11;
      temp = fabs(result)+*errest;
      while (*errest!=0. && temp == fabs(result))
      {
        *errest *= 2.;
        temp = fabs(result)+*errest;
        }
      }
      return result;
}


#include "function.h"


int [*] main()
{
   double [host]a=0., [host]b=2., [host]abserr=0.,
          [host]relerr=1.e-11, [host]errest, [host]bad point,
          [host]sflag, [host]time, result;
   int [host]nofun, [host]pflag;


   time = ([host]MPC_Wtime)();
   result = pquanc8(fun, a, b, abserr, relerr, &errest,
                  &nofun, &pflag, &badpoint);


   time = ([host]MPC_Wtime)()-time;
   [host]:
     if(pflag)
       printf("pquanc8:\nBad singularity at %e\n",
              badpoint);
     else
       printf("pquanc8:\nresult=%e errest=%e nofun=%d time=%es\n",
              result, errest, nofun, time);


   time = ([host]MPC_Wtime)();
   [host]: result = quanc8(fun, a, b, abserr, relerr,
                   &errest, &nofun, &sflag);
   time = ([host]MPC_Wtime)()-time;
   [host]:
     if(sflag)
       printf("quanc8:\nBad singularity at %e\n",
              b-modf(sflag,NULL)*(b-a));
     else
```

```
printf("quanc8:\nresult=%e errest=%e nofun=%d time=%es\n",
    result, errest, nofun, time);
}
```

The preceding pquanc8 routine does not contain a serial code for calculating the number of points to be assigned to each processor and for processing the lists of subintervals. The code is kept in the files partition.h and interval.h respectively, and included in the mpC program with the include directives. Other two files included in the program are

- quanc8.h, which contains the C code of the quanc8 routine. The file is used in the program to compare the quanc8 execution time with the execution time of pquanc8.
- function.h, which contains the definition of a function fun for integrand $f(x)$.

The full code of the mpC application can be found in Appendix C.

9.4. SIMULATION OF OIL EXTRACTION

This section presents an example of a regular real-life problem—the simulation of oil extraction—in a heterogeneous parallel environment. In particular, the problem was to port a Fortran 77/PVM application, written to simulate oil extraction (about 3000 lines of source code), from a Parsytec supercomputer to a local network of heterogeneous workstations.

The oil extraction process by means of nonpiston water displacement is described by the following system of equations:

$$m \times \frac{\partial S_w}{\partial t} + \mathrm{div}(F_w(S_w) \times K(S_w) \times \mathrm{grad}(P)) = q \times F_w(\overline{S}), \qquad (9.1)$$

$$m \times \frac{\partial S_w}{\partial t} + \mathrm{div}(F_w(S_w) \times K(S_w) \times \mathrm{grad}(P)) = q \times F_w(S_w), \qquad (9.2)$$

$$\mathrm{div}(K(S_w) \times \mathrm{grad}(P)) = q, \qquad (9.3)$$

where

$$K(S_w) = -k \times \left(\frac{k_w(S_w)}{\mu_w} + \frac{k_0(S_w)}{\mu_0} \right), \qquad (9.4)$$

$$F(S_w) = \frac{k_w(S_w)/\mu_w}{[k_w(S_w)/\mu_w] + [k_0(S_w)/\mu_0]}. \qquad (9.5)$$

The initial and boundary conditions are

$$S_w|_{t=0} = s, \quad P|_{t=0} = P_0, \qquad (9.6)$$

$$\frac{\partial S_w}{\partial n}|_\Gamma = 0, \quad \frac{\partial P}{\partial n}|_\Gamma = 0. \qquad (9.7)$$

Equation (9.1) is the water fraction transport equation at the sources, and equation (9.2) is the water fraction transport equation in the domain. Equation (9.3) is the elliptic pressure equation. The solutions of this system involve water saturation, S_w (the fraction of water in the fluid flow), and pressure in the oil field, P. These equations include coefficients for the medium's characteristics: the coefficient of porosity (m), the absolute permeability (k) and nonlinear relative phase permeabilities of oil ($k_o(S_w)$) and water ($k_w(S_w)$), the viscosities of oil (μ_0) and water (μ_w), the function of sources/sinks (q), critical and connected values of water saturation (S and $\bar{S}$) and the strongly nonlinear Bucley-Leverett function ($F_w(S_w)$).

The numerical solutions were sought in a domain with conditions of impermeability at the boundary (9.7). This domain was a subdomain of symmetry singled out from the unbounded oil field being simulated. The numerical algorithm was based on completely implicit methods of solving equations (9.1) through (9.3). That is, equations (9.1) and (9.2) were solved by the iterative secant method, while the (α–β)-iterative algorithm was employed to solve equation (9.3). The (α–β)-elliptic solver was an extension of the sweep method for the many-dimensional case. It did not need any a priori information about problem operators and was sufficiently general purpose. By this algorithm the solution being sought was obtained via eight auxiliary functions calculated iteratively. It was useful to include a relaxation parameter into the equations for some coefficients in order to reduce the number of (α–β)-iterations.

The standard seven-point ("honeycomb") scheme of oil/water well disposition was simulated as shown in Figure 9.14. The computational domain was approximated by a uniform rectangular grid of 117×143 points.

The parallel implementation of the algorithm for running on MPPs was based on computational domain partitioning. The domain was divided into equal subdomains in one direction along the Y-coordinate, with each subdomain being computed by a separate processor of an executing MPP.

That domain distribution was more successful in reducing the number of message-passing operations in the data parallel (α–β)-algorithm than the domain distributions along the X-coordinate or along both coordinates.

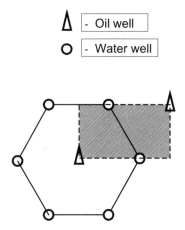

Figure 9.14. The seven-point "honeycomb" scheme of oil/water well disposition.

In each subdomain the system (9.1) through (9.3) was solved as follows: At every time level, the water saturation was found by solving equations (9.1) and (9.2) using the pressure values from the previous time level. Then, from the just obtained water saturation, a new pressure was calculated at the present time level by solving equation (9.3). This procedure was repeated at each subsequent time level.

The main difficulty of this parallel algorithm was estimation of the optimal relaxation parameter ω for the $(\alpha-\beta)$-solver because this parameter varies while dividing the computational domain into different quantities of equal subdomains. Employing a wrong parameter led to slow convergence or in some cases to nonconvergence of $(\alpha-\beta)$-iterations. Numerous experiments allowed finding the optimal relaxation parameter for each number of subdomains.

The parallel algorithm above was implemented in Fortran 77 with PVM as a communication platform and demonstrated good scalability, speedups, and parallelization efficiency while running on the Parsytec PowerXplorer System—an MPP consisting of PowerPC 601 processors as computational nodes, and T800 transputers as communicational nodes (one T800 provides four bi-directional 20 Mbits/s communication links).

Table 9.2 presents some results of the experiments for one time level. The parallelization efficiency is defined as $S_{real}/S_{ideal} \times 100\%$, where S_{real} is the actual speedup achieved by the parallel oil extraction simulator on the parallel system, and S_{ideal} is the ideal speedup. S_{ideal} is calculated as the sum of speeds of processors of the executing parallel system divided by the speed of a base processor. All speedups are calculated relative to the original sequential oil extraction simulator running on the base processor. Note that the more powerful are the communication links and the less powerful are the processors, and the higher efficiency is achieved.

TABLE 9.2. Performance of the Fortran/PVM parallel oil extraction simulator on the Parsytec PowerXplorer System

Number of Processors	ω	Number of Iterations	Time (s)	Real speedup	Efficiency
1	1.197	205	120	1	100%
2	1.2009	211	64	1.875	94%
4	1.208	214	38	3.158	79%
8	1.22175	226	26	4.615	58%

TABLE 9.3. Relative speeds of workstations

Workstation Number	Relative Speed
1	1150
2	575
3–4	460
5–7	325
8–9	170

The parallel oil extraction simulator was thought to be part of a portable software system that would run on local networks of heterogeneous computers and provide a computerized working place of an oil extraction expert. Therefore a portable application efficiently solving the oil extraction problem on networks of computers was required.

Our first step was to port the Fortran/PVM program to a local network of heterogeneous workstations based on 10 Mbits Ethernet. Our weakest workstation (SPARCclassic) executed the serial application a bit slower than PowerPC 601, while the most powerful one (UltraSPARC-1) executed it more than six times faster. In general, nine uniprocessor workstations were used, and Table 9.3 shows their relative speeds.

Table 9.4 shows some results of execution of the Fortran/PVM program on different two-, four-, six-, and eight-workstation subnetworks of the network. For every subnetwork in this table the speedup is calculated relative to the running time of the serial program on the fastest workstation of the subnetwork. (The total running time of the serial oil extraction simulator while executing on different workstations can be found in Table 9.5.) The visible degradation of parallelization efficiency is explained as caused by the following: slower communication links, faster processors, and an unbalanced workload of the workstations.

The first two are unavoidable, while the third can be avoided by slight modification of the parallel algorithm implemented by the Fortran/PVM program.

TABLE 9.4. Performance of the Fortran/PVM parallel oil extraction simulator on subnetworks of workstations

Subnetwork (Workstation Number)	ω	Number of Iterations	Time (s)	Ideal Speedup	Real Speedup	Efficiency
{2, 5}	1.2009	211	46	1.57	0.88	0.56
{5, 6}	1.2009	211	47	2.0	1.52	0.76
(2, 5–7}	1.208	214	36	2.7	1.13	0.42
{2–7}	1.21485	216	32	4.3	1.27	0.30
{2, 3, 5–8}	1.21485	216	47	3.8	0.87	0.23
{1–8}	1.22175	226	46	3.3	0.41	0.12

TABLE 9.5. Performance of the serial oil extraction simulator for 20s iterations

Processor Type	Ultra SPARC-1	SPARC 20	SPARC Station 4		SPARC 5			SPARC Classic	
Workstation number	1	2	3	4	5	6	7	8	9
Time (s)	18.7	40.7	51.2	51.2	71.4	71.4	71.4	133	133

That is, to provide the optimal load balancing, the computational domain should be decomposed into subdomains of nonequal sizes, proportional to relative speeds of participating processors. To be exact, the number of grid columns in each subdomain is the same, while the number of rows differs. This modified algorithm is hard to implement in portable form using PVM or MPI but can easily be implemented in mpC.

Regarding the relaxation parameter, it is reasonable to assume its optimal value to be a function of the number of grid rows, and to use its own relaxation parameter $\omega = \omega(N_{row})$ for each subdomain. While distributing the domain into different quantities of subdomains with equal numbers of grid rows, a sequence of optimal relaxation parameters can be found empirically. Now using the experimental data and piecewise linear interpolation, the optimal parameter ω can be calculated for any N_{row}. Note in Table 9.6 that this approach gives a high convergence rate and good efficiency of the parallel $(\alpha–\beta)$-solver with relaxation (see the numbers of iterations).

Table 9.6 shows experimental results of execution of the mpC application on the network of workstations. In the experiments the mpC programming environment used LAM MPI 6.0 as a communication platform. As can be seen, the mpC application demonstrates much higher efficiency in the het-

TABLE 9.6. Performance of the mpC parallel oil extraction simulator on subnetworks of workstations

Subnetwork (Workstation Number)	Number of Iterations	Time (s)	Real Speedup	Efficiency	Time of 205 Iterations	Speedup on 205 Iterations	Efficiency on 205 Iterations
{2, 5}	324	41.6	0.98	0.63	28.2	1.44	0.92
{5, 6}	225	38.8	1.84	0.92	36.4	1.96	0.98
{2, 5–7}	279	26	1.57	0.58	19.7	2.07	0.77
{2–7}	245	17.9	2.27	0.54	15	2.71	0.63
{2, 3, 5–8}	248	20.2	2.01	0.54	17	2.39	0.64
{2, 3, 5–8}^{a}	260	32.8	1.24	0.33	26.8	1.52	0.40
{2–9}	268	21	1.94	0.40	16	2.54	0.53

^{a}The computational domain was forcedly divided into equal subdomains.

erogeneous environment than its PVM counterpart. To estimate the pure contribution of load balancing in the improvement of parallelization efficiency, we ran the mpC application on a subnetwork {2, 3, 5, 6, 7, 8} with a forcedly even domain decomposition, which resulted in the essential (more than 1.5 times) efficiency degradation (compare rows 5 and 6 in Table 9.6). Note that the mpC application only dealt with processor speeds and distributed data by taking into account only this aspect of heterogeneity.

9.5. SUMMARY

We have demonstrated that a wide range of scientific problems can be efficiently solved on heterogeneous networks of computers. We considered the design of the parallel block cyclic algorithm of matrix multiplication on heterogeneous NoCs and its portable implementation in the mpC language. We also considered parallel algorithms solving on the heterogeneous NoCs a more demanding linear algebra problem: Cholesky factorization of a symmetric, positive-definite matrix.

We introduced a relatively simple approach for assessing a heterogeneous parallel algorithm via comparing its efficiency with the efficiency of its homogeneous prototype. We also presented two design approaches for parallel algorithms that solve regular problems on heterogeneous NoCs. The first approach involved a one-process per-processor configuration of the parallel program with the workload unevenly distributed over the processes. The second approach involved a mutliple-processes per-processor configuration of the parallel program, when the workload is evenly distributed over the processes while the number of processes on each processor is proportional to its speed. We expreimentally compared the approaches and described their portable mpC implementation.

We discussed the results of the experiments with the N-body mpC application described in Section 7.1, showing them to be an example of an inherently irregular problem. We showed that a heterogeneous parallel algorithm solving such a problem would be naturally deduced from the problem itself rather than from the parallel environment executing the algorithm. We also provided in detail a design of the parallel adaptive quadrature routine for numerical approximation to definite integrals on heterogeneous NoCs and its portable mpC implementation.

We concluded in recalling an experience of solving a real-life regular problem—that of oil extraction, which we simulated in a heterogeneous parallel environment. While all the experiments presented in the chapter were conducted on relatively small heterogeneous NoCs, heterogeneous parallel computing make sense on large heterogeneous networks as well. Indeed, recent experiments with an mpC application simulating a supernova explosion, carried out by researchers at the Russian Academy of Sciences on a heterogeneous network of some 500 processors, have proved that a very complex scientific problem can be efficiently solved on a large heterogeneous NoC.

## CHAPTER 10

Business and Software Engineering Applications

10.1. ACCELERATION OF DISTRIBUTED APPLICATIONS

10.1.1. Introduction

CORBA is widely used to develop and integrate highly complex distributed technical applications in industries as diverse as health care, telecommunications, banking, and manufacturing. CORBA is supported on almost every combination of hardware and operating system in existence, and is available from a large number of vendors, CORBA supports a large number of programming languages; CORBA-based distributed applications fall within the client/server programming paradigm. A typical CORBA-based application server provides a number of operations that can be invoked by remote clients.

A particularly important quality of the service, provided by the remote server, is the execution time of the remote operations. The total time of execution of a remote operation includes the time of communication between the client and server and the time of computation on the server side. In computationally intensive operations the maximal effect comes from an acceleration of the computations on the server side of the hardware, which is typically a heterogeneous network of diverse computers.

There are two ways that a speedup of execution is usually achieved in remote operations on a network of computers. The first is to balance the workload of available computers. This means that the CORBA implementation starts up the server providing the requested operation on the computer that is the fastest at the moment of the receipt of the request. The second is a multithreaded implementation of the remote operation and its execution on a shared memory multiprocessor computer if the latter is available.

Yet another way for efficient implementation of a remote operation is its parallel execution on the network of computers. Theoretically, this could provide speedup independent of the availability of a multiprocessor computer. In practice, this option is not used for two good reasons. The first is the lack

Parallel Computing on Heterogeneous Networks, by Alexey Lastovetsky
ISBN 0-471-22982-2 Copyright © 2003 by John Wiley & Sons, Inc.

of experience-based integration of distributed memory parallel computing into CORBA-based distributed applications. The second, and more important, is that the technologies and tools for parallel computing on heterogeneous networks are only in their early stages, and so are not as mature and widespread as those for homogeneous multiprocessors.

In this section we show that computationally intensive remote operations in CORBA-based distributed applications can be easily and greatly accelerated with a help of tools for parallel computing on heterogeneous clusters. IONA's Orbix is used as a particular implementation of CORBA, and the mpC language is used for parallel implementation of such remote operations.

10.1.2. Distributed Application of a "Supermarket Chain"

Consider a distributed application dealing with a chain of supermarkets. Let us assume that each cash register in the supermarkets sends information about all baskets of items purchased by customers to a central information center where the information is accumulated and stored.

A single basket of items is stored in the form of a file record, so that each individual file contains data about a fixed number of baskets. All of the files when compiled together show the full information about the contents of customer baskets during a certain period of time. That data dump is used for extraction of diverse useful information, and any supermarket can contact the central information center for one or another (piece of) information.

That service is implemented by a CORBA-based application server providing a set of corresponding remote operations. In particular, a supermarket can inquire of the central information center about the optimal distribution of items over a given number of sections. A fragment of the CORBA IDL specification of the full service relevant to this particular request is as follows:

```
typedef short Item;
typedef sequence<Item> Basket;
typedef sequence<Item> Section;
typedef sequence<Section> Distribution;
interface central_office
{
   void BasketOfItems(in Basket b);
   Distribution getDistribution(in short number_of_sections);
   void Hello();
   void Bye();
   ...
};
```

Say a client invokes operation `BasketOfItems` to add a basket to the server's data store. Each physical item in the basket is represented by its numerical code, so that the basket is represented by a sequence of codes of purchased items.

To get an optimal distribution of items over a given number of sections, the client invokes the operation `getDistribution`, passing the number of sections as an input parameter. Each individual section is represented by a sequence of items belonging to the section so that each item appears in one and only one section. The operation returns a sequence of sequences of items representing the requested distribution.

To initialize a session with the remote server, the client invokes operation `Hello`; to finalize the session, it invokes operation `Bye`.

Operation `getDistribution` is computationally intensive and implements the following algorithm:

- First it reads all files one by one and computes a vector, S, and a matrix, P, representing the mappings $S:I \to N$ and $P:I \times I \to N$ respectively, where

    I is a set of all stock items,

    N is a set of positive integers,

    $S(i)$ is the total number of baskets containing item i, and

    $P(i,j)$ is the total number of baskets containing both item i and item j.
- Then it uses the mappings to divide set I into m nonintersecting subsets $I_0, \ldots, I_{m-1}$, where m is the total number of sections and each item of m is that most frequently bought, $i_0, \ldots, i_{m-1}$, and so will head a separate section. Distribution of the remaining items over the sections can be described by the following pseudocode:

```
delete i₀, ... ,i_{m-1} from I
for (k=0; I is not empty; k=(k+1)%m)
{
    find i so that P(i,i_k)==max{P(I,i_k)}
    add i to I_k
    delete i from I
}
```

Intuitively this algorithm tries to include in each section at least one very popular item surrounded by the items that most often accompany this popular choice in customers' baskets. It is assumed that such a distribution will stimulate customers to buy items of secondary necessity and reduce the total shopping duration. As the data store is very large and input–output operations are relatively slow, the execution time of the algorithm is practically equal to the time of computation of the mappings S and P.

Note that a more accurate distribution can be obtained by considering not only the popularity of single items and their pairs but also that of their triplets, fours, and so on. But the consideration leads to significantly more computations and hence much slower algorithms. Thus, although the presented algorithm is computationally intensive, it performs the minimal volume of computation that is necessary to solve the problem.

Both the client and server parts of the described distributed application were originally implemented in Orbix 3 C++ programming system.

10.1.3. Parallel Implementation of the Remote Operation `getDistribution`

The traditional, purely serial implementation of the application server will cause the operation `getDistribution` to become very slow from the client's point of view. Yet the application server normally runs on a network of computers whose total performance is quite high. Therefore a parallel implementation of operation `getDistribution`, which enables it to use effectively all of its available performance potential, could accelerate the operation.

An obvious parallel modification of the original serial algorithm is to compute the mappings S and P by all available processors in parallel. The parallel algorithm exploits the following observation: Let m be the total number of stock items. Let P_i be an $m \times m$ matrix representing the popularity of pairs of items, which is computed by processing a set B_i of baskets of items. Let P be an $m \times m$ matrix representing the popularity of pairs of items, which is computed by processing the set $\cup_i B_i$. Let $B_i \cap B_j = \{\}$ for any $i \neq j$. Then $P = \Sigma_i P_i$. Similarly, if S_i is a vector of popularity of single items computed by processing B_i, S is a vector of popularity of single items computed by processing $\cup_i B_i$, and $B_i \cap B_j = \{\}$ for any $i \neq j$, then $S = \Sigma_i S_i$.

Thus the problem of computation of the mappings S and P can be parallelized by partitioning the entire set of baskets of items into nonintersecting subsets. Each subset is processed independently. The resulting mappings are obtained by a simple combination of the mappings computed for each individual subset.

Let us assume that the data store consists of a big number of files, each containing the same number of basket records. Let m be the total number of stock items. Then the algorithm of parallel computing the mappings S and P on a heterogeneous cluster of p processors can be summarized as follows:

- The entire set of n files is partitioned into p nonintersecting subsets. There is one-to-one mapping between these subsets and the processors. The number of files in the ith subset is proportional to the relative speed of the ith processor.
- The ith processor computes an m-element vector of the popularity of single items, S_i, and an $m \times m$ matrix of the popularity of pairs of items, P_i, by processing its subset of the entire set of files.

- Vectors S_i and matrices P_i are gathered to the host-processor.
- The host-processor computes
  - the resulting vector of the popularity of single items, S, as a sum of vectors S_i,

$$S = \sum_{i=0}^{p-1} S_i;$$

  - the resulting matrix of the popularity of pairs of items, P, as a sum of vectors P_i,

$$P = \sum_{i=0}^{p-1} P_i.$$

The parallel algorithm was easily implemented in mpC. As the mpC language is a strict extension of ANSI C, the corresponding parallel mpC code is obtained by a very slim modification of the original serial C code used in the Orbix C++ implementation of the application server.

The key fragments of the parallel mpC code appear as follows:

```
nettype ParallelDataMining(int p, int f[p])
{
   coord I=p;
   node {I>=0: f[I];};
};
...
repl p, num_of_files, *files;
repl double *speeds;
...
recon TestCode();
MPC_Get_processors_info(&p, speeds);
Partition(p, speeds, files, num_of_files);
{
   net ParallelDataMining(p, files) pdm;
   ...
}
```

In this code the network type definition describes a performance model of the implemented parallel algorithm. It introduces the following components:

- The name `ParallelDataMining` of the network type.
- A list of parameters, including the integer scalar parameter n and the vector parameter f of n integers.
- A coordinate variable, I, ranging from 0 to n-1.

Finally, it associates abstract processors with this coordinate system and declares relative volumes of computations to be performed by each of the processors. It is assumed that *i*th element of vector f is equal to the number of files processed by *i*th abstract processor.

The execution of the `recon` statement is that all physical processors running the program execute in parallel some relevant test code, and the time elapsed by each of the real processors is used to refresh the estimation of its performance. The library function `MPC_Get_processors_info` returns the number of available physical processors (in the variable p) and their relative speeds (in the array `speeds`). Based on the number and relative performances of the actual processors, function `Partition` computes how many files of the data store each actual processor will handle. After this call, `files [i]` will be equal to the number of files processed by *i*th actual processor.

The next key line of the code defines the abstract network `pdm` of the type `ParallelDataMining` with actual parameters p—the actual number of physical processors, and `files`—an integer array of p elements containing actual numbers of files to be processed by the processors. The remaining computations and communications will be performed on this abstract network. The mpC programming system maps the abstract processors of `pdm` to the real parallel processes of the program. This mapping is based, on the one hand, on the current estimation of the speed of physical processors and, on the other hand, on the performance model of the parallel algorithm. The programming system does the mapping at runtime and tries to minimize the execution time of the parallel algorithm. In order to guarantee that all physical processors will be involved in computations, we assume that the mpC program has been started so that each physical processor runs precisely one process of the program.

The remaining modifications of the original Orbix implementation of the application server are minor and rather technical. They are aimed at smooth integration of the mpC parallel environment into the Orbix distributed environment.

Code implementing operations `Hello` and `Bye` is modified to initialize and finalize the mpC programming environment respectively. Code implementing operation `getDistribution` is additionally modified to enable the passing of input data (the number of sections) from the Orbix framework of the application server to the mpC inserted component, and output data (the recommended distribution) from the mpC component back to the Orbix layer. The input data are passed to the mpC program as an external argument, and a temporary file is used for passing the result computed by the mpC program to the main Orbix body of the application server.

In general, the modifications integrating the mpC parallel application into the Orbix distributed application are fairly obvious and easy to make. Although a deeper integration of the two technologies, say, on the language level, may be possible, this does not seem to be a reasonable course of action. A deeper integration might prove to be more sophisticated, but it would not provide any visible improvement in the quality of services compared to the light integration scheme we used above.

10.1.4. Experimental Results

Now we look at some results of experiments with supermarket chain applications.

A small network of workstations was used in the experiments. The client ran on an IBM RS6000 workstation, the serial application server ran on a 4-processor Sun E450 workstation, and the parallel application server ran on a network of two 4-processor Sun E450 workstations and one 6-processor HP 9000/K570 workstation. Table 10.1 shows relative speeds of these computers obtained by executing the serial test code specified by the `recon` statement of the mpC program.

The data store consisted of 60 files each containing 8000 basket records. Up to 100 different stock items could appear in a single basket. The client code invoked the remote operation `getDistribution` to get an optimal distribution of the 100 items over five sections and measured the execution time of the operation. This time obtained for different configurations of the application server are presented in Table 10.2.

There were four configurations that only differed in the way of execution of the operation `getDistribution`:

- The original serial version of this operation was executed on a Sun workstation.
- The mpC parallel version of the operation was executed on the same 4-processor Sun workstation.

TABLE 10.1. Cluster of workstations executing the application server

Workstation Number	Model	Number of Processors	Relative Speed
1	Sun E450	4	2658
2	Sun E450	4	3280
3	HP 9000/K570	6	6067

TABLE 10.2. Execution time of the remote operation getDistribution invoked to calculate an optimal distribution of 100 stock items over five sections

Workstations in Execution of Remote Operation	Mode of the Remote Operation	Execution Time (s)
1	Serial	332
1	Parallel	168
1, 2	Parallel	96
1, 2, 3	Parallel	42

- The mpC version was executed on the cluster of the two 4-processor Sun workstations.
- The mpC version was executed on the cluster of the two 4-processor Sun workstations and one 6-processor HP workstation.

As is obvious, the parallel configurations of the application server provided better performance.

10.2. PARALLEL TESTING OF DISTRIBUTED SOFTWARE

10.2.1. Motivation

The case study we present here demonstrates the use of heterogeneous parallel computing to accelerate the testing of a complex distributed programming system such as Orbix 3, which is IONA's implementation of the CORBA 2.1 standard.

Orbix 3 is a distributed programming system most used by corporate programmers around the world. As any software system has bugs, wider and more intensive use of a software system elicits more bugs during its operation. Orbix 3 is not an exception to the rule. Every day its users report new bugs that affect the functionality or performance of the Orbix 3 software. A dedicated team of software engineers is constantly working on the bugs and making appropriate changes in the Orbix 3 code.

The maintenance process includes running an Orbix 3 test suite before and after any changes made in the Orbix 3 source code in order to

- see if the bug has been fixed, and
- check that the changes themselves do not introduce new bugs into the software.

The test suite consists of many hundreds of test cases. Each fixed bug results in one more test case added to the test suite. This test case should examine the problem associated with the bug and demonstrate that the problem has been solved. Thus the number of test cases in the test suite is constantly growing.

The serial execution of a test suite on a single machine might take from 9 to 21 hours depending on the particular machine and its workload. The test suite must be run against at least three major platforms. For each platform the test suite must be run at least twice, namely before and after the corresponding changes are made in the Orbix 3 source code. Thus, on average, the best time for running a test suite is 90 hours per bug. Often, however, it takes longer. For example, if a bug is reported in some minor platform, the test suite should be run against all major platforms and the minor platform. If the bug has enough complexity, the very first solution of the problem may introduce new bugs, and hence more than one solution will have to be tested during the work on the bug.

In terms of time, serial running of the test suite is the most expensive part of the maintenance process. So its acceleration could significantly improve the overall performance of the maintenance team. Since the local network of computers available to the maintenance team includes more than one machine for each major platform and most of the machines are multiprocessor workstations, parallel execution of the test suite seems to be a natural way to speed up its running.

10.2.2. Parallel Execution of the Orbix Test Suite on a Cluster of Multiprocessor Workstations

As all major platforms, against which Orbix 3 should be tested, are Unix clones, an immediate idea is to use the GNU make utility for parallel execution of different test cases of the test suite. On Unix platforms, the ' -j ' option tells make to execute many jobs simultaneously. If the ' -j ' option is followed by an integer, this is the number of jobs to execute at once. If this number is equal to the number of available processors, there will be as many parallel streams of jobs as processors. As the utility assigns jobs to parallel streams dynamically, the load of the processors will be naturally balanced.

This simple approach has several restrictions. One is that it can only parallelize the execution of a set of jobs on a single multiprocessor machine. Another restriction is that if some jobs in the set are not fully independent, the straightforward parallelization may not guarantee their proper execution. For example, a number of jobs may share the same resources (processes, databases, etc.) whose state they both change and depend on in their behavior. Such jobs should not be executed simultaneously, but the GNU make utility provides no direct way to specify that constraint.

A typical test case from the Orbix 3 test suite builds and executes a distributed application (see Section 10.1 for an example of distributed application). The test suite usually includes the following steps:

- Building executables of the server(s) and clients of the distributed application.
- Running the application.
- Analyzing the results and generating a report. The report shows whether the test case passed or failed, and includes the start time and end time of its execution.

On completion of the execution of the test suite, all individual reports produced by the test cases are summarized in a final report.

During the serial running of the test suite on a single computer, the test cases share the following resources:

- Basic system software such as compilers, interpreters, loaders, utilities, and libraries.
- An Orbix daemon through which servers and clients of Orbix distributed applications interact with one other. The daemon is started up once, before the test suite starts running.
- An interface repository, which stores all necessary information about server interfaces. This information can be retrieved by clients to construct and issue requests for invoking operations on servers at run time.

What happens if multiple test cases are executed simultaneously on the same computer? Can the sharing of these resources cause unwanted changes in their behavior?

The basic system software should cause no problem. Each test case just uses its own copy of any compiler, interpreter, loader, utility, or static (archive) library. As for dynamic shared libraries, their simultaneous use by multiple test cases should also cause no problem. This is simply because a dynamic shared library is by definition a library whose code can be safely shared by multiple, concurrently running programs so that the programs share exactly one physical copy of the library code and do not require their own copies of that code.

There further should be no problem with sharing one physical copy of the Orbix daemon by multiple concurrently running distributed applications. This is because that sharing is just one of the core intrinsic features of the Orbix daemon. Moreover, in terms of testing, simultaneous execution of multiple distributed applications is even more desirable than their serial execution as it provides more realistic environment for functioning Orbix software.

Problems may occur if multiple concurrently running test cases share the same interface repository. In order to specify the problems, let us briefly outline how interfaces and interface repositories may be used in the Orbix 3 test suite.

In order to stress object orientation of the CORBA distributed programming technology, the server components of CORBA-based distributed applications are called server objects or simply *objects*. The CORBA Interface Definition Language (IDL) permits interfaces to objects to be defined independent of an objects implementation. After defining an interface in IDL, the interface definition is used as input to an IDL compiler, which produces output that can be compiled and linked with an object implementation and its clients.

CORBA supports clients making requests to objects. The requests consist of an operation, a target object, zero or more parameters, and an optional request context. A request causes a service to be performed on behalf of a client, and the results of executing the request are returned to the client. If an abnormal condition occurs during execution of the request, the exception is returned.

Interfaces can be used either statically or dynamically. An interface is statically bound to an object when the name of the object it is accessing is known at compile time. In this case the IDL compiler generates the necessary output to compile and link to the object at compile time. In addition clients that need to discover an object at runtime and construct a request dynamically can use the Dynamic Invocation Interface (DII). The DII is supported by an interface repository, which is defined as part of CORBA. By accessing information in the interface repository, a client can retrieve all of the information necessary about an object's interface to construct and issue a request at runtime.

In Orbix 3 an interface repository is implemented as a CORBA server object. As a CORBA server, it is registered with an Orbix daemon under the name IFR. Usually it is registered as an automatically launched shared server. This means that the IFR will be launched once by the Orbix daemon on the very first request for its services, and will be shared by all clients associated with this Orbix daemon.

Orbix 3 provides three utilities to access the IFR. Command `putidl` allows the users to add a set of IDL definitions to the IFR. This command takes the name of an IDL file as an argument. All IDL definitions within that file are added to the repository. Command `rmidl` removes from the repository all IDL definitions given as its arguments. Command `readifr` allows the user to output IDL definitions currently stored in the repository. Note that the IFR is a persistent object maintaining its state, namely the contents of the interface repository, even though the server process in which it resides is terminated and relaunched.

The Orbix 3 test suite contains a number of test cases dealing with the IFR, including

- test cases checking functionality of the IFR utilities,
- test cases checking functionality of the DII, and
- test cases just using the IFR not written to test any IFR-related feature.

A test case that checks the functionality of one or another IFR utility typically performs one or more IFR utilities, and compares the resulting contents of the interface repository with some expected contents. Obviously it is not safe to simultaneously execute more than one such test case. IDL definitions that are added to the IFR by one test case may be deleted by the another, and vice versa, resulting in contents equally unexpected by all of the concurrently running test cases.

In general, it is not safe to concurrently run multiple test cases dealing with the IFR if at least one of them changes the contents of the interface repository. In this case other test cases will encounter unspecified and occasional changes in the state of the IFR, which typically results in their failure.

As all test cases dealing with the IFR do change its contents, we can conclude that in order to guarantee their expected behavior, execution of all those test cases should be serialized. One simple way to serialize access to the interface repository by concurrently running test cases is via a mechanism for mutual exclusion. Such a mechanism acts as a lock protecting access to the IFR. Only one test case can lock the mechanism at any given time and thus acquire an exclusive right to access the IFR. The other competing test cases must wait until this test case unlocks the mechanism.

This approach automatically serializes test cases that should not be executed concurrently. Unfortunately, it cannot guarantee the best execution time if the test suite is running in parallel on a multiprocessor computer. Let us run the test suite on a p-processor Unix workstation ($p > 1$) so that we have p parallel streams of running test cases. Let n and m be the total number of test cases and the number of IFR-related test cases respectively. We can assume that all IFR-related test cases are distributed evenly across the streams. We also assume that in each stream IFR-related test cases go first. Then, until all IFR-related test cases are completed, there will be only one running test case at any given time. Correspondingly the total execution time will be

$$t \approx \sum_{i=1}^{m} t_i + \frac{\sum_{i=m+1}^{n} t_i}{p},$$

where t_i is the execution time of the ith test case (we assume that first m test cases are IFR-related). However, if

$$\sum_{i=1}^{m} t_i \leq \frac{\sum_{i=m+1}^{n} t_i}{p-1},$$

then exactly p test cases can be executed in parallel at any given time, and the optimal total execution time will be

$$t_{\text{opt}} \approx \frac{\sum_{i=1}^{n} t_i}{p}.$$

Another disadvantage of this approach is that it is hard to extend it from a single multiprocessor workstation to a cluster of workstations.

We turn now to another approach to parallel execution of the Orbix 3 test suite that is oriented on a cluster of Unix workstations and yet suitable for a single multiprocessor Unix workstation as a particular case of such a cluster. It is based on the idea of using a parallel program to run on an instrumental cluster of workstations and work as a test manager. This program does the following:

- Accept a test suite as an input parameter. Individual test cases in the test suite are considered as atomic jobs to be scheduled for execution among available physical processors.
- Automatically partition the test suite at runtime into as many parallel streams of test cases as physical processors available. This partitioning is performed to

- balance the load of physical processors based on the actual relative speed of workstations and the average execution time of each test case, and

- exclude parallel execution of test cases using the same interface repository. It is assumed that each workstation of the instrumental cluster will run its own Orbix daemon and its own interface repository registered with the Orbix daemon.

- Launch all the streams in parallel so that each workstation runs as many streams as it has processors.

- Wait until all streams of test cases complete.

- Collect local reports from the streams and produce a final report on the parallel execution of the test suite.

The test manager is implemented in the mpC language. Therefore it uses the relevant mpC means to detect the number of physical processors and their actual relative speed at runtime.

The average execution time of each test case is calculated based on information about the test suite, which is stored in a file accepted by the test manager as an input parameter. This file has one record for each test case. The record includes the name of the test case, the total number of its runs, and the total execution time of the runs. A simple `perl` script is used to generate and update this file by processing a final report on the execution of the test suite. Recall that such a report includes the start and end time for each test case.

Another input parameter of the test manager is a file storing information about restrictions on parallel execution of test cases. In general, the file includes a number of separated lists of test cases. Each list represents a group of test cases that should not be concurrently running on the same workstation. In our case the file includes only one list of all test cases using the interface repository. As each workstation of the instrumental cluster runs its own Orbix daemon and its own interface repository, the restriction is equivalent to the restriction that prohibits concurrently running multiple test cases using the same interface repository.

So the algorithm of partitioning of the test suite for parallel execution on p physical processors can be summarized as follows:

- It assumes that the test manager consists of p parallel processes, and each workstation runs as many processes as it has physical processors. Each process manages a stream of serially executed test cases. It launches the test cases and produces a local report on their completion. In the mpC program, the group of processes is represented by an mpC network. So abstract processors of this mpC network manage the parallel execution of the test suite performing the corresponding parallel algorithm.

- The abstract processors first detect the total number of workstations, nc, and divide themselves into nc nonintersecting groups, so that each group consists of abstract processors running on the same workstation. In other words, the abstract processors recognize the structure of the instrumental cluster of workstations and their mapping to the cluster.

- Each group of abstract processors then selects a lead. Each group of test cases, which should not be simultaneously executed on the same workstation, is distributed among the lead processors as follows. At each step the next test case is assigned to a lead processor, which minimizes the ratio:

$$\frac{\Sigma_i t_i + t}{s},$$

where t_i are the average execution times of the test cases assigned to the lead processor, t is the average execution time of the scheduled test case, and s is the relative speed of this lead processor.

- The remaining test cases are distributed among all p abstract processors as follows: At each step the next test case is assigned to an abstract processor that minimizes the ratio

$$\frac{\Sigma_i t_i + t}{s},$$

where t_i are the average execution time of test cases that have been assigned to the abstract processor, t is the average execution time of the scheduled test case, and s is the relative speed of this abstract processor.

After the test suite is partitioned, each abstract processor generates a number of shell scripts and executes them. The scripts manage serial execution of test cases assigned to the abstract processor.

The real mpC code of the test manager appears as follows:

```
#include <stdio.h>
#include <stdlib.h>
#include <mpc.h>
#include <sys/utsname.h>
#include <string.h>

#define MAXFILENAME 256
#define VERY_BIG (10000000.0)

typedef struct
{
    char name[MAXFILENAME]; // name of test
    double time;            // average execution time in seconds
} Test;
```

```
typedef struct
{
   int m;       // number of test cases in stream
   int *tests; // test[i] is ID of i-th test case in stream
} Stream;


// Function to partition test suite into p concurrent streams.
// Input parameters: p, s, cluster, nc, tests, m, groups.
// Output parameter: strm.
void Partition (
   int p,          // Total number of processors and
   double *s,      // their relative speeds.
   int *cluster,   // cluster[i] is computer where i-th processor
                   // belongs. Computers are represented by
                   // integers 1,2,...,nc.
   int nc,         // Total number of computers.
   Test *tests,    // tests[i] represents i-th test case in
                   // test suite.
   int m,          // Total number of test cases in test suite.
   int *groups,    // groups[i] is group where i-th test case
                   // belongs. Groups are represented by integers
                   // 0,1,... Group 0 contains test cases that can
                   // run in parallel with any other test case.
                   // Each of remaining groups consists of test
                   // cases that cannot run simultaneously on the
                   // same computer.
   Stream **strm   // (*strm)[i] represents stream of test cases
                   // to run on i-th processor.
)
{
   int i, j, k, l, *leaders;
   double *load, maxload;

   leaders = calloc(nc, sizeof(int));
   load = calloc(p, sizeof(double));
   *strm = calloc(p, sizeof(Stream));
   for(i=0; i<p; i++)
      (*strm)[i].tests = calloc(m, sizeof(int));

   for(i=1, j=1, leaders[0]=0; j<nc && i<p; i++)
   if(cluster[i]>j)
      leaders[j++] = i;
for(i=0, k=0; i<m; i++)
   if(groups[i])
   {
```

```
   for(j=0, maxload=VERY_BIG; j<nc; j++)
    if((load[leaders[j]]+tests[i].time)/s[leaders[j]] < maxload)
    {
      k = leaders[j];
      maxload = (load[k]+tests[i].time)/s[k];
    }
   load[k] += tests[i].time;
   (*strm)[k].tests[((*strm)[k].m)++] = i;
  }
for(i=0, k=0; i<m; i++)
  if(groups[i] == 0)
  {
    for(j=0, maxload=VERY_BIG; j<p; j++)
      if((load[j]+tests[i].time)/s[j] < maxload)
      {
        k = j;
        maxload = (load[k]+tests[i].time)/s[k];
      }
    load[k] += tests[i].time;
    (*strm)[k].tests[((*strm)[k].m)++] = i;
  }
}


void [net SimpleNet(p)w]getClusterConfig(int **cluster, int *nc)
{
  struct utsname un;
  char names[p][MAXFILENAME];
  char myname[MAXFILENAME];
  repl i, s=0;

  *cluster = calloc(p, sizeof(int));
  uname(&un);
  strcpy(myname, un.nodename);
for(i=0; i<p; i++)
  [w:I==0]names[i][] = [w:I==i]myname[];
[w:I==0]:
{
  int j, k;
  for(j=0, *nc=0; j<p; j++)
  {
    if((*cluster)[j])
      continue;
    else
      (*cluster)[j] = ++(*nc);
    for(k=j+1; k<p; k++)
```

```
        if((*cluster)[k]==0 && !strcmp(names[j], names [k]))
           (*cluster)[k] = *nc;
      }
   }
   *nc = * ([w:I==0]nc);
   ([(p)w])MPC_Bcast(&s, *cluster, 1, p, *cluster, 1);
}


void [net SimpleNet(n)w]getTestSuite(char *log, repl *m, Test **tests)
{
   FILE *fp;
repl i, s=0;

[w:I==0]:
{
   char name[MAXFILENAME+20];
   fp = fopen(log, "r");
   for(*m=0; fgets(name, MAXFILENAME, fp)!=NULL; (*m)++);
   fclose(fp);
}
*m = * [w:I==0]m;
*tests = calloc(*m, sizeof(Test));
[w:I==0]:
{
   int i, runs, time;

   fp = fopen(log, "r");
   for(i=0; i<*m &&
       fscanf(fp, "%s %d %d", (*tests)[i].name, &time, &runs)!=EOF; i++)
   {
      (*tests)[i].time = (double)time/((runs>0)?runs:1);
      if(!(*tests)[i].time)
         (*tests)[i].time = 1.;
   }
   fclose(fp);
}
for(i=1; i<*m; i++)
   (*tests)[i] = [w:I==0]((*tests)[i]);
}


void [net SimpleNet(n)w]getGroups(char *file, repl m,
      Test *tests, int **groups, int *ng)
{
   FILE *fp;
   repl s=0;
```

```
*groups = calloc(m, sizeof(int));
[w:I==0]:
{
   int i;
   char name[MAXFILENAME+20];

   fp = fopen(file, "r");
   if(fp!=NULL)
   {
      *ng = 1;
      while (fscanf(fp, "%s", name)!=EOF)
      {
         if(name[0]=='#')
         {
            (*ng)++;
            continue;
         }
         for(i=0; i<m; i++)
            if(!strcmp(name, tests[i].name))
            {
               (*groups)[i] = *ng;
               break;
            }
      }
      fclose(fp);
   }
   else
      *ng = 0;
   }
      ([(n)w])MPC_Bcast(&s, *groups, 1, m, *groups, 1);
      *ng = *[w:I==0]ng;
}


int [*]main(int argc, char **argv)
// 2 external arguments:
// argv[1] - file with history of execution of the test cases;
// argv[2] - file with groups of test cases that cannot
// simultaneously run on the same computer.
{
   repl p;
   repl double *speeds;

   recon;
   MPC_Processors_static_info(&p, &speeds);
   {
```

```
net SimpleNet(p) w;
[w]:
{
   Stream *strm;
   repl *cluster, nc, *groups, m, ng;
   Test *tests;

   ([(p)w])getClusterConfig(&cluster, &nc);
   ([(p)w])getTestSuite(argv[1], &m, &tests);
   ([(p)w])getGroups(argv[2], m, tests, &groups, &ng);
   Partition(p, speeds, cluster, nc, tests, m, groups, &strm);
   {
      char command[MAXFILENAME];
      char script[MAXFILENAME];
      char root[MAXFILENAME];
      char view[MAXFILENAME];
      FILE *fp;
      int i, j, mycoord;

      mycoord = I coordof w;
      [host]:
      {
         FILE *logs;

         logs = fopen("log_list", "w");
         strcpy(root, getenv("TESTROOT"));
         strcpy(view, getenv("CLEARCASE_ROOT")+6);
         for(i=0; i<p; i++)
         {
            sprintf(script, "%s/bin/script_%d", root, i);
            fprintf(logs, "%s/all/par_test_%d.log ", root, i);
            fp = fopen(script, "w");
            fprintf(fp, "(%s/bin/mkinnetsubs tests -", root);
            for(j=0; j<strm[i].m; j++)
            fprintf(fp, " %s/all/%s", root,
                    tests[(strm[i].tests)[j]].name);
            fprintf(fp, ") >> %s/all/par_test_%d.log 2>&1",
                    root, i);
            fclose(fp);

   strcpy(command, "chmod a+x ");
   strcat(command, script);
   system(command);
}
fclose(logs);
```

```
        }
            view[] = [host]view[];
            root[] = [host]root[];
            strcpy(command, "cd /view/");
            strcat(command, view);
            strcat(command, root);
            strcat(command, "/all");
            system(command);

            sprintf(script, "%s/bin/script_%d", root, mycoord);
            strcpy(command, "cleartool setview -exec ");
            strcat(command, script);
            strcat(command, " ");
            strcat(command, view);
            system(command);
        }
    }
  }
}
```

Note that the test manager is launched from a wrapper script that

- initializes the mpC programming system on the instrumental cluster of workstations,
- launches the parallel test manager on the cluster,
- waits until the test manager completes its work, and
- merges reports produced by parallel streams into a single final report.

10.2.3. Experimental Results

The system for parallel testing of the Orbix 3 software significantly accelerated execution of the Orbix test suite. For example, parallel execution of the test suite on a cluster of two 4-processor workstations, each running Solaris 2.7, provided a speedup that varied from 6.8 to 7.7. In terms of wall time, this would be, for example, 1:41 instead of 12:52.

10.3. SUMMARY

In this chapter we demonstrated that heterogeneous parallel computing can be applied not only to solutions of scientific problems but also to improve the performance of business distributed applications. It can be also used in software engineering practice to optimize the maintenance process.

Our experience in integration of the mpC-based technology of heterogeneous parallel computing and the CORBA-based technology of distributed computing has proved that the integration can be easily made and does not require changes in the combined technologies. It appears that parallel computing technologies and distributed computing technologies are quite ready to work together, but more practical experience of their integration for solutions of real-life problems is needed.

The mpC *N*-Body Application

A.1. SOURCE CODE

The text of the mpC *N*-body program presented in Sections 7.1 and 9.2 is broken down into two source files. The first file contains mpC-specific code of the application. The name of this file must have extension mpc (e.g., nbody.mpc). The contents of this file are as follows:

```
#include <stdio.h>
#include <stdlib.h>
#include <mpc.h>


typedef double Triplet[3];
typedef struct{Triplet p; Triplet v; double m;} Body;


nettype Nbody(int m, int k, int n[m])
{
   coord I=m;
   node { I>=0: bench*((n[I]/k)*(n[I]/k));};
   link { I>0: length*(n[I]*sizeof(Body)) [I]->[0];};
   parent [0];
   scheme {
     int i;
     par (i=0; i<m; i++) 100%%[i];
     par (i=1; i<m; i++) 100%%[i]->[0];
   };
};


repl M;          // The number of groups
double [host]t;  // The time variable
repl int tgsize; // The number of bodies in a test group


#include "serial_code.h"
```

```
void [net Nbody(m, 1, n[m]) g] ShareMasses (void *masses)
{
   double mass;
   repl i, j;
   typedef double (*pArray)[m];

   mass = (*(pArray)masses)[I coordof i];
   for(i=0; i<m; i++)
     for(j=0; j<m; j++)
       [g:I==i](*(pArray)masses)[j] = [g:I==j]mass;
}


void [net Nbody(m, 1, n[m]) g] ShareCenters(void *centers)
{
   Triplet center;
   repl i, j;
   typedef Triplet (*pArray)[m];

   center[] = (*(pArray)centers)[I coordof i][];
   for(i=0; i<m; i++)
     for(j=0; j<m; j++)
       [g:I==i](*(pArray)centers)[j][] =
       [g:I==j]center[];
}


void [*]main(int [host]argc, char **[host]argv)
{
   // Get the number of groups on the host-process
   // and broadcast it to all processes
   M = [host]GetNumberOfGroups(argv[1]);


   {
     repl N[M]; // Array of group sizes
     Body *[host]Groups[[host]M];

     // Initialize N and Groups on the abstract
     host-processor
     [host]: InputGroups(argv[1], M, &N, &Groups);

     // Broadcast the group sizes across all processes
     N[] = [host]N[];
```

```
   // Set the size of test group to the size of the smallest
   // group in the system of bodies
   tgsize = [?<]N[];
   {
      Body OldTestGroup[tgsize], TestGroup[tgsize];
      typedef Body (*pTestGroup)[tgsize];

      TestGroup[] = (*(pTestGroup)Groups[0])[];
      OldTestGroup[] = TestGroup[];
      recon UpdateGroup(tgsize, &OldTestGroup,
                        &TestGroup, 1, NULL, NULL, 0);
}
{
  net Nbody(M, tgsize, N) g;

  int [g]myN, // Size of my group
      [g]mycoord; // My coordinate in network g

  mycoord = I coordof g;
  myN = ([g]N)[mycoord];
  {
     double [g]Masses[[g]M]; // Masses of all groups
     Triplet [g]Centers[[g]M]; // Centers of mass of all groups
     Body [g]OldGroup[myN], // State of my group at time t
          [g]Group[myN]; // State of my group at time
          t+DELTA
     repl [g]gc, // Counter of groups in the system of bodies
          [g]bc, // Counter of bodies in group
          [g]gsize; // Size of group

     //Scatter groups
     for(gc=0; gc<[g]M; gc++)
     {
        [host]: gsize = N[gc];
        {
           typedef Body (*pGroup)[[host]gsize];
           [g:I==gc]Group[] = (*(pGroup)Groups[gc])[];
        }
     }
  }

// Visualize the system of bodies on the computer display
// associated with the abstract host-processor
[host]: FirstDrawGroups(argc, argv, M, N, Groups);
```

```
// Compute masses of the groups in parallel
for(bc=0, Masses[mycoord]=0.0; bc<myN; bc++)
  Masses[mycoord] += Group[bc].m;


// Communicate to share the masses among abstract
// processors of network g
([([g]M, [g]tgsize, [g]N)g])ShareMasses(Masses);


// Main loop of the parallel algorithm
do
{
  OldGroup[] = Group[];

  // Compute centers of masses of the groups in parallel
  Centers[] = 0.0;
  for(bc=0; bc<myN; bc++)
    Centers[mycoord][] +=
    (OldGroup[bc].m/Masses[mycoord])*(OldGroup[bc].p)[];


// Communicate to share the centers among abstract
// processors of network g
([([g]M, [g]tgsize, [g]N)g])ShareCenters(Centers);


// Update the groups of bodies in parallel
([g]UpdateGroup)(myN, &OldGroup, &Group, [g]M,
                &Centers, &Masses, mycoord);
        // Increment the time variable t
        t += DELTA;

        // Gather all groups to the abstract host-processor
        for(gc=0; gc<[g]M; gc++)
        {
          gsize = [host]N[[host]gc];
          {
            typedef Body (*pGroup)[gsize];
            (*(pGroup)Groups[gc])[] = [g:I==gc]Group[];
          }
        }


        // Visualise the groups on the computer display
        // associated with the abstract host-processor
        if(DrawGroups([host]M, [host]N, Groups)<0)
          MPC_Exit(-1);
```

```
        } while(1);

        [host]: DrawBye(M, N, Groups);
      }
    }
  }
}
```

The name of the second source file must be source_code.h. This file contains serial routine code and is included in the program with the include directive. In particular, this file contains GUI code implementing visualization of the system of bodies. The GUI code is based on the Xlib library. The contents of this file are as follows:

```
#include <stdio.h>
#include <math.h>
#include <string.h>


//The number of bodies in groups of default system of bodies
#define N0 200
#define N1 100
#define N2 400
#define N3 200
#define N4 600


#define X 0
#define Y 1
#define Z 2
#define Vx 3
#define Vy 4
#define Vz 5
#define MASS 6
#define ALPHA 0.5
#define BETA 0.5
#define GAMMA 6.67e-11
#define POINTSIZE 1.e7
#define MASSUNIT 1.e23
#define XMAX 800.
#define YMAX 800.
#define ZMAX 800.
#define BOXSIZE 120.
#define EPS 0.001
#define CRITICAL_R 10.
```

```
#define INTERVAL 1
#define MAXGROUPS 9 /*9*/
#define MAXBODIES 600 /*600*/
#define DELTA 360.


double [host]wtime;
void Merging(), SingleBody();


void UpdateGroup(int n, Body (*OldGroup)[n], Body (*Group)[n],
                int m, double (*Centers) [m][3],
                double (*Masses)[m], int mycoord)
{
  int j, k;
  double sigma[3], gma[3], F[3], Fabs, r, r2, dr[3];
  double dV[n][n][3];


  for(j=0; j<n; j++)
    if((*OldGroup)[j].m>0.)
    {
      sigma[]=0.;
      for(k=0; k<n; k++)
        if(j<k&&(*OldGroup)[k].m>0.)
        {
          Body jbody;
          dr[] = ((*OldGroup)[k].p)[]-((*OldGroup)[j].p)[];
          r2 = [+](dr[]*dr[]);
          r = sqrt(r2);
          if(r/POINTSIZE < sqrt(((*OldGroup)[k].m+
            (*OldGroup)[j].m)/MASSUNIT)+CRITICAL_R)
          {
          (jbody.p)[] = dr[];
          (jbody.v)[] =-
                    ((*OldGroup)[k].v)[]+((*OldGroup)[j].v)[];
          jbody.m = (*OldGroup)[k].m;
          SingleBody(&jbody);
          dV[j][k][] = (jbody.v)[];
          sigma[] += dV[j][k][]/DELTA;
          }
          else
          {
          Fabs = GAMMA*(*OldGroup)[k].m/r2;
          sigma[] += Fabs*(dr[]/r);
```

```
    }
}
else if(j>k&&(*OldGroup)[k].m>0.)
{
    dr[] = ((*OldGroup)[k].p)[]-((*OldGroup)[j].p)[];
    r2 = [+](dr[]*dr[]);
    r = sqrt(r2);
    if(r/POINTSIZE<sqrt(((*OldGroup)[k].m+
                (*OldGroup)[j].m)/MASSUNIT)+CRITICAL_R)
    sigma[] -= ((*OldGroup)[k].m/(*OldGroup)[j].m)
            *dV[k][j][]/DELTA;
        else
        {
            Fabs = GAMMA*(*OldGroup)[k].m/r2;
            sigma[] += Fabs*(dr[]/r);
        }
    }
    gma[] = 0.;
    for(k=0; k<m; k++)
        if(k!=mycoord)
        {
            dr[]=(*Centers)[k][]-((*OldGroup)[j].p)[];
            r2=[+](dr[]*dr[]);
            Fabs=GAMMA*(*Masses)[k]/r2;
            r=sqrt(r2);
            gma[]+=Fabs*(dr[]/r);
        }
        sigma[] += gma[];
        ((*Group)[j].v)[] += sigma[]*DELTA;
        ((*Group)[j].p)[] += (sigma[]*DELTA/2.+(ALPHA*
                            ((*Group)[j].v)[]+BETA*
                            ((*OldGroup)[j].v)[]))*DELTA;
        ((*Group)[j].p)[Z] -= BETA*sigma[Z]*DELTA*DELTA;
    }
    Merging(*Group, n);
}


void Merging(Body *rs, int n)
{
    int i, j;
    double dr[3], r2, r;
    for(i=0; i<n; i++)
        if(rs[i].m>0.)
            for(j=i+1; j<n; j++)
                if(rs[j].m>0.)
```

```
        {
        dr[] = (rs[j].p)[]-(rs[i].p)[];
        r2 = [+](dr[]*dr[]);
        r = sqrt(r2);
        if((int)(r/POINTSIZE)<=(int)(sqrt(rs[i].m/MASSUNIT)/2)+
           (int)(sqrt(rs[j].m/MASSUNIT)/2))
        {
        double m;


        m = rs[i].m+rs[j].m;
        (rs[i].p)[] = ((rs[j].p)[]*rs[j].m+
                       (rs[i].p)[]*rs[i].m)/m;
        (rs[i].v)[] = ((rs[j].v)[]*rs[j].m+(rs[i].v)[]
          *rs[i].m)/m;
        rs[i].m = m;
        rs[j].m = 0.;
        (rs[j].p)[] = 0.;
        (rs[j].v)[] = 0.;
        }
      }
}


int GetNumberOfGroups(char *fname)
{
   FILE *pf;
   int i, M;


   if(fname!=NULL)
   {
     pf = fopen(fname, "r");
     if(pf==NULL)
     {
       printf("Can't open file '%s'\n", fname);
       return -1;
     }
   }
   if((i = fscanf(pf, " Number of groups = %d",&M))<1 ||
     M<=0 || M>MAXGROUPS)
   {
     fclose(pf);
     if(i<1)
       printf("Cannot read number of groups from file '%s'\n",
              fname);
```

```
    else
      printf("Number of groups = %d\n", M);
      return -1;
    }
    fclose(pf);
    }
  else
    return 5;
}


int InputGroups(char *fname, int m, int (*N)[m],
                Body *(*Groups)[m])
{
  FILE *pf;
  int i, j;
  double x0, y0, z0;
  double r, phi, xi;
  #define PI2 6.2831854

  if(fname!=NULL)
  {
    pf = fopen(fname, "r");
    if(pf==NULL)
    {
      printf("Can't open file '%s'\n", fname);
      return -1;
    }
    fscanf(pf, " Number of groups = %*d", &m);
    if((i = fscanf(pf, " Group sizes ="))<0)
    {
      fclose(pf);
      printf("Cannot read groups' sizes from file '%s'\n",
             fname);
      return -1;
  }
    for(i=0; i<m; i++)
      if((j = fscanf(pf, " %d", *N+i))<1 ||
        (*N)[i]<=0 || (*N)[i]>MAXBODIES)
      {
      fclose(pf);
      if(j<1)
        printf("Cannot read size of group #%d from '%s'\n",
               i, fname);
      else
```

```
        printf("Size of group #%d = %d\n", i, N[i]);
      return -1;
    }
    fclose(pf);
  }
  else
  {
    (*N)[0] = N0;
    (*N)[1] = N1;
    (*N)[2] = N2;
    (*N)[3] = N3;
    (*N)[4] = N4;
  }
  for(i=0; i<m; i++)
  {
    (*Groups)[i] = calloc((*N)[i], sizeof(Body));
    if((*Groups)[i]==NULL)
    {
      printf("Cannot allocate storage for group #%d\n", i);
      return -1;
    }
  }
}
for(i=0; i<m; i++)
{
  switch(i)
      {
      case 0: x0 = y0 = BOXSIZE/2.; break;
      case 1: x0 = BOXSIZE*1.5; y0 = YMAX-BOXSIZE/2.;
      break;
      case 2: x0 = XMAX/2.; y0 = YMAX/2.; break;
      case 3: x0 = XMAX-BOXSIZE/2.; y0 = BOXSIZE/2.;
      break;
      case 4: x0 = XMAX-BOXSIZE/2.; y0 = YMAX-
      BOXSIZE/2.; break;
      case 5: x0 = BOXSIZE*1.5; y0 = YMAX/2.; break;
      case 6: x0 = XMAX-BOXSIZE/2.; y0 = YMAX/2.;
      break;
      case 7: x0 = XMAX/2.; y0 = YMAX-BOXSIZE/2.;
      break;
      case 8: x0 = XMAX/2.; y0 = BOXSIZE/2.; break;
      }
  for(j=0; j<(*N)[i]; j++)
  {
    r = (BOXSIZE/2./RAND_MAX)*rand();
    phi = (PI2/RAND_MAX)*rand();
```

```
        ((*Groups)[i][j].p)[X]  =  (x0+r*cos(phi))*POINTSIZE;
        ((*Groups)[i][j].p)[Y]  =  (y0+r*sin(phi))*POINTSHZE;
        ((*Groups)[i][j].p)[Z]  =  0.;
        ((*Groups)[i][j].v)[]  =  0.;
        (*Groups)[i][j].m  =  (j==(*N)[i]/2)?50.*MASSUNIT
                                          :0.5*MASSUNIT;

      }
   }
   return 1;
}



void SingleBody(Body *body)
{
   double r2, r, a, dt=DELTA, t, k1[3], k2[3], vk1[3],
   vk2[3],
      ak[3], ar[3];
   int i=1;


   r2 = [+]((body->p)[]*(body->p)[]);
   a = GAMMA*body->m/r2;
   r = sqrt(r2);
   ar[] = a*((body->p)[]/r);
   vk1[] = (body->v)[]+ar[]*dt;
   k1[] = (body->p)[]+vk1[]*dt/2.+(body->v)[]*dt;
label:
   vk2[] = (body->v)[];
   k2[] = (body->p)[];
   ak[] = ar[];
   for(dt/=2., t=0.; t<DELTA; t+=dt)
   {
      i++;
      vk2[] += ak[]*dt;
      k2[] += vk2[]*dt/2.+(ALPHA*vk2[]+BETA*(vk2[]-
      ak[]*dt))*dt;
      r2 = [+](k2[]*k2[]);
      r = sqrt(r2);
      a = GAMMA*body->m/r2;
      ak[] = a*(k2[]/r);
   }
   if(fabs(vk2[X]-vk1[X])<=EPS*fabs(vk2[X]) &&
      fabs(vk2[Y]-vk1[Y])<=EPS*fabs(vk2[Y]) &&
      fabs(vk2[Z]-vk1[Z])<=EPS*fabs(vk2[Z]) &&
```

```
         fabs(k2[X]-k1[X])<=EPS*fabs(k2[X])  &&
         fabs(k2[Y]-k1[Y])<=EPS*fabs(k2[Y])  &&
         fabs(k2[Z]-k1[Z])<=EPS*fabs(k2[Z]))
  {
     (body->p)[] = k2[];
     (body->v)[] = vk2[]-(body->v)[];
     return;
  }
  else
  {
     vk1[] = vk2[];
     k1[] = k2[];
     goto label;
  }
}


#pragma keywords ANSI
#include <X11/Xlib.h>
#include <X11/Xutil.h>
#include <X11/Xos.h>
#include <X11/bitmaps/icon>
#pragma keywords SHORT


#define WIDTH XMAX
#define HEIGHT YMAX


Display *[host]display;
int [host]screen;
Window [host]win;
GC [host]gc;
XEvent [host]report;
XFontStruct *[host]font_info;
char *[host]fontname="9x15";
void [host]DrawBody();
void [host]DrawText();
void [host]SayGoodBye();


int [host]FirstDrawGroups(int argc, char **argv, int m,
                          int *N, Body **Groups)


  unsigned width=WIDTH, height=HEIGHT;
```

```
    int x=0, y=0;
    unsigned border_width=4;
    unsigned display_width, display_height;
    char *window_name="Groups Demo";
    char *icon_name="galaxy";
    Pixmap icon_pixmap;
    XSizeHints size_hints;
    unsigned long valuemask=0;
    XGCValues values;
    char *display_name=NULL;
    int i, j, k;


    wtime = MPC_Wtime();
    if((display = XOpenDisplay(display_name)) == NULL)
    {
       printf("FirstDrawGroups: cannot connect to Xserver %s\n",
              XDisplayName(display_name));
       return (-1);
    }
    screen = XDefaultScreen(display);
    win = XCreateSimpleWindow(display, XRootWindow
                              (display,screen), x, y,
                              width, height, border_width,
                              XBlackPixel(display, screen),
                              XBlackPixel(display, screen));
icon_pixmap = XCreateBitmapFromData(display, win,
                                    icon_bits,
                                    icon_width,
                                    icon_height);
size_hints.flags = PPosition|PSize|PMinSize;
size_hints.x = x;
size_hints.y = y;
size_hints.width = width;
size_hints.height = height;
size_hints.min_width = width;
size_hints.min_height = height;
XSetStandardProperties(display, win, window_name,
                       icon_name, icon_pixmap, argv,
                       argc, &size_hints);
XSelectInput(display, win, ExposureMask|KeyPressMask|
             ButtonPressMask|StructureNotifyMask);
if((font_info = XLoadQueryFont(display, fontname)) == NULL)
{
```

```
      printf("FirstDrawGroups: cannot open %s font\n", fontname);
      return -1;
}
gc=XCreateGC(display, win, valuemask, &values);
XSetForeground(display, gc, XWhitePixel(display, screen));
XSetLineAttributes(display, gc, 1, LineSolid,
                   CapNotLast, JoinMiter);
XSetFillStyle(display, gc, FillSolid);
XSetFont(display, gc, font_info->fid);
XMapWindow(display, win);
      while(1)
      {
        XNextEvent(display, &report);
        switch(report.type)
        {
        case Expose:
          while(XCheckTypedEvent(display, Expose, &report));
          for(i=0; i<m; i++)
            for(j=0; j<N[i]; j++)
              if(Groups[i][j].m>0.)
                DrawBody(&gc, (int)(Groups[i][j].m/MASSUNIT),
                              (int)((Groups[i][j].p)[X]/POINTSIZE),
                              (int)((Groups[i][j].p)[Y]/POINTSIZE),
                              (int)((Groups[i][j].p)[Z]/POINTSIZE));
              DrawText(t);
              XFlush(display);
              return 1;
          case ConfigureNotify:
              break;
          case ButtonPress:
          case KeyPress:
            return 1;
          default:
            break;
      }
    }
}


int [host]DrawGroups (int m, int *N, Body **Groups)
{
    int i, j, k, size;
    XEvent event;

    event.type = Expose;
```

```
   XSendEvent(display, win, False, 0L, &event);
   while(1)
   {
      XNextEvent(display, &report);
      switch(report.type)
      {
         case Expose
            while (XCheckTypedEvent (display, Expose, &report))
               ;
            XClearWindow(display, win);
            for(i = 0; i<m; i++)
               for(j = 0; j<N[i]; j++)
                  if(Groups[i][j].m>0.)
                     DrawBody(&gc,(int)(Groups[i][j].m/MASSUNIT),
                             (int)((Groups[i][j].p) [X]/POINTSIZE),
                             (int)((Groups[i][j].p) [Y]/POINTSIZE),
                             (int)((Groups[i][j].p) [Z]/POINTSIZE));
            DrawText(t);
            XFlush(display);
            XSendEvent(display, win, False, 0L, &event);
         return 1;
            case ConfigureNotify:
            break;
            case ButtonPress:
            case KeyPress:
               XFreeGC(display, gc);
               XCloseDisplay(display);
               return 1;
            default:
               break;
      }
   }
}


void [host]DrawBody(GC *gc, int m, int x, int y, int z)
{
   int xx, yy, r;

   r = (int)(sqrt((double)m)/2);
   for(xx=x-r; xx<=x+r; xx++)
      for(yy=y-r; yy<=y+r; yy++)
         if((xx-x)*(xx-x)+(yy-y)*(yy-y)<=r*r)
            XDrawPoint(display, win, *gc, xx, yy);
}
```

```
void [host]DrawText(double t)
{
    char text[25];
    int len, wid;
    double gt, wt;

    sprintf(text, "Real time = %.1f hours", gt=t/3600.);
    len = strlen(text);
    wid = XTextWidth(font_info, text, len);
    XDrawString(display, win, gc, (int)((WIDTH-wid)/2),
                20, text, len);
    sprintf(text, "Wall time = %.1f seconds",
            wt=MPC_Wtime()-wtime);
    len = strlen(text);
    wid = XTextWidth(font_info, text, len);
    XDrawString(display, win, gc, (int)((WIDTH-wid)/2),
                40, text, len);
    sprintf(text, "Rate = %.1f sec/h", gt?wt/gt:0.);
    len = strlen(text);
    wid = XTextWidth(font_info, text, len);
    XDrawString(display, win, gc, (int)((WIDTH-wid)/2),
                60, text, len);
}


void [host]SayGoodBye(void)
{
    char text[50];
    int len, wid;

    sprintf(text, "Good bye! See you soon.");
    len = strlen(text);
    wid = XTextWidth(font_info, text, len);
    XDrawString(display, win, gc, (int)((WIDTH-wid)/2),
                (int)(HEIGHT/3), text, len);
    XFlush(display);
}
```

A.2. USER'S GUIDE

A typical session to run the *N*-body application includes the following steps (see Appendix D for a full mpC user's guide):

- Open a virtual parallel machine, vpm,

```
mpcopen vpm
```

- Translate your mpC program into two C files

```
mpcc -I/usr/openwin/include -het nbody.mpc
```

The first file, nbody_host.c, will contain code only run by the
abstract host-processor. In particlular, this file will contain all the GUI
code. The second file, nbody_node.c, will contain code executed by the
remaining abstract processors not involved in visualization. Use the full
name of the file nbody.mpc if it is not in the current directory. Use a
directory other than /usr/openwin/include if necessary (i.e., use the
directory where X Windows system holds its include files on the host
workstation).

- Copy files nbody_host.c and nbody_node.c from the current directory to the $MPCLOAD directory

```
cp nbody_host.c nbody_node.c $MPCLOAD
```

- Broadcast these files from the host workstation to all other workstations
involved

```
mpcbcast nbody_host.c nbody_node.c
```

- Produce executable nbody on all workstations involved

```
mpcload -het -o nbody nbody.c -lm -host -
L/usr/openwin/lib -lX
```

Use a directory different from /usr/openwin/lib if necessary (i.e.,
use the directory where X Windows system holds its libraries on the
host workstation). Use an option different from -lX if necessary (i.e.,
use the proper name for the X library; it may be -lX11 or something
else).

- Run the application

```
mpcrun nbody -- text_file
```

The only external argument of the application is the name of data file,
text_file. This file should contain input data for the application, for
example,

```
Number of groups = 8
Group sizes = 300 500 600 400 350 100 300 200
```

The input data conveys to the application that it should model the evolution of a system of eight groups consisting of 300, 500, 600, 400, 350, 100, 300, and 200 bodies respectively. The application will generate the system. If no external argument is given, the application will model a default system of five groups of bodies.

The Block Cyclic Matrix Multiplication Routine for Heterogeneous Platforms

B.1. SOURCE CODE

The text of the mpC program for parallel block cyclic matrix multiplication presented in Section 9.1.1.3 is broken down into four source files.

The first file contains the declaration of the ParallelAxB network type. The name of the second source file must be ParallelAxB.mpc. The contents of this file are as follows:

```
#define H(a, b, c, d, p) h[(a*p*p*p+b*p*p+c*p+d)]
typedef struct {int I; int J;} Processor;
nettype ParallelAxB(int p, int r, int n, int l, int w[p], int h[p*p*p*p])
{
    coord I=p, J=p;
    node {I>=0 && J>=0: bench*(w[J]*H(I, J, I, J,
    p)*(n/l)*(n/l)*n);};
    link  (K=p, L=p)
    {
        I>=0 && J>=0 && I!=K : length*
            (w[I]*H(I,J,I,J,p)*(n/l)*(n/l)*(r*r)*sizeof(double) [I,J]->[K,J];
        I>=0 && J>=0 && J!=L && (H(I, J, K, L, p)>0) :
        length*
            (w[J]*H(I,J,K,L,p)*(n/l)*(n/l)*(r*r)*sizeof(double)) [I,J]->[K,L];
    };
    parent[0];
    scheme
    {
        int k;
        Processor Root, Receiver, Current;
        for(k = 0;  k < n;  k++)
        {
            int Acolumn = k%l, Arow;
            int Brow = k%l, Bcolumn;
```

```
    par(Arow = 0; Arow <1; )
    {
        GetProcessor(Arow, Acolumn, p, h, w, &Root);
        par(Receiver.I = 0; Receiver.I < p; Receiver.I++)
          par(Receiver.J = 0; Receiver.J < p;
          Receiver.J++)
            if((Root.I != Receiver.I || Root.J != Receiver.J) &&
                Root.J != Receiver.J)
              if(H((Root.I),(Root.J),(Receiver.I),(Receiver.J),p) > 0)
              100/(w[Root.J]*((n/1))) %%
                [Root.I, Root.J] -> [Receiver.I, Receiver.J];
        Arow += H((Root.I),(Root.J),(Root.I),(Root.J),p);
    }
    par(Bcolumn = 0; Bcolumn < 1; )
    {
        GetProcessor(Brow, Bcolumn, p, h, w, &Root);
        par(Receiver.I = 0; Receiver.I < p; Receiver.I++)
          if(Root.I != Receiver.I)
            (100/(H((Root.I),(Root.J),(Root.I),(Root.J),p)*(n/1))) %%
            [Root.I, Root.J] -> [Receiver.I, Root.J];
        Bcolumn += w[Root.J];
    }
    par(Current.I = 0; Current.I < p; Current.I++)
    par(Current.J = 0; Current.J < p; Current.J++)
          (100/n) %% [Current.I, Current.J];
    }
  };
};
```

The second file contains the `main` function. The name of this file must have extension `mpc` (e.g., `hmxm.mpc`). The contents of this file are as follows:

```
#include <math.h>
#include <stdio.h>
#include <stdlib.h>
#include <mpc.h>
#include "ParallelAxB.mpc"
#include "Load_balance.mpc"
#include "hmxm_i.mpc"


int [*] main(int [host] argc, char** [host] argv)
{
  repl int p, r, n, l, *w, *h, *trow, *lcolumn;
```

```
repl double* speeds;
int [host] opt_l;
double [host] time_i, Elapsed_time;


p = [host]atoi(argv[1]);
r = [host]atoi(argv[2]);
n = [host]atoi(argv[3]);


/*
 * Update the estimation of the processors speeds
 */
{
  repl int i, j;
  repl double x[r*r], y[r*r], z[r*r];
  for (i = 0; i < r; i++)
    for (j = 0; j < r; j++) {
      x[i*r+j] = 2.;
      y[i*r+j] = 2.;
      z[i*r+j] = 0.;
    }
  recon rMxM(x, y, z, r);
}


/*
 * Detect the speed of the physical processors
 */
speeds = (double*)malloc(sizeof(double)*p*p);
MPC_Get_processors_info(NULL, speeds);


/*
    * w — widths of rectangular areas in generalized block
    * h — heights of 'horizontal-neighbours' sub-rectangles
    * trow — Top rows of rectangular areas in generalized block
    * lcolumn — Left columns of these rectangular areas
    */
w = (int*)malloc(sizeof(int)*p);
h = (int*)malloc(sizeof(int)*(p*p*p*p));
trow = (int*)malloc(sizeof(int)*p*p);
lcolumn = (int*)malloc(sizeof(int)*p);


/*
 * Determine the optimal generalized block size
```

```
*/
[host]:
{
 int i;
 double algo_time, min_algo_time = DBL_MAX;
 for (i = p; i < n; i++) {
  DistributeLoad(p, speeds, i, w, h, trow, lcolumn);
  algo_time = timeof(net ParallelAxB(p, r, n, i, w, h) paxb);
  if (algo_time < min_algo_time) {
   opt_l = i;
   min_algo_time = algo_time;
  }
 }
}


/*
  * Start timing the algorithm
  */
time_i = [host]MPC_Wtime();


/*
  * Broadcast the optimal generalised block size
  */
l = opt_l;


/*
  * Determine widths, top rows, top columns of the rectangular
  * areas in generalized block, and the heights of their
  * 'horizontal-neighbours' sub-rectangles
  */
DistributeLoad(p, speeds, l, w, h, trow, lcolumn);
free(speeds);


{
 /*
  * Create the mpC network
    */
 net ParallelAxB(p, r, n, l, w, h) g;
 int [g] icoord, [g] jcoord;
```

```
/*
 * Initialize the matrix elements and execute the algorithm
 */
[g]:
{
 int x, y, i, j, s, t, MyTopRow, MyLeftColumn;
 double *a, *b, *c;



 a = (double*)malloc(sizeof(double)*(n*r)*(n*r));
 b = (double*)malloc(sizeof(double)*(n*r)*(n*r));
 c = (double*)malloc(sizeof(double)*(n*r)*(n*r));
 icoord = I coordof g;
 jcoord = J coordof g;



 MyTopRow = trow[icoord*p + jcoord];
 MyLeftColumn = lcolumn[jcoord];



 for (x = MyTopRow; x < n; x+=l)
  for (y = MyLeftColumn; y < n; y+=l)
   for (i = 0; i < H(icoord, jcoord, icoord, jcoord, p); i++)
    for (j = 0; j < w[jcoord]; j++)
     for (s = 0; s < r; s++)
      for (t = 0; t < r; t++) {
       a[(x*r*n*r) + y*r + (i*r*n*r) + j*r + (s*r*n) + t] = 2.;
       b[(x*r*n*r) + y*r + (i*r*n*r) + j*r + (s*r*n) + t] = 2.;
       c[(x*r*n*r) + y*r + (i*r*n*r) + j*r + (s*r*n) + t] = 0.;
      }



 ([(p, r, n, l, w, h) g])ComputeAxB(
             icoord, jcoord, a, b, c, trow, lcolumn);
 {
   free(w);
   free(h);
   free(trow);
   free(lcolumn);
   free(a);
```

```
    free(b);
    free(c);
  }
  ([(0)g])MPC_Barrier();
 }
}


/*
 * Print the algorithm execution time
 */
[host]:
{
  Elapsed_time = MPC_Wtime() - time_i;
  printf("Problem size=%d, time(sec)=%0.6f, time(min)=%0.6f\n",
         n*r, Elapsed_time,
         Elapsed_time/60.);
}
}
```

The name of the third source file must be hmxm_i.h. This file contains the definitions of functions rMxM, Height, GetProcessor, and ComputeAxB. The contents of this file are as follows:

```
/*
  * This function is used in recon to update the estimation of
  * the processors speeds
  */
int rMxM (double *a, double *b, double *c, int r) {
  int l, m, t;
  for (l = 0; l < r; l++)
    for (m = 0; m < r; m++)
      for (t = 0; t < r; t++)
        c[l*r + m] += a[l*r + t] * b[t*r + m] ;
      return 0;
}


/*
  * This function gives the height of `horizontal-neighbours' sub-rectangles
  * for different pairs of rectangles in generalized block
  */
int Height(int top_row_1, int bottom_row_1, int top_row_2, int bottom_row_2)
```

```
{
  if ((top_row_1 >= top_row_2) && (bottom_row_1 <= bottom_row_2))
    return (bottom_row_1 - top_row_1);
  if ((top_row_1 <= top_row_2) && (bottom_row_1 >= bottom_row_2))
    return (bottom_row_2 - top_row_2);
  if ((top_row_1 <= top_row_2) && (bottom_row_1 >= top_row_2)
        && (bottom_row_1 <= bottom_row_2))
    return (bottom_row_1 - top_row_2);
  if ((top_row_1 >= top_row_2) && (top_row_1 <= bottom_row_2)
        && (bottom_row_1 >= bottom_row_2))
    return (bottom_row_2 - top_row_1);
  return 0;
}




/*
  * This function returns the coordinates of the root processor in the
  * processor grid. The inputs to this function are the row and column
  * of the root processor, the number of processors, the widths of
  * the rectangular areas in the generalized block, and the heights of
  * the 'horizontal-neighbours' sub-rectangles
  */
int GetProcessor(const int row, const int column,
                 const int p, const int *h,
                 const int *w, Processor* proc)
{
  int x, y, i, j, tempy;
  int *trow = (int*)malloc(sizeof(int)*p);
  for (i = 0; i < p; i++)
    trow[i] = 0;
  for (x = 0; x < p; x++)
  {
    tempy = 0;
    for (y = 0; y < p; y++)
    {
      int hi = H(x, y, x, y, p);
      int wi = w[y];
      if (x)
        trow[y] += H((x-1), y, (x-1), y, p);
      for (i = 0; i < hi; i++)
        for (j = 0; j < wi; j++)
          if (((row >= (trow[y] + i)) && (row < (trow[y] + hi)))&&
              ((column >= (tempy + j)) && (column < (tempy + wi))))
          {
            proc->I = x;
```

```
            proc->J = y;
            free(trow);
            return 0;
          }
      tempy += w[y];
    }
  }
  free(trow);
  return 0;
}




/*
 * This function performs the computations and communications
* of the parallel algorithm
*/
void [net ParallelAxB(p, r, n, l, w, h) g]
  ComputeAxB(int icoord, int jcoord, double *a, double *b,
             double *c, int *trow, int* lcolumn)
{
  int MyTopRow, MyLeftColumn;
  int m, s, t, x, y, z;
  repl int i, j, k;
  repl Processor Me, Root, Receiver;



  Me.I = icoord;
  Me.J = jcoord;
  MyTopRow = trow[(Me.I)*p + Me.J];
  MyLeftColumn = lcolumn[Me.J];



  for (k = 0; k < n; k++) {
    int Acolumn = (k%l);
    int Brow = (k%l);
    /*
     * Processor P(k,j) broadcasts a(k,j) to P(*,j) vertically
     */
    for (j = 0; j < n; j++) {
      int Bcolumn = (j%l);
      GetProcessor(Brow, Bcolumn, p, h, w, &Root);
      {
```

```
flex subnet[g:(J==(Root.J))] cSubnet;
[cSubnet]:
{
  int am_I_root = 0;
  double temp[r*r];



  if ((Me.I) == (Root.I)) {
    am_I_root = 1;
    for (x = 0; x < r; x++)
      for (y = 0; y < r; y++)
        temp[x*r + y] = b[k*r*n*r + j*r + x*n*r + y];
  }
  temp[] = [cSubnet:(I==(Root.I) && J==(Root.J))] temp[];



  if (!am_I_root)
    for (x = 0; x < r; x++)
      for (y = 0; y < r; y++)
        b[k*r*n*r + j*r + x*n*r + y] = temp[x*r + y];
  }
 }
}
/*
* Processor P(i,k) broadcasts a(i,k) to P(i,*) horizontally
*/
for (i = 0; i < n; i++) {
 int Arow = (i%l);
 GetProcessor(Arow, Acolumn, p, h, w, &Root);
 {
  flex subnet
    [g:(Height(Arow,Arow+1,trow[I*p+J],trow[I*p+J]+H(I,J,I,J,p))>0)]
    rSubnet;



  [rSubnet]:
  {
    int am_I_root = 0;
    double temp[r*r];
    if (((Root.I) == (Me.I)) && ((Root.J) == (Me.J))) {
      am_I_root = 1;
      for (x = 0; x < r; x++)
```

```
            for (y = 0; y < r; y++)
                temp[x*r + y] = a[i*r*n*r + k*r + x*n*r + y];
        }



        temp[] = [rSubnet:(I==(Root.I) && J==(Root.J))]temp[];



        if (!am_I_root)
          for (x = 0; x < r; x++)
            for (y = 0; y < r; y++)
              a[i*r*n*r + k*r + x*n*r + y] = temp[x*r + y];
      }
    }
  }
  for (x = MyTopRow; x < n; x+=1)
    for (y = MyLeftColumn; y < n; y+=1)
      for (i = 0; i < H((Me.I),(Me.J),(Me.I),(Me.J),p); i++)
        for (j = 0; j < w[(Me.J)]; j++)
          for (s = 0; s < r; s++)
            for (m = 0; m < r; m++)
              for (t = 0; t < r; t++)
                c[x*r*n*r+y*r+i*r*n*r+j*r+s*n*r+m] +=
                a[x*r*n*r+i*r*n*r+k*r+s*n*r+t] * b[y*r+k*r*n*r+j*r+t*n*r+m];
  }
  return;
}
```

The name of the fourth source file must be `Load_balance.mpc`. This file contains the definition of function `DistributeLoad`. The contents of this file are as follows:

```
int DistributeLoad(int p, double *speeds, int l, int *w,
                   int *h, int *trow, int* lcolumn)
{
  int i, j, k, x, y, csum[p], tsum = 0;
  double total = 0.;
  for (i = 0; i < p; i++)
  {
    csum[i] = 0;
    for (j = 0; j < p; j++)
      csum[i] += speeds[j*p + i];
```

```
  tsum += csum[i];
}
for (i = 0;  i < p;  i++)
 for (j = 0;  j < p;  j++)
 {
   double temp = (speeds[i*p+j]/(double)csum[j])*l;
   if (temp < 1.0)
    temp = 1.0;
   temp = floor(temp);
   H(i,j,i,j,p) = temp;
 }
for (j = 0;  j < p;  j++)
{
 total = 0.;
 for (i = 0;  i < p;  i++)
  total += H(i,j,i,j,p);
 if (total > 1)
 {
   int ind = 0;
   for (i = 0;  i < p;  i++)
    if (H(i,j,i,j,p) > 1.0)
    {
     ind++;
     H(i,j,  i,j,p) -= 1.0;
     if ((total - ind) == 1)
      break;
    }
 } else if (total < 1)
 {
   int ind = 0;
   for (i = 0;  i < p;  i++)
   {
    ind++;
    H(i,j,i,j,p) += 1.0;
    if ((total + ind) == 1)
     break;
   }
 }
}
total = 0.;
for (i = 0;  i < p;  i++)
{
 double temp = ((double)csum[i]/(double)tsum)*l;
 if (temp < 1.0)
  temp = 1.0;
```

```
  temp = floor(temp);
  w[i] = temp;
}
for (i = 0; i < p; i++)
 total += w[i];
if (total > 1)
{
  int ind = 0;
  for (i = 0; i < p; i++)
   if (w[i] > 1.0)
   {
     ind++;
     w[i] -= 1.0;
     if ((total - ind) == 1)
       break;
   }
} else if (total < 1)
{
  int ind = 0;
  for (i = 0; i < p; i++)
  {
   ind++;
   w[i] += 1.0;
   if ((total + ind) == 1)
       break;
  }
 }
  for (i = 0; i < p; i++)
   for (j = 0; j < p; j++)
   {
     trow[i*p+j] = 0;
     for (k = 0; k < i; k++)
       trow[i*p+j] += H(k, j, k, j, p);
   }
  for (i = 0; i < p; i++)
  {
   lcolumn[i] = 0;
   for (x = 0; x < i; x++)
     lcolumn[i] += w[x];
  }
  for (i = 0; i < p; i++)
   for (j = 0; j < p; j++)
    for (x = 0; x < p; x++)
     for (y = 0; y < p; y++)
      {
```

```
      int height = CommonHeight(trow[i*p+j], trow[i*p+j]+H(i,j,i,j,p),
            trow[x*p+y], trow[x*p+y]+H(x,y,x,y,p));
      if (height > 0)
        H(i,j,x,y,p) = height;
      }
  return 0;
}
```

B.2. USER'S GUIDE

Outlined below are the steps to run this mpC application (see Appendix D for the full mpC user's guide):

• Create a new virtual parallel machine, say, *vpm*,

```
mpccreate vpm
```

• or open the existing virtual parallel machine *vpm*,

```
mpcopen vpm
```

A newly created virtual parallel machine is opened immediately after successful completion of the mpccreate command.

• Compile the mpC sorce code

```
mpcc hmxm.mpc
```

• Copy the file hmxm.c produced by the mpC compiler into the $MPCLOAD directory

```
cp hmxm.c $MPCLOAD
```

• Broadcast the file hmxm.c to other computers constituting the virtual parallel machine

```
mpcbcast hmxm.c
```

• Produce the executable on each participating computer

```
mpcload -het -o hmxm hmxm.c
```

- Run the executable

```
mpcrun hmxm
```

- The output will be of the form

```
Problem size=108, time(sec)=0.262353,
time(min)=0.004373
```

The Parallel Adaptive
Quadrature Routine

C.1. SOURCE CODE

The text of the mpC parallel adaptive quadrature routine presented in Section 9.3.4 is broken down into five source files.

The first file contains the most principal code of the application. The name of this file must have extension mpc (e.g., pquanc8.mpc). The contents of this file are as follows:

```
#include <stdlib.h>
#include <stdlib.h>
#include <mpc.h>
#include <math.h>


#include "quanc8.h"
#include "partition.h"


typedef struct Interval
{
    double *x, *f;
    double qprev;
    struct Interval *next;
} *IntervalList;


#include "interval.h"


double [*]pquanc8(double (*fun)(double), double [host]a,
        double [host]b, double [host]abserr,
        double [host]relerr, double *[host]errest, int *[host]nofun,
        int *[host]flag, double *[host] badpoint)
{
```

```
double [host]area=0., [*]result=0., [host]absarea,
       [host]stone, [host]step, [host]minstep,
       [host]cor11=0., [host]esterr, [host]tollerr,
       [host]qleft, [host]qright, [host]qnow,
       [host]qdiff, [host]prevleft=0.;
int [host]repeat=0, [host]maxrepeat=2;
double *[host]f, *[host]x;
IntervalList [host]ints, [host]nextints;
repl int p;
repl double *speeds;

if(a==b)
   return result;

// Initialization for first interval
[host]:
{
   *flag = 0;
   *errest = 0.;
   *nofun = 0;
   stone = (b-a)/16.;
   minstep = stone*relerr+abserr;
   InitFirstInterval(fun, a, b, &x, &f);
   *nofun=9;
}
MPC_Processors_static_info(&p, &speeds);
{
   net SimpleNet(p) s;
   int [s]myn;
   repl [s]nints, *[s]ns, *[s]dsp, [s]src=0;
   double *[s]nodes, *[host]times;
   double *[s]mynodes, *[s]myvalues, [s]mytime;
   [s]:
   {
      ns = malloc(p*sizeof(int));
      dsp = malloc(p*sizeof(int));
   }
   [host]: times = malloc(p*sizeof(double));

   ints = ([host]CreateInterval)(x, f, 0., NULL);
   nints = 1;

   //Main loop of the algorithm
   for(step=stone; ints!=NULL; ints=nextints,
```

```
      step/=2.0)
{
   // Calculate points, where integrand should be evaluated
   // at this iteration, proceeding from list ints of nints
   // subintervals of width step, contribution of which into
   // the integral is still to be estimated. Store the points
   // in array nodes.
   [host]:
   {
      int j, k;
      struct Interval *i;

      nodes = malloc(nints*8*sizeof(double));
      for(i=ints, k=0; i!=NULL; i=i->next)
         for (j=1; j<16; j+=2, k++)
            nodes[k] = i->x[j] = (i->x[j-1]+i->x[j+1])/2.;
   }
   nints = [host]nints;


   // Become alert if the left end point of left subinterval
   // does not change from iteration to iteration
   [host]:
      if(fabs(prevleft-nodes[0])<relerr*fabs(prevleft)
         || fabs(prevleft-nodes[0])<abserr)
      repeat++;
      else
      {
         prevleft = nodes[0];
         repeat = 0;
      }
   // Convergence test
   if(repeat>maxrepeat && step<minstep)
   {
      *flag = 1;
      *badpoint = [host]nodes[0];
      [s]: break;
   }
   [s]:
   {
      int k;


      // Calculate the number of points assigned to each
      // processor and store it in array ns; the number is
```

```
   // proportional to the processor's relative speed
   Partition(p, speeds, ns, nints*8);


   // Distribute the points across processors
   myn = ns[I coordof myn];
   mynodes = malloc(myn*sizeof(double));
   myvalues = malloc(myn*sizeof(double));
   for(k=1, dsp[0]=0; k < p; k++)
     dsp[k] = ns[k-1]+dsp[k-1];
   ([(p)s])MPC_Scatter(&src, nodes, dsp, ns, myn, mynodes);


   // Evaluate the integrand at the points in parallel and
   // measure the time taken by each processor
   if(myn)
   {
     mytime = MPC_Wtime();
     for(k=0; k<myn; k++)
       myvalues[k] = (*fun)(mynodes[k]);
     mytime = MPC_Wtime()-mytime;
   }
   else
     mytime = 0.;
}


// Calculate the actual relative speed of processors
// and store it in array speeds
times[] = mytime;
[host]:
{
   int j;
   double temp;


   for(j=0, temp=0; j<p; j++)
     if(ns[j] && times[j] > temp*ns[j])
       temp = times[j]/ns[j];
   for(j=0; j<p; j++)
     if(ns[j])
       speeds[j] = temp/times[j]*1000.*ns[j];
}
[s]: ([(p)s])MPC_Bcast(&src, speeds, 1, p, speeds, 1);
// Gather the function values to host-processor storing
// them in array nodes
([([s]p)s])MPC_Gather(&src, nodes, dsp, ns, myn, myvalues);
```

```
// Complete computation of all elements of list ints that
// represents a set of subintervals of width step, whose
// contribution into the integral is still to be estimated
[host]:
{
    int j, k;
    struct Interval *i;
    for(i=ints, k=0; i!=NULL; i=i->next)
        for (j=1; j<16; j+=2, k++)
            i->f[j] = nodes[k];
}



// Increase number of function values
*nofun += ([host]nints)*8;



[s]free(mynodes);
[s]free(myvalues);
[host]: free(nodes);



// Calculate an estimate of the integral over each
// interval in list ints. If the interval is acceptable,
// add its contribution to the result. If not, bisect it
// and add 2 new subintervals to a list of subintervals to
// be processed at next iteration of the main loop
[host]:
{
    struct Interval *i;


    for(i=ints, nextints=NULL, nints=0; i!=NULL; i=i->next)
    {
        CentralQuanc8Calculation(i, step, &qleft, &qright);
        qnow = qleft+qright;
        qdiff = qnow - i->qprev;
        area = area+qdiff;
        esterr = fabs(qdiff)/1023.0;
        absarea = fabs(area);
        tollerr = fmax(abserr, relerr*absarea)*(step/stone);


        if(esterr <= tollerr) //Interval convergence test
        { // Interval converged. Add contributions into sums.
```

```
            result += qnow;
            *errest += esterr;
            cor11 += qdiff/1023.0;
            free(i->x);
            free(i->f);
          }
          else
          { // No convergence. Bisect interval i and add its
            // subintervals to list nextints of intervals to be
            // processed at next iteration of the main loop
            nextints = BisectInterval(i, nextints, qleft, qright);
            nints += 2;
          }
        }
      }
      [host]FreeList(ints);
    }
  }
  [host]:
  {
    double temp;
    result += cor11;
    temp = fabs(result)+*errest;
    while (*errest!=0. && temp == fabs(result))
    {
      *errest *= 2.;
      temp = fabs(result)+*errest;
    }
  }
  return result;
}


#include "function.h"


int [*] main()
{
  double [host]a=0., [host]b=2., [host]abserr=0.,
         [host]relerr=1.e-11, [host]errest, [host]badpoint,
         [host]sflag, [host]time, result;
  int [host]nofun, [host]pflag;


  time = ([host]MPC_Wtime)();
  result = pquanc8(fun, a, b, abserr, relerr, &errest,
                   &nofun, &pflag, &badpoint);
```

```
time = (([host]MPC_Wtime)()-time;
[host]:
  if(pflag)
    printf("pquanc8:\nBad singularity at %e\n", badpoint);
  else
    printf("pquanc8:\nresult=%e errest=%e nofun=%d time=%es\n",
           result, errest, nofun, time);


time = (([host]MPC_Wtime)();
[host]: result = quanc8(fun, a, b, abserr, relerr,
                       &errest, &nofun, &sflag);
time = (([host]MPC_Wtime)()-time;
[host]:
  if(sflag)
    printf("quanc8:\nBad singularity at %e\n",
           b-modf(sflag,NULL)*(b-a));
  else
    printf("quanc8:\nresult=%e errest=%e nofun=%d time=%es\n",
           result, errest, nofun, time);
}
```

The name of the second source file must be `partition.h`. This file contains serial routine code for calculation of the number of points to be assigned to each processor and is included in the program with an `include` directive. The contents of this file are as follows:

```
// Calculates distribution of n units of computation across
// p processors proportional to their powers
  void Partition(int p, double *powers, int *ns, int n)
{
  int k, sum, imaxfrac, max, imax;
  double totalpower, *fracs, maxfrac;


  fracs = calloc(p, sizeof(double));
  for(k=0, totalpower=0.0; k<p; k++)
    totalpower += powers[k];
  for(k=0, sum=0; k<p; sum+=ns[k++])
  {
    ns[k] = (int)((powers[k]/totalpower)*n);
    fracs[k] = (powers[k]/totalpower)*n-ns[k];
  }
```

```
  sum = n-sum;
  while(sum>0)
  {
     for(k=0, maxfrac=0., imaxfrac=0; k<p; k++)
       if(maxfrac<fracs[k])
       {
          maxfrac = fracs[k];
          imaxfrac = k;
       }
     ns[imaxfrac]++;
     sum--;
     fracs[imaxfrac]=-1.0;
  }
  free(fracs);
  for(k=0, sum=0; k<p; k++)
    if(!ns[k])
    {
       ns[k]++;
       sum++;
    }
  while(sum>0) {
     for(k=0, max=0, imax=0; k<p; k++)
       if(max<ns[k])
       {
          max = ns[k];
          imax = k;
       }
     ns[imax]--;
     sum--;
  }
}
```

The name of the third source file must be interval.h. This file contains serial routine code for processing lists of subintervals and is included in
the program with an include directive. The contents of this file are as
follows:

```
struct Interval *CreateInterval(double *x, double *f,
                                double qprev,
                                struct Interval *next)
{
  struct Interval *i;
```

```
  i = malloc(sizeof(struct Interval));
  i->x = x;
  i->f = f;
  i->qprev = qprev;
  i->next = next;
  return i;
}


IntervalList BisectInterval(struct Interval *i,
                            IntervalList ints,
                            double qleft, double qright)
{
  struct Interval *left, *right, *cur;
  int j;

  right = CreateInterval(malloc(17*sizeof(double)),
                         malloc(17*sizeof (double)),
                         qright, NULL);
  for(j=0; j<9; j++)
  {
    right->x[2*j] = i->x[j+8];
    right->f[2*j] = i->f[j+8];
  }
  left = CreateInterval(i->x, i->f, qleft, right);
  for(j=0; j>-9; j--)
  {
    left->x[2*j+16] = i->x[j+8];
    left->f[2*j+16] = i->f[j+8];
  }
  if(ints == NULL)
    return left;
  for(cur = ints; cur->next != NULL; cur = cur->next);
    cur->next = left;
  return ints;
}


void FreeList(IntervalList list)
{
  IntervalList l;

  for(; list!=NULL; list=l)
  {
```

```
    l = list->next;
    free(list);
  }
}


void CentralQuanc8Calculation(struct Interval *i,
                              double step,
                              double *qleft,
                              double *qright)
{
  static double w[] = {3956./14175., 23552./14175.,
                      -3712./14175., 41984./14175.,
                      -18160./14175.};


  *qleft = (w[0]*(i->f[0]+i->f[8])+
            w[1]*(i->f[1]+i->f[7])+
            w[2]*(i->f[2]+i->f[6])+
            w[3]*(i->f[3]+i->f[5])+
            w[4]*i->f[4]
           )*step;
  *qright = (w[0]*(i->f[8]+i->f[16])+
             w[1]*(i->f[9]+i->f[15])+
             w[2]*(i->f[10]+i->f[14])+
             w[3]*(i->f[11]+i->f[13])+
             w[4]*i->f[12]
            )*step;
}


void InitFirstInterval(double (*fun)(double), double a,
                       double b, double **x, double **f)
{
    int j;


    *x = malloc(17*sizeof(double));
    (*x)[0]  = a;
    (*x)[16] = b;
    (*x)[8]  = ((*x)[0]+(*x)[16])/2.;
    (*x)[4]  = ((*x)[0]+(*x)[8])/2.;
    (*x)[12] = ((*x)[8]+(*x)[16])/2.;
    (*x)[2]  = ((*x)[0]+(*x)[4])/2.;
    (*x)[6]  = ((*x)[4]+(*x)[8])/2.;
```

```
      (*x)[10]  =  ((*x)[8]+(*x)[12])/2.;
      (*x)[14]  =  ((*x)[12]+(*x)[16])/2.;
      *f = malloc(17*sizeof(double));
      for(j=0;  j<9;  j++)
        (*f)[2*j]  =  (*fun)((*x)[2*j]);
}
```

The name of the fourth source file must be function.h. This file supplies a function fun for the integrand $f(x)$ and is included in the program
with an   include directive. An example of the contents of this file that
provides a function fun for the integrand $f(z) = z / \int_0^{z+0.5} |\sin(16x)| dx$ is as
follows:

```
double infun(double x)
{
    return fabs(sin(16*x));
}
double fun(double x)
{
    double y, errest, flag;
    int nofun;

    y = quanc8(infun, 0., x+0.5, 0., 1.e-10, &errest, &nofun, &flag);

    return x/y;
}
```

The name of the fifth source file must be quanc8.h. This file contains the
quanc8 C code presented in Section 9.3.3.

C.2. USER'S GUIDE

A typical session to run the *N*-body application includes the following steps
(see Appendix D for a full mpC user's guide):

• Open a virtual parallel machine, vpm

  mpcopen vpm

• Translate your mpC program into a C file

  mpcc pquanc8.mpc

- Copy file `pquanc8.c` from the current directory to the `$MPCLOAD` directory

  ```
  cp pquanc8.c $MPCLOAD
  ```

- Broadcast this file from the host workstation to all other workstations involved

  ```
  mpcbcast pquanc8.c
  ```

- Produce executable `pquanc8` on all workstations involved

  ```
  mpcload -het -o pquanc8 pquanc8.c
  ```

- Run the application

  ```
  mpcrun pquanc8
  ```

The mpC User's Guide

D.1. DEFINITION OF TERMS

The following terms are used in this document:

- *Computing space* (a language term)—a set of processes of the parallel program able to play the role of abstract mpC processors.
- *Virtual parallel machine* (an implementation term)—a parallel computing environment used to execute mpC programs. A virtual parallel machine (VPM) is defined by
  - a set of networked computers,
  - the total number of processes constituting the computing space, and
  - a mapping of the processes to the computers.
- *Host workstation* (an implementation term)—any workstation or PC that may be used as a user's working place. The user can launch mpC applications only from the host-workstation's terminal.

D.2. OUTLINE OF THE MPC PROGRAMMING ENVIRONMENT

The basic configuration of the mpC programming environment includes a *compiler*, a *runtime support system* (RTS), a *library*, and a *command-line user interface*. All these components are written in ANSI C.

The mpC compiler translates an mpC program into an ANSI C program with calls to RTS. The compilation unit is a source mpC file. The mpC compiler uses optionally either the SPMD model of target code, when all processes constituting a target message-passing program run the identical code, or a quasi-SPMD model, when the source mpC file is translated into two distinct target files: the first one is for the host process and the second one is for the other processes.

RTS manages the computing space and provides all necessary communications. RTS encapsulates a particular communication package (currently, a small subset of MPI). It ensures platform-independence of the other compiler components.

The library consists of a number of useful nodal, network, and basic functions.

The user interface consists of a number of commands for creation of a VPM and execution of mpC applications on the VPM. The creation of a VPM includes detection of the performance characteristics of the NoC that are saved in a file used by RTS. The VPM creation command runs a special parallel program detecting the number of processors in each SMP computer of the NoC, the speed of the processors, as well as the speed of communication links connecting the computers (optionally).

All processes constituting the target program are divided into two groups—a special process, a *dispatcher*, playing the role of the computing space manager, and ordinary processes, *nodes*, constituting the computing space. The dispatcher works as a server accepting requests from nodes. Notice that the dispatcher does not belong to the computing space.

D.3. SUPPORTED SYSTEMS

The components of the mpC programming environment have been written so as to avoid problems with its installation on any Unix system that has a C compiler supporting ANSI C. It has been successfully installed on many Unix platforms including:

- Sun workstations running Solaris 2.3, 2.4, 2.5, 2.6 or SunOS 4.1 with gcc versions 2.6.3, 2.7.0, 2.7.2, 2.8.1 and SPARCworks Professional C 3.01;
- HP9000 workstations running HP-UX 9.07 with gcc version 2.7.2 or c89, or running HP-UX 10.20 with gcc version 2.8.1;
- DEC Alpha running OSF/1 V3.2 with gcc version 2.7.2;
- PC running Red Hat Linux 4.0, 5.2 with gcc versions 2.7.2 and 2.8.1;
- PC running FreeBSD 3.0, 3.4 with gcc version 2.7.2.

The mpC compiler has been written so as to avoid problems with compilation of the generated code on any Unix system that has a C compiler supporting ANSI C.

RTS has been written so as to ensure its correct working for any implementation of MPI supporting full MPI 1.1 standard as an underlying communication platform. Two main free implementations of MPI, LAM MPI and MPICH, have been the most intensively tested.

The basic version of the command-line user interface has been written so as to work correctly for two implementations of MPI—LAM MPI and MPICH.

D.4. THE MPC COMPILER

The command

```
mpcc [options] filename
```

is used to compile an mpC program. The `mpcc` command processes an input file through one or more of three stages: preprocessing, analysis, and generation of one or two target C files. A standard C preprocessor is used for preprocessing. The most recommended C preprocessor is GNU `cpp`. Only one input file may be processed at once. The suffix .mpc is used for mpC source files, and the suffix .c is used for generated C files. `mpcc` puts the generated C files into the current directory.

D.4.1. Options

All options must be separated. For example, option -hetmacro is quite different from -het -macro. All options different from those described below are considered preprocessor's options.

```
-v
```

Verbose mode. The compiler prints to standard output the compilation time (in seconds) and the version of the compiler. If a syntax error is detected, the compiler produces a message specifying the parser's restart point.

```
-E
```

Performs only the preprocessing stage.

```
-analyse
```

Performs only the preprocessing and analyzing stages. Does not generate the target code.

```
-mess
```

Does not buffer messages, and prints a message immediately after the error is detected. If a syntax error is detected, the compiler will print some additional messages not printed in the default mode.

```
-const
```

Evaluates constant subexpressions (default).

```
-no_const
```

Does not evaluate constant subexpressions. This option is mainly useful if the generated code should be inspected. Some compile-time checks are not performed, and some errors are not detected in this mode.

```
-k<mode>
```

This option specifies one of the four parser modes. <mode> may be SHORT, ANSI, LONG, and ALL. SHORT is the default mode. This mode only allows the short form of the mpC keywords. The LONG mode only allows the full form of the mpC keywords. The ALL mode allows both forms of the mpC keywords. The ANSI mode only allows the ANSI C keywords. For example,

- While net and mpc_net are identifiers in the ANSI mode, they will be mpC keywords in the ALL mode;
- net is an identifier in the LONG mode and an mpC keyword in the SHORT mode;
- mpc_net is an identifier in the SHORT mode and an mpC keyword in the LONG mode.

This option supports incorporation of legacy C code into mpC applications.

```
-macro
```

Does not use RTS macros in the generated C code. The generated C code with macros is shorter but may be more difficult to understand.

```
-out
```

Directs output of the mpC compiler to a standard output instead of the C file.

```
-het
```

Generates two target C files. By default, for a source mpC file foo.mpc the compiler generates one C file, foo.c. Option -het makes the compiler generate two target C files: foo_host.c, containing the code for the host-process, and foo_node.c, containing the code for the other processes.

```
-Woff
```

Does not print warnings.

```
-Wsome
```

Prints only the important warnings (default).

-Wall

Prints all warnings, including:

- Warnings about possible errors in declarations (-Wdecl, default).
- Warnings about possibly incorrect data initialization (-Winit, default).
- Warnings about operand sizes whose correctness cannot be checked at compile time (-Wsize).
- Warnings about operand distributions whose correctness cannot be checked at compile time (-Wdistr, default).
- Warnings regarding the location or usage of statements (-Wstats, default).
- Warnings regarding the declaration or usage of labels (-Wlab).
- Warnings regarding the declaration/usage of formal parameters, function arguments or network-type arguments (-Wargs).

D.4.2. Pragmas

A #pragma directive of the form

```
#pragma keywords <mode>:
```

has the same affect on the mpC keywords as option -k described above. It allows the application programmers to use the same header file in both C and mpC source files.

D.5. HOW TO START UP

Any workstation that may be used as a working place of the user is called a host workstation. The user may launch mpC applications only from host workstations.

To start working with the mpC environment, the user must have it installed on each computer of the NoC (see D.11 for installation guide).

The user should become an authorized user with the same name on each of the computers.

The user should make sure that on each computer of the NoC the user's home directory has a Unix configuration file .rhosts with names of all computers of the NoC.

On each computer in the user's home directory a file responsible for the shell environment (for example, .cshrc if C shell is used) should be modified to determine environmental variables WHICHMPI, MPIDIR (also LAMHOME when using LAM 6.3), MPCHOME, MPCTOPO, and MPCLOAD.

Note that sometimes different files should be modified for local and remote invocation of the shell. For example, if Bourne shell is used on a PC running Red Hat Linux 4.0, both .bashrc and bash_profile should be modified, one for local and the other for remote invocation.

There are a small number of restrictions depending on the value of WHICHMPI used:

- When using LAM MPI, it may be necessary to determine the environmental variable TROLLIUSHOME setting it to the same value as MPIDIR.
- When using LAM 6.3, the environmental variable LAMHOME must be set to the same value as MPIDIR.
- When using LAM 6.3, it may be necessary to determine the environmental variable MPIFLAGS setting it to -lamd.
- When using MPICH, the environmental variable MPCHOME must be set to the same value on all computers of the NoC. To ensure this, the user may need to use the Unix ln command to make the necessary hard or soft links.
- When using MPICH, the environmental variable MPCLOAD must be set to the same value on all computers of the NoC. To ensure this, the user may need to use the Unix ln command to make necessary hard or soft links.
- When using MPICH, the user should have write access to the directory $MPIDIR/bin/machines (equally, $MPIDIR/util/machines) on each host workstation.

On each computer the directories $MPCTOPO, $MPCTOPO/log, and $MPCLOAD must be created. Different users should not share the directories. Binary incompatible computers must not share any of these directories. The user must have write access to these directories.

On each computer the directories $MPIDIR/bin, $MPIDIR/lib, $MPCHOME/bin, $MPCHOME/lib, and $MPCLOAD should be added to PATH. To avoid name conflicts, the directory $MPCLOAD should be the first in the search path.

In addition, directories $MPIDIR/lib and $MPCHOME/lib should be added to the ld path (by modifying LD_LIBRARY_PATH for Solaris, LPATH for HP-UX and so on).

D.6. VIRTUAL PARALLEL MACHINE

The next step is the description of the VPM, which will execute mpC applications. The description is provided by a manually written VPM description file, which should be in the $MPCTOPO directory. The name of this file is just considered as the name of the specified VPM.

D.6.1. VPM Description File

A VPM description file consists of lines of three kinds. Lines beginning with the symbol # are treated as comments. Lines containing one of the symbols {or} are used to specify the hierarchy of clusterization. All other lines should be in the following format:

```
<name> <number_of_processes> <number_of_processors>(opt)
```

where

- `<name>` is the name of the computer as it appears in the system /ets/hosts file
- `<number_of_processes>` is the number of processes of the computing space that will be running on this computer, and
- `<number_of_processors>` is a bracketed integer constant which specifies the number of physical processors of the SMP computer.

While the mpC programming environment can automatically determine the number of processors of each computer during creation of the VPM, the user may specify the number of processors explicitly. The host workstation must go first in the file. The abstract host-processor will be mapped to a process running on this workstation.

For example, the following file describes a VPM that consists of three workstations (alpha, beta, and gamma) each running five processes, and the host workstation is alpha:

```
# three workstation each running 5 processes
alpha 5
beta 5
gamma 5
```

The following example describes a VPM with the same total number of the processes, but running on a single workstation. It may be useful for debugging mpC applications:

```
# simple VPM for debugging
alpha 15
```

The following more complicated example describes a VPM with clusterization:

```
# four 1-processor workstations...
omega 1 #...including cluster:
{
  alpha 5
```

```
  beta 5
  gamma 5
}
# and one 2-processor server
serv 10 [2]
```

Note that the actual total number of running processes is greater than the number specified in the description file. A process for the dispatcher is added automatically and runs on the host workstation. The mpC abstract host-processor is always mapped to the host workstation.

D.7. ENVIRONMENTAL VARIABLES

D.7.1. WHICHMPI

Currently, $WHICHMPI should be:

- LAM, if you use a LAM implementation of MPI;
- LAM6.3, if you use version 6.3 of LAM MPI implementation;
- MPICH_P4, if you use a MPICH implementation of MPI configured with the ch_p4 communications device;
- MPICH, if you use a MPICH implementation of MPI configured with any valid communications device not having to be ch_p4.

WHICHMPI should be set to a proper value on each host workstation.

D.7.2. MPIDIR

$MPIDIR is a directory where MPI has been installed. MPIDIR should be set to a proper value on each computer of the NoC.

D.7.3. MPCHOME

$MPCHOME is a directory where the mpC programming environment has been installed. MPCHOME should be set to a proper value on each computer of the NoC.

Subdirectory $MPCHOME/bin holds all executables and scripts of the mpC programming environment.

Subdirectory $MPCHOME/h holds all specific mpC header files as well as the header mpc.h containing declarations of the mpC library and embedded functions.

Subdirectory $MPCHOME/lib holds the RTS object files mpcrts.o and mpctopo.o.

With WHICHMPI set to MPICH, MPCHOME should have the same value on all the computers. If mpC has been installed in different directories on different computers, the Unix ln command can be used to make all the necessary hard or soft links.

D.7.4. MPCLOAD

$MPCLOAD is a directory for C files, object files, libraries, and executables needed for user's applications. MPCLOAD should be set to a proper value on each computer. Different users should not share the directories. Binary incompatible computers must not share the directory. The user should have write access to the directory.

With WHICHMPI set to MPICH, MPCLOAD should have the same value on all the computers. In particular, the Unix ln command can be used to make all the necessary hard or soft links.

D.7.5. MPCTOPO

$MPCTOPO is a directory for VPM description files and system files produced by the mpC programming environment. MPCTOPO should be set to a proper value on each computer. The mpC programming environment saves a file specifying the current VPM in subdirectory $MPCTOPO/log. Different users should not share the directories. Binary incompatible computers must not share the directories. The user should have write access to these directories.

D.8. HOW TO RUN MPC APPLICATIONS

To run an mpC application on a described VPM, the user should proceed as follows:

- Create a VPM with the mpccreate command. Immediately after the creation, the VPM is opened.
- If the VPM has been created earlier, open it using the mpcopen command.
- Put all C files necessary to produce the executable file into the $MPCLOAD directory on the host workstation, and broadcast them from the host workstation to the other computers using the mpcbcast command.
- Create an executable file on each computer using the mpcload command.
- Run the executables using the mpcrun command.

Additionally,

- `mpctouch` displays the status of the VPM and all its processes,
- `mpcclean` cleans the VPM,
- `mpcclose` terminates the work with the VPM, and
- `mpcmach` prints the VPM's name.

For sample sessions with the mpC programming environment see Section D.10.

D.8.1. mpccreate

The command

```
mpccreate <name>
```

creates a new VPM with the name given by its argument. The command uses the `$MPCTOPO/<name>` description file as a specification of the VPM. The command produces all necessary files required by the RTS and environment for the VPM.

In particular, this command creates the `$MPCTOPO/<name>.topo` file that contains a description of the performance characteristics of the VPM and is used by the RTS at runtime. For each SMP computer, the file contains two lines of the form:

```
# <name_of_computer>
s<number_of_processors> p<performance> n<number_of_processes> ...
```

where `<name_of_computer>` is the computer's name as it appears in the `$MPCTOPO/<name>` description file, `<number_of_processors>` is the number of identical physical processors in the computer, `<performance>` is an integer number characterizing the performance of one physical processor, and `<number_of_processes>` is the number of processes running on the computer. The rest of this line specifies communication characteristics of the computer. We recommend checking of the file after creation of the VPM, since the automatically detected characteristics can be rough enough if the background workload of the NoCs is essential and uneven during the working of the `mpccreate` command.

Once created, the VPM is accessible to be opened by `mpcopen`. Note that `mpccreate` is an expensive command performing a lot of computations and communications, so it may take a few minutes to create a new VPM.

D.8.2. mpcopen

The command

```
mpcopen <name>
```

initializes a VPM specified by its argument. The VPM must have been created earlier. Having been opened, the VPM is accessible for mpcbcast, mpcload, mpcrun, mpcclean, mpctouch, mpcmach, and mpcclose.

D.8.3. mpcbcast

The command

```
mpcbcast  [<file1>  <file2>  ...  ]
```

broadcasts files listed from the directory $MPCLOAD on the user's workstation to the directory $MPCLOAD on the other computers of the current VPM. Only file names without paths must be given.

D.8.4. mpcload

The command

```
mpcload  [-het]  -o  <target>  [<file1>.c  <file2>.c  ...  ]
         [<file01>.o  <file02>.o  ...  ][<file11>.a  <file12>.a  ...  ]
         [<options_to_all_nodes>][-host][<options_to_host_only>]
```

produces executable <target> in the directory $MPCLOAD on each computer of the current VPM. Do not use a path in <target>.

The command produces the executable from .c, .o, and .a files. The name of each of these files should use either no path or the full path. In the first case, the file will be only searched in the directory $MPCLOAD.

Option -het must be used if computers of the VPM are not binary compatible. The user may use the option even if all the computers are binary compatible.

Option -host separates general options, applied to all nodes, from specific options, only applied to the abstract host-processor's code. In addition, if this option appears then:

• The executable for the abstract host-processor will be produced from files whose names have suffix _host;

• The executable for the other nodes will be produced from files whose names have suffix _node.

<options_to_all_nodes> and <options_to_host_only> may be any proper C compiler options. Note that if option -c is used, and hence <target> is an .o file, then option -host will not be allowed.

D.8.5. mpcrun

The command

```
mpcrun <target> [- <params>]
```

runs the mpC application <target> on the current VPM passing parameters <params> to this application. Do not use a path in <target>.

D.8.6. mpctouch

The command

```
mpctouch [-p]
```

checks the status of the current VPM and prints it. The VPM may be ready or busy. With option -p, the status of all nodes is printed.

D.8.7. mpcclose

The command

```
mpcclose
```

closes the current VPM.

D.8.8. mpcclean

The command

```
mpcclean
```

cleans the current VPM and makes it ready to run a new mpC application. This command should be used in the case of abnormal termination of the previous command or mpC application.

D.8.9. mpcmach

The command

```
mpcmach
```

prints the name of the current VPM.

D.8.10. mpcdel

The command

```
mpcdel <name>
```

deletes a VPM specified by its argument, which means deleting all system files associated with this VPM.

D.9. HOW TO DEBUG MPC APPLICATIONS

Debugging mpC applications is not yet an easy task, but it is much simpler than debugging MPI applications due to the absence of indeterminism. There are at least three levels of debugging.

At the top level, we suggest including in the mpC code calls to `MPC_Global_barrier` and `MPC_Barrier` to split the program execution into small debuggable portions. Use `MPC_Printf` to output process coordinates and expression values. Note that some `MPC_Printf` messages may be lost if errors breaking message-passing subsystem occur. It is also possible to use `printf`, but the output from remote computers may be lost. We strongly recommend starting with debugging on a single workstation. All error messages include either position in the mpC source file or ` '0,0'`, if the error takes place in the dispatcher process.

At the middle level, we suggest to include `printfs` and barriers in the C code generated by `mpcc`. This is a more complex procedure, as the user needs to understand the logics of the generated C code and RTS kernel calls.

At the low level of debugging, the user can turn kernel tracing on and/or use debugging MPI utilities. To turn tracing on, the user should close the current VPM, set MPCDEBUGMODE to 1 or 2, and then reopen the VPM.

To debug an application, which hangs without error messages, first use MPI utilities to find all the processes that do not respond (for example, LAM MPI's `mpitask`). They often "die" due to a simple "C error", such as an uninitialized variable, dividing by zero and so on. The trace is useful for finding the point in the code where the error occurs. When all processes are alive, the MPI utility will show operations where all the processes are blocked.

D.10. SAMPLE MPC SESSIONS

D.10.1. A Simple Session

Let file `sum_vec.mpc` contain the following mpC code:

```
#include <stdio.h>
nettype Star(n) {coord I=n;};
```

```
#define M 4 /*number of the processors*/
#define N 3 /*dimension of the vectors on the each
processor*/
#define NM N*M /*dimension of the source vectors*/
void [*]main() {
   int [host]x[NM], [host]y[NM], [host]z[NM], [host]i;
   void [*]parsum(),[*]parsum1();
([host]printf)("<host input vectors>\n");
for(i=0;i<NM;i++) {
  x[i]=i;
  y[i]=-i;
}
([host]printf)("x=");
for(i=0;i<NM;i++)([host]printf)(" %d",x[i]);
([host]printf)("\ny=");
for(i=0;i<NM;i++)([host]printf)(" %d",y[i]);
([host]printf)("\n");
parsum((void*)x, (void*)y, (void*)z);
([host]printf)("<host result vector>\n z=");
for(i=0;i<NM;i++)([host]printf)(" %d",z[i]);
([host]printf)("\n");
}
void [*]parsum(int [host]x[M][N], int [host]y[M][N],
               int [host]z[M][N])
{
   net Star(M) Sn;
   int [Sn]dx[N], [Sn]dy[N], [Sn]dz[N];
   int [Sn] i,[host]j,[host]l;
   dx[]=x[];
   dy[]=y[];
   dz[]=dx[]+dy[];
   z[]=dz[];
}
```

The program sums up two vectors on M abstract processors using function
parsum. This function creates an mpC network with M abstract processors,
scatters portions of vectors, calculates the sum, and gathers results to the host.
In addition, suppose that the user works on a workstation beta. We assume
that the user wants to execute the application on this single workstation and
that the corresponding VPM has not been created yet. Therefore, the user
should first create the VPM. To do this, the user creates the following description file beta5 in the $MPCTOPO directory:

```
# my own workstation only
beta 5
```

Then the user creates the VPM with name beta5:

```
mpccreate beta5
```

On the console of beta something like

```
mpccreate: net definition /home/mpc/topo/beta5.def is created.
mpccreate: scheme /home/mpc/topo/beta5.ts is created.

LAM 6.0 - Ohio Supercomputer Center

mpccreate: wait for creation 'beta5'
mpccreate: parallel machine 'beta5' is created.
```

will appear. Note that immediately after the creation, the VPM is opened. Then, the user compiles the mpC file:

```
mpcc sum_vec.mpc
```

and copies the output file sum_vec.c to the $MPCLOAD directory:

```
cp sum_vec.c $MPCLOAD
```

As the user wants to execute the application on the beta workstation only, he can skip the step of broadcasting sum_vec.c. Then the user makes an executable sum_vec:

```
mpcload -o sum_vec sum_vec.c
```

Finally, the user runs the application:

```
mpcrun sum_vec
```

On the console of beta something like

```
<host input vectors>
x= 0 1 2 3 4 5 6 7 8 9 10 11
y= 0 -1 -2 -3 -4 -5 -6 -7 -8 -9 -10 -11
<host result vector>
z= 0 0 0 0 0 0 0 0 0 0 0 0
```

will appear. Then the user may check the status of beta5

```
mpctouch
```

On the console of beta something like

```
mpctouch: Ready!
```

will appear.

D.10.2. More Complicated Session

Let a VPM that will run the application gal-buf.mpc is already opened. The following command produces two target C files—one for the abstract host-processor, with calls to Xlib displaying data in the graphical form, and the other for the abstract processors not involved in graphically displaying data:

```
mpcc -I/usr/openwin/include -het gal-buf.mpc
```

Note that the absolute application name should be used if gal-buf.mpc is not in the current directory. If X Windows system stores its include files on the host workstation in a directory different from /usr/openwin/include, use that directory instead.

The above command will produce files gal-buf_host.c and gal-buf_node.c in the current directory. To make these files accessible to the mpC programming environment, copy them into the $MPCLOAD directory:

```
cp gal-buf_host.c gal-buf_node.c $MPCLOAD
```

Broadcast these files from the host workstation to the other computers of the VPM:

```
mpcbcast gal-buf_host.c gal-buf_node.c
```

Produce executable gal-buf on each computer of the VPM:

```
mpcload -het -o gal-buf gal-buf.c -lm -host -L/usr/openwin/lib -lX
```

Note that if X Windows system stores its libraries on the host workstation in a directory different from /usr/openwin/lib, use that directory instead. Use an option different from -lX if necessary (i.e., use the proper name for the X library; it may be -lX11 or something else).

Launch the application:

```
mpcrun gal-buf -- input_file
```

The file input_file contains input data for the application.

Note that the absolute name of the input file should be used if it is stored in a directory different from the directory which was the current directory when you were opening your VPM.

■ BIBLIOGRAPHY

Adams, J. C., W. S. Breinerd, J. T. Martin, and J. L. Wagener, *Fortran 95 Handbook*. MIT Press, 1997.

Basic Linear Algebra Subprograms Technical (BLAST) Forum Standard. Basic Linear Algebra Subprograms Technical (BLAST) Forum, University of Tennessee, Knoxville, August 21, 2001.

Blackford, L., J. Choi, A. Cleary, E. D'Azevedo, J. Demmel, I. Dhillon, J. Dongarra, S. Hammarling, G. Henry, A. Petitet, K. Stanley, D. Walker, and R. Whaley, *ScaLAPACK User's Guide*. SIAM, 1997.

Culler, D., R. Karp, D. Patterson, A. Sahay, K. Schauser, E. Santos, R. Subramonian, and T. von Eicken, LogP: Towards a Realistic Model of Parallel Computation, *4th ACM SIGPLAN Symposium on Principles and Practice of Parallel Programming*, San Diego, CA, May 1993.

Fagg, G., A. Bukovsky, and J. Dongarra, HARNESS and fault tolerant MPI, *Parallel Computing* 27(11), 2001.

Forsythe, G. E., M. A. Malcolm, and C. B. Moler, *Computer Methods for Mathematical Computations*. Prentice-Hall, 1977.

Fortran—Part 1: Base Language. ISO/IEC 1539–1:1997 on December 15, 1997.

High Performance Fortran Language Specification. Version 1.1. High Performance Standard Forum, Rice University, Houston, November 10, 1994.

High Performance Fortran Language Specification. Version 2.0. High Performance Standard Forum, Rice University, Houston, January 31, 1997.

Metcalf, M., and J. Reid, *Fortran 90 Explained*. Oxford, 1990.

MPI: A Message-Passing Interface Standard, Message Passing Interface Forum, June 12, 1995.

Nichols, B., D. Buttlar, and J. P. Farrell, *Pthreads Programming. A POSIX Standard for Better Multiprocessing*. O'Reilly, 1996.

OpenMP C/C++ Application Program Interface (API). OpenMP Architecture Review Board, March 2002.

WILEY SERIES ON PARALLEL AND DISTRIBUTED COMPUTING
Series Editor: Albert Y. Zomaya

Parallel and Distributed Simulation Systems / Richard Fujimoto

Surviving the Design of Microprocessor and Multimicroprocessor Systems: Lessons Learned / Veljko Milutinović

Mobile Processing in Distributed and Open Environments / Peter Sapaty

Introduction to Parallel Algorithms / C. Xavier and S.S. Iyengar

Solutions to Parallel and Distributed Computing Problems: Lessons from Biological Sciences / Albert Y. Zomaya, Fikret Ercal, and Stephan Olariu (*Editors*)

New Parallel Algorithms for Direct Solution of Linear Equations / C. Siva Ram Murthy, K.N. Balasubramanya Murthy, and Srinivas Aluru

Practical PRAM Programming / Joerg Keller, Christoph Kessler, and Jesper Larsson Traeff

Computational Collective Intelligence / Tadeusz M. Szuba

Parallel and Distributed Computing: A Survey of Models, Paradigms, and Approaches / Claudia Leopold

Fundamentals of Distributed Object Systems: A CORBA Perspective / Zahir Tari and Omran Bukhres

Pipelined Processor Farms: Structured Design for Embedded Parallel Systems / Martin Fleury and Andrew Downton

Handbook of Wireless Networks and Mobile Computing / Ivan Stojmenoviić (*Editor*)

Internet-Based Workflow Management: Toward a Semantic Web / Dan C. Marinescu

Parallel Computing on Heterogeneous Networks / Alexey L. Lastovetsky